# LIFE OF
# THE DUKE OF DEVONSHIRE

Emery Walker Ph. sc.

The Marquess of Hartington
in the year 1888
From the painting by The Lady Abercromby in the National Portrait Gallery

# THE LIFE OF
# SPENCER COMPTON

## EIGHTH DUKE OF DEVONSHIRE

BY

## BERNARD HOLLAND, C.B.

IN TWO VOLUMES

VOL. I

*WITH PORTRAITS AND OTHER ILLUSTRATIONS*

SECOND EDITION

## LONGMANS, GREEN AND CO.

39 PATERNOSTER ROW, LONDON

NEW YORK, BOMBAY, AND CALCUTTA

1911

FIRM is the man, and set beyond the cast
Of Fortune's game, and the iniquitous hour,
Whose falcon soul sits fast,
And not intends her high sagacious tour
Or ere the quarry sighted ; who looks past
To slow much sweet from little instant sour,
And in the first does always see the last.
                                    —FRANCIS THOMPSON.

# PREFACE

My chief thanks are due to the present Duke of Devonshire, who entrusted me with this work, and placed all the letters and other documents connected with it at my free disposal. It may be well to say that, beyond this, his Grace is responsible for nothing whatever which is contained in this book. I also wish to express my gratitude to all those who have permitted me to see and use letters, or have given me information orally or otherwise. I am much indebted to Mr. Henry Cavendish, who, before I began the work, over two years ago, had sorted and arranged, as a labour of love, the tangled correspondence which lay at Devonshire House in rich confusion, and has helped me much in other ways.

BERNARD HOLLAND.

*September* 1911.

# CONTENTS

CHAP.                                                                          PAGE

   I. Lineage and Early Years . . . . . 1

  II. First Years in Parliament . . . . 21

 III. Visit to the United States of America . . 39

 IV. The War Office, 1863-1866 . . . . 55

   V. 1866 to 1868 . . . . . . . 67

 VI. The Liberal Government of 1868 to 1874 . 73

 VII. The Interregnum of 1874 . . . . . 130

VIII. Lord Hartington's Leadership . . . 152

 IX. The Eastern Question . . . . . 168

  X. The Afghan War and South Africa . . 215

 XI. Parnellism, Radicalism, and Toryism . . 241

 XII. The Elections of 1880 and their Results . 255

XIII. Mr. Gladstone and Lord Hartington . . 282

XIV. The India Office . . . . . . 296

 XV. Irish Affairs . . . . . . . 328

XVI. Egypt . . . . . . . . 360

XVII. Internal Politics, 1882-1883 . . . . 369

XVIII. The War Office, 1883-1885 . . . . 407

# LIST OF ILLUSTRATIONS

THE MARQUIS OF HARTINGTON, M.P., IN THE
YEAR 1888 (*Photogravure*) . . . . *Frontispiece*
*From the painting by the Lady Abercromby in the
National Portrait Gallery.*

HARDWICKE HALL . . . . . . *Facing p.* 2
*From a photograph by R. Keene, Ltd., Derby.*

THE COUNTESS OF BURLINGTON . . . . „ 10
*Painted by T. Lucas, after her death, from a miniature.*

FAMILY GROUP BY P. BAUGNUT IN THE YEAR
1852 . . . . . . . . „ 17
*From a lithograph.*

HOLKER HALL IN LANCASHIRE, NOW THE PRO-
PERTY OF LORD RICHARD CAVENDISH . . „ 76
*From a lithograph.*

MAP OF THE ANGLO-EGYPTIAN SOUDAN . *At end of Volume*
*By permission of the Controller of His Majesty's
Stationery Office.*

# LIFE OF THE
# DUKE OF DEVONSHIRE

## CHAPTER I

### LINEAGE AND EARLY YEARS

CAVENDISH village sits remotely on the Suffolk bank of the river Stour, and looks now much as it must have looked five hundred years ago. Sir John, of Cavendish, who had acquired the manor of that name by his marriage with Alice daughter of John de Odyngseles, became Chief Justice of England in the reign of Edward III., and was elected in the fourth year of the next reign to be Chancellor of the University of Cambridge. His son, John, in the year following, slew, or rather completed the slaying, for the Lord Mayor began it, of the Kentish Radical leader, Wat Tyler, in Smithfield, in young King Richard's presence, and was immediately knighted. The Suffolk crowd, led by Jack Straw, on the other hand, captured, at Bury St. Edmund's, Sir John Cavendish—who had just been appointed Commissioner for suppressing a Yorkshire rising—dragged him, together with his friend and host, John of Cambridge, Prior of the Monastery, to the market-place, and there rudely beheaded both lawyer and priest.

After these illustrious and stormy episodes the name

and manor of Cavendish descended from the Chief Justice
through four or five undistinguished generations, to Thomas
Cavendish, ' Clerk of the Pipe,' who died in 1523, leaving
two sons. The elder, George, entered the service of Cardinal Wolsey, 'abandoning,' as Wolsey said, 'his own
country, wife and children, his own house and family, rest
and quietness, only to serve me.' He remained with the
Cardinal through his disgrace, and till his death; then
returned to Suffolk, where he lived retiredly, and wrote the
beautiful and touching Memoir of his Lord. King Henry
VIII. so far recognised the fidelity of George Cavendish to
his fallen master that he gave him six of the late Cardinal's
best cart horses, a cart, £10 in respect of unpaid wages,
and £20 more as a donation.

His younger brother, William, like Halbert Glendinning
in Scott's Border romance, embraced the winning cause.
His portrait at Hardwicke Hall gives the semblance of a
cautious, solid, and hard-headed man of business. In 1530
he was a Royal Commissioner engaged in the work of
dissolving monasteries. He was rewarded by a knighthood
and by grants of confiscated lands here and there, most
of which he sold in order to concentrate his possessions in
Derbyshire. He died in the reign of Queen Mary, having
apparently accommodated his own religious opinions to
hers, as he was sworn in to her Privy Council. His first
two wives gave him daughters, but no sons. His third
wife was the famous Derbyshire heiress, Elizabeth Hardwicke, then a widow. She brought to Cavendish her
father's lands, and those of her first husband, also in that
county, and bore to him three sons. She was a strong
woman and mighty builder. Hardwicke Hall, near Chesterfield, remains, tapestry and all, very nearly as she left it;
and she built Oldcotes, and completed the then existing
House of Chatsworth, standing in a fair wide valley

HARDWICKE HALL

among the Derbyshire hills.[1] After the death of Sir William Cavendish she married twice again, her fourth husband being Talbot, Earl of Shrewsbury. Queen Elizabeth must have thought highly of her loyalty, discretion, and power of withstanding illustrious and pathetic charm, for she entrusted Mary Queen of Scots for years to her keeping, and to that of her last husband. The eldest son of this great woman died without legitimate offspring. The second was William, afterwards first Earl of Devonshire. The third was Charles Cavendish of Welbeck Abbey, father of the Marquis, afterwards Duke of Newcastle, illustrious in the Civil Wars, from whom again descend in the female line the present owners of Welbeck, the Cavendish-Bentincks, Dukes of Portland.

The House of Cavendish was thus, by policy and by marriage, solidly founded in a single generation. The son of the founder was made Earl of Devonshire, at Salisbury in 1618, by King James I. The jealous said that £10,000 were paid by the new Earl to the needy monarch. There is a theory that Derbyshire was intended to supply the title, and that Devonshire got into the patent by a clerical error.

The third Earl of Devonshire, who on his mother's side was of the Bruces of Elgin, and so brought some Scottish - Norman blood into an extremely English family, was educated by that early Tory-Socialist, the philosopher Hobbes, with whom he travelled for three years on the Continent.[2] This education, or his own

---

[1] The present Chatsworth House was built by the first Duke of Devonshire at the beginning of the eighteenth century. There is a legend that it was predicted to ' Bess of Hardwicke' that she would die when she ceased to build. Building operations were at last stopped by a long frost, and she died (see *Letters of Horace Walpole*).

[2] Some twenty-five years earlier Hobbes had been the tutor of the second Earl, and had travelled also with him, and was afterwards his private secretary. The philosopher, indeed, was a life-retainer of the family, and lived for years at Chatsworth and Hardwicke, only requiring, as he said, board and lodging, and some tobacco.

temperament, made him one of the strongest Royalists of
his time.  He voted courageously against the attainder of
Strafford, was himself one of eight peers impeached by the
House of Commons in 1642, and spent his fortune freely
during the war in the cause of Charles I.  His younger
brother, Charles Cavendish, played a gallant part in the
North, until, advancing against the indomitable Eastern
Counties, he was slain in an encounter with Cromwell's
cavalry at Gainsborough on the 28th July 1643.  Waller's
magniloquent lines on this event are too finely tempting
not to quote :—

> 'Here lies Charles Ca'ndish ; let the marble stone
> That hides his ashes make his virtues known ;
> Beauty and valour did his short life grace,
> The grief and glory of his noble race.
>
> .   .   .   .   .   .
>
> Two loyal brothers took their Sovereign's part,
> Employed their wealth, their courage, and their art
> The elder did whole regiments afford,
> The younger brought his courage and his sword.
> Born to command, a leader he begun,
> And on the rebels lasting honour won.
> The horse, instructed by their general's worth,
> Still made the King victorious in the North.
> Where Ca'ndish fought the Royalists prevailed ;
> Neither his judgment, nor his courage failed ;
> The current of his victories found no stop
> Till Cromwell came, his party's chiefest prop.
> Equal success had set these champions high,
> And both resolved to conquer or to die ;
> Virtue with rage, fury with valour strove ;
> But that must fall which is decreed above ;
> Cromwell, with odds of number and of fate,
> Removed this bulwark of the Church and State.
>
> .   .   .   .   .   .
>
> Thus fell the young, the lovely, and the brave,
> Strew bays and flowers on his honoured grave.'

One might quote also from Walter Scott's splendid
Cavalier lyric :—

> 'There Erin's high Ormonde, and Scotland's Montrose,
> And Derby and Cavendish, dread of their foes.'

The third Earl of Devonshire died in 1684. He shared in the scientific tastes which, in the Restoration period, were, together with a relaxed morality, part of the reaction against religious excesses, and was an original member of the Royal Society. His son, the fourth Earl and first Duke, who was born in 1640, had an active and varied career. He took part in the sea-fight against the Dutch on the 4th June 1665. As Lord Cavendish, in the House of Commons, he distinguished himself as an active opponent of the Court and Catholicising party, and was an 'Excluder' in those political fights of 1680 and 1681, which turned upon the attempt to prevent the Duke of York from succeeding to the throne. He was not, however, so extreme in action as were Shaftesbury, Russell, and others, who went to the verge of rebellion. When he visited Lord Russell in prison, between his condemnation and execution, Cavendish offered to change clothes with him and so give him a chance of escape, but Russell declined the offer. In 1684 he succeeded to the Earldom. In April 1687 he struck with a cane, at Whitehall, in the very presence of James II., a quarrelsome Kentish Tory,[1] Colonel Colepeper, who had told him that Exclusionists had no right to show their faces at Court. For this dire offence he was fined £30,000 by the Court of King's Bench. He withdrew to Chatsworth, and avoided payment until the Revolution took place, after which the conviction was cancelled. The Earl of Devonshire was, naturally, one of the chief leaders in the movement which substituted William III. for James II. Removing the politics of his race from a Cavalier to a Whig foundation, he largely determined the destinies of his descendants, including the subject of the present

[1] This was a sequel to a former affray, also at Whitehall, which Mr. Evelyn witnessed. See Evelyn's *Diary* of 9th July 1685, and *Dictionary of National Biography*, articles 'Cavendish' and 'Colepeper.' Burnet says that Cavendish first broke with the Court on account of some disappointments there.

Memoir. In 1694 he was created Duke of Devonshire.
His wife was a daughter of the Duke of Ormonde, chief of
the ancient Norman-Irish house of the Butlers. Between
1687 and his death in 1707, he built the existing magnificent
house at Chatsworth. He was a patron not only of horse-
racing, but also of arts and letters, and even deigned to
write verse himself. His morals were notoriously relaxed,
as were those of most wealthy noblemen in the Restoration
period.[1] Bishop Burnet calls him a 'libertine,' but adds,
' He was ambitious and had the courage of a hero, with an
unusual proportion both of wit and knowledge.' Evidently
he was a man of force and vigour, of large notions, and
adventurous in various fields of life. His mother was Lady
Elizabeth Cecil, daughter of the second Earl of Salisbury.

The second Duke married Rachel, daughter of the beheaded Lord Russell, and thus increased the Whig strain
in the family. It was of their son, the third Duke, that
Dr. Johnson said, ' He was distinguished before all men
for a dogged veracity.' The Sage, on another occasion, said
of this Duke, ' He was not a man of superior abilities, but he
was a man strictly faithful to his word. If, for instance, he
had promised you an acorn, and none had grown that year
in his woods, he would not have contented himself with that
excuse; he would have sent to Denmark for it.' ' This,'
observes Boswell, ' was a liberal testimony from the Tory
Johnson to the virtue of a great Whig nobleman.'

The fourth Duke was Lord-Lieutenant of Ireland in
1755, and, for a few months in 1756–57, was First Minister
in a stop-gap Administration formed in consequence of
the refusal of Pitt to serve under the Duke of Newcastle.
On Pitt's reconciliation with Newcastle, Devonshire re-

---

[1] Lord Oxford called the Duke, in the elegant diction of the day, ' a patriot
among men, a Corydon among ladies.' He was also a bold gambler. One night,
as Lord Cavendish, M.P., at the Duchesse de Mazarin's rooms at Whitehall, he
lost at cards £1000, all his horses, and all his plate, and had to put off an
intended journey to France.

signed in favour of the latter. A brother of this Duke, Lord John Cavendish, was a member of the Rockingham Governments of 1765 and 1782. In the last-mentioned short-lived Administration he was Chancellor of the Exchequer. He refused to serve under Shelburne after the death of Rockingham, and, in 1783, moved the resolution censuring the terms of peace, which caused Shelburne's resignation. He was again Chancellor of the Exchequer under the brief Government of the Duke of Portland. Edmund Burke, in his letters, bestows high praise upon this Cavendish, commending his scholarship, his sound judgment, power of memory, and business capacity. He was, Burke says, 'of great integrity, great tenderness and sensibility of heart, with friendships few and unalterable, of perfect disinterestedness, the ancient English reserve and simplicity of manner.'[1] Walpole said of this Lord John that under an appearance of modesty he had a confidence in himself which nothing could shake. In the schism among the Whigs caused by the French Revolution, the Cavendishes went with Burke, and not, like the Russells, with Fox.

A strange eighteenth-century scion of the race was the scientist, Henry Cavendish. He was famed not only for his scientific discoveries, but for an astounding excess of the 'hereditary taciturnity' ascribed to the Cavendishes. He could hardly endure to speak at all, or to be seen by man, still less by woman, and, to quote Lord Brougham, who certainly did not share in this infirmity, 'probably uttered fewer words in the course of his life than any man who ever lived to fourscore years, not at all excepting the monks of La Trappe.' He must have resembled his distant kinsman, the late Duke of Portland.

[1] Burke, however, writing to Lord Rockingham, wished that Lord John Cavendish could be 'induced to show a certain degree of regular attendance on business,' and added that Lord John 'ought to be allowed a certain reasonable proportion of fox-hunting, but anything more is intolerable.'

The fourth Duke, the transient Prime Minister, by marrying Lady Charlotte Boyle (the Baroness Clifford), daughter of the Earl of Cork and Burlington, added Lismore Castle and large Irish estates to the Cavendish possessions. This glorious heiress also brought Bolton Abbey, Londesborough, Chiswick, Burlington House, in Piccadilly, and other property in England, especially in Derbyshire.[1] The fourth Duke died in 1764. His eldest son, the fifth Duke, married in 1774 the irresistibly delightful and lovely Georgiana, daughter of Earl Spencer. It is of her that Nathaniel Wraxall writes in his *Memoirs*:—

'I have seen the Duchess of Devonshire, then in the first bloom of youth, hanging on to the sentences that fell from Johnson's lips, and contending for the nearest place to his chair. All the cynic moroseness of the Philosopher and the Moralist seemed to dissolve under so flattering an approach.'

'This charming person' (Wraxall elsewhere writes) 'gave her hand at seventeen years of age to William, Duke of Devonshire, a nobleman whose constitutional apathy formed his distinguishing characteristic. His figure was tall and manly, though not animated or graceful; his manners always calm and unruffled. He seemed to be incapable of any strong emotion, and destitute of all energy or activity of mind. As play became indispensable in order to rouse him from this lethargic habit, and to

---

[1] Lady Charlotte Boyle was descended from the 'great Earl of Cork' (1566–1643), described by Sir Richard Cox as 'one of the most extraordinary persons either that or any other age hath produced.' The great Earl's eldest son married (1635) Lady Elizabeth Clifford, daughter and heiress of the fifth Earl of Cumberland. She brought Bolton Abbey and Londesborough (in Yorkshire) into the possession of the Boyles, whence they passed through Lady Charlotte Boyle into that of the Cavendishes.

Through Lady Elizabeth Clifford's marriage in 1635, and Lady Charlotte Boyle's marriage in 1748, the Barony of Clifford, created in 1628, came into the Cavendish family. After the death of the sixth Duke, without offspring, in 1858, this Barony fell into abeyance between his sisters, the Countesses of Carlisle and Granville:

The present Earl of Cork descends from a younger son of the 'great Earl.' The Boyles were a family of small landowners, first in Herefordshire and then in Kent, when the Cavendishes were a small Suffolk family.

awaken his torpid faculties, he passed his evenings usually at Brookes' engaged at whist or faro.  Yet beneath so quiet an exterior, he possessed a highly improved understanding ; and on all disputes that occasionally arose among the members of the Club, relative to passages of the Roman poets or historians, appeal was commonly made to the Duke, and his decision or opinion was regarded as final. Inheriting with his immense fortune the hereditary probity characteristic of the family of Cavendish, if not a superior man, he was an honourable and respectable member of society.  Nor did the somnolent tranquillity of his temper by any means render him insensible to the seduction of female charms.'

This fifth Duke died in 1811, leaving one son, the sixth Duke, and two daughters, one of whom married the sixth Earl of Carlisle, the other the first Lord Granville.  The sixth Duke never married, and died on the 17th January 1858.  He was a collector of books and coins, and he built the great conservatories at Chatsworth.  He took little part in politics, and rarely spoke in the House of Lords.  Upon his death the title and estates reverted to his cousin William, Earl of Burlington, the grandson of Lord George Cavendish, the fourth Duke's third son, in whose favour the Earldom of Burlington, extinct in 1753, had been revived in 1831.  The first Earl of Burlington, of the Cavendish line, had for wife the daughter and heiress of the seventh Earl of Northampton, through whom Compton Place and the valuable Eastbourne estate were annexed to the Cavendish possessions.  From another son of this first Earl descend the Cavendishes, Barons Chesham.

Lord Burlington in 1829, at the age of twenty-one, married the still younger Lady Blanche Georgiana Howard, daughter of the sixth Earl of Carlisle, and thus grand-daughter on her maternal side to the fifth Duke and to the 'beautiful' Georgiana.  Her children therefore descended from the main stream of the family by two re-uniting channels, and were doubly Cavendish. The Countess of Burlington died on the 27th April 1840, leaving her husband without her when he was only thirty-two years old. He survived her for fifty years, and did not marry again.

She also left four children. The eldest was Spencer Compton, born on the 23rd July 1833. He became, in 1891, the eighth Duke of Devonshire, and he is the subject of this Memoir. Two other sons, Frederick and Edward, were born in 1836 and 1838. There was one daughter, Lady Louisa, born in 1835. Spencer Compton was not the first-born. He had an elder brother who died at less than three years old.

## II

Lord Burlington succeeded to the Devonshire title in 1858, and his eldest son then became Marquis of Hartington, a title created in 1694. Till then his title was Lord Cavendish, and by the name of "Cavendish," or by affectionate diminutives, he was called by his near relatives throughout life.

Lord Burlington, before and after he succeeded to the Dukedom, lived quietly, chiefly occupied in the care of his own estates, though undertaking many public duties. He was chairman of the Railways Commission in 1865, Lord-Lieutenant first of Lancashire and then of Derbyshire, Chancellor first of London and then of Cambridge University. He was a naturally silent man of almost excessively reserved disposition, with warm family affections, and a high standard of conduct.

Holker Hall, in North Lancashire, where Lord Burlington lived with his children, was once the property of a branch of the Lowther family, who intermarried with the Cavendishes in the eighteenth century. It had eventually

THE COUNTESS OF BURLINGTON

*(Painted by* T. LUCAS, *after her death, from a miniature)*

fallen to the share of the first Lord Burlington. The house, now partly old and partly modern, stands in a wildly beautiful country between the last slopes of the Westmoreland Hills and dreamy levels of sand and sea, the northern limit of Morecambe Bay.[1] The place is still secluded, and must have been far more so before the industrial developments of Barrow and the residential developments of Ulverstone had taken place. Lord Burlington liked the quiet and silent life, and then lived almost entirely at Holker. He infinitely preferred it to Chatsworth, after he had inherited that palace in 1858, and never failed to celebrate Christmas in his old home.

Sometimes, however, he had to visit London, and then his children wrote letters to him. A few of those from his eldest son have been preserved. They chiefly contain news about various animals, and narratives of sport; on one day the precise number and weight of trout caught in the river, on another 'a beautiful run with the hounds at an awful pace from Bigland woods to the side of Windermere.' Lord Burlington himself, as a boy, had been unhappy at Eton, and he sent his sons to no school. They were taught in earliest years by a governess, Miss Hastings, and later mainly, apparently, by Lord Burlington himself, who had at Cambridge achieved the remarkable feat of being both second wrangler and one of the first few men in the classical tripos. Probably they learned more than they would have done had they gone to Eton or Harrow. But the upbringing may have developed a certain innate tendency towards shyness and silence, and an indisposition for exchange of ideas. The Cavendishes were never inclined to talk for talking's sake, or unless they had something concrete or humorous to say, and

---

[1] One wing of Holker Hall was destroyed by a fire in 1871, and was then rebuilt on a rather larger scale than that of the previous structure.

they found no difficulty or embarrassment whatever in the longest spaces of complete silence.[1]

On 23rd July 1850, Lord Burlington noted in his diary :—

'This is my beloved Cavendish's birthday. He is seventeen. He is, I feel, a most delightful boy, full of life and animation. I trust he has strong religious feelings, but he is certainly fond of amusement. I am anxious he should go to a Tutor for a few years before Cambridge, if I can find one on whom I can rely.'

The tutor was found, though not till the spring of 1851, in the shape of the Rev. Mr. Conybeare, of Axminster in Devonshire, who took two or three pupils at a time. As Cavendish was to go to Cambridge in October, he only had a few months' tutoring. Before his departure for Devonshire Lord Cavendish made his first public speech. It was at a tenants' dinner. Lord Burlington told his tenants that 'Protection' was gone, offered them a re-valuation of their farms, and urged them to farm with vigour and energy. 'Cav's health was drunk, and he returned thanks for the first time.'[2] On 14th May 'Cav went off this morning to Axminster. It is my first real separation from him,' wrote his father.

At Axminster Cavendish was improved in the classics, translating from Demosthenes and Thucydides and Juvenal, whom he liked 'very well,' also in original English composition. 'Mr. Conybeare has given me,' he wrote to his father, 'some English composition to do, which is horrible—"The adventures of an Athenian drachma between 500 and 400 B.C." I have made a beginning, but

---

[1] This faculty is well illustrated by the well-known tale about the fifth Duke and his brother, the inn on the North Road, the three-bedded room, and the corpse. See the works of Sir Algernon West, Mr. George Russell, and other raconteurs.

[2] Lord Burlington's diary for 3rd March 1851.

get on very slow.' A little later, 'Mr. Conybeare goes on plaguing me with English composition, which I hate mortally.' This hate proved lasting. To the end of his life it was a torment to him to compose a speech. He thought it 'great humbug being here,' and that he learned much more at home; nor was he consoled by having 'a nice little drive, like a good boy, with Mrs. Conybeare, in a little pony carriage which I had the honour of driving,' nor by the fact that a school-inspector, 'a Mr. Tidling, or something like that, and a brace of curates, dined here last night.' In the middle of July, indeed, Cavendish wrote to his father that he was 'in a horrible passion. Mr. C. asked me this morning if I had set my heart very much on grouse shooting, and said he thought it was a great pity to interrupt the course of reading.' However, if his father should decide in favour of Axminster as against Bolton Moors, he would accept his fate, and 'not be desperately disappointed.' Fortunately the moors carried the day.

Cavendish began his Cambridge career in October 1851. He had rooms in Trinity College, in Neville's Court, on what is called the 'iron-gate staircase,' first floor. He was, as boys of rank usually then were, entered as a 'fellow commoner,' which involved various distinctions of a boring kind. He resisted in his third week a temptation to which he afterwards frequently succumbed. 'Almost everybody is going to Newmarket, but I shall not. How very good of me! Because I do not see any sort of harm in it.' In revenge some hunting and shooting at once offered itself; he found 'very little time to read; and the day vanishes most unaccountably,' a phenomenon familiar to undergraduates. But he succeeded in attending some lectures. 'Stupid old C. is still bothering away at the life of Herodotus,' and there was some

mathematical lecturing also which he thought less unreasonable. Academic work was not to his taste. However, by
means of a two months' summer reading party in Nor-
mandy, and a virtuous residence at Cambridge, free from
temptations, during a Christmas vacation, Cavendish succeeded in taking a tolerably good place in the second
class of the mathematical tripos. In a letter dated 1st
February 1854, a cousin, Colonel William Cavendish, who
was on the staff of Queen Victoria, says that at the Queen's
dinner he had just met the Vice-Chancellor of Cambridge,
who said:—

'Cavendish could have taken the highest honours
without any extra work. He is the cleverest man Cambridge had, but had not confidence in himself, but passed
very high indeed with a week's reading.'

The statement must perhaps be taken with some
discount, as the Vice-Chancellor was in the glorious
position of dining at Windsor. Cavendish belonged to
the Union Society, by his father's desire, but never spoke
in the debates, and perhaps never attended any. In this
respect he resembled two later Trinity undergraduates,
both from Scotland, each of whom became Prime Minister
—Arthur Balfour and Henry Campbell, afterwards Sir
Henry Campbell-Bannerman.

Lord Cavendish lived mainly with the set of young men
whose centre was the Athenæum Club, a Cambridge institution which, notwithstanding its name, has no connection
with learning, literature, or the fine arts. Lord Welby, so
long the distinguished permanent Under-Secretary at the
Treasury, was at Trinity at the same time as Cavendish,
and, like him, belonged to the Athenæum set.

'The members of the Club,' he writes, 'lived much
together, though differing much in their daily pursuits.

We used to dine a great deal out of hall, small parties in our own rooms, but the evening life was spent at what we called Athenæum teas or suppers, which took place about 9 o'clock, and were followed by card-playing till 12, and, in college, much later. The gambling was not excessive. The set I speak of was an idle set. I scarcely recall what would be called a reading man among them. Practically they all went out as Passmen, but Cavendish always read to a certain degree, certainly more than the majority of his companions, and he took the Honour degree. I need hardly say that the idle set in which he lived did not distinguish themselves in after life. I don't think that there was one of them who made a name for himself in any line. On the whole they were gentlemen, manly in pursuits and ideas, *insouciants*, taking life easily as it came, without ambition, and with but little culture. Freddy Cavendish, who was a great friend of mine, came up just before Cavendish went down, and Spencer [1] came up a little later. He and they were the only ones that, to use a sporting phrase, came through their horses.'

It was, in fact, the set which has always existed in the free and untutored life of Trinity, entirely outside the intellectual pursuits of Cambridge, and it has its merits. Lord Welby adds :—

'The Cavendish of that day had a good deal of the character which distinguished him in after life. There was about him an utter absence of ostentation, and, I need not add, not an atom of swagger, or any reliance on rank. In this set there was a good deal of chaff, and Cavendish had his share of it, and took it with perfect good nature. He did not, as far as I recollect, shine in talk, but I think we all recognised and respected a sound male common-sense, and, as you would expect, he was always a gentle-man. I remember we were struck by one point about him. As was natural, the " tufts " lived a good deal among

---

[1] The late Earl Spencer, afterwards Lord Hartington's political colleague.

themselves, and they of course took up Cavendish. They were at the time rather a namby-pamby set, and it was soon evident that he preferred the larger and freer life of the more numerous set of which I have spoken. We, of course, knew what a great position was before him, but I don't think that, if we had thought about it, we should have anticipated for him so great a career as fell to him, but he had no predominant influence, as far as I recollect, among us. Nor do I recollect that he had any very intimate friends.'

Lord Burlington visited Cambridge in December 1851, and notes in his diary :—

'It has been a great delight to me seeing my beloved boy again, looking very well, and seemingly very happy. He is not reading quite as much as I could wish, but certainly not very idle. Most of his acquaintances do not read much.'

A year later Lord Burlington notes that his son—

'has certainly scarcely acted up to my expectations of him at Cambridge, but still is by no means thoroughly idle. He is extremely fond of society, and enjoys being with his companions so much that I am afraid he will never make up his mind to submit to the restraint which hard reading requires. In other respects I am well satisfied with him. He seems thoroughly happy here at home with us, and is very fond of his sister and brothers.'

In after life Lord Hartington sometimes expressed regret that he had wasted his educational opportunities. Once, when Duke of Devonshire and Chancellor of Cambridge University, he had occasion to deliver an address to an audience of undergraduates, and advised them, among other things, to attend to their studies. Observing the symptoms of a general smile he added, 'Perhaps you think that I did not do much work myself

FAMILY GROUP BY P. BAUGNUT IN THE YEAR 1852

when I was an undergraduate. It is true and I regret it. All through life I have had to work with men who thought three times as quick as I did, and I have found this a great disadvantage.'

But he could never have been a 'reading man.' He belonged to that class of Englishmen who, as Sidonia, in Disraeli's novel, unexpectedly remarks, are so like the ancient Greeks, because they know no language but their own, and live in the open air. During his life Lord Hartington got through an immense amount of indoor and official work, but it was always despite his true inclinations. He accepted work unwillingly, though, from a strong sense of *noblesse oblige*, he did it thoroughly, and he was always charmed by any prospect of release from the bonds of official captivity. His home education at Holker enabled him to express himself in sound and solid English, and his mathematical training there and at Cambridge improved, no doubt, his power of attention, his accuracy, and his sense of logical order and distribution of a subject.

Lord Cavendish left Cambridge early in 1854, and entered the House of Commons in 1857. The intervening years were spent in the amusements and pursuits of a young man of high position. Hunting, his dominant passion, and shooting filled the year from autumn to spring, and visits at great country houses. All fashionable doors that he cared to enter were open to him in the London season, and once or twice he went abroad.

His first visit to Paris was in April 1854. He virtuously spent some hours in the Louvre, and, as he cautiously wrote to his father, thought that ' perhaps a slight taste for pictures may be beginning to show itself.' These early blossoms never came to fruit. He attended a ball at the Elysées Palace, and was introduced to the British Ambassador, Lord Cowley, and by him to Napoleon III. Also by others 'to a host of swells, and I am going to dine to-morrow with a female of that species, the Marquise de C. . . .' The weather was lovely and the Tuileries Gardens were 'perfectly beautiful.' In the summer of the same year he visited Berlin, and admired the town and the gardens of Sans Souci. At Dresden he was a good deal in the picture-gallery, 'trying hard to give myself a taste for the arts, and I think I succeed a little.' Also he travelled down the Rhine, but 'was not particularly struck of a heap by the beauties of the said river.'

In 1855 Lord Cavendish, who had since 1852 been captain of the Ulverstone troop of Lancashire Yeomanry, became an officer in a newly embodied 2nd Derby Militia, or 'Chatsworth Rifles.' It was an extremely Cavendish troop. Colonel William Cavendish was in command, Lord Cavendish was major, Lord George Cavendish and William Cavendish (second Lord Chesham) were captains, and Edward Cavendish joined later. Headquarters were at Chesterfield, and about this period he saw a good deal of the then reigning sixth Duke of Devonshire. In September 1855 he visited the family castle of Lismore in Ireland. He writes to his father that he was very glad that he had been able to go there, 'both because it has seemed to please the Duke so much, and because it has been a time I would not have missed for a good deal. I have been very much struck with the real affection the people of all classes seem to have both for the Duke and for Uncle Morpeth.' The occasion was a visit to Lismore of the Earl of Carlisle, who was then Lord-Lieutenant of Ireland.

Lord Cavendish continues : ' It seems to have been one of the Duke's great wishes to receive Uncle Morpeth here in this way. I am sure it must have done good to everybody, and though the people are Irish, and I suppose make the most of their feelings, I really believe that they would do anything for either of them.'

Some letters from the sixth Duke show his affection for his young kinsman, and his constant desire for his company. As soon as Cavendish came of age the Duke gave him an allowance of £2000 a year.

In August 1856, the Crimean War being finished, took place the coronation at Moscow of the new Czar of Russia, Alexander II. Lord Granville was sent to attend the ceremonies as a special Ambassador representing the Queen on the occasion, and invited his young cousin, Lord Cavendish, to accompany him as one of his staff. There was a family interest in this, for the sixth Duke of Devonshire, then still living, had been the head of a similar mission, and had been accompanied by Lord Burlington, at the coronation of the late Czar Nicholas. The mission travelled in a warship to Cronstadt, and after a stay of two weeks at St. Petersburg, arrived at Moscow at the beginning of September. 'The entry of the Czar was very magnificent. The prettiest part of the procession were the Circassian Cavalry in chain armour.' The mission, Lord Cavendish adds, were at first 'in a state of perpetual presentation to some member of the Imperial Family. They take place at all hours of the day, and last a long time, and are very tiresome. When we are not being presented we are at some Ambassador's levee, or other function, and I have not had time yet to see a single thing in Moscow.' He saw a review of 115,000 troops, and was much impressed by their appearance, especially by that of the cavalry, who were 'much better mounted than any of ours.' Russian officers told him that none of these troops had been in the Crimea, and that no such fine troops were there, but Cavendish patriotically remarks, 'I suppose they are made of the same kind of stuff, and

would have been beaten as well.' There were two great
State balls in the Kremlin.

'The first was for the swells, of whom, I believe, there
were more than 2000. It was very splendid and cut out
ours at the Palace considerably. The last ball was for everybody in Moscow, and there were said to be 20,000 people.
There were certainly immense numbers, but no crowd; the
place was quite big enough to hold them. It was a curious
sight as they were all in their national costumes or uniforms,
and there were a great many of them, included between
English attachés and Tartars from the great Wall of
China.'

Then came a great sham fight, which he liked 'better
than anything else.' It gave one, he thought, 'a very
good notion of a battle.' Also he saw some forms of
field sport which struck him as strange and alien to
English practice.

A General Election took place in the spring of 1857,
and it was arranged that Lord Cavendish should stand
for North Lancashire. He stood as a supporter of
Lord Palmerston's Government, then in power, and was
returned without difficulty. He thus began, at the
age of twenty-four, a political career which was to
last, in one House of Parliament or in the other, until
his latest appearance in the House of Lords in the
summer of 1907, a period of fifty years. During
almost the whole of that time he was either in office or
taking a leading part in opposition, and most of the period
was crowded with important events relating to home and
foreign policy. If this book, as it is to be feared, is
too long, it is the fault not so much of the writer as of
the subject.

# CHAPTER II

## FIRST YEARS IN PARLIAMENT

IT will be convenient to the reader to be reminded of the state of the political world at the time when Cavendish entered the House of Commons. It was a period of comparative calm. Lines dividing parties were less well marked, and issues less deeply dividing, than they were in the previous period, marked by Catholic Emancipation, the first Reform Bill, and the Repeal of the Corn Laws, or than they became in the period following the death of Palmerston and the second Reform Bill. The middle class battle for power had been won, and the mass of the people were not yet on the political field. The Whig Government of Lord John Russell, after a brief interval of Tory administration, had been followed at the end of 1852 by the Coalition Government of Lord Aberdeen, comprising Whigs or Liberals, such as Russell and Palmerston, and the group of leading Peelites. This Government drifted into the Crimean War. Lord Palmerston, then Home Secretary, had urged Lord Aberdeen to take strong and timely steps, to make clear declarations as to the point at which England would resist by arms the Russian advance, and to enforce them by demonstrations in action. He believed that if this had been done, the Russian Government would have paused in its course, and that war might have been avoided. It was part of this policy that the fleet should be sent to the Dardanelles and, if necessary, to the Black

Sea. This step was eventually taken, but too late to save the Turkish fleet from destruction at Sinope on 30th November 1853, the event which precipitated the war. Palmerston accepted the maxim 'si vis pacem para bellum.'[1] The Aberdeen Cabinet was led by a good man of tremulously indecisive mind, and it was weak, though full of talents. It contained some men of sensitive conscience, but deficient in sound judgment and understanding of human affairs.

Lord Aberdeen's Government sustained a crushing defeat in the House of Commons in January 1855, on Roebuck's motion to appoint a Select Committee to inquire into the condition of the army in the Crimea, and, especially, into the alleged defects in the supply departments. Lord Derby and Lord John Russell having successively failed to form a new Administration, Lord Palmerston undertook the task, and succeeded triumphantly. Save for a year and a half Palmerston remained Prime Minister until his death, at eighty-one, in the autumn of 1865.

Lord Palmerston led the nation with vigour and success to the end of the Crimean War, in 1856, and, in 1857, encountered with prompt energy the storm of the Indian Rebellion. Under his first consulship also was initiated the complete and formal transfer to the Crown of the government of India.[2] He was extremely popular with the middle-class electorate of the time. He spoke and acted exactly in accordance with their taste. His gay good humour, congenial to the age of Dickens and Leech, amused them; his sporting tastes won their sympathy; he flattered their pride and made them feel—and it was true—that England was playing

---

[1] See *Life of Lord Palmerston*, by Evelyn Ashley, vol. ii. chap. 10.
[2] The transfer was completed by Lord Derby's Government.

a great rôle on the stage of the world. But he was disliked by the Radicals, led by Bright and Cobden, and until 1859, so long as Whigs like Russell and Peelites like Gladstone remained outside his Government, he was weak in the House of Commons.

In the spring of 1857 Cobden moved a resolution condemning the Government's forcible action in obtaining redress by naval force from the Viceroy of Canton for the seizure of a ship under the British flag engaged in the opium trade. The resolution was carried against the Government by a combination of Tories, Peelites, and Radicals. Palmerston at once appealed to the country, and the election followed at which, as a Palmerstonian, young Cavendish began his political career. 'An insolent barbarian,' ran the Prime Minister's election address, 'wielding authority at Canton, has violated the British flag, broken the engagements of treaties, offered rewards for the heads of British subjects in that part of China, and planned their destruction by murder, assassination, and poisons.' Palmerston also reminded the nation that it was he who had finished the Crimean War, when others had shirked that duty. This sporting appeal was triumphant. 'The "*fortuitous* concourse of atoms*,*" as he called his opponents when they denied having *combined* against him, was scattered to the winds.'[1] Bright and Cobden lost their seats in the melée, the Peelites were almost extinguished as a party, and a solid majority was returned to support the patriotic Prime Minister.

Early in 1858 Palmerston had a worse parliamentary fall. His bill, introduced, in consequence of the Orsini attempt to murder Napoleon III., with the intent to make England a somewhat less hospitable home to

[1] Evelyn Ashley's *Life of Lord Palmerston*, vol. ii. p. 346.

assassins, was defeated by a new 'fortuitous' combination of Tories, the few remaining Peelites, and the Radicals, led respectively by Disraeli, Gladstone, and John Russell. This time Lord Palmerston resigned, and Lord Derby, with Disraeli as Chancellor of the Exchequer, undertook the Government. He was supported by a minority in the House of Commons, and was really kept in power for a space by the personal quarrels in the opposing camp.

Mr. Gladstone had become one of the two or three foremost men in the political life of the time. He was, in 1859, fifty years of age, twenty-five years younger than Lord Palmerston, and twenty-four years older than Lord Hartington. He was one of that group of Tory Intellectuals who had been severed from the main body of the party by the schism of 1846, due to the action of Sir Robert Peel in electing to repeal the Corn Laws. Until 1859 Gladstone, with a diminishing band of friends, hovered between the two main parties. He was Chancellor of the Exchequer in Lord Aberdeen's Coalition Government. When Lord Palmerston was forming the next Government in February 1855, Gladstone, with Sidney Herbert and Sir James Graham, after doubts and refusals, accepted office, but resigned two weeks later, finding that Palmerston was too sensible to resist any longer the general desire that there should be an inquiry into the Crimean supply arrangements.[1] Mr. Gladstone told Prince Albert that this concession would allow the House of Commons to succeed in 'a most unconstitutional, most presumptuous, and most dangerous course,

---

[1] Upon this Peelite secession, Lord John Russell, who had resigned in January *because* Lord Aberdeen's Cabinet refused to accept the Roebuck inquiry, entered Lord Palmerston's Cabinet, in February, as Colonial Secretary. He resigned again in July over the peace negotiations, and was out of office till 1859. His career is most confused.

after which it would be impossible for the Executive ever
to oppose again the most absurd and preposterous
demands for inquiry.' It was a strange view to take.
Probably the sub-conscious reason of resignation was
antipathy to Palmerston, and growing dislike to the
continuance of the war.

He denounced the policy of Palmerston in breaking
off the negotiations begun at Vienna in the spring of
1855, and persevering in the war until the fall of Sebas-
topol in September and the acceptance by Russia of the
full Black Sea conditions. The Duke of Argyll, in his
*Memoirs*, says that he is unable to commend the course
taken by his friend Mr. Gladstone in this affair, namely,

'to be responsible not only for beginning the war, but
for giving it the significant direction of an attack upon
the naval arsenal and fleets of Sevastopol, to continue
that attack till it led to great loss and almost to disaster,
and then suddenly to desert the cause, and to denounce
both the feelings and the arguments on which that cause
depended.' [1]

Gladstone was conspicuous in those attacks upon
Palmerston which led to the dissolution of 1857, and to
the resignation of 1858. He allied himself in these assaults
with Disraeli on the one side, and Bright and Cobden on
the other. In 1858 he was asked by Lord Derby to
join his Cabinet as Indian or Colonial Secretary of State,
and all but accepted the offer. But he knew that he was
disliked, almost more than any Radical, by a section of
the Tory party, and he deeply distrusted Disraeli, who,
having already, in 1852, acted as leader, had a prior
claim to lead the House of Commons ; and he had,
perhaps, also a foreboding which made impossible his
reunion with men of Conservative principles or tempera-

[1] *Autobiography of the Duke of Argyll*, vol. ii. p. 28.

ments.  His mind, however, was almost exactly balanced on the line between acceptance or refusal.  Had Lord Derby decisively set aside Disraeli's claim, and strongly pressed Gladstone to accept the Exchequer *with* the Leadership of the House, the offer would probably have been accepted.  This was a price which Lord Derby would not, or could not pay.[1]

Mr. Gladstone, however, gave outside support to Lord Derby's Government.  It was, apparently, with him, at this time, rather a question of persons than of parties.  For the time being, in his eyes, Palmerston was the enemy of all that was virtuous.  Writing to Sydney Herbert, in December 1856, he said : ' I am undeniably conscious of the greatest objection to Lord Palmerston, and were it in my power to sign the warrant for turning him out, I would do it with all the ink which is now in my pen.[2]  I do sincerely believe him to be a most demoralising and a most destructive Minister.'  In a letter to Sir James Graham, in 1858, he called Palmerston ' the worst Minister the country has had during our time.'[3]  Not only did he assail Palmerston in Parliament, but anonymously, and still more violently, in the *Quarterly Review*.  In 1858 he made an extra-ordinarily fierce personal attack in the October number.  ' Lord Palmerston,' he wrote, ' can hardly fail to see that a number of those who formerly supported him, amply sufficient in numbers, if their resolution hold, to give effect to their intention, have written this sentence upon the tables of their hearts, " *Come what may, Lord Palmerston shall not again be Minister.*" '

The resolution did not hold.  In less than a year from the day when Gladstone underlined these words he was

[1] Greville says that Derby could not reconcile his followers to an alliance with the 'detested Gladstone,' and see in Lord Morley's *Life of Gladstone* the curious exchange of letters with Disraeli.

[2] *Life of Sydney Herbert*, by Lord Stanmore, vol. ii, p. 67.

[3] Parker's *Life of Sir James Graham* : letter of February 14, 1858.

serving himself under Palmerston, though certainly not
'with a quiet mind.' The following passage from the
same article may be quoted because it shows the reaction in
Gladstone's mind against the strong Palmerstonian foreign
policy, which explains much that Gladstone himself said
and did in later times. The violent animosity roused in
his mind by Palmerston's methods of asserting the power
and maintaining the influence of England is to be remembered in connection with later events with which
Lord Hartington's career was so closely connected. He
wrote on this occasion :—

'The quarrel between them' (*i.e.* men like the writer
and Lord Palmerston) 'is no lover's quarrel. The proscription is no personal proscription. It is the determination
of a great and serious issue, too long neglected and misunderstood, but now at least deliberately handled and, to
all appearance, finally disposed of. It is the proscription,
not of a person, but of a system of misgovernment at
home and abroad ; of a system which, because it despised
or made light of rights, was sure to mismanage interests ;
a system which at home was favourable neither to permanence nor to progress, and which abroad united the
dangers of violence with those of poltroonery ; a system
which has happily vanished with its authors and instru-
ments from the seat of power, but which has left for itself
a bad memorial in remembered slights and insults, in the
uneasiness and suspicion which it has introduced or aggravated in the whole range of European diplomacy, and in
the spirit of jealousy and even of hatred which it has
engendered towards England.'

The writer also attacked the Minister warmly on the
ground of his complete indifference, or even hostility, to
political reform and domestic legislation.[1] Gladstone's wrath

---

[1] This was too true. See the amusing conversation, worthy of a Disraeli
novel, between Lord Palmerston and young Mr. Goschen, on the subject of a
legislative programme, in Mr. Arthur Elliot's *Life of Lord Goschen*, vol. i. p. 65.

against Palmerston had been sharpened by the Erastian principles of the latter, his addition of Low Church bishops to the Bench (eighteen bishops had voted in support of what Gladstone called 'the sanguinary and shameful proceedings at Canton'), and the passing of the Divorce Act of 1857, to enable the middle classes to share in the privilege of being divorced, hitherto confined to the wealthy sufferers from marriage.[1]

Palmerston was practical and placable. Gladstone, in a speech made after Palmerston's death, said truly that his was 'a nature incapable of enduring anger or the sentiment of wrath.' He had even offered a place in his Administration to Cobden. He knew that Gladstone disliked him and his policy, and would be a difficult colleague, and he considered him to be a 'dangerous' character. But, in order to complete the strength of his Government, he needed Gladstone's financial ability and reputation ; and he felt justly confident that he would be master in his own Cabinet, and that he could, as he would have said, ride this delicate and sensitive horse with a light hand. He therefore asked and obtained Gladstone's assistance as Chancellor of the Exchequer when he formed a new Administration after the defeat and resignation of Lord Derby in 1859. Mr. Gladstone explained, rather superficially, to his constituents that, having helped to overthrow Lord Palmerston's Ministry in 1857, he had thought it to be his duty to support that of Lord Derby, and that, having failed to save the Conservative Government, he considered himself to be at liberty to accept Lord Palmerston's offer. Lord Aberdeen wrote to Sir

---

[1] Lord Palmerston narrated, in a characteristic speech, that 'one prominent opponent of the Divorce Bill said to me, "You shall never pass the Bill." I replied, " Won't we ?"' The opponent was, probably, Mr. Gladstone. (Ashley's *Life of Lord Palmerston*, vol. ii. p. 347.)

James Graham [1] that the wish expressed in a speech by Lord Palmerston that he might see the Austrians driven out of Italy by the war 'has secured Gladstone, notwithstanding the three articles in the *Quarterly* and the thousand imprecations of late years.' As Shakespeare makes Hotspur say, 'Thought is the slave of life.' This Austro-Italian reason weighed no doubt, yet it seems to be, on the whole, one of those so readily accepted or invented by the intellect to justify the changes of the wayward will. Perhaps the 'subliminal' Gladstone felt that the existence and character of Disraeli had made his own reunion with the Tory party impossible ; that by belonging to Palmerston's Government he might diminish evil and promote good ; that his one chance of leading a great party was to take office in 1859 ; that the age of both Lord Palmerston and Lord Russell made it obvious that the succession would soon be open, and that the general tendency of things pointed to a long predominance of the Liberal party. Mr. Gladstone, on more than one occasion, made a kindly use against political opponents of the words ascribed by Milton to the fallen Angel—

> 'Ease would recant
> Vows made in pain as violent and void.'

When he took office in June he may have applied it in his own mind to the vows registered in October. He might have used a still finer Shakespearean quotation :—

> 'Time, whose million'd accidents
> Creep in 'twixt vows, and change decrees of kings,
> Tan sacred beauty, blunt the sharp'st intents,
> Divert strong minds to the course of altering things.'

Mr. Gladstone began as a Tory and, after he had passed the mid-line of life, definitely became a Liberal, subject to remains of Toryism on certain matters. At no time did he

[1] Parker's *Life of Sir James Graham.* vol. ii. p. 388.

approximate to the Whig temper.  A great lady once said
that the pulse of the Tory beats ten times more to the
minute than does that of the Whig.  So does the pulse of
the Radical.  Lord Hartington, in his later years, referring
in conversation to the incompatibility between himself and
Mr. Gladstone, said, ' You see, he was a Peelite, and I was
a Palmerstonian.'  This expresses much.  The divergence
between Palmerston and Gladstone towards the end of the
Crimean War was the foundation of the later divergence
between Gladstone and Hartington at the time of the
' Eastern Question.'

## II

In January 1858 Lord Burlington became Duke of
Devonshire.  His son, therefore, entered upon his second
session under the title of Marquis of Hartington.  He did
not for long remain unexhorted to unwelcome action.  On
the 7th May, the Speaker, Mr. Denison, wrote that he had
been wanting to see him for the last day or two—

' but you are very wild and keep at a distance, out of shot.
I wish to persuade you to enter the arena and to descend
like a Young Eagle *in reluctantes dracones*.  Unless I felt
sure that you would speak well, and do yourself credit, and
do honour to your family and your name, I should not
invite you to the undertaking.  But I am very confident
about it, and I think, after a little while, you will like the
sport in my forest as well as that on the Scotch hills.'

Probably the indolent young eagle was more reluctant
than the dragons, and nothing could be extracted from him
this year but a very short speech on a dry and local subject.
The Speaker wrote to the Duke of Devonshire that—

' it was done in good taste, and just in such a way as
to please the House and to make a favourable impression,

which it did most completely. I see that he has the gift of giving utterance to his thoughts in a parliamentary style. It is, therefore, entirely in his power to obtain complete success if he choose to do so. I trust such will be his choice.'

His second speech was on a great occasion. Lord Derby, after a precarious ministerial existence, advised the dissolution of Parliament. The General Election took place in May 1859, and, though the Conservatives made a net gain of seats, they found themselves when Parliament reassembled still in a minority of about forty. Lord Palmerston, meanwhile, had succeeded in achieving what he called a 'reconciliation of sections,' and was now prepared to overthrow the Government and to take office. The Whigs have always been anxious to maintain the 'apostolical succession,' and Palmerston commanded the rising Cavendish to move an amendment to the Address expressing want of confidence. Lord Hartington, now aged twenty-six, rose, on the 7th June, in a House crowded with members full of the delicious excitement which precedes a straight party fight to decide the possession of the great offices. He grounded his action on the precedent suggested to him by his chief, that of the Tory resolution on the Address which led to the overthrow of Lord Melbourne's Government in 1841. He then pointed out that, in their recent appeal to the country, the Government had not rested their case upon any particular measure. They had simply asked the country to give to them a majority in the House of Commons instead of a minority.

'I hope,' he continued, 'that the decision of the challenge which has thus been thrown down, and which we accept, will, at the conclusion of this debate, be received by both parties in a spirit of fairness and of honour. For myself, I can say, and I believe that in so doing I speak the sentiments of almost all the members on this side of the House, that, if we are defeated in the division on this amendment, we shall cheerfully and willingly bow to the decision of the House. We shall then know what is our position as an Opposition. We shall know that it will not be for hon. members on this side of the House to aspire to guide the counsels of the country, but that it will be their part, while they exercise all the vigilance and watchfulness which is the duty of an Opposition, to give to the Government, as far as lies in their power, the undivided support of the House of Commons in the complicated and difficult state of the relations which they will have to carry on with foreign countries. If, on the other hand, this amendment should be successful, then I cannot imagine that it will be otherwise than satisfactory to Her Majesty's Government to be released from a position which they have already declared that, under such circumstances, they are no longer willing to occupy. I have no doubt that it will be satisfactory to them that the state of things which has existed for the last two Sessions should cease.'

The standard of conduct here laid down for an Opposition is certainly that which Lord Hartington did his best to observe when he led the Opposition between 1875 and 1880. He continued his speech by illustrating, from various recent instances of surrenders, compromises, and non-observance of pledges and principles, the demoralising weakness of a Government in a minority in the House of Commons, and resting on sufferance. Government had been able to pass no measures of domestic reform, and had to justify its existence on the ground of foreign policy. But the recent outbreak of the war between Austria and France proved that they had not been able to maintain the peace of Europe. He said—

'England, at the beginning of the year, occupied as proud and as high a position in the Councils of Europe as it was ever her lot to enjoy. We were as powerful as ever we were; we had come successfully out of the Indian War; we were at peace with the whole world; and I cannot but think that it was then an object of the greatest importance and necessity for any nation in Europe to retain the respect and friendship of England. I think that England was then in a position to speak with authority and power to all the nations of Europe, and it is impossible to conceive how, if the Government had so spoken, the war could have broken out.'

The speaker learned in 1870 that it is not easy for an English Government, even a strongly supported one, to arrest the outbreak of a Continental war. Lord Hartington referred to the reconciliation of the divided sections of the Liberal party. 'We have learned,' he said, 'a lesson from adversity, and the leaders of all sections of our party are prepared to co-operate for the advancement of what they consider the good of their country.' The end of his speech was on sound party lines.

'We shall be told, no doubt, that this is a party move. I admit that it is a party move. I admit that, in a crisis of our domestic and foreign affairs such as at present, I would rather see a party in office which, while it represents most fully and exactly the thoughts and feelings of all educated Englishmen, has at the same time always given a steady and consistent support to every measure of social and political reform. I would rather place power in the hands of such a party than in the hands of a party whose very name and being are antagonistic to all progress. I would rather see in office the successors and inheritors of that policy of peace and non-interference which was advocated by Fox and Grey, than the inheritors of that warlike, interfering, and subsidising policy which characterised the Administrations of Castlereagh and Pitt. I admit that in this sense it is a party move, but I deny that it is a move undertaken for the political aggrandisement of any set of individuals. Office holds out no great temptations to any statesman at this crisis in the national affairs. With the increase in our armaments, which I suppose every Government will think it necessary to continue, there must necessarily be an increase of taxation. With increase of taxation, we shall probably have discontent throughout the country. There is nothing, in truth, but a heritage of trouble for statesmen, whatever Government may be in power. This is no field for any but the noblest ambition.'

The speech was well received. The Tory leader said that Lord Hartington had 'really opened all the grounds on which a resolution expressing a want of confidence in a Government ought to be moved.' He was glad that—

'the noble Lord, in the manly and promising speech which he has made, has . . . not condescended to intrude upon the House the trash of which we have heard so much with regard to the conduct of the elections, the corruption of the constituencies, and the compacts with foreign Powers and Hierarchies. Perhaps the noble Lord thought the subject had been exhausted by a master. . . . I am glad to find that this question is, at least, to be discussed in the spirit of gentlemen with high party views, and on broad constitutional principles.'

Disraeli wrote that evening to the Queen that 'Lord Hartington spoke like a gentleman.'

Some letters to the father of the speaker show how favourable an impression this speech produced. The Speaker wrote :—

'Hartington has done very well indeed. He has made a capital speech. I was certain that, whenever he chose to make the attempt, he would entirely succeed. He has entirely succeeded, and has thoroughly justified all my expectations. He possesses a power of speaking rarely shown by persons who have had so little practice. It gave me the greatest pleasure to hear him. While I am writing

Disraeli has spoken of the "manly and promising speech" of the noble Lord, cheered by both sides.'

Another experienced member, Mr. Ellice, who had suggested to Palmerston that the amendment should be moved by Hartington, wrote to the Duke that—

'it was the best first speech I have heard since Lord Derby's, and in saying this, pray believe that I have no desire to flatter him, or to exaggerate his success. He must now follow it up for the sake of "his Order," as Lord Grey would have said, and of his country. . . . I hope that you will live to see him Minister of the country.'

Lord John Russell also wrote to the Duke. He said :—

' Hartington has only to go on in order to become not only a very good speaker, but a man to influence the course of the House of Commons in times to come. This, to an old worn-out Whig, is a promise and a consolation.'

Lord Palmerston, who had already written to Hartington to congratulate him on his 'excellent speech,' and to say that 'nothing could be better as to language, topics, and delivery,' also wrote to the Duke of Devonshire. He said that he had—

' not been able to propose any office at present to Lord Hartington because of the great number of persons whom a general reconciliation of sections brings on the lists of candidates for official appointments. But to say the truth I am scarcely sorry for it ; for it seems to me that a young man in Lord Hartington's position, and possessed of the abilities and attainments which he has displayed, would be better employed by taking part in the general business of the House of Commons, than by confining his attention and thoughts to the details of one particular department.'

This debate ended in the defeat of Lord Derby's

Government by 323 to 310.  Mr. Gladstone did not speak, but he voted against Lord Palmerston and for the Tory Government, so that, for the last time for many years, he and Lord Hartington went into opposite lobbies.  Lord Derby resigned and, after Lord Granville had been asked, but had failed, to form a Government, Lord Palmerston became Prime Minister for the second time, and Mr. Gladstone, as has been said, accepted the post of Chancellor of the Exchequer.

Lord Hartington did not follow up his début, and appears to have remained quite silent until the 2nd May 1861, when he stated his reasons for voting for the repeal of the excise duty on paper.  They were that, in the preceding year, the House of Commons had passed a Bill to effect this object, and the House of Lords had rejected it.  The tax was therefore now being levied contrary to the expressed desire of the House of Commons, and 'upon the authority of a body which never had, and ought not to have, the control of the taxation of the country.  The rejection of the measure last year furnished ground for a quarrel between the two branches of the Legislature which might have been dangerous to the Constitution.'  If the Budget were now passed as it stood, the possibility of such a collision would be at an end.  It would no longer be 'in the power of any demagogue, sincere and earnest, though he might be mistaken, to say that this duty, pressing severely on a branch of industry, was retained by the sole authority of the House of Lords.'  The question really was, in 1861, whether a remission of taxation should be made by way of abolition of the paper duty, which brought in £1,400,000 a year.  There had been a terrible trouble about this paper duty, and over the action of the House of Lords in 1860.  Lord Palmerston had then expressed open sympathy with the House of Lords, and that of Lady

Palmerston, sitting in the gallery of that House during the debate, was almost indecorously manifest.  Palmerston did not wish to lose the revenue, which he required to meet the interest of a loan for fortifications to which Gladstone had refused to consent.[1]  In July 1860 Gladstone all but resigned because the Cabinet would not take strong action against the House of Lords.  However, on the 2nd July 1860, Lord Palmerston was able to write to the Queen that 'Mr. Gladstone, having failed to become master of the Cabinet by a threat of resignation, will in the end yield to the almost unanimous decision of his colleagues.'  Gladstone himself wrote to Sir James Graham on the 22nd July 1860 : 'Concessions have been made beyond my expectation at the last moment and under great pressure.  On the other hand, I cannot view without uneasiness what I have to yield.  On both sides the strain is great.  I fear it cannot last long.  Never at any time of my life have I had such a sense of mental and moral exhaustion.'  He was therefore grateful to those who supported him in the final settlement of this difficulty in the following year.  He wrote to the Duke of Devonshire on the 4th May 1861 :—

'Two years ago I took the liberty of congratulating you on your son's having made the best speech, in the most arduous and critical circumstances, that I ever heard delivered by a man of his age in the House of Commons. On Thursday night, having understood that he was to speak somewhat later, I unfortunately did not hear him.  But, having read the report of his speech, I could not but be struck with the warm and generous tone of the support which he gave to measures not unimportant in themselves and to me entirely vital.'

The only contribution to debates made by Lord Hart-

[1] See Parker's *Life of Sir James Graham*, vol. ii. p. 396.

ington in 1862 were some short remarks as to the mode
of meeting the distress in Lancashire due to the cotton
famine caused by the American Civil War.   In the autumn
of 1862 he crossed the sea to visit that scene of volcanic
action.

# CHAPTER III

## VISIT TO THE UNITED STATES OF AMERICA

THE long series of controversies and events which led to the Civil War had passed into actual fighting with the attack by the Southerners on Fort Sumter, in April 1861. By the middle of the following summer the Confederate armies were holding a defensive line of great length extending from Texas to the Atlantic at the mouth of the river Potomac. In July 1861 the Federals had been badly defeated at Bull Run and at Manasses, thirty miles from Washington. Early in 1862 the Federals had considerable success in the more western area of operations, and captured New Orleans, but in Virginia and Maryland a series of fierce battles were fought, with no decisive results, between April and July, over the hundred miles of country which lie between the rival headquarters of Washington and Richmond. This area, a distance not much greater than that which separated London and Oxford in the English Civil War, was throughout the centre of the storm. On 29th August, five days after Lord Hartington landed at New York, the Southerners, under 'Stonewall' Jackson, defeated General Pope on the old battleground of Bull's Run, and drove his army towards Washington. M'Clellan, who had been moving by another route, along the peninsula which lies between York River and James River, on Richmond, was recalled to cover Washington, before which he took up a strong defensive position. The battle of Antietam or Sharpsburgh was fought by Lee and Jackson against M'Clellan on 17th September. It was an indecisive fight.  Lee had to recross the Potomac, but, in revenge, he captured the Federal fort at Harper's Ferry, made 12,000 men prisoners of war, and took many guns and great military stores.  It was considered by the military authorities that M'Clellan had failed to make the most of his opportunities, and he was superseded in November by Burnside.  This general attempted on 13th December to storm the heights held by the Confederates at Fredericksburg, and was repulsed with enormous loss.  He was then himself superseded, and so the bloody and indecisive campaign of 1862 came to an end.  In September 1862, President Lincoln issued a Proclamation to the effect that, in any Rebel State which did not return to allegiance before the 1st of January, the slaves would be declared free without compensation to their owners.  The Emancipation declaration was issued on that day.  These were the main events which occurred about the time of Lord Hartington's visit to America.

He left England about the middle of August 1862, and arrived at New York on the 24th.  He was joined there by his brother, Lord Edward Cavendish, who was then stationed with his regiment in Canada.  The following quotations are from letters which Lord Hartington wrote to his father.

At New York the travellers made the acquaintance of a Mr. Duncan, who had lived a good deal in England. 'His sister-in-law was there, who is a Southerner and married to a Southerner, but she is a strong Unionist, which is said to be very uncommon.  Her husband is in the South, and cannot get away.  She is by way of being a very clever individual, and talks like a book; but she is rather too clever for me.'  Recruiting for the army was going on vigorously; 'the bounty they are giving is enormous, in some cases £60 and £70 and £80.'

'We dined last night with Mr. Belmont, whom I think Freddy knows. They are all very low indeed, as they have reason to be, for they appear to have got a most awful licking on Saturday last at Bull's Run, and again at Manasses. General Stahl, who is said to be killed, was here only a fortnight since, and was very much liked. He was a great friend of the Belmonts, and I distinguished myself last night by announcing his death to her at dinner, which they had intended to conceal from her till afterwards. She was a good deal shocked, but, I am happy to say, she did not make a scene. I have had several conversations with people about the war, and Freddy will be glad to hear that, at present, I am inclined to be more a Unionist than I was, but I don't think I shall give you any of my opinions at present. The most surprising thing is the moderation with which they still talk of the South, and, I believe, if they could lick them, and the South would come back to-morrow, they would be willing to forget everything that had happened, and go on as usual. The South, on the contrary, appears from what one hears to hate the North more than the devil. They certainly are not pleased with us at present; but most of those I have seen allow that they have no complaint to make of the Government. Individually, they are as civil as it is possible for them to be, and I think those I have seen very agreeable. All those that I have talked to hate the Abolitionists a great deal worse than the South. . . . Nobody here seems to have any confidence in any of the generals. It is quite wonderful how they bear having all the news kept back from them. All Sunday the only news was a despatch from Pope in which he made out that he had had the best of the fighting; but now it appears that they were beaten everywhere, M'Dowell almost cut to pieces, and Washington in very great danger. However, the communications of the army with Washington seem to be safe now, and I don't think a regular siege seems to be expected. If they could, the Confederates would probably have made a sudden dash at it, but, if they cannot do that they are much more likely to cross the Potomac and stir up secession in Maryland. There certainly does not appear to be any idea of giving up here, and I suppose, in the end, they must have the best of the fighting by their superior numbers and money, but as to subduing the South, they do not seem to expect it, and most of them say they see no possible end to it. There are as many people here as usual, which is strange, but most of the young men who used to be here are with the army; in fact, I believe they don't think much of any young man who can go and does not.'[1]

At a party which Lord Hartington attended, a lady suddenly pinned something to his coat, then vanished in the crowd. The Englishman, who supposed this to be a usual part of the proceedings, found himself the object of surprised or hostile glances. Then some one asked him, 'Why are you wearing a rebel badge?' A most impossible American version of this tale is that a young rebel beauty dared the English lord to wear these colours for her sake at a Ministerial reception, that he accepted her challenge, and received several invitations to a duel in consequence.

After leaving New York, Lord Hartington and his brother spent a few days in the White Mountains and at Boston, and then visited Quebec and Montreal, where they were joined by a Canadian friend, Mr. Rose, well known later as Sir John Rose, who wished to see something of events in the South. With him they went to Washington. There—

'We called on Mr. Seward (the Secretary of State), who was very civil but rather prosy, and began by telling us a long story of how he tried to go to the Derby but couldn't, because he had to dine with the Archbishop of Canterbury. He took Mr. Rose and me to the President,

---

[1] Lord Hartington to his father, 2nd September 1862.

who was also very civil, and also told us stories.[1]  I said
I supposed we had come at a bad time to see the country,
and he said, "Well! he guessed we couldn't do them much
harm."  I never saw such a specimen of a Yankee in my
life.  I should think he was a very well-meaning sort of
a man, but, almost every one says, about as fit for his
position now as a fire shovel.  He didn't talk much about
the war, and I should suppose that Seward did much as
he liked with him.'[2]

Lord Hartington was evidently misjudging by the
certainly strange outward appearances and by the talk
of American 'society people.'  President Lincoln formed
a more favourable opinion of his young English visitor
than the visitor did of him.  At the beginning of 1880,
when Lord Hartington was leading the Liberal Party,
and the General Election which should have made him
Prime Minister had just been won, Sir John Rose wrote
to remind him 'of poor Lincoln's prophecy, now nearly
thirty years ago.' . . . 'We were talking about you just
after our interview, and he said, in a sort of soliloquy,
that, if you belonged to their country, you would soon be
in the "front row" in some Presidential Caucus, but as the
Old Country didn't "own to" that kind of arrangement, he
predicted that if he lived ten years, he would hear of your
"having about as prominent a position there as standing
on the top rung" could give you with them.'

The Englishmen obtained passes to go anywhere
through the lines, which were then close to Washington.
They drove with Mr. Seward to the forts on the Maryland side.  'It was a very pretty drive,' wrote Hartington
to his father, 'with a beautiful view back to Washington
and the Capitol, and in front over the Maryland country.'

---

[1] The President began the interview by saying, 'Hartington! Well, that
rhymes to Partington.'

[2] Lord Hartington to his father, 29th September 1862.

They visited a New York regiment which Mr. Seward's son had just left a bank to join.

'We found the regiment in camp close to one of the forts. They had only arrived a day or two and were employed in making themselves comfortable. They were a very fine-looking lot of men indeed, mostly farmers and country people from Western New York, quite as respectable a looking lot as any of our volunteers. They seemed very jolly and in good spirits, but they have had no drill whatever, and I don't see who is to give it to them. The sentry at the Colonel's tent was sitting on a camp-stool and reading the newspaper. I believe a few of the officers have been in other volunteer regiments, but I could not make out that they had a single regular officer among them. It seems a great pity that such fine material should be thrown away, as they very likely may be, by having utterly incompetent officers. All this time there are old regiments which are reduced to seventy or eighty men, but they will not fill them up, but go on raising new ones from some rotten reasons about bounties and length of service and that sort of thing ; but really because the State Governors like to have the appointment of the new officers. . . . Seward talked away all the time, but I was not very much impressed by his arguments. He has given up all idea of finishing the war in ninety or any particular number of days, and says it is now only a question of which will be exhausted first. He says the North have no idea of giving up (and I must say their new levies do not look like it, for they are getting as many men as they can arm or clothe, and a much better class than the first), and that both in men and money the North will be able to outlast the South. I understand nothing about it, and I can't find anybody except Seward who even pretends that he does, as far as having an idea of what the end of it is to be. They mix up in the most perplexing manner the slavery question, which they say makes theirs the just cause, with the Union question, which

is really what they are fighting for.   They say they cannot
spare the South, that they cannot do without the ports and
the Mississippi, and that if they once let it go, they would
split up into half-a-dozen small republics.   I think this
is what they are really fighting for, and I am not sure, now
that their blood is really up, that they won't go on till they
do beat the Southerners by pure exhaustion.

'As to Seward's grumblings about England, I think
I never heard a man talk such nonsense, and I think I shut
him up, or should have done if he ever let any one talk
besides himself.   The proclamation about the slaves had
come out the same morning.   He didn't talk much about
it, and I have not heard much of it.   I don't think anybody
gives it much importance, and it is supposed to be only
a little political business to keep the "infernal radicals,"
as I hear most people call them, quiet.   We went the next
day to see the Capitol, but only to see the outside, as it
is full of wounded.   I believe there are 1500 or 2000 there,
almost all wounded in the arms.   Most of the churches are
full, and a great many of the private houses too.   The city
looks, of course, exactly like a camp.   You see hardly anything but soldiers and baggage-waggons, and stores moving
up to the troops.   I forgot to say that we saw some of the
forts, which looked very strong.   Washington is now completely surrounded by them, I think there are between forty
and fifty, and, if they can only keep a large enough force
to hold them, I suppose it would be almost impossible to
take the place.   The place is in very good order now, very
different from what it was last winter, I imagine.   No drink
is allowed to be sold, and, though the place is full of
soldiers, it is very quiet.   I believe they have 150,000 men
in the lines round Washington.   On Wednesday we dined
with Seward, and met Mr. Everett and others.   I rather
liked Mr. Everett.   I think he wished to be remembered to
Freddy.   We went on Friday by rail to Sandy Hook, within
a mile of Harper's Ferry. . . . We spent the afternoon
at Harper's Ferry.   We were introduced to lots of officers,
General Sumner among others, who is a fine old fellow.

We saw Maryland Heights, which completely command Harper's Ferry, and the loss of which the other day lost them 12,000 men and heaps of stores.  They are all very angry at the surrender, and said it was a disgraceful thing.

'We went on Saturday to Sharpsburg, where M'Clellan's headquarters were.  They lent us some horses there, and we rode over the ground where the battle of Antietam was fought the week before.  Of course most of the traces were removed, but there was a good deal left.  The hottest places were marked by the larger size of the graves, and the number of dead horses lying about still. The greater part of the ground is open, and was cultivated, with strong snake fences, but there was some wood.  This was where the fight was most severe, and in about seven or eight acres of wood there is not a tree which is not full of bullets and bits of shell.  It is impossible to understand how any one could live in such a fire as there must have been there.  The Confederate position was strong, and they all acknowledge that they fought like devils.  It appears to have been as near as possible a drawn battle, though the Confederates retired the next day.  Both armies slept where they had slept the night before, and neither the dead nor many of the wounded were moved from the ground till next day.  It was certainly the biggest battle they have fought, and both sides must have fought well.  I should have liked to see it, and we might have seen it perfectly from a hill without danger. We stayed that night at the Headquarters.  One of General M'Clellan's aides-de-camp put us up in his tent, and they were extremely hospitable and jolly.  The General came in late at night and sent for us, and we had a long talk with him.  I liked him very much.  He was very quiet and modest, and did not swagger at all about his victory, though he does consider it one.  He is certainly the best specimen I have seen among their officers, and is a gentleman, whatever else he may be. All his staff worship him, and most of the officers I have talked to seem to have the greatest confidence in him. He asked after our Freddy, and I told him that he was very strong for the Union, which pleased him much. He does not conceal his opinion about Pope and the politicians, and hates the Abolitionists well. We also saw Burnside, whom we also liked, but not near so much as M'Clellan. He is a jolly, noisy sort of fellow, and they call him the Pirate, which he certainly resembles very much with a great revolver swinging about from his belt. He talked a great deal, and is about the only man whom I have heard approve of the emancipation proclamation, and he does not much, but he says he thinks the whole thing has got beyond them now, that no man can tell how it will end, and is becoming every day what he calls "Providential"; and that they have nothing to do but go on fighting and see what happens.'[1]

Lord Hartington and his brother after leaving Washington went to Chicago, and to some other more western places, and thence again to Canada, visiting Niagara, which 'I admired extremely, much more than I had expected'; also staying at Hamilton, Toronto, and Montreal. Leaving Canada the travellers went to Baltimore, whence Lord Hartington wrote to his father on the 13th December. At that moment a battle near Fredericksburg was daily expected. 'I should not be at all surprised,' he wrote, 'at Burnside getting a most terrific thrashing and losing most of his army; they say here that Lee has got 200,000 men, and in very good order, and of course he can make them fight him whenever he likes.' Baltimore society was divided; but 'rebel' opinion greatly predominated over 'Unionist.' Lord Hartington wrote:—

'Everybody here seems to take the state of things wonderfully coolly. The rebels feel quite certain of a victory, and the Unionists, though I think they are a little

[1] Lord Hartington to his father, 29th September 1862.

uneasy, seem to bear being kept without any news at all a great deal more quietly than we should do in England. We dined with M. Bonaparte on Wednesday, who collected, I believe, all the Union people he could muster here to meet us, but there were only about half-a-dozen of them. They (the Unionists) are more rabid than I have met them anywhere else, I suppose because they come in contact with such rabid rebels. It is rather difficult to get on at all, as neither side can understand one's not sympathising with them. The poor Union men have had a bad time of it here, as all their old friends have cut them, and they don't look as if they knew what to do with themselves. I have seen some of the political prisoners who have just been released. Those I have met are about the most agreeable and clever people I have met in America. I think the Government must have made a great mistake in keeping them locked up for fifteen months, as I believe they were not generally very extreme men when they were arrested, but of course they don't love the Government much more now than they did when they were shut up. I am afraid I am becoming very Southern in my opinions. The people here are so much more in earnest about the thing than the North seem to be, that it is almost impossible not to go a good way with them, though one may think they were wrong at first. I hope Freddy won't groan much over my rebel sympathies, but I can't help them.'

Lord Hartington and his party now wished to visit Richmond and see the Southern side of the war. They were unable to obtain from the Washington authorities passes which would take them across the lines, and resolved to attempt the journey without this assistance, The following letter to the Duke of Devonshire describes this adventurous ride :—

'RICHMOND, *Christmas Day*, /62.

'We arrived here all right on Tuesday last, after a tolerably prosperous journey on the whole. The only mistake was at the beginning. The arrangements had not been properly made, and having gone about twenty miles from Baltimore to a sort of farmhouse, we found that we could not go on at once, but hoped to go on next day. One delay after another kept turning up, and we were kept there till Thursday night. I can't tell you of course how we went, as this may fall into hands not intended to read it, and it might do harm. We rode two nights, being conducted by all sorts of cross-roads and tracks through the woods, and sometimes by no road at all. It was a very hard frost, very cold, but by getting off and walking a good deal, we managed to keep tolerably warm. We put up in the day-time at hospitable houses, and on the second night we crossed the river without any trouble whatever. There were luckily no pickets of any kind about, and we might have come straight through without any difficulty; but they bungled about it. It was very lucky for us that the river was not watched at the time we crossed, as there is a canal which runs parallel to it, and there are only a few culverts under it which are very easily guarded, and if they are, it becomes necessary to swim the canal, which would be disagreeable in a hard frost. When once we got into Virginia, we did the rest of our journey by day, and stopped every evening at somebody's house. Nothing could possibly be more hospitable than the people were; and though they all complained a great deal of having lost everything by the ravages of the Yankees, we usually found quite enough to eat. We arrived at a railway on Monday night, and came on here on Tuesday. It had been settled first that we were to drive most part of the way, but while we were delayed at the farmhouse, we were told that we could not come that way, so we bought horses there, which we sold when we arrived at the railway. We ought to have made a large profit on them, at least in Confederate money, but as they were not looking well after their journey, and as we were in a great hurry about it (the train starting at half-past nine), we only got about the same in Confederate money that we paid in Federal, which

is a loss of about half.  We crossed with five or six others,
but they separated afterwards, and only ourselves and one
other going to South Carolina, did the last part of the
journey, and came on here together.  We had no guide
most of the way through Virginia, but got on pretty well.
One day we lost our way and went to a house to inquire;
we were not only shown the road, but given a most excellent dinner.  We were in several places on the track of the
Federal army in some one of its marches; and the country
looks terribly desolated.  The fences are all pulled down
for firewood, a good many houses burnt, and everything
looking very bare.  Everywhere where we stopped we
heard terrible complaints of the enemy.  All have lost
some of their horses, and some have lost all; a good
many have lost all their slaves; and they have all had
their pigs, cattle, &c., stolen.  In one place they had
burnt a man's wheat, and in this place, which was
near the river, we heard several accounts of murders
committed by the Yankee soldiers on men who were
trying to save their property, and in some cases had
been doing nothing at all.  I dare say the accounts may
be exaggerated, but I saw quite enough to see that the
Federals had done immense mischief, and that they had
not, in the least, shown the respect for private property
which they claim to have done.  The hatred which every
man, woman, and child express for the Yankees is something quite terrible, and I am sure that in Virginia at least
where they have felt so much of the effects of the war, nothing
on earth would ever induce them to submit.  This place
is in a very curious state at present.  In the first place it is
very full, as there are from 70,000 to 80,000 people in it,
instead of 40,000, its usual number.  In the next place
everybody looks extremely shabby and dirty, as they have
had no new clothes since the war began, and are not likely
to get any till it is over.  Everything is immensely dear,
partly on account of the depreciation of the money,
and partly of the scarcity.  The prices at an hotel are
double what they are in the North, and the feeding most

abominable. My coat, which is by no means very new, I have several times been told would be worth over 100 dollars. However they are in good spirits, though they do not think very much of the Fredericksburg victory, as they never had any doubt whatever about it. They do not expect peace for some time, in which I think they are wrong, because they believe too much in the war protestations of the democrats in the North, and I am convinced that they (the democrats) really want peace. As for these people they say they are ready to go on for any length of time, and I believe many of them think the longer the better, because it will widen the breach between them and the Yankees, against whom their hatred is more intense than you can possibly conceive. I have seen several men who say that they were Union men and altogether against Secession, but they are as violent as any others now. They say that the way in which the Federals have carried on the war, the ascendancy of the Abolition party, and many other things, have entirely destroyed every vestige of Union feeling, and I believe that it is so. I don't know at all when this letter will go, or what are the chances of its reaching you, but I must leave a little room in case I have any more to put in. I have been introduced to the Secretary of the Treasury, and Seddon the Secretary of War. The President is not here now, being in the West. We have got a pass to go up to see the army, and are going there on Saturday with Lawley, who is the *Times* correspondent here. We are very unlucky about battles, having arrived ten days after Antietam, and the same time here after Fredericksburg. Both were excellent battles for a spectator. They don't expect any more fighting in Virginia this winter. I hope you are all spending a happy Christmas. We have not had enough to do to-day; but have plenty to do to-morrow, and dine with Mr. Lygon, whom I knew here. To-day C. and I eat our Christmas dinner at a restaurant at our own expense, which was heavy.'

From Richmond Lord Hartington went up to the Confederate camp at Fredericksburg, and spent a week there. 'We saw,' he writes, 'most of the generals and had a very pleasant time.  We saw all the battleground and wished very much, as we did at Sharpsburgh, that we had been in time to see the battle.  We were in some hopes that there was going to be something done while we were there, but it ended in nothing.'  He saw President Jefferson-Davis at Richmond, and several of his Ministers.  'I liked them all very well, and they all talked in a very moderate and sensible way.  They are all quite prepared for a long war ; but are in very good spirits.  Nobody appears to have the least idea of ending the war except in one way; and I am quite convinced that, whatever happens, they can never be brought back into the Union except as conquered provinces, and I think they will take a great deal of conquering before that is done.'  Near Richmond Lord Hartington saw two or three slave plantations.  'The negroes hardly look as well off as I expected to see them, but they are not dirtier or more uncomfortable-looking than Irish labourers.'  In the same letter Lord Hartington says, 'I have certainly become much more Southern since I came here, and it is quite impossible for any one not to admire the spirit of the whole people. Nobody complains about their sufferings or losses, and such unanimity I should think was never seen before.'

This reminds one of the fine passage in the address issued by President Jefferson-Davis in this same year, which runs :—

'This great strife has awakened in our people the highest emotions and qualities of the human soul.  It is cultivating feelings of patriotism, virtue, and courage. Instances of self-sacrifice and of generous devotion to the noble cause for which we are contending are rife throughout the land.  Never has a people evinced a more determined spirit than that now animating men, women, and children in every part of our country. Upon the first call men fly to arms, and wives and mothers send their husbands and sons to battle without a murmur of regret.'

It truly was one of the most gallant fights in all history against a crushing superiority in men and money combined with an equally stubborn resolution.

The travellers next went to Charlestown, and succeeded in getting thence by sea, notwithstanding the blockade, to New York, where they had two or three weeks of pleasant society before sailing for home. In his last letter to his father from America, 17th February 1863, Lord Hartington says :—

'I suppose there will be an early debate in the House of Commons about America, but perhaps it is just as well for me not to be there, as I might be tempted to speak, and my opinions are all so mixed up and confused that I should probably make a mess. Besides, notwithstanding my confusion, I am decidedly very Southern in the main, and, from what I see, that would not at all suit my constituents. How they can be so idiotic as to admire Lincoln and his Emancipation Proclamation, and how they can talk such nonsense as they do about emancipation I cannot understand, and I shall have to tell them so.'

Lord Hartington, no doubt, in time revised these judgments. Romance in this war was on the side of the South, and awoke an echo of the romantic and chivalrous in the hearts of descendants of English Cavaliers. The ruined homes of the gallant Virginian gentlemen appealed more strongly to the heir of a great territorial family than did the rich merchant houses of New York. Many things were distasteful, even to strong Federals, in the polemics of the

Abolitionists. It is generally admitted now that, granting the main end to be right, yet the sudden and complete emancipation of the slaves, and the attempt to turn them at once into full citizens, was an error. The Southern States were certainly resisting an invasion of their constitutional rights. But it was not the destiny of the United States to be disunited. The Northerners were fighting in the cause of the future. Lord Hartington himself, in his own country, was one day to lead in a fierce, though, as it happened, a bloodless fight in defence of the political unity of a nation. A visit to a country in a state of civil war must have been good education in the school of life for a young statesman, vividly impressing on his mind the realities which lie below, and not so far below, political words, phrases, and documents.

## CHAPTER IV

### THE WAR OFFICE, 1863-1866

BEFORE Lord Hartington reached England, Lord Palmerston had addressed the following letter (7th February 1863) to the Duke of Devonshire :—

'Mr. Whitbread, the Lay Lord of the Admiralty, is obliged on account of his health to resign his appointment, and I wish to know from you whether we might look to Lord Hartington as a successor to Mr. Whitbread in that office.

'The office is one of a good deal of labour, but of labour of a highly interesting kind, being connected as it is with the management of the naval service of the country. Lord Hartington has shown much ability whenever he has taken part in the debates of the House, and I feel very strongly that it is of great importance to the country, and is highly conducive to the working of our Constitution, that young men in high aristocratical positions should take part in the administration of public affairs, and should not leave the working of our political machine to classes whose pursuits and interests are of a different kind.'

The arrangement eventually made was that Hartington should begin ministerial life, not as a Lord of the Admiralty, but as Under-Secretary at the War Office, where he took up his duties in April 1863, having secured the necessary re-election in North Lancashire without a contest. The Secretary of State for War was a peer, Lord de Grey,[1] so that the representation of the War Office in

---

[1] Lord de Grey was created Marquess of Ripon in 1871, and was Viceroy of India when Lord Hartington was at the India Office, 1880-82.

the House of Commons devolved upon Lord Hartington. He was then in his thirtieth year, had been six years in Parliament, had only twice spoken in debates of importance, and had been by no means assiduous in his attendance. His appointment shows the advantage then possessed, and still in a less degree possessed, by—to use Palmerston's words—'young men in high aristocratical positions' in this country. There is the danger that things may be made too easy for them, with consequent detriment to character. On the other hand, there is the benefit, if selection is judiciously exercised, that men under this system can arrive at positions of responsibility and command while they are still in full possession of their highest vigour and energy. There is the more advantage in this, since the ingredients of experience, caution, wariness, and reluctance to take a decided course, are abundantly supplied by permanent officials who, after a long ascent, have arrived in their late maturity at the highest posts in the service.

There is an everlasting and natural struggle between the Treasury and the Military and Naval Departments. At this particular period the struggle was emphasised, or made acute, by the fact that the Prime Minister favoured a spirited foreign policy, and consequently, generous expenditure upon armaments, while the Chancellor of the Exchequer not only held the strongest economic views, but suspected and disliked the spirited foreign policy. Both Prime Minister and Chancellor were, moreover, men of dominating character, and each loved to have his own way. The antithesis was amusingly expressed by Disraeli in one of his speeches :—

'Lord, Sir, we need not maunder in antechambers to discover differences in the Cabinet, when we have a patriotic Prime Minister appealing to the spirit of the country, telling it that it must be prepared to defend itself against aggressive ambition, and to show Europe that we are determined to maintain our rights, and when, at the same time, we find his Chancellor of the Exchequer, whose duty it is to supply ways and means by which those exertions are to be supported, proposing votes with an innuendo, and recommending expenditure with a whispered invective.'

Palmerston wrote to Gladstone on the 29th April 1862,[1] commenting on a speech in which the latter had complained that the nation had forced undue naval and military expenditure upon Government and Parliament. Palmerston said that, in the first place, this was not correctly stated, inasmuch as Government and Parliament had been in sympathy with the nation, and, in the next place, if it had been true, he should have seen in it 'rather a proof of the superior sagacity of the nation than a subject for reproach.' Cobden attacked the Prime Minister on the same score in 1861, and said that Lord Palmerston had cost the country a hundred millions. The reply of the Minister was to thank Mr. Cobden for having 'drawn attention to the successful efforts which the Government had made for the preservation of the honour, the safety, and the interests of the Empire.'

That keen observer, Speaker Denison, in a letter to Charles Greville referring to Cobden's assaults on defence expenditure, wrote:[2] 'It is the fault of Cobden's mind to see one object so strongly that his view cannot embrace another at the same time.' Mr. Gladstone, it is generally admitted, also suffered from this defect. In our system, moreover, each great Department is so biassed by its own main *raison d'être* that no one but a strong Prime Minister can make them all subserve the public interest, restraining

[1] Evelyn Ashley's *Life of Lord Palmerston*, vol. ii. p. 413.
[2] See Greville, 11th August 1860.

within due limits the zeal of some to spend and of others
to save. The Prime Minister is like the driver of a four-
horse coach who has to synthesise the energies of his
team. The Treasury was, in this period, so far successful
that the Army Estimates in 1866 were about £2,000,000
less than those in 1862, although higher than those before
the war.

The 'aggressive ambition' feared in these years was
that of Napoleon III. and his army. The Volunteer movement and the expenditure on coast fortifications were
directed against this danger. Expressions in Lord Hartington's speeches and letters show that his own sympathies
as to these matters were strongly with the 'patriotic Prime
Minister,' and against the views of Cobden and the Chancellor of the Exchequer. The first real speech which the
new Under-Secretary for War had to make in that capacity
was in order to introduce the Volunteers Bill of 1863. The
object of this Bill was to give to the Volunteer force, which
had been initiated in 1859, and had already enrolled 159,000
men, some public assistance by way of a permanent staff
of non-commissioned officers and other means. Lord
Hartington, characteristically, arrived late at the House
on the occasion of his first important official speech,
and found there another Minister trying to kill time
with platitudes, but he spoke without any appearance
of nervousness. Lord Granville, who was sitting in the
gallery between the Duke of Somerset and Lord de Grey,
wrote to the Duke of Devonshire, 'We were all much
pleased. His manner excellent. Cool as a cucumber, and
civil at the same time. Somerset and I agree that there is
no reason why, if he chooses, he should not, at some future
time, lead the House of Commons.'

Lord Hartington drew a moral in support of the Bill
from his observations in America. He said that the Army

of the North, which seemed imperfect in discipline and was wanting in *esprit de corps*, had not been found efficient in aggressive warfare ; but the Army of the Southern States was composed of men animated by very much the same feeling, and drawn from the same class as our Volunteer force. To that Southern Army our Volunteers were, he felt persuaded, superior in physical appearance and strength ; in discipline and equipment, too, they were superior ; while he could not bring himself to believe that they were inferior in courage, and it had been seen how the Southern Army had fought in resisting the attacks of the invader. If then England should be invaded, we had at our command 150,000 men as efficient for the purposes of defence as any army which could be called into the field. The movement, he added, was entirely the spontaneous effort of the English people, fostered, encouraged, and brought to perfection by the exertions of such men as Lord Elcho.

A discussion arose in Committee as to the exclusion of Ireland from the operation of the Volunteer system. Some Irish members urged that it was impolitic to continue this exclusion, and unjust, if it were continued, to tax Ireland for the support of English Volunteers. Lord Hartington replied that the Government had no fear of any want of loyalty on the part of the Irish nation, but were unable to allow Volunteer regiments to be formed in Ireland on account of the religious animosity prevailing in that country. It was thought to be undesirable to place arms in the hands of the people when a law existed under which the Lord Lieutenant, by proclamation of a county or district, might deprive them of those arms next day. The fact was, as a subsequent Irish speaker put it, that 'the Government would not trust an Irishman with arms, being apparently of opinion that he would shoot his neighbour with them.' The incident illustrated rather vividly the profound difference between the conditions of Great Britain and Ireland.

In the early sixties some reduction in the strength of the army was effected. It was, however, becoming evident that there would have to be a considerable expenditure upon armaments. The muzzle-loading gun and rifle did their last important services in the Crimea and the Indian Mutiny. By 1863 it was merely a question what kind of breech-loader it would be best to adopt. Investigations and experiments were carried on, but the outbreak of the Austro-Prussian War in 1866, shortly after Lord Harting-ton ceased to be at the War Office, found our army still equipped with the muzzle-loader. The Prussians had chosen for war the moment when their troops were armed with a breech-loading rifle and the Austrians still with a muzzle-loading. The Prussian soldier could fire thrice while the Austrian fired once, and the battle-fields of Bohemia were a convincing proof that any nation which would be saved must re-arm. Steps for the rapid con-version of the Enfield rifle were then taken.

The Crimean War had revealed many defects in military organisation which had to be remedied at a considerable cost. In the period 1863 to 1866 the strength of the army was greater, and the estimates higher, than in the years immediately before the Crimean War. There were during this period no changes of importance in the terms of service, or in the general army system, or in the administrative system connected with the War Office. Reforms of this kind, on any large scale, did not begin till English opinion had once more been startled from its habitual lethargy by the swift and unexpected German victories in the war against France of 1870. These proved that the Prussian successes in 1866 had been due to something else besides superiority in the shape of a quick-firing rifle. But in the preceding years the English organisation was much as it had been in the days of the Duke of Wellington. The Commander-in-Chief, ruling at the Horse Guards, with not very well-defined functions, was the royal Duke of Cambridge, who held that post so long.

Lord Hartington's speeches on the affairs of his department were sound and lucid, and gave satisfaction to the old Prime Minister. In June 1865 a Tory member raised the point that the Secretary of State for War ought to be a member of the House of Commons. Lord Palmerston, in reply, spoke of the manner in which Lord Hartington " acquits himself of his duties, the complete master he makes himself of every subject with which he has to deal, and how fully he understands the whole matter which he has to treat." After Hartington's statement in Committee in the preceding year (1864), Speaker Denison wrote to the Duke of Devonshire :—

'Just now General Peel (the ex-War Secretary) came by me. I said, "Allow me to ask you, and tell me candidly, how did Hartington do last night?" General Peel answered, " He did uncommonly well. He has got a very good head. There was no pretension to fine speaking, but he went through all the points with great clearness. It was very well done indeed." He turned back from his seat, just as he was sitting down, and said, " Let me add that all of us on this side of the House were of the same opinion." It cannot fail to give you pleasure to hear such testimony as this. It gives me real pleasure to write it.'

Lord Palmerston was now considerably endeared to the nation, not only by his spirit and humour, but by his antiquity. It was a joke of the time that Government were going to the country on the cry of ' Palmerston and no Politics ' or ' Palmerston and no Principles.' The General

Elections took place in July 1865, and a Liberal majority exceeding that of 1859 was returned.[1]   Lord Hartington held his seat in North Lancashire without difficulty, and his two brothers, Frederick and Edward, also entered Parliament.   An uncle, Lord George Cavendish, was also returned, so that the family was strongly represented on the Liberal side of the new House of Commons.

The Prime Minister, now in his eighty-first year, did not long enjoy his latest triumph.   He died in October 1865.   His ministerial career had been longer and happier than any in previous English history.   He had spent his youth as a member of the Tory Governments from 1809 to 1828 ; his maturer years in the Whig Administrations of Lord Grey, Lord Melbourne, and Lord John Russell.   He had held office in the Coalition Aberdeen Government, and, with a short break, had himself been Prime Minister for the last ten years of his life.   Lord Palmerston was succeeded in the Premiership by Earl Russell, in the leadership of the House of Commons by Mr. Gladstone.   Other changes soon took place.

In February 1866 Lord de Grey was moved from the War Office to the India Office, and Hartington was promoted to be Secretary of State for War in his stead.   He thus, at the age of thirty-three, entered the Cabinet as one of the chief officers of the State.   The Duke of Cambridge wrote to him that 'no successor could have been selected to fill the post more acceptable or agreeable to me.'   Lord Hartington said in reply, 'I feel that my past services in the Department have not earned for me such sudden and unexpected promotion, and that the responsibility of the office which I have undertaken is one which I

---

[1] Of the members returned at the elections of 1865, 367 were classed as Liberals and 290 as Conservatives.   The net gain of the Liberals at this election was of 24 seats.

would gladly have avoided for some years to come.' Mr. Knatchbull Hugessen wrote to him on this occasion, 'You will fulfil my prophecy and be Prime Minister if you will only stick to political work.' This was the doubt which haunted all his friends.

In the year 1866 there were some rather difficult military questions. It was not easy to obtain sufficient recruits in consequence of the very flourishing and expanding conditions of trade, and Lord Hartington had to constitute a Royal Commission to inquire into this subject. The question of the modernisation of arms was still pending. There was trouble due to the propagation of an active Fenianism among the rank and file of Irish regiments. Some non-commissioned officers were tried by court-martial for enrolling soldiers in the Fenian organisation. Two were condemned to death, though the sentences were commuted, and there was a quarrel between lawyers and soldiers as to the adequacy of the procedure. It was not, however, till the following year that the Fenian conspiracy made necessary some active use of military force in Ireland.

Hartington recreated himself when, for a day or two, he could escape from the toils of office, by hunting or by attending one of the more important race-meetings. This year the Tory chief, Lord Derby, won a bet of £100 from him on the Derby race, and in acknowledging the cheque offered a revenge. 'I shall be quite ready,' he wrote, 'to make the same bet for next year's Derby, laying against all the horses that shall have appeared in public before the first day of Goodwood Races, though the offer on my part is rather a rash one, as there is already a rattling favourite in Hermit.' Lord Derby, it has been observed, would not have turned Homer's report of the chariot-races before Troy into English verse so

spirited had he not been fond of actual horse-racing.
When Mr. Chaplin's famous horse made him lose his
new bet with Lord Hartington in 1867, Lord Derby was
Prime Minister.

The rule of Palmerston had been a period of arrest
in democratic evolution.  Mr. Gladstone wrote to Sir
James Graham on November 27, 1860 : [1]  'We live now
in anti-reforming times.  All improvements have to be
urged in apologetic, almost in supplicatory tones.  I sometimes reflect how much less liberal, as to domestic policy,
is this Government than Sir Robert Peel's, and how much
the tone of ultra-Toryism prevails among a large portion
of the Liberal party.'

In 1858 the short-lived Conservative Government had
played with an Extension of the Franchise Bill, but
nothing had come of this.  Lord Robert Cecil (afterwards Lord Salisbury), in an article in the *Quarterly
Review* in 1866, alleged that Lord Palmerston had staved
off admission of the artisan classes to political power
by throwing other concessions to the pursuing Radicals.

'Just as in 1860 and 1861 the reforming zeal of the
Radicals was bought off by the sacrifice of the paper
duty, so, from 1861 to 1865, it was appeased by the
sacrifice of the gallant Confederacy.  But with the fall
of Richmond, Mr. Bright's heart was set at ease concerning the fate of the Government to which his true
allegiance was given' (that at Washington *i.e.*).  'And
the moment Lord Palmerston was removed by death,
the Government instinctively felt that the time had again
come round for buying off once more their insatiable
ally.  This time there was nothing for it but to produce
a Reform Bill.'

The truth was that, as the events of 1867 showed,
the rise in real power, through their trade-unions, of

[1] See Parker's *Life of Sir James Graham.*

the urban artisan class had made their admission to political power inevitable. The Bill introduced by Lord Russell's Government in the spring of 1866 proposed to reduce the £10 annual house value qualification in the boroughs to one of £7. It was calculated that the change would admit about 400,000 new voters to the electoral body. Lord Hartington spoke in support of this measure in the House of Commons on April 12, 1866. He rested his argument mainly upon the ground that neither party could escape from the pledges which they had given on this subject, a reasoning which never betokens much zeal on the part of those who use it. He said:—

'I would remind the House that, whether they consider those pledges rash or not, they have to be fulfilled. It is all very well to say that no excitement about reform prevails at present. Is it impossible that a contingency might arise in which something might happen to disturb the tranquillity of the country and produce a great political agitation? I am far from saying that it is impossible to resist successfully a great political agitation; but I do say that the only ground on which you should successfully resist agitation should be the high ground of justice, patriotism, and honour; and I say that we cannot build a platform on which to raise ourselves to that height out of broken promises and abandoned pledges.'

Mr. Lowe, he added, in speaking against the Bill, had quoted 'the eloquent and beautiful lines of the poet'—

> 'His honour rooted in dishonour stood
> And faith unfaithful made him falsely true,'

and he expressed his surprise that this quotation should have been made—

'from one of our greatest poets in defence of a policy which, whatever may be said of its expediency, cannot be recommended as one of high and chivalrous honour.

I do not believe that any poet who ever wrote, or any statesman who was ever worthy of the name, and exercised power in this House, would counsel any party, or any member, to cast away pledges so solemnly given as those which we have given, and to which we now desire to give effect.'

This was nearly the only instance of a reference made by Lord Hartington in Parliament to poetry or poets. Perhaps these lines of Tennyson touched him in a special way. Fidelity was indeed a leading characteristic of Lord Hartington. No man was less capable of breaking promises, or of deviating, for reason of personal interest or inclination, from a line of conduct to which he had pledged his word.[1]

A strong group of Liberals, headed by Lowe, opposed the Reform Bill; it got through the second reading by a minute majority, and was finally wrecked upon an amendment which, a year later, appeared to be truly insignificant. A Liberal party, which had been returned in 1865 on no definite issue, but to support Palmerston, was not, as a whole, enthusiastic for reform. Lord Russell's Government resigned on 26th June 1866, and Lord Derby entered upon the third of his short-lived Administrations. Disraeli was again Chancellor of the Exchequer. General Peel succeeded at the War Office to Lord Hartington, who now found himself, much to his pleasure, free for all too short a space from official duties.

[1] Mr. Lowe, on a previous day of the debate, had said that if any member 'had got into a situation incompatible with honour'—*i.e.* by giving pledges opposed to his real conviction—'he should get out of it. If he remain in it he will be in that position described by one of our greatest poets,' and he then quoted the above lines, and added, ' I hope therefore we shall not hear that hon. gentlemen are pledged to act contrary to their consciences, and to do what they believe will be injurious to their country.' The poet, by using the word 'falsely,' instead of some such word as 'strongly' or 'nobly,' seems to agree with Mr. Lowe rather than with Lord Hartington. But, if so, was he right? It is an open question in ethics,

# CHAPTER V

## 1866-1868

SOON after the resignation of the Liberal Government the war for supremacy in Germany between Prussia and Austria broke out.  Prussia then had a population of 20,000,000.  Within three weeks of the declaration of war she had in the field 400,000 men and 900 guns, with 317,000 trained men in reserve as a second line.[1]  The campaign ended in six weeks in a complete, well-deserved, and well-used victory for the rising Power.  Lord Hartington visited Berlin in September, and saw, on the 20th of that month, the entry of the King of Prussia and his victorious army.

'I should say,' he writes to his father, 'that the reception of the King and of the army was not very enthusiastic, but perhaps it is not the habit of these people to be very enthusiastic about anything.  They certainly are very modest about their successes, and speak of them as if they were to be attributed more to the blunders and disorganisation of the Austrians than to their own perfection, or even to the needle-gun.  We saw Spandau, the principal arsenal, yesterday, which is not to be compared in any respect to Woolwich, but I think that there are some things which we might learn from them as to the organisation of their army.'

He made the acquaintance of many of the generals, and had some conversation with Bismarck, who 'made himself very agreeable, much more than most of the

---

[1] The German Empire, with a population of 65,000,000, can now (1911) put 1,000,000 men into the field at the opening of a campaign, and 4,000,000 trained men altogether.

people here, who are generally as stiff as pokers.' It was
also necessary to call on 'innumerable princes and officials,
which is very uninteresting, and a great waste of time.'
Thence he travelled to Vienna, visiting on the way the
recent battle-field of Königgrätz.

'As we went,' he wrote to his father from Vienna,
'with Russell, who saw part of the battle, and had been
over the field again with others who had seen other parts
of the battle, we could make out everything very well.[1]
There were not many traces of the fight left now, except
the graves, and they will soon be invisible, as they are
already ploughed over, and only marked by wooden
crosses, which will soon disappear. It is very difficult
to understand how the Austrians got such a licking as they
did, and the position, though a very strong one, was the
worst possible to be beaten in, as they had a river behind
them. They don't quite admit it here, but I should imagine
that their army must have been altogether demoralised,
and a great part of it must have fought very badly.'

Lord Hartington took small part in the debates of
1867. He spoke only on a few minor points in respect
of the franchise and re-distribution bills, wherewith
Disraeli, in a minority in the House of Commons, fusil-
laded by Gladstone, who was much irritated, violently
assailed by some of his own party, reluctantly supported by his chief, and with the unwilling co-operation
of Radicals, was performing his great manœuvre of
'dishing the Whigs.' Hartington made, however, this
session, a speech or two upon matters connected with
the army. In one of these he said that the Prussian-
Austrian War had shown that an efficient infantry soldier
might be obtained by a period of drill not exceeding three
years; indeed much of the Prussian army was composed
of men who had not been in training for more than one

---

[1] Russell was the famous *Times* war correspondent.

year. Much to the pleasure of the Duke of Cambridge, who wrote to thank him, he spoke against the proposal for an immediate abolition of the system of purchasing commissions, on the ground that public opinion was not ripe for the step, and that the means and results of effecting it had still to be carefully thought out. He also spoke against a motion in favour of the entire abolition of flogging as a punishment in the army. He thought it 'almost the only punishment that can be inflicted in time of war, and also an appropriate one, which ought to be inflicted in cases of mutiny and aggravated insubordination.'

On the 9th March 1867, Lord Hartington received a letter from Lord Strathnairn, the General then commanding in Ireland, giving an account of his anti-Fenian operations by means of 'flying columns.' Lord Strathnairn, like Charles Gordon and William Butler, and some other soldiers who had seen Ireland before the land legislation, was convinced that something besides force was required. 'The treasonable associations,' he wrote, 'must be extinguished with the utmost energy and by suitable measures. Then it will be for you statesmen to adopt those remedial measures, the mottoes of which, I hope, will be policy, justice, and, above all, a moderation which will ensure equal rights to adverse parties, without giving either a triumph.'

The winters of 1866 to 1867 and 1867 to 1868 were spent by the Marquis of Hartington mainly in hunting. His chief resort for the last two or three years had been, and now more than ever was, Kimbolton Castle, in the shire of Huntingdon, where his hostess was the splendidly beautiful Duchess of Manchester, who was his most intimate friend, and in 1892 became Duchess of Devonshire.[1]

[1] A friend advanced in years has said to the writer, 'No one knows how gloriously beautiful a woman can be who did not see the Duchess of Manchester when she was thirty.'

About Christmas 1867 Lord Russell, now seventy-five, signified his intention of retiring from the leadership of the Liberal party. In February 1868 Lord Derby resigned the post of First Minister for reasons of health, and was succeeded by Disraeli. Gladstone and Disraeli, men of types as opposite as it would be possible to find, were thus left confronting each other as the chiefs, in every sense, of the two parties. The strategy which had kept the Conservative Government in power with a House of Commons elected to support Palmerston, ceased to be effective as soon as the passing of the reform measure was completed. The schism in the Liberal party was more or less healed, and though there had been some intrigues to keep Mr. Gladstone out of power, they came to nothing. Lord Hartington had heard of them, and of some suggestions of a coalition of Whigs with the Tories, but, as he wrote to his father, he told one of the plotters that whatever these designs might be he would have nothing to do with them. At the end of April 1868, Mr. Gladstone, as fully recognised leader of the party, moved his famous resolutions committing the House of Commons to the disestablishment and partial disendowment of the State Church of Ireland. Lord Hartington spoke in support of the principal resolution, which was carried on a division by a majority of 65. He said :—

'I look on the adoption of the resolution as a measure of justice, and, if the worst anticipations of its opponents should be realised, and if, unfortunately, it should be necessary to continue to rule Ireland with a heavy hand, still we owe it to ourselves to leave no grievance unredressed. It is because I wish to see a firm administration of law as well as conciliatory policy in Ireland, that I most earnestly desire that we shall place the justice of our whole system of government there beyond dispute.'

The Conservative Government did not resign or dissolve at once in consequence of this defeat. The constituencies, as rearranged under the recent reform measures, would not be ready for elections till the autumn. It was therefore agreed that the ascertainment of the will of the nation as to the Irish Church and other matters should be deferred till then. The General Election took place in November 1868. Its result was the return of a Liberal majority of 112. In Lancashire, however, there was a strong dislike to the Irish Church proposals, and all the Liberal candidates were defeated in the four double-membered divisions into which the county, apart from the boroughs, was then divided. Lord Hartington lost his seat in North Lancashire to a son of the powerful House of Stanley. The probability of defeat had for some time been apparent, and there had been a proposal from headquarters that one of the Liberal candidates for North-East Lancashire should be induced to retire in favour of Lord Hartington, and that an arrangement should be made with the Tories that, if they were not opposed in the Northern division, they should not oppose in the North-Eastern. The arrangement, however, did not prove practicable, and Lord Hartington himself disliked it, especially as one of the candidates for the North-Eastern division was young Mr. Shuttleworth (now Lord Shuttleworth), who was, he wrote, 'a personal friend.'

Mr. Gladstone was defeated in South-West Lancashire, the district which had given him hospitality since he lost his seat for Oxford University, but, in anticipation of this possibility, he had already been returned | for Greenwich.

'It is not pleasant,' Lord Hartington wrote to his father, 'to be beaten in this way, and I don't like it, but I can't say that I am very unhappy about it.' There is, perhaps, something stimulating in defeat to the more lethargic temperament.  Before the battle Lord Granville had written to his cousin congratulating him on the energy with which he was working at his 'obdurate constituency.' . . . 'Barring the expense, this contest is the best thing that could have happened to you. It stirs your blood, airs your vocabulary, and adds much to your popularity in the country at large.'  The real Anglo-Saxon temperament, so admirably delineated by Walter Scott in his Athelstane in *Ivanhoe*, requires, perhaps, the actuality of hard fighting to bring it into full play.

## CHAPTER VI

### THE LIBERAL GOVERNMENT OF 1868 TO 1874

THE Conservative Government resigned early in December 1868. Mr. Gladstone undertook to form a new Administration; and it became a question how a place was to be found for a man of Cabinet rank who was not provided with a seat in Parliament. Mr. Gladstone, at first, asked Lord Hartington to accept the Lord-Lieutenancy of Ireland. The terms of the offer were a little enigmatic. ' It may,' he wrote, ' be possible, and desirable, after a time, to make a change in the local government of Ireland, but it is also probable that when such a period arrived there might also be opportunity for other arrangements for our coming into yet closer contact.'

Palmerston once wrote about Napoleon III: ' His mind seems as full of schemes as a warren is of rabbits, and, like rabbits, his schemes go to ground for a moment to avoid notice or antagonism.' Mr. Gladstone's mind, also, was full of underground passages. The idea which here for a moment bolted out, then vanished, was probably that of abolishing the post of Irish Viceroy, and substituting, for social purposes, a royal residence.

Lord Hartington declined this offer, and Mr. Gladstone did not press it, and appointed Lord Spencer to this post. Lord Granville wrote to Lord Hartington: ' The thing which has most agitated Gladstone has been how to act most fairly, and in the most favourable way to your interests. He could not leave the War Office unfilled.'

The result was that the War Office was given to Mr. Cardwell, and Lord Hartington was made Postmaster-General
upon condition that he found a seat before Parliament met
in February.    If he failed to secure one he was to give
up the post.  He accepted the office on these terms, but
he wrote to his father, ' I am not quite pleased about it,
and don't feel sure that I have done right.'

To be Postmaster-General after having been, in Lord
Russell's Government, Secretary of State for War, was a
very considerable fall, both in point of dignity and salary.
There may have been special reasons, but it is not clear why
Lord Hartington could not, upon the same condition of
soon finding a seat, have been appointed to the War Office.
Mr. Gladstone himself, when at the beginning of 1846 he
rejoined Sir Robert Peel's Administration, after his exodus
on the Maynooth question, was for months, indeed until
the fall of that Government, Secretary of State for the
Colonies, without having a seat in the House of Commons.
But a Prime Minister engaged upon the delicate work of
Cabinet-making, is not to be rashly blamed.  It is certain
also that Cardwell proved to be an excellent choice for the
War Office.

At the end of December, Mr. Green Price, member for
the Radnor Boroughs, in Wales, was kind enough to resign
his seat in favour of the Postmaster-General.  There was
a contest, but Lord Hartington was elected for the seat in
March, and reappeared, therefore, in the new House of
Commons very soon after it met.

Lord Hartington held the office of Postmaster-General
for two years.  The only important departmental measure
which he had to carry through Parliament was the transfer
to the State of the undertakings of the Electric Telegraph
Companies, at a cost of nearly £7,000,000.  He was,
however, in 1870, placed in charge of the Ballot Bill, having

been chairman of a Select Committee which had, in fact, reported against both the abolition of hustings' nominations and the introduction of secret voting. He said (9th May 1870), in introducing the measure, that the public nomination was too often ' nothing but an expensive, a mischievous and a useless farce which tends to bring the Constitution of the country, and representative institutions generally, into contempt, and to disgust the most peaceable and intelligent portion of the community with everything connected with elections.' Dickens drew an exact and immortal picture of the hustings' method in his election at Eatonswill. It is safe to say that this mediæval process, as personally experienced, inspired no man with more disgust than the member for the Radnor Boroughs. But to secret voting he was a reluctant convert. He referred, in this speech, to the argument that the act of voting is a public duty and should involve a public responsibility. This view had hitherto, he said, induced him to vote against the system of secret ballot, and still made him reluctant to come to a different conclusion. He said that there could be no more worthy a spectacle in a free country than that of constituencies returning members to Parliament by an open, a pure, a tranquil, and, above all things, a free election. But the essential matter was the freedom of choice; the other attributes of the ideal election were not essential, only desirable. If freedom could not be ensured without sacrifice of open voting, then open voting, for a period at any rate, must be sacrificed. The system of open voting had not hitherto given either pure, or tranquil, or free elections. It was known that in the Colonies, where the ballot had been used for some time,

' when the necessity for secrecy had disappeared, the secrecy itself had disappeared, and that, when no one is disposed to take advantage of the knowledge, every voter votes just as openly and publicly with the ballot as without it. Therefore, I am in hopes that, under a system of ballot, the day may come when not only our desires in respect of purity, tranquillity, and freedom of election may be realised, but openness of voting may be regained.'

Lord Hartington then, in characteristic style, made an excursion into the domain of ethics.

'I really feel scarcely qualified to decide the nice moral point that appears to be involved in the argument, whether it is more wrong to act a lie, or to tell a lie. Those who argue that the ballot will encourage hypocrisy and deception assume, of course, that the voter has some object in telling some one that he is going to vote one way when he is really going to vote another. If he has the desire, under the present system of open voting, to vote one way, and yet in order to fulfil some obligation to another person he votes the other way, that, in my opinion, is acting a lie, whereas, in the case of secret voting, he will tell one. I do not pretend to decide in which case the greater moral guilt is incurred; but I do contend that the encouragement to hypocrisy and deception afforded by the ballot will not be a very long one, because when the voting is once proved to be perfectly secret no one will take the trouble to ask the voter which way he has given his vote.'

Probably the ballot has done more to protect Conservative voters than Liberal ones, because the moral pressure of working class and trade-union collective opinion is infinitely greater than that exercised by wealthier classes upon poorer ones. The tendency to return to virtually open voting is now marked, and is shown by the increasing use of party colours worn by electors at elections. Where parties are fairly balanced the joy of irritating an enemy and pleasing a friend has overcome more selfish considerations.

HOLKER HALL IN LANCASHIRE, NOW THE PROPERTY OF LORD RICHARD CAVENDISH

The measure was not carried through in this session
of 1870, but it became law two years later.


## II

Lord Hartington, in the session of 1870 (2nd May),
spoke in support of the Irish Land Bill which legalised in
Ulster, and extended to other parts of rural Ireland, the
custom by which a tenant whose tenancy was terminated
by the landlord for any cause except non-payment of rent
was enabled to claim compensation for tenant's improvements and goodwill.  He said that :—

'Irish landlords have, as a body, done their duty to
their tenants, while they have, perhaps, put up with
more, and sacrificed more than any body of landlords
either in England or Scotland have done.  But probably
there are some who are inclined to use the power the
law gives them with somewhat more than strict justice,
and even with severity, and they have produced discord
and brought unpopularity and distrust upon all.  I think
the landlords of Ireland would, of all people, be the most
grateful to Parliament for passing this Bill, in which
there is no provision that will oblige them to do more
than the majority of good landlords willingly do now.
I cannot see why the landlords of Ireland, good as I
believe them in general to be, should object to a measure
which will give to the tenants that sense of security
which in fact they now possess, but which the acts of a
few have hitherto prevented them from feeling.'

It would have been better if the legislation of 1870
could have had a still wider scope.  Much misery might
have been saved if the legislation of 1881 had been pressed
in 1870, and if the consequent transfer of holdings from
landlord to tenant thereby made necessary had been begun
earlier.  But public opinion in 1870 was not ripe for larger

measures. Mr. Gladstone himself thought that the Act of 1870 was the last word in Irish agrarian reform, and said a little later that Ireland had now only one grievance left, that of university education. The larger agrarian change had to await the years of wet seasons and agricultural depression, and to be proceeded with when Ireland was in a state of active rebellion. The Act of 1870 only increased the exasperation caused by eviction for non-payment of rent. In the end the few bad landlords, chiefly those who had bought land as pure investment under the Encumbered Estates Act, brought down the social edifice. If ten good men can save a city, ten bad, or unwise ones, can sometimes destroy it.

The passing of the Land Act was accompanied by one of that long series of measures which have dispensed with safeguards of English justice in order to meet the conditions of a country where public opinion has been in sympathy with, and not hostile to, agrarian crime. At the beginning of the year 1870 Lord Spencer had pressed for additional powers to preserve order in Ireland, but the Prime Minister and the majority of the Cabinet were unwilling to proceed in this direction until the remedial measure, the Land Bill, was well on its way. Lord Spencer wrote to Lord Hartington from Dublin on 3rd February 1870 :—

'Individually, I hold a strong opinion that the decision of the Cabinet is not right as to agrarian outrage.

'I feel the difficulty, as you put it, of meeting Parliament with the confession that the law in certain places is powerless without proposing a remedy. I have urged the proposal which Fortescue brought before the Cabinet as strongly as I could, and I cannot but admit that I have considered what I should do in the event of the proposal being rejected.

'I feel much diffidence about pressing my individual

opinion against the wide experience of Mr. Gladstone and others, and I have a horror of making a splash or a kick up.

'The concession made of hanging the threat of exceptional measures over the heads of the ruffians in disturbed districts may lead to stronger measures as the session goes on, and though I think immediate action the right course, I do not feel that I could take so strong a step as that of resignation at the present moment. For, however an unimportant member of the Government I may be, the Tories would make for the moment great use of such a weapon as my resignation, and I feel so very strongly the necessity of getting the Land Bill carried that I would sacrifice a great deal to assist that object—would, in that view, try to avoid any difficulties which might beset the path of Government.

'The mistake is one of omission rather than of commission, and, on so grave a thing as separation from a Government, that consideration has considerable weight with me.

'I need not say that my opinion would be very materially influenced by the decision or strong opinion of one like you, who have wider experience in these matters, and to whose judgment I should attach great weight.'

Lord Hartington, in reply, said that, on the whole, he thought that Lord Spencer would not be justified in resigning at present. He added, 'I consulted my father about my own conduct under the circumstances, and he advised me strongly not to resign or to press you to do so. Therefore I think that, unpleasant as it will be, we must stay in and bear the worst that can be said of us.'

Lord Spencer did not have long to wait for the powers which he desired. When the Land Bill had been well launched, the 'Peace Preservation Bill' was introduced, and was passed very rapidly into law. It received the Royal Assent in April 1870.

Lord Hartington, already, as the son of a great Irish landlord, knew something of Ireland. His knowledge was now to be increased by official experience. Some Cabinet changes took place in December 1870. Mr. Chichester Fortescue (afterwards Lord Carlingford), then Irish Chief Secretary, was moved to the Board of Trade. The Prime Minister wrote on 23rd December to Lord Hartington—

'to place his office at your disposal, and indeed something more, namely to press it on your acceptance. In your position, as well as with your capacity, I make bold, as the saying is, to ask of you to step from a less forward into a more forward rank. I can say with truth that the arrangement I now propose will be the best for the Government; but I wish rather to say, that it is the best, with reference to a longer future of the party, and of the country, than any one Government can be likely to cover, or than I myself can have a personal concern in.

'I need not be long. The Irish Secretaryship has been for some time a most important office. It is likely to continue so; nay, there are contingencies in which it may become greatly more important than it is.

'You will not I hope feel even inclined to refuse this fence. But if you are so inclined I hope that you will not do so without seeing me that I may explain myself more fully.'

Lord Granville wrote on the same day :—

'I presume Gladstone will press you to take the Irish Secretaryship. I also assume that you will be unwilling to do so. Further, that your objections will be personal and social, and not political either as regards yourself, or the public service. I hope very much that you will end by accepting, and, if so, you had better do it at once.

'You have the ball at your feet if you choose to kick it.

'The new office will not have any very great difficulties in starting, but enough to keep your hand in; and I have no doubt it will, during your term of office, give you the same opportunities of distinction and of training, as it did to Peel and Derby.'

No post in the public service within the United Kingdom does, indeed, give so good a training in the art of statesmanship. The work touches all branches of administration in a great and turbulent province, and at the same time exercises the mind in parliamentary tactics. But Hartington was not ambitious, and his cousin was right in his anticipation of the difficulty in getting him to take this fence. Mr. Gladstone's veiled suggestion that the post might be a step towards future leadership was the reverse of an inducement. The following letters show the strength of the resistance which he opposed to the scheme for his advancement :—

CHATSWORTH, CHESTERFIELD,
*24th December* 1870.

MY DEAR MR. GLADSTONE,—I cannot but feel much flattered by your selection of me for the important post of Irish Secretary. Some reports which had reached me before I received your letter had caused me to consider what I would do in the event of such an offer being made to me, and I had resolved that I would decline it. Nothing but the kind and urgent expressions contained in your letter and in one which I have received from Granville could have inclined me even to hesitate in giving this reply.

My objections are of various kinds.

The difficulties of the Irish Education question, even if legislation upon it be postponed for another year, seem to me to be almost insuperable if it is a necessary condition that the support of the Irish members should be retained.

The management of that body is a fact for which I do not feel any aptitude or inclination.

But I am afraid that I must confess that the considerations which weigh most of all with me are of a more private and personal character.  I cannot reconcile myself to giving up almost the whole year to official duties.  I imagine that the Irish Secretary ought to be in Dublin during the greater part of the year when Parliament is not sitting.  This to me, with all my friends and pursuits in England, would be almost banishment for the time.  I presume that it is mainly this obligation which has induced Fortescue to leave the office; but to me as a bachelor the necessity of constant residence in Ireland would be still more irksome.  I should wish, however, to take another day or two to consider the matter fully; and if necessary will come to Hawarden.  Perhaps you would kindly let me have a line to say whether you are anxious to have a very early reply; and further what are in your opinion the necessities of the case as regards residence in Ireland.— Yours very sincerely,  HARTINGTON.

> DEVONSHIRE HOUSE,
> *28th December* 1870.

MY DEAR MR. GLADSTONE,—Your second letter only reached me this morning, as I had left Chatsworth.  I have also received your telegram sent after you had written.  Since writing to you on Saturday, I have thought much on the subject of your offer; and have done my best to overcome the reluctance which I told you that I felt about accepting it.

I am sorry to say that I have not been successful.  The more I think of it, the more I feel that it is not a place which would in any way suit me, and that therefore in accepting it, I could not do justice either to myself or my colleagues.

I need not trouble you by repeating and enlarging my list of objections.  Singly they would appear to you to be trifling, and collectively I doubt not they would still seem to you quite insufficient.  But to my own mind they appear so strong that even if I allowed myself to be persuaded into acceptance against my will, it would be with such reluctance that I feel certain that an office undertaken in such a spirit could only lead to failure.

I am quite aware that in declining this offer I am doing that which may greatly damage my own political prospects. This, however, cannot be of any great importance to any one except myself. I fear, however, that it may be inconvenient to you and to the Government. For this I am very sorry, and I cannot conclude this letter without saying (knowing that you will not misunderstand the spirit in which I say it), that if now or at any future time my present office would facilitate any combination which you may choose to make, it is so far as I am concerned entirely at your disposal. I feel that I have no right to retain an office which is almost a sinecure, when I refuse a place of real work.

I do not know whether after this explanation you will still think it desirable that I should see you at Hawarden. The matter seems to me to be so much more one of inclination and feeling than of reason or argument, that I am afraid it would be useless; but, as you expressed a wish to see me, I shall be ready to come to-morrow if you telegraph to me that you expect me. I should add that I have seen Granville, and, though neither of us has convinced the other, I think that he has used most of the arguments which can be brought to bear on the subject.— I remain, yours sincerely,

HARTINGTON.

In the end, the insistence of the First Minister induced his reluctant subordinate to accept the duty, and Lord Hartington entered upon the work which occupied him until the resignation of the Government rather more than three years later. The experience enabled him to mature those convictions as to Ireland which so much affected his future career. Like other Chief Secretaries he spent part of the year at Dublin, but a much larger part in London doing his work in Parliament and at the Irish Office. The head of the permanent service in Ireland was the Mr. Burke who came, some twelve years later, to a tragic end.

Although the state of Ireland called for the Peace Preservation Act, passed in 1870, the condition of the island was more tranquil than it had been for many years preceding 1870, or than it was for many years following 1874. It was almost, for Ireland, a period of calm between storms. It was, however, Hartington's earliest duty, as it has been that of many Chief Secretaries, to ask Parliament to grant special powers for maintaining 'law and order.' There had been a crop of agrarian outrages in the county of Westmeath and neighbouring districts, due to the existence of a very flourishing local ' Ribbon Society.' Experience showed that these could not be sufficiently dealt with under the ordinary law, reinforced though it was by the provisions of the Peace Preservation Act. It was impossible to obtain evidence or secure convictions against the evil-doers. Lord Spencer and Lord Hartington were agreed that it was necessary to obtain power to suspend ' Habeas Corpus ' for this district, so that the criminal leaders might be arrested and kept in prison without trial and conviction for the public good. When Lord Hartington broached this plan to Mr. Gladstone it was received by him, as Lord Hartington wrote to Lord Spencer, with ' horror and dismay,' and it was by no means easy to win the fight in the Cabinet. On the 15th February 1871, Lord Hartington wrote to Lord Spencer :—

'After two long discussions, we have come to no decision on the Westmeath business. I have not been able to convince the Cabinet that everything has been done which can be done under the existing law. . . . I have some hope that, by hammering away, we may at last get our proposal through, but—besides Gladstone—Gran-

ville, the Chancellor, Lowe, and Cardwell, are all against
it ; the others more or less in its favour.'

As a compromise, the Cabinet agreed to begin by
asking Parliament to appoint a Select Committee to
inquire secretly into 'the nature, extent, and effect of a
certain unlawful combination and confederacy existing
in the county of Westmeath and adjoining districts.'
Lord Hartington, who thought this intermediate proceeding quite unnecessary, and rather absurd, moved the
appointment of the Select Committee in the House of
Commons on the 27th February 1871.   The condition
of Ireland, he said, as regarded agrarian crime, had on
the whole greatly improved.   With his usual frankness, he
attributed this improvement, not to the Liberal 'remedial'
legislation, but to 'the vigour, firmness, and decision'
with which Government had used both the ordinary
powers of the law and the extraordinary powers which
had been placed in their hands by the Peace Preservation
Act.   Vigorous search had been made for fire-arms, and
a large number had been taken out of the hands of the
'disloyal and criminal classes.'   Other strong measures
had been taken.   At no time within memory had the
powers of the law been more vigorously, and at the same
time more impartially, executed.   'We hope and believe,'
he added, 'that time and wise legislation will regenerate
Ireland and, meanwhile, the present Government is
determined to exercise the powers conferred upon them
by Parliament, and to govern Ireland according to law.'

The county of Westmeath, he explained, and districts
near it, were troubled by the operations of a secret
'Ribbon Society,' against which the powers given by the
Act of 1870 had proved inadequate.   He said that he did
not feel in the least that he appeared before Parliament
'in the character of a penitent in a white sheet,' or that

the proposal involved 'any confession of failure on the part of the Government.'  It would, he added, be—

'the height of insanity to suppose that the establishment of religious equality, or the passing of a law regulating the tenure of land, would put a stop to the Ribbon conspiracy.  I cannot see on what possible ground it could be imagined that the establishment of equal and just legislation should have any effect on the minds of men who have a system of laws of their own, not just laws, but the most unjust, the most arbitrary, the most tyrannical, the most barbarous.  I cannot conceive what sympathy such men could have with good legislation.'

It was possible, he said, that the House—

'might, upon the statement I have made, be willing to admit that the case was proved, and to give the Government any powers which they might think fit to ask.  But, Sir, I think that the House, in taking such a course, would evade the responsibility which properly belongs to it—[cries of 'No, no; to the Government']—if they took for granted from any Minister a statement of facts which they themselves have the opportunity of proving to their own satisfaction.'

He wrote next day to Lord Spencer :—

'Last night was very unpleasant.  I was not at all satisfied with my speech, and I don't think that I made as good a case for the committee as I might have done.  However, there is no doubt that the position of having to speak in defence of a course, which I did not think adequate to the occasion, was not an agreeable one, and I am afraid that I showed too plainly that it was not.'

He did indeed ; for he was no actor, and a very bad hand at pretending to think that which he did not think.  In his speech he made out a strong case for immediate legislation, and then had to make the pro-

posal to inquire into its necessity. Mr. Chaplin said in
the debate, that the Chief Secretary had 'performed his
task in a manner most unlike him, his manner showed that
the task he had undertaken was most disagreeable to him.
To shirk responsibility was foreign to the character of
his noble friend.' And Sir Robert Peel said that he had
'listened with pleasure to the speech of an honest man—
it was the speech of a man who was saying that which he
did not quite feel to be right. So honest was it that he
convinced me that he did not approve the policy he had
to advocate.'

Disraeli made upon the Prime Minister one of those
attacks which, under language of brilliant exaggeration,
contained something of *la vérité qui blesse.* The First
Minister, he said, had been returned to power as
the one statesman who could secure the tranquillity
and content of Ireland. Under his influence we have
'legalised confiscation, consecrated sacrilege, and condoned high treason; we have destroyed churches, we
have shaken property to its foundations, and we have
emptied gaols, and now we cannot govern one county
without coming to a Parliamentary Committee.' Such
a committee was, he said, necessary to the Minister,
'after his flashy speeches, as a veil, in order that he
might save his self-love.' The answer was, of course,
that already so frankly given by Hartington, that no one
but a fool could have supposed that the disestablishment
of a Church, or the alleviation of the position of the
stronger tenants by the Act of 1870, would prevent village
ruffians from committing outrages, but that this was no
argument against the intrinsic merit of that legislation.
Disraeli's sarcasms only hit those who had claimed too
much for remedial measures.

The evidence before the Committee proved the existence

of an intolerable state of terrorism based upon murder. Disraeli took the line of asking for information too secret to be produced, in order to show, what indeed was the case, that the Government had information so black that the inquiry was superfluous. 'It will be better,' wrote Lord Hartington to Lord Spencer, 'to endure Dizzy's taunts than to give what ought not to be given.' The Bill suspending Habeas Corpus for this Westmeath region was then brought in. Hartington described the measure, in unsugared language, as—

'a new and unconstitutional one, for formerly Parliament has attempted to deal with this class of crime simply by defining and describing new offences, by giving additional powers to the police and magistrates, and by imposing excessive penalties on those who were convicted of those offences, but the measure which the Government now asks the House to adopt, although an unconstitutional one, and one which will place in the hands of the Government a grave and novel power, is not necessarily a severe one, its object being not so much the punishment as the prevention of crime. . . . The only way that the Government sees of putting an end to this organisation is to put its leaders out of mischief for some time by imprisoning them.'

He attributed the fact that no previous Government had armed itself with this simple and effective weapon, to the extreme jealousy with which Parliament always looked 'upon any interference with the securities which we enjoy for our personal liberties.' English principles of criminal law have rarely worked successfully when applied to the different conditions of Ireland. They rest on the assumption that social opinion is in favour of the detection and punishment of crime, that witnesses will give evidence, and that juries will convict. This Act of 1871 furnished a precedent for the far wider suspension of Habeas Corpus ten years later.

A not very important Irish affair in August 1871 caused a good deal of talking and writing. It was announced that a meeting would be held at the Monument in Phœnix Park outside Dublin, presided over by Mr. Smyth, the M.P. for Westmeath, to 'agitate for the release of the political prisoners still confined in English dungeons.' The people were exhorted to show that they were 'not unmindful of their brothers who were undergoing the horrors of penal servitude in England for their love of Ireland.' It happened that the Prince of Wales and Prince Arthur were, that Sunday, staying at the Viceregal Lodge in the Park, and the leading popular paper had declared that it was 'intolerable that alien Princes should come here in search of welcome while the Power they represent still holds fifty patriots in prison.' These patriots, as Lord Hartington afterwards explained to the House of Commons, were 'not political prisoners at all; they were soldiers who, in addition to the crime of high treason, had committed the offence of breaking the oath of allegiance to their Sovereign, and had also conspired to seize upon, and, in some instances, to murder their brethren in arms. There were also those who had participated in the crimes of Manchester and Clerkenwell.' Other 'political prisoners,' he said, had been already released. The Phœnix Park belongs to the State, and the Irish Government, not very wisely, thought fit, at the last moment, to prohibit the meeting. The people attempted to hold the meeting, and there was a painful collision with the police. Lord Hartington, who was in London, went to see Mr. Gladstone when the sad news arrived, who 'shook his head a good deal and seemed much disturbed in his mind.'[1] The

---

[1] Lord Hartington to Lord Spencer, 8th August 1871.

Chief Secretary, in defending the conduct of the Irish Government in the House of Commons, then sitting, held a weak position, by reason of the concession made, after the riots in 1866, of the right, virtually, of free meeting in Hyde Park, where all kinds of preachers of atheism, treason, and immorality were, and are, allowed to address the public, without much apparent damage. Irish members said that there was one law for London and another for Dublin. Lord Hartington had written to Lord Spencer that 'Gladstone will shake his head and grumble, but will not throw us over,' and, in fact, the First Minister supported his lieutenants well in the debate. But, after this, both Lord Spencer and Lord Hartington had, evidently, something of the feelings of schoolboys who had given offence to their excellent master, and were rather suspiciously watched.

In reply to a question put, about this time, by Mr. Gladstone as to the effects of the release of Irish political prisoners, Lord Hartington wrote :—

'I am sorry to say that I cannot think that it has hitherto had any good effect. It is impossible to detect any sign of gratitude for what has been done. The National Press is as disloyal and as intensely hostile to England in tone as ever, and there is reason to fear that it accurately represents the opinion of the lower classes.

'On the other hand, the middle classes have no doubt been disgusted by the amnesty. I have little doubt that the acquittal of Kelly arose from this cause. Dublin juries have generally done their duty, but the language held on that occasion was this : " How can we be expected to convict political prisoners at considerable risk to our lives and property, if the only result is to enable the Government to earn a little popularity by releasing them in a year or two." '

It was clear that neither the disestablishment of the
Irish Church in 1869, nor the Land Act in 1870, had
achieved the pacification of Irish sentiment.

### III

The Parliament of 1868 to 1874 was the last of those
in which no distinctly organised Irish Home Rule party
existed. Since the days of Catholic Emancipation the
Irish representatives had, in the main, been reckoned as
Liberals, and had supported Liberal Governments, although it was admitted that they, or some of them, held,
on certain subjects, peculiar views which had to be taken
into account. Until the extension of the franchise in 1867
the class of voters in boroughs was still more limited than
in England, by reason of the lesser values of town
properties. The larger farmers of the rural districts, who
possessed the voting qualification, unreduced until 1884,
mostly returned as their representatives members of the
local gentry. The extension of urban franchise in 1867
gave birth to a new democratic movement in Ireland. In
1870 the Home Rule Association was formed under the
chairmanship of Mr. Butt, and the new movement soon
made itself felt.

In January 1872 there was a by-election for the county
of Kerry. Mr. Dease stood as a strictly official candidate,
with the full sanction and support of that Liberal Government which had made the great concession to Roman
Catholic sentiment in 1869, and to the interests of tenant-
farmers in 1870. He was opposed by the Home Rule
Association. They found in Mr. Blennerhassett a rival
candidate with position and means. Lord Kenmare wrote
to the Chief Secretary that 'it is essential that troops
should be in the country a week before the election. The

intimidation is tremendous, and their presence would give confidence.' The Roman Catholic Bishop of Kerry also pressed for troops, 'especially cavalry.' He had publicly denounced the Home Rule agitation. Lord Lansdowne wrote that 'a great many of our voters will stop at home in my part of the county unless they are ensured "whole heads."' Troops were sent. A gunboat was despatched to Valentia to protect from intimidation the tenants of the Knight of Kerry. These precautions were in vain, and the Government candidate was defeated by a large majority. Lord Kenmare, after the election, wrote to Lord Hartington that 'every considerable landlord and almost all the sober-minded among the Catholic clergy, headed by their bishop, gave Mr. Dease their active and hearty support.' 'But,' said Lord Kenmare, 'the election was carried by a vast amount of intimidation, applied in every conceivable form, guided from Dublin through the instrumentality of itinerant orators and local and imported Fenians, and the unsurpassed energy of a powerful section of the priests, who combined to fan Home Rule sentiment into a frenzy.' Nearly at the same time a by-election in County Galway produced like results. Captain Trench, the official Liberal, was severely defeated by Captain Nolan, the Home Ruler. On this occasion there was an election petition, and Judge Keogh, whose language during the proceedings was censured for want of good taste, and was indeed compared by Irish speakers to that of Scroggs and Jefferies, scheduled in his report one archbishop, two bishops, and several priests as guilty of the exercise of undue influence, and several other priests as having intimidated would-be Liberal voters by 'denunciations and threats of temporal injury and spiritual punishment uttered at divine service from the altars.' Other voters had been intimidated by nocturnal visits from laymen armed with secular weapons, or had been prevented by violent mobs from proceeding to the poll. Evidently, like other English institutions, the system of election was not working well under Irish conditions. Elections in Ireland were neither ‘pure,’ ‘tranquil,’ nor ‘free’ even with the ballot system. These phenomena were ominous of storms to come.

Lord Hartington remarked, in the debate in the House upon the language used by Mr. Justice Keogh, that, when he was chairman of the committee which examined the question of voting by ballot, he had come, upon the evidence, to the conclusion that the ‘Irish voter was the last person who was expected to have any influence over his own vote, and that it was a struggle between the landlord and the priest who should take him to the poll.’ It was, probably, one effect of the substitution of voting by ballot for open voting that in Ireland the secret power of the priest, and of the masked secular intimidator, prevailed over the open terrors of the landlord. In any case these elections made it evident that future Irish Governments might have to deal with something different either from occasional Fenian risings, or from chronic subterranean anarchy.

The nominal leader of the Home Rule movement was then Isaac Butt, a Dublin lawyer of some literary distinction. His general idea was the establishment of a provincial Government and Parliament for Ireland empowered to legislate on matters purely Irish, subject in all cases to a power of veto lodged with the Imperial Government, and subject also, in the last resort, to the supreme over-riding power of the Imperial Parliament, in which Ireland would still be represented. He did not face the difficulty that, in that case, Irish members would have power to deal with purely English and Scotch affairs, in which the existence of the Government of the United

Kingdom is often involved, but that English and Scotch
members would have, at most, an indirect and remote
right of dealing with Irish affairs.  His scheme, to make
it complete, or possible, required the reconstitution of the
United Kingdom upon the model of the Canadian Constitution of 1867, involving (1) a central Parliament and
Government representing the whole United Kingdom, (2)
several provincial legislatures for England, Scotland, Ireland, and Wales, (3) a specific division of subjects between
the central and provincial legislatures, (4) the maintenance
of a veto by the Imperial Government upon all provincial
legislation, and (5) judicial means of decision whether a
doubtful question fell within the central or provincial
sphere.

In a debate in the House of Commons on the 2nd May
1872, over a proposal to repeal an old Irish Act, passed in
1793 by Grattan's Parliament, which virtually prohibited
any assembly or meeting being held for political objects,
Lord Hartington, on behalf of the Government, maintained
that the political condition of Ireland still made it desirable
to have such weapons in reserve.  He illustrated his argument by saying that many members of the Home Rule
Association were still connected with the old Fenian
Association, which had attempted rebellion in 1867.  Isaac
Butt denied this, and said that many of those engaged in
the Home Rule organisation were 'men of high position
and large property, who were not likely to lend themselves
to revolutionary projects.' . . . 'Their proposals might be
wild and impracticable, or otherwise, but they were simply
that Ireland should have an Irish Parliament, managing
Irish affairs, under the sovereignty of the Queen, with a
veto given to her Majesty upon every Irish subject, and
the supreme control of the Imperial Parliament to be
exercised in the last resort.'  He believed 'that the whole

Irish people would make their demand at the next General Election in such a form that every Englishman would feel it necessary for the peace of the Empire that the demand should be granted.'

Mr. Gladstone dealt very courteously with this part of Mr. Butt's speech, and treated the question of a distinct Irish Parliament as one which was entirely open to consideration in principle, but presented some difficulties in practice and detail. 'How,' he asked, 'is there to be a federal arrangement between the Parliament, which is imperial and supreme, and any other body, within the area of the United Kingdom?' In England this friendly reception of the subject caused no emotion. It was probably thought to be a ministerial method of evading angry or prolonged debate on a subject still considered to be purely academic. But a well-informed Irish correspondent wrote to Lord Hartington that the Prime Minister's speech had given an 'immense impulse' to the Home Rule cry in Ireland, and was considered there to be a reply to what had been said by the Chief Secretary in the same debate. It certainly seemed to be a recession from the strong position taken by Mr. Gladstone in his speech at Aberdeen in the autumn of 1870, when he said :—

'If the doctrines of Home Rule are to be established in Ireland, I protest on your behalf that you will be just as well entitled to it in Scotland; and moreover, I protest on behalf of Wales. Can any sensible man, can any rational man suppose that, at this time of day, in this condition of the world, we are going to disintegrate the great capital institutions of this country for the purpose of making ourselves ridiculous in the sight of all mankind, and crippling any power we possess for bestowing benefits through legislation on the country to which we belong?'

Gladstone was sensitive to any manifestations of

popular feeling, and the elections in Kerry and Galway may have had their effect. Besides, bred in the school of Canningite Toryism, he had spent much of his vigour in denouncing government exercised by men of one race or religion over men belonging to another. His old and passionate beliefs as to Italy, and Greece, and the Christians in Turkey, could not but affect his views with regard to Ireland.

A few days after this debate of May 1872, there was a question as to giving an appointment which would vacate a certain seat in Ireland then held by a Liberal. Lord Hartington wrote to Lord Spencer that he had told Gladstone that, if the seat were vacant, a Home Ruler would capture it, and added :—

‘I am sorry to say that Gladstone did not seem so much shocked as he ought. His views on Home Rule are much too Liberal, in my opinion, and, if they will only profess to maintain the supremacy of the Imperial Parliament, he does not much mind what they go in for.’

In fact, Gladstone’s views were very much in 1872 what they were in 1886, nor did he ever wholly conceal them. Nothing is more unjust than to accuse him, as he was accused, of a sudden and interested conversion in 1885. But no one believed that he really meant the things which from time to time he said showing his tendency towards Home Rule.

At this time, before the great agrarian fight and its accompanying horrors, many Irishmen of good position and moderate minds were more or less in sympathy with Butt’s movement in the direction of limited self-government. There was a strong and justified feeling that the Government had paid insufficient attention to the opinions and wishes of Irish representatives in really important matters, such as that of the railways, and that promises

were made to obtain Irish assistance in English party conflicts which were afterwards, in deference to English
opinion, not redeemed. Irishmen felt that their country
was in many ways the 'Cinderella of the three sister kingdoms'; neglected by royalty, for instance. No reigning
king had ever visited Ireland, with the exception of hostile
and warlike tours by Richard II. and William III., and
one festive trip by George IV., until Queen Victoria had
made a flying visit or two. Mr. Gladstone had a favourite
and sensible scheme to meet this complaint. He wished
to abolish the Viceroyalty and to provide for the residence
in Ireland during part of each year of the Prince of Wales,
who was to perform the social functions, also to see the
important official papers, and so to have a 'training in
the art of actual government.' It was thought by good
judges, W. E. Forster for one, that this large scheme
would be dangerous, because, admirably though the Prince
might discharge all his duties, he would be connected in
the suspicious Irish mind 'with acts of administration
which must sometimes be stern, and very often would be
unpopular.' For some irresistible reasons this scheme
was dropped. Discussion lasted until the spring of 1873
as to a smaller plan of maintaining a Royal Residence
in Ireland to be occupied for part of the year, for merely
social purposes, by a prince of the royal family ; but this
idea also proved to be impracticable.

In 1872 and 1873 the repose of the Irish Government,
seldom long, was disturbed by another affair, long ago
'fallen silent,' as Carlyle would have said, but the cause at
that time of much excitement and correspondence, the
affair of Father O'Keefe. How Cardinal Cullen, acting as
Legate from Rome, suspended from his functions this turbulent, or martyred, priest ; how the Irish Commissioners
of National Education—without due hearing—followed

in the wake of the Cardinal, and removed him from the management of the parish school; how their decree proved ineffective through the resistance of the exasperated parishioners; and how Her Majesty's Government, in debate, staked their existence upon the support of the Commissioners, and in the end escaped from the affair as best they could—are not these things written in the pages of Hansard?

## IV

An Irish question of real importance, much discussed in these years, was that relating to railways. In 1836 a well-selected Royal Commission had been appointed to consider the way in which a railway system might best be introduced into Ireland. The leading mind on this Commission was Thomas Drummond, the ablest permanent Under-Secretary who ever worked in Dublin Castle. This Commission advised, that for good reasons connected with the economic and social condition of Ireland, the Irish railway system should not be left to hazard and to the conflicts of contending companies, but should be based upon a general and rational plan, should receive financial aid from the State, and, to a large extent, be subject to State control. In other words, they recommended that the continental, and not the Anglo-Saxon, methods should be applied to Irish railways. But in London the idea of *laissez-faire* and competitive enterprise was then becoming rapidly dominant. A measure founded on the report was brought in by the Whig Chief Secretary, Lord Morpeth, in 1839, but it was strongly attacked by Sir Robert Peel, who said that, if the railways would pay they would be made by the spontaneous exertions of the private capitalists of Ireland, but if they would not pay, they should not be made at all. Parliament was then in more sympathy with

these Peelite ideas, where specious economical platitudes
sheltered middle-class interests, than it was with those of
statesmen like Morpeth and Drummond.  The Report of
the Railway Commission, like that of the Irish Poor Law
Commission, like that of the Devon Commission, disappeared into the abyss of oblivion which has swallowed
up so much sound advice supplied by men who have
studied the true needs of Ireland.

In 1847 Lord George Bentinck, the Protectionist Tory,
made a daring attempt to induce the English Government
to rescind their Irish railway policy.  Proposals for State
purchase of Irish railways were discussed by the Railway
Commission of 1867, not altogether unfavourably.  A
Special Commission, appointed by Disraeli in 1868, showed
that purchase could be effected without loss to the State,
and with great advantage to Ireland.  The same proposal
was made in the House of Commons in 1871 and in 1873.
In the latter year no less than seventy-eight Irish peers and
ninety Irish members of the House of Commons signed a
memorial in favour of State purchase, to be followed by
large reductions of railway rates.  The memorial was supported by petitions from every Grand Jury and Municipal
Corporation in Ireland.  In 1874 the proposal was renewed.  On each occasion the proposal was opposed
by the Government, and defeated by large majorities
composed of English and Scottish representatives.  This
treatment of the almost unanimous wish of the Irish
public, in an affair of pure business, was a favourite
theme of Home Rule speakers and writers.  There were
at this period no less than sixty-six distinct railway companies in Ireland, supporting some 500 directors and 170
other officers.  The total gross receipts of all the lines
were no larger than those of a single Scottish Company,
the Caledonian, which had but thirteen directors to main-

tain. The thing was a real scandal. The Irish lines were slowly and badly made, the services inconvenient and disconnected; the rates and fares were excessively high.[1]

Mr. Gladstone committed himself rather deeply in 1867, when he was out of office, and the Irish vote at the coming election was important. He said that no boon to Ireland would be so great as a measure which would secure cheapness of railway transit. One of the Irish speakers, in the debate of 1871, asked why, if this were true, Mr. Gladstone had not introduced in 1869 a measure dealing with the railways instead of the Irish Church Act, which 'injured a large part of the community and did no good to the rest.' This would have been too much to ask. The purchase and nationalisation of Irish railways would have displeased precisely that powerful section of the English Liberals to whom the destruction of the Established Church gave immense delight. Certainly, no one would have been more pleased than Lord Hartington had his chief been wise enough to introduce an Irish Railway Act in 1873 instead of that hopeless measure of University reform which displeased every one, was unsound in itself, and led to a humiliating defeat.

In the debate of 1871 on Irish railways, Lord Hartington made a cautious speech. In the following year, with more experience of Irish affairs, he expressed in Parliament (17th July 1872) as strong an opinion in favour of State action as was possible for the representative of a Government which had decided to take no present action. He said that Ireland had real ground for complaint in the fact that 'this subject had been waiting for consideration during

---

[1] It was shown by the latest inquiry, the Irish Railway Commission which reported in 1910 in favour of State acquisition of the railways, that, although many amalgamations have been effected, things are little better now in many respects.

seven years, and had not received any proper consideration from the House.'  He added :—

'Though I entertain as strong objections as any one to what are called Home Rule principles and arguments, I have never denied that an argument in favour of the demand for Home Rule is furnished by the very small time devoted during the last two sessions to practical questions affecting the interests of Ireland.  Unless the House is prepared in future sessions to devote more time to practical business concerning Ireland instead of the discussion of every imaginable subject, the arguments in favour of Home Rule will, in my opinion, acquire more force.'

At the beginning of the following session (1873), the Cabinet decided to take no action in the matter of Irish railways.  The University Education Bill blocked the way.  Lord Hartington wrote to Lord Spencer on 9th February 1873 :—

'Gladstone is completely frightened, or pretends to be, by the prospect of the Government working the lines.  Childers thinks that there is much to be said on both sides, but with these exceptions, and Fortescue, the whole Cabinet are dead against purchase.  I am very much disgusted, and don't quite know what to do.  I suppose my speech last year went rather far ; at all events, it is known that I am in favour of purchase, and it is quite impossible for me to argue against it.  It will also be almost impossible for me to say nothing, if I am challenged about last year's speech.  I think I shall ask Gladstone whether it may be treated as an open question, and whether I may say that, personally, though I see difficulties, I do not think them insuperable, and that I differ from the majority of my colleagues on the question.  If I cannot say so much as this, I don't very well see how I can remain in.  I believe that it would be one of the best things that could be done for Ireland, and that the

Tories will do it when they come in, and I should not like to do anything which would prevent my giving the best help I can to any one who will do it. Gladstone is disposed to do something in the way of advancing borrowed capital on easy terms to companies which will amalgamate, and agree to certain conditions; but I don't believe in this.'

On the following day Lord Hartington wrote to the Prime Minister :—

'The decision of the Cabinet on Irish railways places me in a very difficult position.

'I suppose that there can be no doubt that I made last session an indiscreet speech on the subject. Some of my colleagues thought so, and it was commented on in the Press, as indicating some favourable intention on the part of the Government. I do not think that it pledged the Government, but it must to some extent have pledged me. Putting that aside, it is perfectly well known to many members that I am in favour of the purchase. Nor, if I were free, could I bring myself to argue against the proposal. I believe that it would be the best thing that could be done for Ireland; and I hope that it may yet be done some day.

'Probably, I shall not be expected to oppose Sir R. Blennerhassett's Bill; but it will be difficult for me to remain silent, if I am challenged on my speech of last year.

'Would it be possible that this should be allowed to be an open question, and that I should be free to state that although I see many difficulties, I do not think them insuperable, and that I do not concur in the decision of the Cabinet? If I cannot say as much as this, I hardly see how I can honourably remain in office.

'I know that you see the political advantages of the measure, although you think the difficulties of detail too great to be overcome. You will therefore appreciate my disappointment at not being able to do anything further in the matter.  But though I must put up with this, I do not see how I could assent to a course which would make me a consenting party to what I entirely disapprove, and would put it out of my power to further a measure which I approve when a more fitting occasion may arise.'

Mr. Gladstone replied that he had read this letter 'with intense concern,' that he had had no conception that this subject of Irish railways involved Lord Hartington in anything like personal embarrassment.  'Indeed, my belief was that you and I were both implicated to almost the same extent by favourable impressions not fairly, yet plausibly, to be construed as pledges, though mine happened to be of the older date, and therefore less in view.'

In 1874, when the Conservatives were in office, this question was again raised in Parliament.  The Government announced that they had no intention of dealing with the matter, although, by Disraeli's action in 1868, they were pledged even more deeply than the Liberals, and the Irish, almost unanimous, were defeated by a crushing majority. Lord Hartington could now speak more freely.  He said :—

'Perhaps I ought to plead guilty to the charge that by too open a statement of my own views I may have raised hopes which I was not able to fulfil.  But certainly I did think that in a country like Ireland, whose industrial resources are not so fully developed as those of England, private enterprise could not be expected to do, in regard to railway management, all that it has done here.  I certainly did think that some reparation might be due to Ireland from us for having sanctioned a system of railways there which did not give the country the fullest advantages which it is entitled to enjoy, and that it was possible, at all events, if the Government undertook to work the railways in a liberal and enterprising spirit, that although some loss at first might ensue, it was not necessary that that loss should be a permanent one.'

But, he added, since it appeared from the speech made by Sir M. Hicks Beach that the Government had, like their predecessors, arrived at the decision to do nothing—

'it would not be fair in me to attempt to gain any popularity in Ireland by holding out now any hope of support from this side of the House to a proposition to which, when we were in office, we were unable to give our assent."

He then appealed to the Irish members not to press on an agitation which, while it could not be successful, might be mischievous as preventing the improvement of Irish railways by voluntary amalgamations and expenditure on improvements and extensions.

## V

Mr. Gladstone's well-intended, but ill-conceived and ill-starred, Irish University Bill came under consideration by the Cabinet in the autumn of 1872.

British statesmen had made a long and unsuccessful attempt to place education in Ireland upon the foundation of English and Liberal ideals, and to blend the unmixable Catholic and Protestant elements in a common system. Model, or mixed, schools had been initiated in 1831, and for some years had achieved a considerable measure of success, and, it was thought, had done good. Sir Robert Peel, in 1845, had founded with State grants the undenominational Colleges at Belfast, Cork, and Galway, to give education of an university kind. It was intended that these Colleges should meet the needs both of Catholics and Presbyterians, the doors of advancement in Trinity College, practically one with Dublin University, being still barred by Church of Ireland tests. Education was given to students, designed for the Roman Catholic priesthood,

by Maynooth College.   Sir Robert Peel had secured a State
endowment to this College, the step which made Gladstone
resign office, in 1845.   A purely examining and degree-
giving machine, called the 'Queen's University,' had also
been created.

The undenominational system, devised with the best
intentions, had been frustrated by the rising tide of Ultra-
montane Catholicism in its world-wide conflict against
Liberalism.   The Irish hierarchy, acting under instructions
from Rome, had condemned and denounced from an early
date both the schools and the colleges.   As late as August
1869, the year of disestablishment of the Church of Ireland,
the Roman Catholic bishops, assembled at Maynooth, had
reiterated their condemnation 'of the mixed system of
education, whether primary, intermediate, or university,'
as 'grievously and intrinsically dangerous to the faith and
morals of Catholic youth,' and had declared that 'to
Catholics only, and under the supreme control of the
Church in all things relating to faith and morals, can the
teaching of Catholics be safely entrusted.'   They called on
their clergy and laity to 'oppose the extension or perpetua-
tion of the mixed system, whether by the creation of new
institutions, by the maintenance of old ones, or by changing
Trinity College, Dublin, into a mixed College.'   Language
could not be more clear or decisive, or notice more distinctly given.

Under the influence of continuous maledictions, branded
as 'godless,' the Galway and Cork Colleges had for many
years withered and declined.   Catholic parents who obeyed
their bishops could obtain no university education for
their sons in Ireland.   The Irish Roman Catholic bishops,
and most of the laity, wished for the establishment and
endowment by the State of a new university under
Catholic control, with Catholic teaching and with a

Catholic atmosphere. They had no desire to interfere with, or injure, or have a share in, the existing institution, which, looked at from one point of view, was Trinity College and, looked at from another, was Dublin University. On the other hand, English nonconformists and radicals, and the Scottish, were violently opposed to State endowment of any Roman Catholic university or college. They were keen to abolish the religious tests which restricted the posts and fellowships of Trinity College and, consequently, the government of Dublin University, to men belonging to the recently disestablished Church of Ireland, and they wished to place the administration of that university on a wider basis. If this were done their idea was that men of all or no religions might happily settle down together in the existing Dublin University, and fight as best they could for the capture and occupation of the posts in it. These were the objects of the Bill brought in by Henry Fawcett in 1871, and again in 1872. Liberal feeling was so strongly behind it that, in 1872, Gladstone was forced to allow the Bill to pass second reading, but, in so doing, he announced that, in committee, the measure would be divided into two parts, one dealing with the abolition of tests, which Government would accept, the other with the future constitution of the university, which they could not accept, because it was matter for Government, and not for a private member, to deal with. It was intimated that, if this procedure were rejected, the Government would resign. By this means they achieved their purpose, but at the point of the bayonet, and almost at the cost of an open mutiny. Fawcett said that, before the threat of resignation, his Bill had obtained an almost unanimous support in the House. That is to say, English and Scottish Liberal opinion was almost unanimous in supporting a measure, relating exclusively to

Ireland, which was condemned by almost all Roman Catholics in Ireland, and all their representatives in Parliament, as having no relation to Catholic wants or claims, and was disliked also by a considerable section of the Irish Protestants. Mr. Gladstone truly said in the debate that Fawcett's proposals were 'totally inadequate as a settlement of the great university question in Ireland,' but now it was evident that the Government must produce a scheme of their own.

How to satisfy Irish Catholics without offending English and Scottish Protestants; it was the problem which had tormented and finally ruined Charles I. The riddle, Mr. Gladstone thought, might be solved by a reform of the existing Dublin University. This was to be divorced from its undivided unity with Trinity College, and to be endowed with £12,000 a year from the revenues of the College and £10,000 a year from the State, in addition to revenue from fees. It was to be governed by a Council composed of men of all denominations, and appointed, at first, by the Act, and, for some time following, by the Crown. Trinity was to be one of the colleges affiliated to it; the colleges at Belfast and Cork were to be two others; the Galway college was to be suppressed. The Roman Catholic college in Dublin, and any other such institutions, were also to affiliate, but to receive no State endowment. The examining 'Queen's University' was to disappear.

Then came the difficulty of teaching in a mixed and State-endowed University. How were Catholic professors to teach Protestants, or Protestant professors to teach Catholics, in controversial subjects such as philosophy, theology, history? Mr. Gladstone met this difficulty by the simple device of prohibiting all university instruction in these perilous sciences, although it might still be given by college lecturers in Trinity or in the Catholic colleges. There were to be no chairs in theology, 'moral philosophy,' or 'modern history.' Thus, for instance, the history of Athens or of Rome before Augustus might be taught, but not that of the Roman Empire, nor, perhaps, the history of Judea, which, though ancient, would partake of theology.

Lord Hartington's view from the first, fully justified by the event, was that this scheme would irritate Irish Protestants and English Liberals, while it would not conciliate Irish Catholics, because it would not give them what they, or, at any rate, what their bishops desired. On the 22nd November he wrote to the Lord-Lieutenant :—

'I am not satisfied with the way the University question is going. Mr. Gladstone produced a plan yesterday containing his ideas, which were generally adopted by the Cabinet in spite of my objections. I am sure they are going on the wrong tack, but I am really not well enough up in the subject, and can't fight Gladstone and the majority.'

On the 29th November he wrote again :—

'. . . I am certainly extremely dissatisfied with the Government plan as it stands. It seems to me that we are upsetting everything, Dublin University and the Queen's University, without putting in their places anything which we can have any confidence will work better. Trinity College certainly is to remain, with part of its income, but it will say, and perhaps with truth, that the character of its examinations and teaching will be lowered. The Queen's University may say the same thing, and perhaps also with truth ; and we do all this without giving any encouragement to the College which the Roman Catholics want, and we have no guarantee that they will accept our scheme as any satisfaction whatever of their grievances. However, I think that the Cabinet have now definitely disposed of my objections, and decided that a central university on Mr.

Gladstone's basis is to be the foundation of the scheme. . . .
I shall wait, of course, to see what the plan looks like,
when more complete, but I don't at present feel at all certain that it is one for which I can be responsible. I dare
say that nothing else is practicable, but I would rather do
nothing at all than propose a plan which may do harm
and cannot do good.'

On the following day Lord Hartington wrote as follows
to Mr. Gladstone :—

'I have expressed such strong opinions in the Cabinet
as to some of the provisions of the Irish University
measure ; and the general opinion of the Cabinet has been
so completely against me, that I think I ought to state to
you what I conceive my position with regard to this subject
to be.

'I feel great doubt whether a Bill founded on the principles which have been adopted by the Cabinet can be one
to which I can assent, or (if I could bring myself to assent
to it) to which I could give my hearty support. Now,
although I hope that, in any case, you would yourself take
the main charge of the Bill, as in the case of the Church
and Land Bills, I suppose that a considerable part in the
conduct of the Bill in the House of Commons would
devolve on me ; and I am quite sure that I should do more
harm than good to the Government if I could not bring
myself, not only to assent to, but to support heartily the
measure.

'I distrust so much (although some things I may have
said in the Cabinet may have led you to form a different
opinion) my own judgment and knowledge in this matter,
that I am not prepared to say that, when the measure has
assumed a more definite shape, my objections may not be
removed or diminished ; and I therefore do not wish (unless
you should think it necessary) to come at present to a final
decision.

'But possibly my own independence might be compro-
mised, if I went on any further without some explanation ;

and possibly also my colleagues might not consider it fair to them if I were to go with them into the consideration of the details of a Bill, as to the main principles of which I (as at present advised) differ from them—to the extent possibly of being obliged to separate myself from them.

'If, therefore, you should think that I ought, before proceeding further, to say Yes or No to the principles which have been adopted by the Cabinet, I shall be quite ready to do so. I think, however, that, before finally deciding, I should consult personally with Spencer, with whom I have been in this, as in all other questions relating to Ireland, in the most confidential communication; but who, as far as I know, does not altogether share in my objections to the proposed course of proceeding.'

Mr. Gladstone wrote so persuasive a reply that Lord Hartington continued in the Administration for the present, but on the 16th December he wrote to Lord Spencer with regard to the now more complete scheme, 'I don't like it any better than I did, but I want to have a consultation before I decide anything final.' Some encroachments were proposed upon a special 'tutorial fund,' in which the Fellows of Trinity College enjoyed a vested interest. Lord Hartington wrote to Lord Spencer on the 16th February 1873: 'It is bad enough to have to rob Trinity College, but I cannot stand the plunder of individuals.' Evidently he was not in sympathy with the socialistic age to come.

Lord Spencer, in a letter to Lord Hartington of 17th February 1873, reported an interview which he had had with the Roman Catholic bishop of Limerick, who had said that, on the whole, the Catholics ought gratefully to accept the measure, protesting, indeed, against the absence of endowment for their college on St. Stephen's Green, but hoping that at some future time Parliament might be disposed to grant this to them. Lord Spencer had told the bishop that the current of public opinion in England and Scotland was setting in with increasing force against State endowment of denominational education, and that he did not think that, in the future, the Roman Catholics would get as much as they now were offered. The bishop asked what Mr. Gladstone would do if the Catholics rejected the proposal. Lord Spencer replied that, in his opinion, he would go on with the measure and pass it, in the full belief that he was proposing the utmost that he could carry, and that the Roman Catholics would eventually find that it was in their interest cheerfully to accept the terms offered to them. Lord Spencer told Lord Hartington that he had heard that certain other bishops were friendly, or at any rate, not decisively hostile to the Bill, but on 2nd March he had to report that a meeting of the Irish bishops had resulted in unanimous opposition to the Bill, which they regarded as a 'glorification of mixed education,' and that they 'would rather see the Government turned out than the Bill passed.'

This resolution of the Irish bishops was made public immediately before the second reading debate began in the House of Commons. The governing body of the existing Dublin University, or Trinity College, had already declared their objection to the scheme on the ground that it would lower the standard of education, and that the proposed mixed Council would not work satisfactorily. Mr. Gladstone should have dramatically withdrawn the Bill as soon as he heard of the declaration of the Roman Catholic bishops, and have thrown upon them, in a magnificent speech, the whole responsibility for its loss. But he went obstinately on, cherishing, it seems, the hope that, although he was opposed by the Irish hierarchy, he might divide the Irish Catholic laity from their episcopate and secure their support,[1] or hoping that the bishops were acting *pro formâ,* under orders from Rome, and might not themselves be sincerely hostile.

Lord Hartington, victim to no illusions, immediately before the debate began, wrote to Lord Spencer :—

'The state of affairs seems to me as depressing as possible, but Gladstone is still in good spirits. The only part of the bishops' proceedings which at all distresses him is their refusal to allow the Roman Catholic College to be a college of the University, which, no doubt, if they persist in, they have the power to do. He has an idea that there is something under the open action of the bishops which is not so unfavourable to the Bill, and I believe the Chancellor is to be sent back to Dublin to see whether he can do anything with Cullen.'

The Bill had encountered a storm of criticism from all sides. 'Never,' said Professor Henry Fawcett, 'had a measure been introduced which had been rejected with so much unanimity. . . . No principle was carried out by the Bill. It was just one of those compromises which, intended to please everybody, ended by pleasing nobody.' Lord Hartington followed Mr. Fawcett in the debate. He said, after explaining that he did not think much of the Professor, that, in his opinion, the Roman Catholics exaggerated the importance of State endowment and recognition. On the other hand, he could not agree with those advocates of undenominational education, 'with whom it seems to be a sacred and cardinal item of faith that not a single sixpence derived from the taxpayer shall be applied to the endowment of any religious institution whatever. I am unable to see the sacredness of this belief.' He himself, he said, as an individual, saw 'nothing wrong, unjust, or sacrilegious in the endow-

---

[1] His speech in the debate pointed to this prospect.

ment of a distinct Roman Catholic University.' This endowment was, however, 'absolutely impracticable': (1) because a majority in the House of Commons was opposed to all denominational endowment whatever, (2) because if an exclusive endowment were given to one religion it must be given to others. He made it quite clear that his own opinion was in favour of endowing a distinct Catholic University. He held this opinion throughout his life, and it was the end to which, although not until 1909, the destinies of Ireland, vindicating his judgment and foresight, have conducted a reluctant England and Scotland.

Lord Hartington did not defend with any warmth the singular part of this measure which forbade the new university to teach metaphysics, ethics, or modern history. He did not, he said, put forward this interdiction as an 'ornament of the scheme.' He had referred, he said, to the Roman Catholics with their exaggerated idea of the importance of State endowment, to the 'fanatic undenominationalists,' and to other fanatics who thought that unless a university was a completely teaching as well as examining body, it was of no use at all. He had not, he said, the 'slightest expectation that anything which he could say would have the slightest effect upon the devoted adherents of these opinions.' He should therefore address himself, not to those who had formed inflexible opinions, but to those who were disposed to look at the question from a 'more practical and reasonable point of view, and to shape this measure rather according to expediency than to some ideal notion of unattainable perfection.' This was his general attitude upon all questions. He received, in this case, the approval of, perhaps, the most lucid thinker on these matters then living in England, Matthew Arnold. Mr. Arnold wrote to Mr. Chichester

Fortescue, a year later, that he and Lord Hartington alone of the late Ministry seemed able to clear themselves—

'where Catholicism was concerned of the conventional notions and supposed necessities of the Liberal party. Religion will affect politics more and more ; and the provision of ideas which the bulk of the Liberal party, whether secularist or nonconformist, has got at present for meeting this state of things, will not carry them far. All the more interest do those inspire who, in questions where religion is concerned, are independent of their party, and in advance of it.'

The Liberal party, by no means incapable of progress, reached thirty-five years later the advanced position occupied in 1873 by Lord Hartington and Matthew Arnold, and gave to the Irish Catholics the university which they desired, accompanied by a denominational endowment.

In this debate of March 1873 the unhappy Bill which, in the absence of all real support, resembled that which Rabelais called a *chimera bombinans in vacuo*, was assailed by representatives of Dublin University, by Irish Catholics, by Scottish Presbyterians, and by some of the less dependent English Whigs and Radicals. Edward Pleydell Bouverie both spoke and voted against it. Vernon Harcourt, another Whig, not yet in office, said that he should only vote for the Bill in the faint hope that it might be made into something more tolerable in Committee, and described, with genial vigour, the clauses which excluded theology, philosophy, and modern history from the teaching of the new university as 'the most hideous deformity ever laid by an English Government upon the table of an English Parliament.' Henry Fawcett, of Cambridge, that academic Radical, was among the fiercest assailants. But the most effective onslaught of all was made by the now dimly remembered Mr. Horsman, then a Liberal of leading, if not of light. He treated Lord Hartington with ponderous wit, and directed fierce invective against the Prime Minister, who had, he said, come into power in 1868 upon the crest of the wave of a movement against the established Irish Church which true, or aboriginal, Liberals had laboured to promote for forty years.

'On Monday night,' said Mr. Horsman, 'it appeared to me that the Chief Secretary, struggling with the speech of the hon. member for Brighton (Fawcett), was not so much a spectacle for gods as an object for the attention of the Royal Humane Society. Not that I would by any means disparage the almost superhuman efforts of the noble Marquess to rise to the occasion. He went at it like a man, and all but crushed the hon. member for Brighton at the outset by declaring that his beau-ideal of a professor in the new university would be a type of man as dissimilar as possible from the Professor of Political Economy at Cambridge. That was a tremendous blow. I wonder that the Professor of Political Economy survived it. I thought the next morning of sending over to inquire after his health. Then the noble Marquess, after having demolished the hon. member for Brighton, proceeded to terrify the unfortunate member for Dublin University (Dr. Ball), who sat opposite him at the moment. After expatiating upon the advantages offered to Trinity College by the Bill, he turned to the other side of the picture, and said, " See what you will lose by its rejection." '

Horsman then battered the Bill in the name of Liberalism throughout the world. He said that the mixed system of education was 'the greatest blessing that the British Legislature ever conferred on Ireland.' He objected ' to make the slightest concession, direct or indirect, to the claims of the Roman Catholic Hierarchy to control the education of the State.' He said that the country would regard a vote for the Bill as ' a vote of confidence in Cardinal Cullen and his priests, and the supporters of the Government know well that when they are sent to their constituents upon it they will be sent to certain execution.'

This was amusing, for a week earlier Cardinal Cullen and his bishops had publicly declared against the Bill, but Mr. Horsman was not going, for that reason, to alter the whole lines of the greatest oration of his life. Never was there a more tremendous sounding of the Protestant-Liberal drum, so repugnant to the ears of Matthew Arnold. This philippic was delivered on the 8th March. On the 8th, Lord Hartington wrote to Lord Spencer that the Liberal Whip counted on a majority of from twenty to twenty-five if things did not get worse, but that Horsman's speech had produced an extraordinary effect upon the Liberals, and that, if a division had been taken immediately after it, the Government would certainly have been beaten. He added :—

'Any mistake on our side, or unforeseen accident, may make matters as bad again, though, for the present, they have partly recovered from the effect of the speech. Glyn only counts about sixteen Irish M.P.'s as likely to vote with us. . . . I must say that I rather hope we may be beaten, for I cannot see what possible good can be expected to result from a Bill passed in the teeth of the Irish representatives.'

The Tory leader was as free from religious prejudice as was Lord Hartington, and had a truer understanding of the Roman Catholic Church than had Mr. Gladstone. In a brilliant and effective, though not quite fair, attack, he exposed the absurd device for the amalgamation of Incompatibles by the omission of Essentials. A university, he said—

'should be a place of light, of liberty, and of learning. It is a place for the cultivation of the intellect, for invention, for research; it is not a place where you should expect to find interdiction of studies, some of them the most interesting that can occupy the mind of man. . . . This is essentially a material age.  The opinions which are now afloat, which have often been afloat before, and which have died away, as I have no doubt these will die in due time, are opposed to all those convictions which the proper study of Moral and Mental Philosophy has long established.  And that such a proposition should be made in respect to a university which has produced Berkeley and Hutchinson makes it still more surprising.  We live in an age when young men prattle about protoplasms, and when young ladies in gilded saloons unconsciously talk Atheism. And this is the moment when a Minister, called upon to fulfil one of the noblest duties which can fall upon the most ambitious statesman, namely, the formation of a great university, formally comes forward, and proposes the omission from public study of that philosophy which vindicates the spiritual nature of man.'

Disraeli said of concurrent endowment, as applied to Churches, that it was 'at least the policy of great statesmen, of Pitt, of Grey, of Russell, of Peel, and of Palmerston.' Mr. Gladstone, he said, 'was a pupil of Sir Robert Peel. He sat in the Cabinet of Lord Palmerston. . . . He suddenly changed his mind' (in the case of the Irish Church), 'and threw over the policy of concurrent endowment, *mistaking the clamour of the Nonconformists for the voice of the nation.*'

The Prime Minister, no doubt keenly enjoying a close and arduous fight, affording the finest opportunities for his subtle skill, followed his great antagonist and made a clever speech with a fine peroration, but, when the division was taken at 2.30 on the morning of 12th March, he was defeated by three votes.  His normal majority was about 90.

A few hours later political England was humming with excitement over the probable fall of a powerful Government.

On the 10th March, the last day but one of the debate, Lord Hartington had written to Lord Spencer that the Cabinet had had some talk about what should be done in the event of a defeat, and that—

'certainly the opinion of a majority of the Cabinet, including Mr. Gladstone, would be in favour of a dissolution. I cannot, however, conceive anything more unfortunate for Ireland than a dissolution at this moment. The Home Rulers would be certain to carry every seat (except the Tory seats), and the priests would probably throw all their influence into the Home Rule movement. Whether matters will be any better next year if the Tories should then dissolve I do not know, but I don't think they could ever be worse than they are now. Let me know how it strikes you.'

Lord Spencer replied that he could not ' conceive how a dissolution would be justified in Ireland. Home Rule would increase in force and gain some formidable allies who conceive that a real grievance exists as to the University question.' Nor did he think that in England the results of a dissolution would be favourable. Mr. Gladstone would really go to the country on the unpopular University Bill, although he might put it ' upon general confidence in himself and his Government.' After the division in the early hours of 12th March Lord Hartington wrote :—

' I think that opinion is tending more towards resignation. On Saturday Gladstone was strong for dissolution, and said, which of course would be almost decisive, that, though he should think it his duty to lead the party in an immediate dissolution, he should retire if it were postponed and were to take place under the Tories. He has said nothing about this to-day, and I imagine is rather changing his mind.  I remain very strong against dissolution, especially as regards Ireland.  Gladstone considers that we are absolutely released by the vote of the Irish members from our pledges on the subject of University Education.  But I think that, if we were to have an election now, it must turn, in Ireland, almost exclusively on this question, and all Irish Liberal members would come back pledged, not only to Home Rule, but to decided opposition to the Government.  If the dissolution is postponed I am afraid there is no hope that matters will be much altered as to Home Rule, but the agitation on the subject of education may subside, and they may not on general questions be hostile to us.  I think also that dissolution will be very unpopular with our party generally, and that they will think that they are being punished for our mistakes.  I also think that if we wash our hands of the University business it will be very difficult to give good reasons for going to the country.  It is true that we have received such a blow that we could not hope to keep any command over the present House, but it will be said that the majority are prepared to support us in every question except one, and that we have ourselves abandoned that one.  As to resignation, I am much afraid that the Tories will not take office, and that, after much backing and filling, we shall come back again, which I think will be most unpleasant. Some, however, think that Disraeli will jump at office on any terms, and that he will be at his old tricks again, getting up caves in our party, and bidding for support in all quarters of the House.  This is, I daresay, very demoralising to the party and the House of Commons, but I don't think that we are responsible for it, and I have no doubt that resignation is our proper course.  If Mr. Gladstone persists in his intention it is no doubt very serious, for I don't see who is to take his place ; but even in such a case I should be very unwilling to dissolve in present circumstances.'

The Cabinet decided in favour of resignation, and

Lord Hartington wrote again to Lord Spencer on the 13th March :—

'You will be glad to hear that we have resigned and not dissolved. It remains to be seen what will next happen. There is a very strong opinion that Dizzy will not be able to form a Government, and that Gladstone will have to come back. So perhaps you will not have to leave after all. Whether I should come back if I am asked, I don't know. I have been longing to be out for a long time, and I think this would be an excellent opportunity to recover my freedom. I don't think Gladstone will make much difficulty about returning, if Dizzy and the Tories fail. I suppose he will have to dissolve soon, as I don't think that after this the present Parliament could be satisfactorily managed.

'If there was a question of returning, I should want to be satisfied as to the course to be taken with reference to Fawcett's Bill; which I see no ground for opposing any further. I also hardly see how I could come in without some pledge about Irish railways; and I am inclined to think that there ought to be some reconstruction of the Cabinet, and some addition to the Whig element. However, it is no use discussing all this, as there may be no question of it, and a great many people think that Disraeli will never let slip the opportunity of taking office.'

Lord Hartington went for a holiday to Kimbolton Castle, had a good gallop, and found that 'Blarney went first-rate.' His dream of escape from office, and more time free for hunting, was not yet to be realised. Two days later, on 18th March, he wrote to Lord Spencer :—

'We are in again, I am sorry to say, not without an attempt on my part to get free. I saw Mr. Gladstone this morning, and told him some of the reasons which induced me to wish to leave. However, finding that there were to be no other changes, and that my leaving now might be attributed to some other reasons than the real ones, I have

agreed to remain for the present; but have given warning
that if I do not feel more comfortable in my office at the
end of the session, I may then have to retire.

'I should be particularly sorry to put you to any
inconvenience; but I have really come to detest office. I
don't know whether I dislike this one much more than any
other; but I think that my position for the remainder of
the session and Parliament will be a disagreeable one, and
after an election it may be worse. However, here we are
again for the present, and it is no use grumbling. We are
not to have a dissolution if we can help it; but of course
it will depend on the conduct of the House. There are
many very awkward questions, which are likely to make
it impossible for us to go on with the present House.'

On the 20th March Lord Hartington heard Disraeli
explain the reasons for which he had declined, when
invited by the Queen, to form an Administration, and, at
the end of his speech, define the functions and predict the
future of the Tory party. Lord Hartington could not have
imagined that he himself was destined to support this
party during many years of his life, until it returned to a
policy which Disraeli did not then consider to be 'indigenous to its native growth.' 'I believe,' said Disraeli—

'that the Tory party at the present time occupies
the most satisfactory position which it has held since
the days of its greatest statesmen, Mr. Pitt and Lord
Grenville. It has divested itself of those excrescences
which are not indigenous to its native growth. . . . We
are now emerging from the fiscal period in which
almost all the public men of this generation have been
brought up. All the questions of trade and navigation,
of the incidence of taxation and of public economy are
settled. But there are other questions not less important,
and of deeper and higher reach and range which must
soon engage the attention of the country. The attributes
of a constitutional monarchy, whether the aristocratic

principle should be recognised in our constitution, and
if so, in what form, whether the Commons of England
shall remain an Estate of the Realm, numerous, but
privileged and powerful, or whether they should degenerate
into an indiscriminate multitude; whether a national
Church shall be maintained, and if so, what shall be its
rights and duties; the functions of Corporations, the
sacredness of endowments, the tenure of landed property,
the free disposal and even the existence of any kind of
property.  All those institutions, and all those principles
which have made this country free and famous, and
conspicuous for its union of order with liberty, are now
impugned, and in due time will become " great and burning" questions.[1]  I think it is of the utmost importance
that when that time arrives, there shall be in this country
a great Constitutional party, distinguished for its intelligence as well as for its organisation, which shall be
competent to lead the people and direct the public mind.
And, sir, when that time arrives, and when they enter upon
a career which must be noble, and which I hope and
believe will be triumphant, I think they may perhaps
remember, and not, perhaps, with unkindness, that I at
least prevented one obstacle from being placed in their
way, when as trustee of their honour and their interests
I declined to form a weak and discredited Administration.'

Mr. Gladstone was obliged to continue his Administration, but all virtue and strength were gone.  Sadly and
aptly he quoted the lines of his favourite Horace :

> ' Neque amissos colores
> Lana refert, medicata fuco ;
> Nec vera virtus, cum semel excidit
> Curat reponi deterioribus.'

It was clear that the Ministry could only last until they
found an opportunity for dissolution better than that presented by the defeat of an universally unpopular measure.

[1] ' Great and burning' was a quotation from Gladstone.

## VI

On 12th August 1873, Lord Hartington received a
letter from Mr. Gladstone which surprised him. The
Prime Minister wrote that Lord Spencer wished to give
up the Viceroyalty on December 1st, and added, 'I understand you do not mean to remain after him, and it would
not be desirable to change both the great functionaries
at once.' He proposed, therefore, that Lord Hartington
should, at the beginning of October, return to the Post
Office, and should be succeeded in Ireland by W. E.
Forster. Lord Hartington replied that he had not been
aware of Lord Spencer's intention to resign, but he
added :—

'You are quite right in supposing that I should not
like to remain in Ireland with another Lord-Lieutenant,
and you will also remember that, when the Government
returned to office last spring, I wished that my resignation should still be accepted. My office is therefore at
your disposal whenever it may be convenient to you.
But I am not at all disposed to go back to the Post
Office. I liked the office well enough when I was there,
but I should not care to return to it after holding a
much more important and interesting office.'

Lord Hartington wrote on the same day, August 14th,
to Lord Spencer, and, after expressing his surprise at the
news of his intended resignation, said :—

'I have told Mr. Gladstone that he is quite right in
supposing that I did not wish to remain after you, and
that, as he knows, I had wished to resign in April, and
that therefore my office was quite at his disposal, but
that I am not at all inclined to go back to the Post
Office. I am, therefore, so far as I know, out altogether,
at which I shall greatly rejoice ; but I must say that I am

not much pleased at the manner in which it has been done. I don't know from whom Mr. Gladstone has heard that I will not stay after you, and the alacrity with which my supposed wishes are now consulted is a contrast to the pressure put on me to stay in April. The fact is that the place is wanted for Forster, who can't stay in his present office, with Bright in office, without offending the Dissenters. I shall be glad to hear what took place between you and Mr. Gladstone, and whether he was as glad to accept your resignation as mine.

'I think we are well out of a troublesome place where no credit is to be gained, but, if you had stayed on, I had quite made up my mind to make a rather more vigorous attempt next year to do something about Local Government reform in Ireland, and I am a little sorry to go without leaving any legislative work whatever behind me. From Mr. Gladstone's letter I imagine that he would like Forster to take the office about October 1st.'

Mr. Gladstone explained that he knew, from what he had heard from Lord Frederick Cavendish, that Lord Hartington desired to give up his present office upon Lord Spencer's retirement, and continued—

'I thought, therefore, that all was plain and smooth before me, when I simply pointed out a way which I hoped (not without some appearance of reason) would be agreeable to you, for retaining your connection with the Cabinet. I do not say no other way is possible ; certainly I would not arrive at that conclusion without looking well about me.

'For surely the question of your total retirement at this moment is a serious one. I put aside entirely my own personal conviction about the claim which the Crown as well as the country has upon the services of men born to great positions and properties, and to hereditary rights of legislation ; for that conviction is, I admit, no argument. But pray review the circumstances of the moment. Ripon's retirement is reasonably, and that of Childers palpably, grounded on private affairs. The other Cabinet and Privy

Council changes are either consequential or (more or less) penal. In this last category your resignation could not be placed. But in what category *would* it stand? To what possible cause could it be referred by the world outside except to the difficulties of the Government, which I believe to be the last cause which would operate on your mind.

'Spencer has made an immense gap in his Northamptonshire life, and is most naturally anxious not to widen it further; but he told me that he felt the topic, to which I have last referred, to be an objection, such, however, as, in the circumstances of his case, I would not admit, far less press.

"I should not have entered on this topic at all were I a younger man, or less anxious to see my way out of office and of public life. But I put aside all reserve in regard to it, being determined for myself to stick close until a good case comes for leaving; and really being prompted, at least to my knowledge, by no other consideration than by the duty and desire to be loyal to the colleagues, and to the party, who have been so kind to me.'[1]

It appeared that the Prime Minister had acted upon a misunderstanding of what the Lord-Lieutenant had said. Lord Spencer, at an interview, had asked Mr. Gladstone whether there were any prospect of a dissolution or resignation at the beginning of 1874, as, if so, he would like to vacate office before the beginning of the expensive Dublin season in the early part of the year. Mr. Gladstone mysteriously had replied that, in December 1873, there would be 'a crisis for the Government.' Lord Spencer thought that he might take this oracle as meaning a dissolution or resignation in December, and, saying nothing more, went abroad for a holiday. When he returned in August he discovered, at an interview with Mr. Gladstone, that his own resignation, as from December, was considered to be a *fait accompli*, and that it had been mentioned to the Queen. Lady

[1] Mr. Gladstone to Lord Hartington, 15th August 1873.

Spencer wrote to Lord Hartington that, when she heard this, she felt 'a little taken aback, and did not think it quite flattering or agreeable to have our departure from Ireland made *so very easy*.'

After receiving Lord Spencer's explanation, Lord Hartington wrote to him on August 18th to say that, notwithstanding Lord Granville's arguments, he did not think that there was any possibility of his changing his own intention to resign. He added :—

'I have not heard a word from Gladstone showing that he would wish me to remain in my present position, and even if he should now turn round and ask either or both of us, or me only, to remain, I think I could not do it. As to the Post Office, the idea of going back to it is more repulsive to me every day, and I can't think that I am bound to give up my independence for such an office as that.'

'I have no doubt that the difficulties have been great, and Granville says that everybody has done his utmost to remove them; that he himself offered to give up the Foreign Office for any other office, &c., and it is not pleasant to be the only one to interpose with personal objections; but I can't help thinking that the change from the Irish Office to the Post Office would be nothing short of humiliation, and that it can't be for the advantage of the Government itself that any of its members should submit to that. I don't suppose that Gladstone intended it, but it presents itself to me in that light.'

It must be remembered that Lord Hartington had been Secretary of State for War seven years earlier, in 1866, and had already made one steep descent, in 1868, to the Post Office, which, although a more distinguished office now than it was in 1873, is still, to judge by Cabinet promotions, less an object of ambition than is the Local Government Board or the Board of Trade. Lord Hartington's successor at the Post Office had not even been given a seat in the Cabinet.

Both Lord Spencer and Lord Hartington felt that the Prime Minister had shown too much 'alacrity' to *believe* that they wished to retire.   Hartington wrote again to Mr. Gladstone from Walmer Castle, on the 18th August, that he had consulted his host, Lord Granville, but, as yet, saw no sufficient reason to change his mind, although he was very unwilling to take any step which should embarrass the Government, even slightly.   He would delay his final decision for a few days, until he had heard again from Lord Spencer, and had consulted his father.

Lord Granville wrote on the 19th August to Lord Hartington to say that he had had a letter from Mr. Gladstone which—

'entirely disposes of the "alacrity" theory, as far as regards wishing you and Spencer to be out of Ireland.   But what I do not know is how far he is committed now, after having considered you and Spencer determined to resign. I had a letter from Spencer in which he adopts rather an indignant attitude about the "alacrity," but is, as usual, as high-minded as possible.   I have little doubt that, if you withdraw from the Government, whether owing to your fault, or to a fault of Gladstone's, it will be detrimental to you, and an immense blow to the Government, and, in saying this, I divest myself of every iota of personal feeling in the matter.'

Lord Hartington was not yet quite satisfied, but on the 21st August he wrote to Lord Spencer :—

'I feel sure that there has been some considerable mis-understanding about the whole thing; and that Mr. Gladstone has done what he rather hastily assumed would be most agreeable to both of us.   Whether what is done can be undone is, however, another question.'

On the 22nd, Lord Granville explained the confusion more fully in a letter to Lord Hartington :—

'Under high steam pressure to reconstruct, at a moment when everybody was vanishing, and most desirous to secure Bright, no doubt appears to have occurred to him (Mr. Gladstone) that Spencer had resigned, and that you were determined not to stay without him. He spoke to Bright accordingly, and gave a hint, without committing himself, to Forster. . . . You once used the word "penal." I can only give you my positive assurance that I have never heard him in his frequent observations do anything but praise your character, qualities, and gifts, or make any complaint, excepting about your Parliamentary attendance, concerning which I imagine there may be a speck on the sun.'

The reconstruction of the Ministry, partly for 'penal' and partly for 'consequential' reasons, was on so extensive a scale that mistakes were certainly to be excused. Lowe was removed from the Treasury, which the Prime Minister himself now took, to the Home Office ; Ayrton was removed from the Cabinet altogether ; Bruce left the Home Office and became a Peer and President of the Council ; Lord Ripon and Mr. Childers retired, for private reasons, from the Cabinet. John Bright entered it. Vernon Harcourt and Lyon Playfair, both lately hostile critics, were given posts in the Administration. But the incident illustrates the inaccuracy of Mr. Gladstone's mind in certain respects, his predisposition, recorded by his most devoted adherents, to believe that to be true which he wished to be true, and the consequent embarrassment in which he involved from time to time the plain-minded Whig noblemen, educated at Cambridge University, who honestly endeavoured to follow this great man through the bewildering phases of his strange career.

However, the question of change was adjourned for the

present, and Lord Hartington remained at the Irish Office until the resignation of the Liberal Government. He had been thwarted in his desire to reform the Irish railway system, and he had met with great difficulties in obtaining any time for minor Irish business in a congested House of Commons. Explaining this to Lord Spencer in a letter of April 1872, he said humorously, 'I think the Chancellor told you I was becoming a Home Ruler. I am getting stronger every day.'

One day in the autumn of 1873 Sir Arthur Helps, in writing to Lord Hartington upon a business matter, said—

'I have been staying for two or three days with the Recluse of Hughenden. He spoke very kindly of you, and, indeed, he seems to me to be very fair, that is, in private speech, towards all his political opponents.'

The Recluse was now to reach the acquisition of solid power, so long deferred, during years of combat against the dominant tide of Liberalism, that it came too late for the fulfilment of the visions of the author of *Coningsby* and *Sybil*, and too late to yield much enjoyment or satisfaction to a weary and lonely spirit.

## CHAPTER VII

### THE INTERREGNUM OF 1874

On the 24th January 1874 appeared Gladstone's manifesto announcing the immediate dissolution of Parliament. He based his action upon the weakening of the position of the Government, due to the defeat on Irish University education and manifested in the results of recent by-elections. This, he said, made it desirable to obtain a general decision from the country. No programme was put forward save that of reduction of local taxation and abolition of income-tax. Disraeli, in his answering manifesto, said that it would have been better, during recent years, if there had been more energy in foreign policy and less in domestic legislation. He also said :—

'There is reason to hope, from the address of the Prime Minister, putting aside some ominous suggestions which it contains as to the expediency of a local and subordinate Legislature, that he is not, certainly at present, opposed to our national institutions or to the maintenance of the integrity of the Empire. But, unfortunately, among his adherents, some assail the monarchy, others impugn the independence of the House of Lords, while there are those who would relieve Parliament altogether from any share in the government of one part of the United Kingdom.'

Disraeli, in whom the brooding predominated over the discursive intellect, had certainly a good eye for tendencies. There was in him something of

> " . . . the prophetic soul
> Of the wide world dreaming of things to come."

The elections took place in February 1874. Liberals lost many seats, and the cumulative result was that the Conservatives had in the new Parliament a majority of about fifty over Liberals and Irish Home Rulers combined. In Ireland fifty-eight men pledged to Home Rule were returned. Soon after the meeting of Parliament they declined to answer the Liberal Whip, and declared themselves to be a distinct and independent party. They were still led by old Isaac Butt. Charles Parnell did not enter Parliament till a year later.

When the results of the elections were ascertained the Gladstone Government resigned office. At their last meeting as a Cabinet, on 17th February, the Prime Minister announced that he—

'would no longer retain the leadership of the Liberal party, nor resume it, until the party had settled its differences. He would not expose himself to the insults and outrages of 1866–8, and had a keen sense of the disloyalty of the party during the last three years. He would sit as a private member, and occasionally speak for himself, but he would not attend the House regularly nor assume any one of the functions of leader.'[1]

Mr. Gladstone added more satisfying reasons on other occasions. He pleaded, on behalf of retirement, his age (he was now sixty-five), his desire to spend his remaining days in tranquillity, and, at any rate, in freedom from political strife ; his inability to agree with certain tendencies of the Liberal party, especially in religious matters. He consented, under pressure by his colleagues, to defer for a while the final step. The public were informed that his need for rest was so pressing that he could appear only occasionally in the present session, and that it was an open

---

[1] Letter from a member of the Cabinet, quoted in Lord Morley's *Life of Gladstone*, vol. ii. p. 497.

question whether he would be able to lead at all in later sessions. A voice from the past hailed with joy this provisional retreat. Earl Russell wrote to Lord Hartington: 'I look to you in the Commons, assisted by Forster and Goschen, to lead the business of our party. I can never look to Gladstone any more as a leader. With great abilities, he and Granville have led the Whig party of Lord Grey to destruction and dispersion.' But how could the party of Lord Grey be an eternal and unchanging fact? The fall in the franchise level in 1867 had brought upon the field of action two new forces—the English and Scottish artisans and the Irish Nationalists. Mr. Gladstone held the Whigs and the Radicals together till 1886 with difficulty but with success. Then he broke up the party by his attempt to restore self-government to Ireland, and to eliminate from the Imperial Parliament the Irish members who had, since 1874, ceased to form part of the Liberal organisation.

Gladstone was sincere in his wish to retire. Probably, however, in any case, the desire would not have lasted long. Like Achilles, he—

> " Pined in dull repose, and his full heart
> Panted for war's loud din. "

And unfortunately for his dream of rest, the session of 1874 assumed an ecclesiastical character. There was a Scottish Church Patronage Bill, and an Endowed Schools Bill, and the Bill for the Regulation of Public Worship, intended, Disraeli said, to suppress ceremonies practised by certain of the Anglican clergy, and described by him as the 'Mass in masquerade.' Lord Salisbury, in the debates on this Bill, said that there existed three schools in the Church, 'the Sacramental, the Emotional, and the Philosophical.' Disraeli described the characteristics of these schools as being 'ceremony, enthusiasm, and free speculation.' In so far as Hartington could be said to belong to any school, it was to the last-mentioned. Lord Arthur Russell kept a note of conversation which illustrates this way of thinking :—

'We were at Chatsworth in 1875. Bishop Temple at dinner wondered how all the scientific men adopted Darwin's theories without evidence, only on his authority. His were simply fanciful theories without facts to support them, and nobody who had not witnessed, as he had done, the strange fact, could have foreseen that men trained in observation would adopt them so readily and without enquiry. The Duke and Cardwell, who did not appear to wish for controversy, were silent.

'After dinner I was in the smoking-room with Hartington. After a long silence he said, "The Bishop says that scientific men adopt hastily and without sufficient evidence all the modern ideas about evolution! Why, surely, it is only because these ideas explain facts, and because they are based on facts and on evidence, that scientific men do adopt them, and they would not adopt Darwin's explanations if they were not supported by evidence. Is it not so?"' [1]

Lord Hartington took no part in the ecclesiastical debates of 1874, and there is nothing to show that at any time he took the slightest interest in any purely ecclesiastical question. As to the relations between Church and State, and the ideal of a Church, his views were probably not very different from those of Sir William Harcourt. [2]

It was a curious feature of these debates that, while Lord Salisbury in the House of Lords and Disraeli in the House of Commons exchanged some bitter repartees,

---

[1] The writer is indebted for this note to Mr. Harold Russell, the son of Lord Arthur Russell.

[2] Once, when ecclesiastical questions were invading the political area, Lord Hartington said to a private secretary, 'Can you explain to me what " transubstantiation " means, that they are talking about?'

although colleagues, Harcourt, as the Erastian and anti-ritualistic champion, ran a-tilt against Mr. Gladstone in the House of Commons. Mr. Gladstone found scant sympathy for his views in Parliament; the second reading of the Bill was carried without even a division. He was now concerned to refute the popular notion that ritualism prepared the way for conversion to the Church of Rome. In October 1874 he published an essay denying this tendency, on the ground that modern developments of the Roman Church exercised, for a sound Churchman, an influence not attractive, but repelling. This was followed in November by his famous pamphlet, entitled *The Vatican Decrees in their Bearing on Civil Allegiance. A Political Expostulation.* There was an immense sale of this injudicious and hastily written production. In one sense these fierce attacks upon the decisions of the Vatican Council of 1870 were well timed. They effaced, or diminished, the adverse impression which Mr. Gladstone's attempt to propitiate the Irish Hierarchy, and his opposition to the very popular Public Worship Bill, had caused in Protestant England. They proved, what is true, that no one is so strong an opponent of Rome as a real Anglican. Strange that a statesman who, in 1874, laid it down in the clearest and strongest terms that allegiance to spiritual Rome was incompatible with civil allegiance, should, in 1886, have attempted to establish a Roman Catholic Government in Ireland! Had he then admitted to himself that he was mistaken in the denunciations of 1874? It may be, all secular prudence was forgotten in the intense antagonism excited in his mind by the uncompromising and far-reaching assertion made in the Vatican Decrees that authority descends from above, and does not ascend from below. He was, besides, under the weird influence of Lord Acton, a mortal foe to Rome; he had been offended by the conduct of the Irish Hierarchy towards the University Bill; and, possibly, fuel was added to the fire of indignation by the fact that his old Anglican ally, Manning, now Roman Archbishop of Westminster, had, at the great Council, been so powerful an advocate of the doctrine. To a cool Whig diplomat, Odo Russell, the Roman policy appeared to be sound, from a mundane point of view, and Hartington certainly felt not a spark of excitement about it, or, consequently, of indignation against it.

## II

On the 30th June 1874, the case for Irish Home Rule was, for the first time since the collapse of O'Connell's 'Repeal' movement, formally submitted to the House of Commons by Isaac Butt and his followers. It was presented in moderate tone and reasonable form. Mr. Butt moved—

'that it is expedient and just to restore to the Irish Nation the right and power of managing all exclusively Irish affairs in an Irish Parliament, and that provision should be made at the same time for maintaining the integrity of the Empire, and the connection between the countries, by reserving to this Imperial Parliament full and exclusive control over all Imperial affairs.'

Mr. Butt said that fifty-nine Irish Members of Parliament entirely assented to this proposition, which was based upon resolutions adopted at a representative Conference held in Dublin.

His practical proposal was that there should be no change in the existing composition of the Imperial Parliament, but that the Irish members should meet as a distinct Parliament for distinctively Irish affairs. They were not to vote upon English or Scottish questions in the Imperial Parliament.

Mr. Gladstone was not present at this debate, and Lord Hartington spoke on behalf of the Liberal Opposition. These words must not be forgotten by the reader :—

'In honour and in honesty,' he said, 'the Imperial Parliament were bound to tell the Irish people that, while giving every consideration to the just claims of Ireland, they could only look at this question from an Imperial point of view; and that they were convinced that, whatever might be the effect of that proposal upon the internal affairs of that country, they could never give their consent to the proposal. . . . It may be said that this is a strong declaration, but at the same time a very safe one on my part, seeing that the party to which I belong are at present in a hopeless minority in this House, and that they have therefore nothing either to hope or to fear from the support of Irish members. But I can say for myself—and I think that I may say the same for those who sit round me—that no motive of personal ambition, no consideration of party advantage, could ever induce us to purchase the support of honourable members representing Irish constituencies by any sacrifice which in our opinion would endanger the union between the two countries. I know that it may be said that protestations of this kind are of little avail, that, when the exigency of the moment demanded, they might be easily evaded and set aside. It is, therefore, of all the more importance that I should express my firm conviction that, if any members sitting on this side of the House were so reckless as to show a symptom on their part of a disposition to coquet with this question, there would instantly be such a disruption and disorganisation of parties that they would find that they had lost more support from England and Scotland than they could ever hope to obtain from Ireland.'

This was plain speaking, and a fair warning, and

it was an exact forecast of what was to happen twelve
years later. Lord Hartington added that he did not see
how it was possible to set up a federal system unless
the kingdoms were first separated; that, in his opinion,
the proposition, if accepted, must lead to complete separation; and that, though Mr. Butt denied this, he (the
Marquis of Hartington) was *not willing to risk the
integrity of the Empire on the assertion of any one, however
well-meaning he might be*. A demand, he said, for separation proceeding from an Irish Parliament and Government
would not be so easily met, by force, as were present
discontents and possible risings. After pointing out
financial and administrative difficulties inherent in the
particular scheme suggested by Mr. Butt, he concluded
his speech by saying :—

'It remains for the people of Ireland to consider
whether, by accepting the inevitable—and I think that
they will, by the result of this discussion, discover that
it is inevitable—by entering freely and cheerfully into
all our counsels, they will secure to themselves a far
greater share of influence in their own affairs than they
have ever yet possessed since the Union, and get a very
large share in all the imperial concerns of England, or
whether, by advocating what is impracticable, by placing
themselves in hopeless opposition to the ascertained
wishes of the vast majority of the people of England
and the Legislature, they will reduce to insignificancy
their influence in the councils of the nation, and compel
us to legislate for them without their aid, and, perhaps,
sometimes in opposition even to their just rights.'

What inspired the last words? Was it a reminiscence
of the treatment of the railway question and the University
question? The Irish people have chosen the second
alternative offered by Lord Hartington; probably by the
nature of things they could do no otherwise. Whether

they would have gradually abandoned it, had every English statesman adhered to the position taken up by Lord Hartington, one cannot say.  Lord Hartington perhaps deemed it necessary to speak so strongly and explicitly, and to foretell certain disruption to the party which should accede to the Irish demand, because Mr. Gladstone before the last election had uttered some enigmatic words which might, or might not, mean a concession.

An Irish speaker, who followed, said that Lord Hartington's was almost the only speech delivered in the debate 'that really touches our case so as to call for serious answer.'  True it is that most of the English speakers, after the English manner, had met sentiments based on history, nationality, and religion, with statistics of the increase of pigs, sheep, poultry, railway passengers, and investments in savings banks in Ireland within a given period of years. As Ireland had during this period been under English government, these statistics, it was felt, were obviously the effects of that cause, and, although certainly not very magnificent in themselves, completely destroyed the case for Home Rule.  Sir Michael Hicks Beach observed in the debate on Butt's motion that Lord Hartington had said—

'with a manly courage that did him honour, as the representative of what remained of the Liberal party of England —that nothing could persuade them to assent to the proposal.  The present Government would be unworthy to occupy their position if they did not state with equal emphasis their sincere and firm resolve, caring not for place or power, or for the fleeting breath of popular favour, to oppose in any and every way what they believed would conduce to the destruction of the United Kingdom and the disintegration of the Empire.'

The motion was rejected by the great majority of 458 to 61, both English parties combining to defeat it.

### III

Mr. Gladstone's resolution to retire was strengthened by the events of the session of 1874. On the 13th January 1874 he addressed to Lord Granville the following letter, which was also communicated to the Press :—

11 CARLTON HOUSE TERRACE,
*13th January* 1875.

MY DEAR GRANVILLE,—The time has, I think, arrived when I ought to revert to the subject of the letter which I addressed to you on March 12.

Before determining whether I should offer to assume a charge which might extend over a length of time, I have reviewed, with all the care in my power, a number of considerations, both public and private, of which a portion, and these not by any means insignificant, were not in existence at the date of that letter.

The result is that I see no public advantage in my continuing to act as the leader of the Liberal party; and that, at the age of sixty-five, and after forty-two years of a laborious public life, I think myself entitled to retire on the present opportunity. This retirement is dictated to me by my personal views as to the best method of spending the closing years of my life.

I need hardly add that my conduct in Parliament will continue to be governed by the principles on which I have heretofore acted ; and whatever arrangements may be made for the treatment of general business and for the advantage or convenience of the Liberal party, they will have my cordial support. I should, perhaps, add that I am at present, and mean for a short time to be, engaged on a special matter, which occupies me closely.—Believe me always sincerely yours, W. E. GLADSTONE.

The experiment of carrying on the Opposition without a definite leader constantly present had not been a success during the session of 1874. But the existing division

between Whigs and Radicals made the choice of a new
leader difficult, nor was there any man whose reputation and influence was decidedly superior to that of
others.   Sir William Harcourt had played a leading
part in the session of 1874; he was a first-rate fighter
and debater; he had great power of affection for those
whom he liked, and of fidelity to comrades in battle;
but he was not popular, did not possess smooth or in-
gratiating manners; and was too much of a Whig to
please the Radicals.   He entertained no idea that the
leadership could fall, on this occasion, to himself; from
the first moment he worked, like Lord Granville, to secure
it to Lord Hartington, and, a more difficult business, to
compel Hartington to accept it.   Two days after the
announcement of Mr. Gladstone's final decision, Harcourt wrote to Hartington :—

'I hope now that there is no doubt or hesitation as
to your being the man to take the helm in the House of
Commons.   In my humble judgment any other arrangement is *absolutely impossible* and would disastrously fail.
All I can say is that, as an integer of the party, I will
work heart and soul to the best of my ability to help
you in the difficult task before you.   It depends entirely
upon your pluck and determination whether the Whig
or the Radical flag is to be hoisted to the fore.   If the
latter, the party is irretrievably broken up.   You ought
to save us from this, and I feel confident that you
will.'

To this Lord Hartington replied from Kimbolton Castle
on January 17th :—

'I have to thank you for your letter; the more because
since last March you have taken a position in the House of
Commons which certainly would entitle you to consider
yourself a candidate for the vacant place.   The time since
Gladstone's retirement is short, but I have already heard

enough to convince me that, if leadership of the Opposition as a whole is to be attempted at all, it must be brought about, not by its assumption by myself or any one else, or by the dictation of the late Cabinet, but by the party itself after consultation and consideration of the many difficulties of the position.

'I do not myself feel certain that leadership of the Opposition as a whole is either possible or desirable, and that an arrangement which would recognise the real state of affairs among us might not be preferable. The Opposition consists of Whigs, Radicals, and Home Rulers, and a recognition of that fact would save us from many embarrassments, and might possibly enable us to resist any really mischievous policy of the present Government, at least as efficiently as if we were nominally united. However, other things are no doubt being discussed everywhere at this moment, and a few days will probably show what the wishes of the various sections of the Opposition are.

'The only point on which I have at all made up my own mind is that I would not accept the nominal leadership of the Opposition, unless the proposal was made with the general concurrence of the leading men in and out of the late Government.'

Sir William Harcourt replied :—

'As for myself, I assure you most sincerely that no thought of any pretensions of my own have ever crossed my mind. I know but too well how totally unfit I am for such a situation. But you must allow me to tell you frankly how much I dissent from the policy—or rather no-policy—which your letter indicates.

'As you are aware, I have always regretted the want of firmness and decision which the late Cabinet (who are the natural leaders of the party) exhibited last spring. I still think that the mischiefs which have since happened are mainly due to that cause. The difficulties are now far

greater than they were then, as always happens by postponing evils which ought to be faced.

'It seems that the same persons still shrink from the
responsibility of decision, and the consequences I foresee
will be nothing else but the irretrievable dissolution of the
Liberal party.   If, as I suppose, Lord Granville is accepted
by all as the chief, it seems to me he in concert with Bright
ought to recommend a course to the party, and, if that were
done with decision, I believe it would be accepted cheerfully.   To fling the thing down to be scrambled for in a
general meeting will expose us all to ridicule and confusion.
If there are to be three recognised sections of the Liberal
party, are they to have three separate heads—*e.g.*, you,
Forster, and Butt.   This would be a bad imitation of the
French Assembly.

'In my judgment the moderate Liberals are the majority
of the party.   I should class them about thus : 70 Home
Rulers, 70 Radicals, and about 150 Whigs, or whatever you
please to call them.   I cannot see that the 150 are to yield
tamely to the dictation of the 70 Radicals.   Yet this is
likely enough to happen if the 70 know their own mind
and the 150 do not.

'We are " drifting " into final disruption, as it seems to
me, for want of courage.   And there will soon be no party
at all.   Parties which do not believe in their own existence
have already ceased to exist because they deserve to do so.
It is idle to talk of "party discipline" in such a situation,
for we are all mere disintegrated atoms.

'I can quite understand the wisdom of waiting a little
to gain time to feel the pulse of the party, but I am sure
in the end that a definite proposal should be made and
adhered to.

'I have written and spoken to no one but you, and do
not intend to do so.   I am glad to be out of London, and
intend to be so as much as I can till the meeting of Parliament.   I suppose I shall learn then if there still survives any
party to which I can pretend to belong.   If not I shall tie
on my life-preserver and bob about on the waves.   Of all

things in the world I am sure the least wise is to "let things slide."'

One or two other possible leaders had been discussed, but it became clear that the practical choice lay between Lord Hartington and William E. Forster. There was much resemblance in important matters between the two men. Both were large-natured, sincere, courageous, straightforward, and public-spirited. Both saw things as they were, and not as they might have wished them to be. Neither was ever a prey to illusions, or to intellectual subtleties. They liked each other, and were usually allies on political questions. Mr. Forster by descent and education was, no doubt, a more 'democratic' Liberal than Lord Hartington. He had, however, as Minister for Education, incurred the displeasure of the Nonconformist section of the party by concessions to the advocates of denominational religious teaching, which were embodied in the Education Act of 1870.[1]

Lord Hartington still was strongly convinced that Forster should be invited, and even compelled, to accept the vacant post. He wrote to Lord Granville on the 21st January 1875, from Kimbolton Castle :—

'I return Playfair's letter. The more I think of it, the more glad I shall be if the party will consent to take Forster, and he will consent to take the place.

'My suggestion to you was not exactly that we should do without a leader, but that the Whigs or moderate Liberals should have one, the Radicals another, and the Irishmen a third. I think that there is hardly any impor-

---

[1] Mr. Gladstone was opposed to the idea of Mr. Forster's succession. He thought him 'Liberal over about half the circumference. In economy, peace and war, national vanity, territorial aggrandisement, he partakes, I think, the follies of our countrymen.' (Letter to Lord Granville in *Life of Lord Granville*, vol. ii. p. 148.) Mr. Forster was more 'advanced' than was Lord Hartington on questions like the franchise. and also, perhaps, a more decided Imperialist, at that time.

tant question on which the Whigs and Radicals will not vote against each other ; Disestablishment, Household Suffrage in Counties, Education, Land Laws, &c. ; and the position of a nominal leader seeing his flock all going their own way without attending to him, will not be comfortable. If each section had its own leader and its own organisation, it seems to me that there might be more real union and co-operation on points where we could agree than if we were nominally united; when each section would complain and quarrel every time the party organisation was not used to support its views. However, this must not come from me, as it would look as if, not being able to get the leadership of the party, I wanted to get that of the Whigs.

'I still think that there is no necessity for your intervention at present. The active men are evidently for Forster. If they can get him accepted, so much the better; I would much rather that he should try what looks like an impossibility than that I should ; if they fail, it will be from the opposition of the Radicals rather than that of the Whigs, and if the Radicals would then be obliged to come to me, it will be to some extent better than if I had been put forward by my own friends.

'Therefore I should let Playfair, Fawcett, and Co. have their own way as far as possible.

'I don't know what Vernon Harcourt is doing. If he is working for me, it will probably help Forster.'

His next letter to Lord Granville was intended to be shown to some of the leading men in the party. It ran thus :—

*22nd January* 1875.

MY DEAR GRANVILLE,—You will remember that when I saw you a week ago in London I told you that I thought it extremely doubtful whether the party is at present capable of anything like real organisation, and that the nominal leadership, whoever might undertake it, would be an extremely thankless and unsatisfactory task. I said at

the same time that through the papers, and in various
ways, we should probably in a week know the wishes and
ideas of the party. The subject has certainly been
sufficiently discussed in the interval; and everything I
have heard or read increases my disinclination to be
brought forward as a candidate for the leadership.
The difficulties and unpleasantness of the position seem
to be ignored; and the party occupies itself in deploring,
not its own condition, but the deficiencies of its possible
leaders. A duty, which nothing but absolute necessity and
loyalty to the party could induce any one to undertake,
is offered as a great favour to one or other of us, with
many lamentations over our unfitness. Although, if it
came to a vote, it is possible that the numerical majority
might be in my favour, I cannot help seeing that if certain
objections could be removed or diminished, Forster would
be preferred. The position, which I have never courted,
would under such circumstances be intolerable. The
objections to Forster would certainly be diminished, if not
entirely removed, if he were the only candidate in the
field; and I shall be glad if you will say to Adam, and
any other members of the party whom you may consult,
that, as far as I am concerned, I decline to be placed in
opposition to him.

'If Forster should wish to adopt the same course and
to retire in my favour, I think that it may fairly be urged
upon him that the objections to him are not, as in my
case, personal, and must be diminished at all events, by
my withdrawal; that whatever may be done there will be
some irreconcilables who will break off; and that being by
almost general consent personally the fitter man of the
two, he is more bound to face the difficulties and submit
to the annoyances of the position than I, having only to
look for a sort of toleration in consequence of certain
accidents of my position, can be.

'I should wish Forster to be told that if he becomes
leader, I, for one, should be willing to act under him and to
give him any support in my power. That we could vote

together on all questions, I am afraid is at present impossible; but that is one of the difficulties of our position, and would not be a greater one under one leader than another.—Yours very truly,       HARTINGTON.

*Private.*

I believe that my letter to you expresses my real feelings and intentions, and that nothing will now induce me to have my name put up in opposition to Forster. I hope that you will decide to show it to Adam and other colleagues in London. I was half inclined to write direct to Adam, but thought this would not be fair to you as we have been in consultation throughout.

I got your two letters to-day. I return Adam's, which strengthened my previous intention.

I send you Vernon Harcourt's opinions. I suppose he will have to look about. I am sorry you don't come to Althorpe till Tuesday, as I shall have to leave either Tuesday night or Wednesday morning if I am to attend the Sussex dinner, and I shall hardly see you. Please tell me if you think I had better go. If the question is still unsettled, I think I had better send an excuse; but if you agree with me and I retire at once in favour of Forster, I think I had better go and put a good face on it, and say something which may be of use to Forster.

It will really be a great relief to my mind to be out of it; and not only on idle grounds. I should never have liked it; but I don't think I could endure the toleration I should have to put up with.       H.

Lord Granville wrote from Longleat on the 22nd January :—

'I agree with all you say about the bore of being leader, but that is a different thing from what ought to be done. If the Nonconformists agree to support Forster, which has again become more doubtful, his appointment would probably go smoother at first than yours. But, once in your saddle, you would unite the party longer, and be much better able to play the reticent and expectant part which Gladstone rightly thought the proper one at this moment. And the aristocratic element, which at first might be a disadvantage, would in the end tell in your favour. We may be reduced to your expedient of a Cerberus at last, but it should be avoided if possible.'

The question was already almost settled in the way adverse to Lord Hartington's anxious hope. Lord Frederick Cavendish wrote to his brother on the 23rd that there 'is little doubt that you will be asked to be leader.' 'Although,' he added, 'the position is not a particularly attractive one at this moment, I do not think you can well refuse it if the party is unanimous in its application.'

The fatal news reached Lord Hartington, in his Huntingdonshire retreat, on the 31st January. 'My dear Harty Tarty,' wrote Lord Granville, resorting to, or improvising, a nickname, 'you are in first. I have had a long conversation with Forster, the upshot of which is that he will absolutely refuse to be proposed.'

The final sentence of doom was communicated by the following letter, in a beautifully neat and precise hand, dated from the Reform Club, 3rd February 1875 :—

MY DEAR LORD HARTINGTON,—I am very glad, not on your account so much as on our own, that, at a meeting of members of the House of Commons of the Liberal party held here this day, a resolution has been passed offering you the honourable position of leader of the party in the House of Commons. From the tone of the meeting, and from the number of members present at it, I hope and believe you will find yourself supported by a strong and loyal party, with whom you will be able to render services to the country which will compensate you for the sacrifice you are now called on to make.—I am, very faithfully yours, JOHN BRIGHT.

The victim of the sacrifice received with a heavy heart, no doubt, a number of congratulations which still repose among the papers at Devonshire House. 'How I shall get on Heaven only knows,' he wrote to his father. A man who had a positive dislike for assemblies, and speech-making, and paper-work, and for much sitting in the oppressive atmosphere of the House of Commons, was forced by destiny, entirely against his will, into a position in which he would be compelled to talk and write to all kinds of people, to get up a number of subjects, and to make speeches on them in the House of Commons, to be perpetually in or near that Chamber watching proceedings, and, a still worse infliction, to attend public dinners and huge provincial assemblies. He was modest to an excess as to his own intellectual capacities and oratorical powers, yet he was obliged to succeed in the leadership to the most immediately effective orator of the age, who had moreover that natural gift so essential to political success, of making his own personality stand out in bold relief, and impressing it upon the soft popular imagination. This predecessor had retired from the leadership, but not from Parliament, nor even from the front Opposition bench. So often as he chose to reappear there it was certain that, even without intention on his part, his would be the central figure on the Liberal side. Lord Hartington was not flexible by nature, nor could he pretend to share, or make himself believe that he shared, in opinions which were not his own. Yet, as he knew, a large and turbulent section of the Liberal party held convictions to which he was opposed.

Among the letters is the following from Mr. Gladstone, who urges very finely the great argument of *noblesse oblige*. This argument, in effect, throughout Lord Hartington's career made him overcome many a repugnance and resist many an adverse inclination. No one felt more than he did the true feudal doctrine that great property and social position are only rightly held on tenure by public service.

Mr. Gladstone wrote :—

HAWARDEN CASTLE, CHESTER,
*February 2, 1875.*

MY DEAR HARTINGTON,—You will perhaps consider that I am out of court, and not in a condition to lay upon others the burden I have myself eschewed. Nor do I place my own title high : although one of my grounds of action has certainly been that difficulties, and grave ones, existed for me which did not exist for others.

You may possibly recollect the opinion I gave you (close to the spot where I am now writing), at the time when you handsomely agreed to take the Irish Office. It was plain that this must come. During the fretful agitation of the last eighteen or twenty days my opinion has not for a moment varied as to what ought to be, and what I think, by hook or by crook, will be.

I both admit, and plead, that the leadership of the Liberals in both Houses ought to be and cannot help being, light and negative rather than positive, in a degree unknown at least in the House of Commons for the last forty-five years. We approached nearly to this in 1867 after the important defeat. In 1868 it altered its character, solely because the great Irish question came up in force.

Let me explain. What is good, and what is less good, is that you have continued to give the public an inadequate idea of your force. You have not been a good attendant in Parliament, relatively to your *political* rank. Your real and undeniable modesty has worked in the same direction as the comparatively small number of your appearances. Those who are now choosing you, and can choose no one but you, partly on negative grounds, will be perhaps surprised, certainly pleased, when they come to know by experience the quantity of available material, pith, and manhood that is in you. I am using a great freedom in writing thus. But I do not think you are one to require, or much to care for, apologies, in critical circumstances.

I think that, as an equitable man, viewing all circumstances of the past and future, you will be disposed to admit that the public, that your country, has some unpaid claims upon you. I do not think you will be able strongly to urge that there is any other person in particular who ought to take that which is now thrust upon you. The diffidence, which is your best defence, will nevertheless not suffice to make a good and complete defence. While the demand upon you will be lighter, much lighter, than usual, the reasons for not declining to meet it are certainly stronger than usual.

One circumstance in this case will, I think, bring you some compensatory pleasure. Your family has, for a series of years, been much at the head of all families belonging to the Liberal aristocracy of England, for its exertions and distinctions in the cause; and your assumption of the post will give, as well as take, honour where it is due.—Believe me, with all good wishes, sincerely yours,

W. E. GLADSTONE.

Lord Hartington replied :—

DEVONSHIRE HOUSE,
*Feb.* 3, 1875.

MY DEAR MR. GLADSTONE, — I have only a few moments before post time, but I am unwilling to lose a day in thanking you for your most kind and friendly letter received this morning. You know enough of me to be sure that I was not ambitious of the honour which has fallen upon me, I can scarcely tell how; but at the same time I have felt, ever since the matter has been discussed, that if the post were offered to me with the concurrence of any of my late colleagues and the large majority of the party, in fact in such a manner as to offer at least a possibility of success, it would be incumbent on me to accept it. I feel very little doubt that at first, at all events, I shall find the greatest difficulty in discharging even the formal part of my new duties; but I shall certainly make every effort in my power to justify your opinion, and bring as little discredit as possible on the party.  You must excuse this most hasty note, and believe me, yours sincerely,

HARTINGTON.

It is the more satisfactory to be able to quote these letters, because events in coming years strained the political relations between the two men.  Yet, even when the strain was severest, their correspondence never lost the tone which it had at first, that of kindliness on the part of the older man and respect on the part of the younger.

Lord Hartington was in his forty-third year when he took over the command of the Liberal party in the House of Commons.  He had sat in that House for nearly eighteen years, and had spent about eight of these in office, more than five of them in the Cabinet.  No one, perhaps, then in the House, of a corresponding age and position, had made so small a number of speeches.

'I need hardly say,' he wrote to his Lancashire supporter, Mr. John Fell, 'that I have no confidence in my ability to discharge even tolerably such arduous duties as those which I have undertaken; but I am in hopes that for a session or two there may not be much need for energetic leadership; and it is possible, as you suggest, that some sections of the Liberal party may work more cordially under the present arrangement than they would otherwise have done.'

# CHAPTER VIII

## LORD HARTINGTON'S LEADERSHIP

AFTER the retreat of Mr. Gladstone the political audience had, no doubt, the feeling expressed in the lines—

> 'As in a theatre the eyes of men,
> After a well-graced actor leaves the stage,
> Are idly bent on him that enters next—'

Two days after the meeting at the Reform Club Lord Hartington made his first speech as Leader of Opposition in the debate upon the Address. He spoke rather nervously, and began by a characteristically expressed apology for the position in which he so unwillingly found himself. He was well aware, he said, that, standing in the place which he had seen occupied by Lord Palmerston, Mr. Disraeli, and Mr. Gladstone, he could not hope or pretend to take the part which was taken by those distinguished men in the discussions of the House, or to exercise the influence which they had exercised over its deliberations. It might, however, be convenient that there should be—

'some individual who should be to some extent responsible for the conduct of public business on this side, and, if his humble services could in any way tend to the convenience of the House or to the despatch of business, they should, however inefficient, be cheerfully rendered.

'I have now the satisfaction of passing from this subject, and I hope that it may never again be necessary

for me to advert to a subject which must be so unimportant and uninteresting to the House as anything
personal to myself must be.'

The Government's legislative proposals were, he said,

'on the whole, of a wise, a salutary, and a beneficent
character. They are proposals eminently adapted to be
considered by the Legislature of a prosperous and contented country in a time of peace and quietness.'

This was civil, and Disraeli, in replying, said :—

'It has long been the boast of the House of Commons
that, even when political passions run high and party
warmth becomes somewhat intense, there should exist
between those members of both parties who take any
considerable share in the conduct of business, sentiments
of courtesy, and, when the public interest requires it, even
of confidence, which tend very greatly to facilitate the
business of the country to the public advantage. I trust
that feeling will in our time never cease, and I can truly
say, without making or intending to make any observations
of a personal or invidious nature, that it is matter of satisfaction to us that the chief business of our opponents is
to be conducted by one who, in the course of many years
in this House, has obtained equally our respect and our
regard.'

On the 1st March Lord Hartington spoke on the Peace
Preservation (Ireland) Bill. This measure consolidated the
provisions, with some omissions and relaxations, of
various expiring Acts directed towards the same object of
adjusting English criminal law to Irish conditions. The
new Chief Secretary, Sir Michael Hicks Beach, always a
friendly opponent of his predecessor, took occasion to
praise the 'fairness and firmness' of the Irish administration of Lord Spencer and Lord Hartington, 'often under
very critical and difficult circumstances.' Lord Hartington

supported the proposals of the Government, and, it was said at the time, was 'more ministerialist than the ministerialists.' He referred to the substitution by secret societies, or bodies of people acting in the same spirit, of a law of their own for the law of the land. Comparisons, he added, 'are often made between the amounts of crime in England and in Ireland,' but the difference was this :—

'In England, crime is an attack by an individual on other individuals, in Ireland, it is an attack by society, or a large part of society, upon individuals. It is the same in whatever shape it may show itself, whether the victim be the landlord who is using the rights over his property which the law gives him ; whether it be the tenant who, having been lawfully inducted into his farm, is endeavouring honestly to make his living there ; whether it be the employer of labour who chooses to exercise some discretion in the choice of the persons whom he employs ; or whether it be the labourer himself who wishes to take his labour to the best market. You find that the spirit of agrarianism interferes in every one of these cases, and seeks to impose a law of its own, a traditional law, perhaps, but one which has never been sanctioned by the State, and is in actual opposition to the law of the State.'

Lord Hartington then referred to the measures passed by Mr. Gladstone, and said that he was able to support the Government 'with a clearer conscience and a better courage' than he could have done, had he not known that the British Parliament had 'done all that lay in its power to do substantial justice to Ireland.'

He spoke again on the 7th July upon a subject of importance. This was the Bill, introduced by Mr. George Trevelyan, for extending the household franchise to the counties. Lord Hartington abstained from voting. He could not, he said, vote against the second reading of the

Bill because he was not prepared to meet by a direct negative the principle embodied in it. 'I do not,' he said, 'rest my assent to the Bill upon the doctrine of the Rights of Man. I rest it solely upon this—that I see no convenience or wisdom in excluding permanently from the franchise any class, unless it can be shown that they are less fully qualified to exercise it wisely than the class we have enfranchised in the boroughs.' He thought, however, that the extension must be accompanied by a simultaneous redistribution of seats. No scheme for this was before the House, and it was evidently a measure which must proceed from the Government. Redistribution was always a difficult matter by reason of local prejudices and conservative spirit, and nothing could enable any Government to carry through a large and satisfactory measure, but an amount of energy and interest in the question in the country, which did not, it appeared to him, at present exist. He doubted, moreover, whether the enfranchisement of the agricultural labourer, in his present state of political education, might not lead to an excessive Conservative reaction. This last was an interesting observation, and may be considered in connection with the fear expressed, at a later date, by Mr. Goschen that the agricultural labourer would not be able to appreciate sound economic doctrines.

Mr. Gladstone did not speak on this occasion, but he gave his vote for the Bill. Before the debate he had written to Lord Hartington :—

'My own course is predetermined to the extent, at least, of my own vote. Yours is more difficult, but I do not see that, if you determine to vote for Trevelyan's Bill, you can on that account be expected to place it on the *menu* of your party, which, however, is not overcrowded."

On the whole politics ran very smoothly in London while the earth rolled round the sun in the year 1875, and Lord Hartington secured a firm seat in his saddle before he had to cross difficult country.  He captained his side well, leaving special questions to men of special knowledge, and interfering in debate only where general party policy had to be indicated.  His leadership was good because he was unmoved by passion, even-tempered, and indifferent, even averse, to the acquisition of personal glory.  He would not have said, like Charles Gordon, 'I would rather be dead than praised,' but to be praised would certainly have bored him.  In every sound organisation there should be calm at the centre and activity in the circumference; an agitated spirit at the heart of the machine destroys the balance. It is an advantage of the hereditary aristocracy, taking the word in a wide sense, that it supplies to the service of the State the less perturbable temper.  Those whose social does not depend upon their political distinction, to whose career office is incidental but not essential, who 'nor hope to rise, nor fear to fall,' can take an unimpassioned view of practical questions more easily than can those whose 'will to live,' in a political sense, is closely interwoven with the matter.  A sound defence of hereditary honours and of great territorial property rests on this foundation, especially in the case of a country which is but the central province of a vast empire largely controlled, defended, and guided in foreign relations, in the last resort, from offices in Downing Street and Whitehall.[1]  The larger the sphere of action the greater is the need of calm prudence on the part of those who control affairs, because the more widespread are the disasters which may arise from errors of judgment and factious passions.

[1] The word 'controlled' does not, of course, apply to the 'self-governing' dominions as it does to India, the Crown Colonies, and Protectorates.  But it is true of the vast majority of the population of the British Empire.

One may add in favour of, at least, a mixture of aristocracy in political leadership the argument given four
centuries ago by Baldassar Castiglione, in his book *Il
Cortigiano*, that—

'nobleness of birth is, as it were, a bright lamp, which
discovers and exposes actions both good and bad; and
influences and encourages to virtue, as well with the fear
of reproach, as with the hope of glory. And whereas this
splendour of nobility does not discover and illustrate the
actions of such as are meanly descended; hence are they
destitute of that encouragement, as also of that fear of
reproach, and think themselves obliged to rise no higher
than the fountain, nor to surpass the pattern set them by
their ancestors, whereas the nobly-born think it a scandal
not to advance at least as far as the bounds marked out by
their predecessors.'

The view of this far-away courtier, statesman, and
diplomatist may sound old-fashioned, but there is always
something true in the thought of a man of the world who
has seen intimately the way in which practical governmental
affairs are conducted, whether he lives in the sixteenth
century or the twentieth. The present danger, however, is
that, careers being more open, men of high extraction
should have too little proper ambition, and men of humbler
extraction should have more than their brains can carry.
After all, as Lord John Russell once said of the true British
aristocracy, 'they are strong in ancient associations and in
the memory of immortal services,' and, while they endure,
they should not forget that it is their duty to emulate the
deeds of their ancestors, even if present conditions make
travel or amusements more agreeable than politics, or
than naval, military, diplomatic, and other imperial em-
ployments.

## II

At the end of 1875 began the development of foreign
and imperial policy which marked the closing years of
Disraeli's career.  The stages were the purchase of the
Suez Canal shares, the assumption by the Queen of the
Imperial title in India, the treatment of the near-Eastern
question, the first annexation of the Transvaal, the second
Afghan War, and that intervention in Egypt, jointly with
France, by the deposition of the Khedive Ismail, which
was one of the chief steps leading to the virtual inclusion
of North-eastern Africa within the British Empire.

Disraeli had a firm conception of his own rôle in
England, and of the rôle of England in the world.  He
took a wide-reaching view of affairs.  He had spent most
of his days in the comparative leisure of Opposition ; had
not blunted his genius by official details ; and had had time
to brood over ideas.  He regarded life, no doubt, not from
the standpoint of an earnest ethical reformer, but from the
Shakespearean point of view as a deeply interesting drama.
England, he believed, should play a leading part, corresponding to her greatness, in the Councils of Europe.  He
believed in conscious will, and in strength, and he thought
that it should be shown and used.  He believed in the
power of ideas, made manifest, over imagination, and of
imagination over feelings and actions.  He would have
said, with Napoleon, 'the world is governed by Imagination.'  He believed that the policy of statesmen guiding,
or following, the destinies of an empire should be bold,
decided, consistent, not too scrupulous, not influenced by
transient events, nor by sentimental-humanitarian considerations.  In his farewell address to his constituents, on
leaving the House of Commons in 1876, he said finely :—

'Throughout my public life I have aimed at two chief results. Not insensible to the principle of progress, I have endeavoured to reconcile change with that respect for tradition which is one of the elements of our social strength, and, in external affairs, I have endeavoured to develop and strengthen our Empire, believing that combination of achievement and responsibility elevates the character and condition of a people.'

In November 1875 was announced the purchase of a dominant interest in the Suez Canal shares by the British Government from the insolvent Khedive of Egypt. The necessary four millions of money were provided, pending ratification by Parliament, by the House of Rothschild. Lord Hartington wrote on the 28th November to Lord Granville that Mr. Gladstone had been at Chatsworth, and—

'was much excited by the Egyptian news. He thought Parliament ought to be summoned immediately, and was inclined to disapprove of the transaction both financially and politically. He thinks that it is almost certain to lead to difficulties with the other Powers, and that we should have resented justly any other Government acquiring an overwhelming share in the Canal. It seems, however, to be well received in the country, and I should think may turn out to be a most successful coup.'

To Mr. Gladstone he wrote on 11th December :—

'I should be very much obliged to you if you have time to send me a line to say whether you have at all altered your opinion respecting the Suez Canal purchase. I have to speak next week at Sheffield and cannot avoid saying something on the subject. I propose, as well as I can, to follow Granville's advice, and not to commit myself at all events to approval, until we have further information. The only thing of importance which appears to me to have occurred since the first announcement, has been the publication of the despatches in the French

Yellow Book. Lord Derby seems to have given to the French Minister the best explanation which the transaction is capable of. Last summer he seemed to regret that a work of so much international importance, and in which we are so much interested, should be in the hands of a private company, and especially of a company the shareholders of which were mainly French. Recently the Khedive was trying to dispose of his shares, and it was possible that they would be acquired by Frenchmen. It was, according to Lord Derby, principally to prevent this that the Government stepped in. It would be difficult, I think, to persuade the country that our interests would not be endangered if the company were to become exclusively French, and, if there was no other means of averting this, I think that the purchase would be approved by many who would not concur in much that has been written in the papers about the bold and wise policy of the measure. The Speaker has been here and is inclined to think that it was right. He thinks, however, that they should have summoned Parliament at once; and also that they will have some difficulty in defending the measure on so limited a ground as that which I have mentioned. He thinks that they ought to have (perhaps they have) communicated at once with other Powers, and proposed to make use of the interest which they have acquired in the Canal, for the purpose of making some arrangement for securing its free navigation by the whole world.

'There seems now to be very little doubt that the measure is generally approved; and unless we can attack it upon very strong grounds, we should, I think, weaken ourselves seriously by the attempt.

'However, in the total absence of explanation by the Government of the history and motives for the transaction, there can be no reason for committing ourselves prematurely to an opinion upon it.'

Mr. Gladstone was, from the first, strongly opposed to the purchase of the shares. He saw, however, that the national approval of the step was too strong to be resisted.  He did not, in his own words, as yet 'see signs that the people were escaping from their gross delusion' on this subject.[1]  Mr. Goschen thought that the step was bad business commercially, an opinion which shows how an excellent man of business may err, but that politically it was a good one, since the shares might have been bought by some foreign rival.[2]  Several other leading Liberals shared in the general national feeling, and approved the Disraelian action.

When Parliament met, the Prime Minister defended the purchase as a stroke of high policy 'consistent with the ancient policy of England.'  The Canal was, he said, an essential link in 'the great chain of fortresses which we possess, almost from the metropolis to India.'  His speech contained a characteristic passage on the way in which the world is governed.  He was replying to the objection that, even if all the control of the Suez Canal were in other hands, yet, in the last resort, British use of the Canal could be maintained by superior naval force.  He said :—

'If the government of the world was a mere alternation between abstract right and overwhelming force, I agree there is a good deal in that observation ; but that is not the way in which the world is governed.  The world is governed by conciliation, compromise, influence, varied interests, the recognition of the rights of others, coupled with the assertion of one's own ; and in addition a general conviction, resulting from explanation and good understanding, that it is for the interest of all parties that matters should be conducted in a satisfactory and peaceful manner.

---

[1] Letter to Lord Hartington, 14th February 1870.
[2] *Life of Lord Granville*, vol. ii. p. 158.

Mr. Gladstone attacked the purchase, but with caution, barely veiling under criticism of methods strong hostility to the transaction itself. Disraeli justly said that the debate had shown that had his old rival been Prime Minister, the shares would not have been purchased. Lord Hartington held to his first opinion. He said that he had always thought that—

'looking at the matter. from a practical point of view, there was a great deal to be said in favour of the course which the Government had taken. . . . It was an unmistakable declaration, stronger than could be made in any despatch, that, whatever might be decided by the Great Powers of Europe as to the future destiny of the Turkish dominions, Her Majesty's Government were aware of the great interest this country has in Egypt and in the security of our communications with our Indian possessions, and that they were not disposed to abandon those interests, but rather disposed to strengthen and consolidate them. I thought then, and still think, that a declaration such as that, made in deed, and not in word, was not inopportune.' [1]

His criticism was that the Government had not, in speeches and despatches, laid sufficient stress upon this political aspect of the question. This view was entirely different from that of Mr. Gladstone, who had attacked the purchase on the ground that it gave, or might appear to give, to England a 'selfish interest' in the Canal distinct from that of other Powers, and this divergence anticipated a division of opinion as to Egypt which, some years later, increased the causes of division between Mr. Gladstone and Lord Hartington. The debate showed that Lord Hartington was by no means under the influence of his former chief, and present 'follower,'

---

[1] Debate on 21st February 1876.

and that he disagreed with him as to fundamental principles of imperial policy.

From the financial point of view the purchase of the shares has been highly successful. The shares bought for £4,000,000 were valued in 1909 at over £30,000,000. From the political point of view the purchase was one of the great steps which brought vast regions in North-eastern Africa within the sphere of the British Empire. In assailing this policy Mr. Gladstone wrote most prophetically in the *Nineteenth Century*:[1]—

'Our first site acquired in Egypt, be it by larceny or be it by emption, will be the almost certain egg of a North African Empire that will grow and grow until another Victoria and another Albert (the lakes) come within our boundary, and till we finally join hands across the Equator with Natal and Cape Town, to say nothing of the Transvaal and Orange River on the South, or of Abyssinia or Zanzibar to be swallowed by way of *viaticum* on our journey.'

The dream or vision of men like Disraeli or Cecil Rhodes was the nightmare of men like Gladstone. *Ducunt volentem fata, nolentem trahunt.* He was himself, a few years later, the reluctant instrument of accomplishing the next great step in this voyage of empire, the occupation of Egypt.

### III

The Act enabling the Queen to assume the title of Empress of India was the next development of Disraelian policy. Mr. Gladstone at once plunged into opposition

---

[1] The article, appearing in August 1877, was called 'Aggression on Egypt,' and referred to some suggestions made at the time in favour of establishing British control over Egypt.

to this proposal. 'Even in this House of Commons,' he wrote to Lord Hartington, 'the most reactionary, the most apathetic, and the least independent in which I have ever sat, there is, I think, much to be done on the unfortunate subject of the Titles Bill.' One of his suggestions[1] was the possibility of 'postponing the whole subject with a view to collecting the opinions and feelings which may prevail in the several remote portions of the Empire.'

Lord Hartington felt some doubt as to the wisdom, or the taste, of the step, but did not wish to offer formal opposition. He did, however, move, on the 16th March, an amendment directed against the assumption of the 'style and title' of Emperor. The letters show that he would not have done so much, had not a certain re-publican-liberal member threatened to move an amendment of his own, if none were moved from the front bench. The Queen was informed of this reason for the official amendment. There was evidence, Lord Hartington said in the debate, of an increasing distaste for the title on the part of a large portion of the public. He thought, himself, that it was open to objection on the ground of taste.

' It is perfectly true that an addition may be made to a noble structure which shall in no way change its character, but even make it more harmonious. But if you put to an old English castle a Grecian portico or an Italian façade, I venture to think that there will be a change.'

It was obvious to his hearers that the Liberal leader spoke officially and without conviction ; the Tory Chancellor of the Exchequer said that he could 'understand the reluctance with which the noble lord has been obliged to state the reasons which have induced him to take a course which, we may infer from many of his observations, was against his own judgment.'

[1] 11th March 1876, to Lord Granville.

One of the reasons stated by Lord Hartington was that in years to come this imperial title might 'overshadow and ultimately absorb the ancient and royal title of the Crown.' So far no tendency of this kind has become visible. If reason were to prevail over sentiment, and words were made to correspond with facts, the title would be 'British Emperor and King of the United Kingdom.' In India, at any rate, a title was rightly assumed, or rather legalised—for it was already in common use—which expressed correctly the relation of the Crown to native princes, the sovereigns of States as large in some cases as the smaller European kingdoms. Mr. Gladstone opposed the measure at all its stages. A Tory speaker dared to say that the Government of India was in fact, and in the last resort must be, so long as the English remained there, of the nature of dominion from above. Mr. Gladstone replied to this :—

'If it be true, and it is true, that we govern India without the restraints of a law except such law as we make ourselves—if it be true that we have not been able to give to India the blessings and benefits of free institutions, I leave it to the right honourable gentleman to boast that he is about to place that fact solemnly upon record. By the assumption of the title of Empress I, for one, will not attempt to turn into glory that which, so far as it is true, I feel to be our weakness and our calamity.'

This was in the spirit of Cobden who, in a speech twelve years earlier, had said that to hold India was 'a perilous adventure, quite unconnected with Free Trade, wholly out of joint with the recent tendency of things, which is in favour of nationality and not of dominion.' Mr. Gladstone once wrote that English rule was only tolerable as resting on the willing consent of the Indian populations, and said that 'we are bound to study the maintenance of our power in India *under the present and all proximate circumstances* as a capital demand on the national honour.'[1] The system of India was repugnant to his fundamental ideas.

In a later speech, Mr. Gladstone said, with some caution, that he did not prophesy that evils were sure to arise from the adoption of this measure, but that we were 'making room for them, and if they do not arise it will not be owing to our prudence and judgment, but to the beneficent influence of a Higher Power that, we trust, watches over the destiny of this country.' He was finely answered by Disraeli in that speech in which he made the often-quoted remark that 'Asia is large enough for the destinies of both Russia and England,' and added, 'but, whatever may be my confidence in the destiny of England, I know that empires are only maintained by vigilance, by firmness, by courage, by understanding the temper of the times in which we live, and by watching those significant indications that may easily be observed.' The people of India, even in villages, were not unaware, he said, 'of the advance across the plains of Asia of the power of a prince who bore the title of Kaiser.'

'The nations and populations that *can* pronounce the word Emperor, and habitually use it, will not be slow to accept the title of Empress. That is the word which will be used by the nations and populations of India, and, in announcing, as Her Majesty will do by her Proclamation, that she adopts that title, confidence will be given to her Empire in that part of the world, and it will be spoken in language which cannot be mistaken that the Parliament of England have resolved to uphold the Empire of India.'

The great word was spoken in the living language of high pageantry at the Durbar held by the Viceroy outside

---

[1] Article in *Nineteenth Century*, August 1877.

the old capital of the Moguls in the first week of the year 1877.

These strokes of imperial policy filled Gladstone with dark foreboding.   He wrote to Hartington :—

'Dizzy has never wanted courage, but his daring is elastic, and capable of any amount of extension with the servility of the times.   He has fallen upon a period singularly favourable to its exercise.'

Now began the supreme struggle for the soul of England between the descendant of cool and wary Italian Jews and the descendant of hot-blooded and combative Scottish yeomen and burghers.   Hartington was a high-born Englishman, and was in political sympathy with neither ; even less, perhaps, in his heart, with Gladstone than with Disraeli.   In private life he would certainly have preferred to spend an evening in the company of Disraeli, who, in addition to his more serious qualities, was a man of this world, very amusing, and able to talk about 'people,' and even horses, in an intelligent manner.   With Mr. Gladstone Lord Hartington never could 'get on' in conversation, so once he said.

# CHAPTER IX

## THE EASTERN QUESTION

In the summer or early autumn of 1875 began an insurrectionary movement among the Christians who formed part of the population of the Turkish provinces of Bosnia and Herzegovina. It was a manifestation of wide unrest among populations both Slav and Greek. Moved by their own reasons the three Imperial Powers, centred at St. Petersburg, Vienna, and Berlin, agreed upon the 'Andrassy Note' calling upon the Turk to reform his ways of government. This was sent on 30th December 1875 to London, Paris, and Rome with a request for co-operation. The Queen's Speech on February 1876 announced that her Majesty had considered it to be her duty not to stand aloof from these efforts, and had accordingly, 'while respecting the independence of the Porte,' joined in urging upon the Sultan 'the expediency of adopting such measures of administrative reform as may remove all reasonable cause of discontent.'

A certain division of opinion or sentiment between Lord Hartington and Mr. Gladstone made itself felt in the debate on the Address (8th February 1876). Hartington quoted Palmerston to prove that 'the right of the Powers to interfere diplomatically is preserved.' But he trusted that the papers to be laid on the table would 'show that the intervention has not exceeded the limits pointed out by Lord Palmerston.' He quoted also a speech made by Gladstone in 1856, in which he had said that it would be 'the work of many generations' to carry out Turkish reforms. 'Those words,' said Lord Hartington, 'are as true now as they were twenty years ago, and convey a salutary and somewhat needed warning against undue impatience with regard to events which have recently occurred.' Disraeli defended the Government rather elaborately for having recommended the Porte to give consideration to the Andrassy Note. He hoped that the Opposition leader would feel that there was no foundation for his fear that the Government had rashly embarked upon a limitless intervention. Mr. Gladstone said that he failed to see where in Lord Hartington's speech the Prime Minister had discovered any disposition to censure the support given to the Austrian Note. The object of the Crimean War, he said, had been to repress Russian ambition, but not to uphold the integrity of the Turkish Empire except, strictly, upon condition of the internal reform of that Empire.

This debate raised an issue upon which much subsequent discussion turned. By one of the two treaties of Paris, that of March 1856, England, Austria, and France had jointly and severally bound themselves to a guarantee of the 'independence and territorial integrity' of the Turkish Empire. Another article in the same treaty recited the intention of the Sultan to introduce reforms for the benefit of his Christian subjects. Conservative speakers maintained that there was no essential connection between these two articles, that we had guaranteed independence and integrity, not for the sake of the Turkish rulers, but for the sake of our own interests and those of European peace and the balance of power, and that, although under the treaty we had a right to remonstrate with the Turks as to Christian grievances, we could not allow these grievances to be

remedied by an armed interference of other Powers which
might very probably lead to permanent occupation.    It
was argued that, even had there been no guarantee, the
interests of the British Empire made it necessary that
Constantinople, and the northern country protecting the
access to that city, should not be allowed to fall into
the hands of any Power, least of all into those of Russia.
Gladstone, on the contrary, who loved to argue on the
subject of 'covenants,' held that the guarantee of integrity and independence stood or fell with the execution
of reforms by the Turks, and that British interests were
falsely understood, or wrongly made paramount, if they
involved the continued ill-government of Christians in the
Turkish dominions.    When it was said that his own Government, in 1871, had solemnly renewed all the stipulations of
the Treaty of 1856, his reply was that he was not then
aware that the promised reforms had never been carried
out by the Sultan.

During the spring and summer of 1876 the conflagra-
tion was spreading in the European dominions of the
Sultan.    An incipient rising in Bulgaria was suppressed
by Turkish irregular troops with ferocity of the old
Oriental kind.    This took place in May, and in June the
dreadful story was known to England through the correspondent of the *Daily News*.    The Consuls of France and
Germany were murdered by a Turkish mob at Salonica.
Servia and Montenegro were arming, and threatened war.
A powerful pan-Slavic movement was influencing the restless educated classes in Russia.[1]    The Austrian Government felt the invariable desire of a civilised Power to
substitute its own administration for a state of anarchy just
beyond its frontier.

---

[1] If Tolstoi is right it did not touch the Russian peasant.  See last chapter of
*Anna Karanina*.

The Andrassy Note of remonstrance to the Porte met with no success. In May, Bismarck, Andrassy, and Gortschakoff met at Berlin. The result was the Berlin Memorandum, which was sent on 11th May 1876 to London, Paris, and Rome. This Memorandum was much stronger than the Andrassy Note. The Turks were required to give guarantees of reform, and specific measures were suggested. There was a menace of the use of force if the steps required were not taken. France and Italy agreed to join in this document; the English Government refused. On May 19th, Lord Derby informed our Ambassador at Berlin that his Government declined to accept a plan in the preparation of which it had not been consulted, and in the success of which it did not believe. The Russian Government in June proposed to Lord Derby that the Turks should be compelled to grant administrative autonomy to the European provinces. In this also the English Government declined to concur, although in the following September they themselves made almost identically the same proposals to the Sultan.

Servia and Montenegro began war in July against the Turkish Empire, that war which, a little later, Lord Beaconsfield averred to have been made, in fact, by the 'secret societies of Europe,' who had also, he hinted, instigated the Bulgarian movement. Servia was assisted by a number of volunteer combatants from Russia. In the same month the English Mediterranean fleet was strengthened, and part of it was moved to Besika Bay.

In the autumn of 1876, further overtures for co-operation were made by the Russian Government. On September 26th they proposed to England that force should be used to arrest the Servian war, and to end Turkish misrule. Bulgaria, it was proposed, should be occupied by Russian troops, Bosnia by Austria, the united fleets should enter the Bosphorus. Or, if the English Government thought it sufficient, naval action only should be taken. Lord Derby replied that the Cabinet would not accept the idea of an armed demonstration. The British Government proposed, instead, a Conference at Constantinople, and laid down for its basis definite proposals for reforms. The Powers agreed. Lord Salisbury was appointed to be our representative, and left London towards the end of October. On November 2nd the Czar 'pledged his sacred word of honour,' at Livadia, to the British Ambassador, 'in the most earnest and solemn manner that he had no intention of acquiring Constantinople, and that, if any necessity obliged him to occupy Bulgaria, it would only be provisionally, and until the peace and safety of the Christian population were secured.'

Notwithstanding these assurances, Lord Beaconsfield used menacing language in his speech at the Guildhall on November 9th. He spoke, with unmistakable meaning, of the resources of England and her power to maintain 'a righteous war.' The message was telegraphed to Moscow, and, on the next day, the Czar, in that ancient and sacred city, declared publicly that, if the Conference should fail, he was firmly determined to act independently, and could rely upon Russia to respond to his summons. The Constantinople Conference met and failed. The Turk rejected proposals for giving a modified autonomy to the provinces, which were based upon the lines laid down by the British Government. The Russian Government then addressed a Note to the Powers inviting them to consider what steps should be taken. The result was a colourless Protocol signed by representatives of all the Powers at London on 31st March 1877. This was no more than an invitation to the Porte to carry out, itself, certain reforms which it had promised, with vague and distant threats of future action if nothing were done.   The British Government made the Protocol still feebler by attaching to it a declaration that, in the event of Russia and Turkey not reciprocally disarming and keeping the peace, the Protocol should, so far as England was concerned, be null and void.   Had the Turks been wise they would have accepted this document.   Instead, they met it with a protest, as being derogatory to the dignity and independence of the Turkish Empire.

The classes ruling in Turkey and Russia had now, in fact, reached that temper at which war becomes certain, and despatches and declarations are no more than manœuvres for superior moral position.   On April 12, 1877, the Czar ordered his long-mobilised armies to cross the Asiatic frontiers, and, in Europe, to move on the Danube. On the 1st May Lord Derby signed a despatch expressing the regret of the British Government that Russia had taken isolated action, and pointing out that the Powers had assumed, in the Protocol, that time would be given to the Turks to carry out reforms.

## II

One may turn from these great events to mark their reverberations in the world of English politics.   Benjamin Disraeli made his last speech in the House of Commons on the 7th August 1876.   In it he laid down the foundation of his policy.   He said, 'What our duty is at this critical moment is to maintain the Empire of England.'   When the Earl of Beaconsfield, on the 9th November, at the Guildhall, spoke of a 'righteous war,' he shot a bolt straight at the heart of the position held by his great rival, in whose eyes, a war to defend Turkish territory from Russian armies would, after the Bulgarian massacres, have been a crime of enormous turpitude. On the 6th September 1876 appeared his pamphlet, *The Bulgarian Horrors and the Question of the East*, the work of five days, during three of which he was in bed with lumbago.[1] He described the Turkish race as 'the one great anti-human specimen of humanity'; and declared that there was not 'a criminal in a European gaol nor a cannibal in the South Sea Islands' who would not be indignant when he heard of their recent conduct. Forty thousand copies were sold in three days. On this same 6th September Lord Beaconsfield wrote to thank Lord Hartington for a gift of grouse amicably sent from Bolton Abbey to Hughenden Manor. His letter breathes a calm not unpleasantly contrasting with the storm of polemical writings.

HUGHENDEN MANOR, 6th September 1876

MY DEAR LORD,—It is very kind of you to remember me; one likes to be remembered. I am sorry I shall not meet you so often in future, but we may meet perhaps more frequently in those secret societies where we sometimes encounter each other, when we ought to be, as Madame de Stael said, 'conspiring on the public place.'

Two days ago I had a letter from Dunrobin asking me to go there on the 25th to meet the Young Court. It is, of course, quite impossible for me to go to the Highlands, as I am chained here, and, indeed, ought to be at Whitehall, though that would be too dreary in August and September. Even Derby goes home every night to his *placens uxor.*

I really have only had one week's holiday, which I spent at the Bradfords' at Castle Bromwich, the most charming old house, smaller, but like Holland House, and with gardens two hundred years old; full of yew terraces and avenues of variegated holly, and formal glades. We drove over one day to see Drayton, by which I was struck; a stately place,

---

[1] See *Life of Gladstone*, vol. ii. p. 551.

abounding in art; quite worthy of the man who created it. The country is not beautiful, but that is nothing. One likes beautiful scenery when one is travelling, or on a visit. You never look at your own lands, as, in town, you never look out of your own window.

I shan't be able to go to Doncaster, or win back my money, which I lost last year by G—— putting me on a horse with a broken leg. He deserves to become one himself for such conduct.

I hope you are well, and that you will win in all your encounters; except, of course, at St. Stephen's, and I am, sincerely yours,                              BEACONSFIELD.[1]

Lord Beaconsfield took at this time a gloomy view of the situation. He wrote to his War Secretary, Gathorne Hardy, 'We have been stabbed in the back, and the arts of faction, abusing the noble enthusiasm of a great part of the people, have endangered, and more than that, our highest national interests and European peace.' He said the same thing 'on the public place,' at Aylesbury a little later in the speech in which he spoke of 'sublime sentiments,' and of 'designing politicians,' who made use of them for 'sinister ends.' This letter, and another recently published,[2] show that Beaconsfield at this time would have liked to effect, in case of a Russian-Turkish war, a British naval and military occupation of Constantinople, and to hold the place as 'a material guarantee' till the end of the war.

Later in autumn, when well-to-do Englishmen, tranquillised by rural pursuits, reassembled in town, there was a visible reaction in London and elsewhere in favour of

---

[1] In the following year Lord Beaconsfield, acknowledging further grouse, repeated his first phrase with an agreeable variation. He said, 'I like to be remembered by those whom I like, and you have the happy habit of reminding me of your existence in a very pleasant manner.'

[2] *Memoir of Lord Cranbrook*, vol. i. pp. 372 and 376.

the Government. Lord Granville wrote on October 27th from Walmer Castle to Lord Hartington that—

'Gladstone has been here for a few hours to-day. He was low and piano about politics. He seems to understand the state of public opinion. In the course of observations he said that you and I did not give the offence which he did to many, that it was impossible to find fault with anything we had done since the change of Government had taken place, and yet it was clear that there was no Liberal reaction. He had felt convinced that nothing could produce this but some great question, and that, at one time, he believed this Eastern Question would have done so.

'I am afraid he sees a good many adventurers, and he has written a defence of the Russians in Central Asia which I should have thought unnecessary.

'Hugessen rushed in this morning and addressed Gladstone and me, "I have been dreadfully annoyed at the mis-report of my speech at Deal. I told them that I had been advised by my friends not to defend Gladstone, he was so unpopular. But I answered 'I like popularity, but I prefer being honest, &c. &c.'"'

In Gladstone's mind, as Lord Selborne said, all motives 'seemed to move together, with equal or almost equal power.' This was why he produced impressions so different upon men who knew him well; Lord Clarendon, who had been his Cabinet colleague, for instance, regarded him in 1860 as an 'audacious innovator,' with 'an insatiable desire of popularity' and 'a fervent imagination which furnished facts, and arguments in support of them,' and thought him 'a far more sincere Republican than Bright, for his ungratified personal vanity makes him wish to subvert the institutions and the classes that stand in the way of his ambition.'[1] This view reflects impressions dominant

---

[1] *Greville's Memoirs*, 1852-60, vol. ii. p. 291.

among the older Whigs. Disraeli thought, or at any rate once said, that his rival was inspired by a 'bitter personal envy.' Gladstone's own letters and diaries, quoted by Lord Morley, give a different impression. As in the case of Cromwell, his outward acts produced upon many contemporaries all the effect of ambition and egotism, while his private correspondence reveals a simple and humbly God-fearing nature. There was manifold action in that many-celled brain. Gladstone was a strong party politician, and burned to defeat Disraeli, as Achilles to defeat Hector, but he was also a warrior of the crusading kind. He believed that he was leading the sound-hearted people to fight in the cause of freedom against allied powers of darkness, the spirit of Judaism incarnate in Disraeli, the spirit of ancient Rome acting through the Vatican, the spirit of Islam embodied in the Sultan, and the spirit of imperialism latent in the English aristocracy.[1] He believed himself to be God's instrument. This was the belief of Oliver Cromwell, and, in his own queer but sincere way, that of the last President of the Transvaal Republic. It gives immense force to him whom it possesses, but it exposes his mind to grave dangers. Trust in special guidance, a different thing from Christian fatalism, is apt to silence the voice of reason, and when reason is hypnotised, the guiding power, supposed to be divine inspiration, may possibly be, subtly disguised, the operation of the unconscious, underlying, natural self. It may, after all, be safer to accept, like Hartington, common reason as the guide vouchsafed to men in practical business, whether concerned with an annual budget or with the freedom of captive races. Perhaps the virtuous and excellent Conservative, W. H. Smith, was right, who, as some letters in the

---

[1] See the interesting extracts from diaries and letters given by Lord Morley in his *Life of Gladstone*, vol. ii. pp. 551, 557, 571, 577, 597, 612, 615, 617.

Memoir by Sir H. Maxwell show, prayed for general guidance in political conduct, but never assumed that he had received it. It is a delicate question. Some still follow the earliest Christian teaching, and draw a line of demarcation between religious life and secular affairs. Gladstone's attitude appealed most potently to a vast number of modern English Christians who, like the Jews of old, take an exactly opposite view.

The outrages in Bulgaria excited in this country an emotion infinitely stronger than did cruelties not less ferocious suffered in later days by Armenian Christians at the hands of Turks in Asia, and by Jews at the hands of Christians in Russia. Why was this so? In the Bulgarian case the miseries were due to the action, or inaction, of rulers whom the English Tory party were inclined to support in the supposed interests of the British Empire, and a little, perhaps, out of secret sympathy with any ruling caste. Thus the fire of commiseration was blown into intenser flame by the everlasting wind of party antagonism. The nonconformist minister was made more ardent in the cause by the comparative apathy of his neighbour, the established priest. But a group of Anglicans were among the foremost leaders of the movement. An ancient sympathy with the Eastern Churches, as communities with an 'historic episcopate,' but independent of, and opposed to Rome, had been vivified by the recent decrees of the Vatican Council, and Gladstone himself was fresh from a violent collision with that Rock.

On the other hand, the importance attached by the Tories to the safeguarding of Constantinople may not be very intelligible to the younger generation. But the road to India had not then been secured by the occupation of Egypt, nor had a far-Eastern war and internal troubles revealed the weaknesses of Russia, nor had the rising naval, military, and economic strength of the German Empire as yet revolutionised the older ideas as to the natural rivals and allies of England. Almost till the close of the nineteenth century the suspicion of the English was still directed towards the side of Russia and of France. It must also be remembered—and this is easily forgotten—that the men of middle age in 1876 were those who, in their youth, had been under the influence of the feelings connected with the Crimean War.

## III

Lord Hartington spent some weeks of September and October 1876 in a visit to Vienna, Pesth, and Constantinople. War between Servians and Turks was proceeding. The Turks defeated the Servians in several actions, and towards the end of October the road to Belgrade lay open. The Russian Government intervened, and the Turks consented to an armistice. Hartington gave some account of his journey in two letters to his father. At Vienna he saw—

'a good deal of Count Andrassy, who is a very pleasant sort of man, and talks very freely about everything. He seems to take things pretty easily, and thinks that they will settle themselves somehow in the East. I should say that he is not absolutely opposed to an Austrian occupation of Bosnia, though I do not think that he wishes it, but is no doubt much opposed to any extension of virtually independent Turkish provinces. I have no doubt they have a good deal of trouble with their Slavs, but he has got many good reasons to give against the multiplication of such independent States in that quarter. I don't suppose, however, that he would object to a certain amount of autonomy, so that it did not mean separate Governments with armies, &c., of their own.'

He found that all those whom he met at Vienna were opposed to Gladstone's policy, 'or rather they don't admit that it is a policy at all, and agree that, although something strong must be done in Turkey, it is impossible altogether to get rid of Turkish administration at present.'

Lord Hartington then went to Pesth, where he was received with great hospitality by some friends of Count Andrassy. 'The place appears to be making most extraordinary progress since the granting of the Constitution some years ago, and the building both there and at Vienna is something wonderful. It is a beautiful town, and the Danube there is magnificent.' Thence he went by boat and rail to Varna, and so by sea to Constantinople. An Englishman living in Servia and some Austrian officers on the river-boat assured him that the Servians were 'the most peaceful people on earth and hate the war. It seems to have been instigated by the Russians and some politicians. They say that hundreds of them mutilate themselves to escape service, and that they shoot the Russian officers when they get a chance.' At Constantinople Lord Hartington saw 'Lots of people, but I am not sure whether I am much the wiser.' He liked the British Ambassador, Sir Henry Elliott, but thought that he was probably 'too much tied up with the old Turkish and anti-Russian policy to be the best possible adviser or organ of the English Government at this time.' He saw also the Austrian and Italian Ambassadors, and some important Turks. The Grand Vizier 'is a fine, and, I believe, honest old Turk, but not much inclined to reform.' He saw the Foreign Minister, 'a shrewd old gentleman,' and Midhat Pasha, who 'talked as if he were a great radical,' but looked like 'a cunning old fellow' who might use language to Europeans very different from that which he used among Turks. He also had an interview with the Sultan, 'who looks intelligent enough, and very like an Armenian merchant, but he was very shy and only said a few sentences.' He met, also, Said Pasha, a high official, who had been educated partly in England. 'He is extremely intelligent, and said to be about the best Turk going, but I should say that even he is extremely prejudiced, and has no idea of the amount of change which is required in order to satisfy Europe.' There was no doubt, he thought, that the Sultan was in favour of reforms, and that Said would be the best man to carry them out, but would probably be thwarted by the other officials.

Spare time was spent in the bazaars, and in walking about Stamboul, 'certainly a wonderful and curious sight. We saw some of the Sultan's new palaces on the Bosphorus, which are magnificent, and on the whole very handsome, though I daresay not in the best taste. If the unhappy creditors could see how most of their money has gone, they would be still more angry than they are now about the Bulgarian atrocities.'

Lord Hartington wrote his impressions of the political situation at some length in this letter to his father. His remarks are adequately summed up in the following extract from a letter which he received from his brother Frederick, on his return, dated 20th October 1876:—

'We met the Gladstones at Castle Howard last week. He was full of the Turkish question, and convinced in his own mind that strong pressure was necessary to keep the Government straight. He regarded Disraeli as the real controller of our foreign policy, and considered that we had fair notice in the Aylesbury speech of what that policy would be under his guidance. . . .

'As he was anxious to hear what your impressions were, I thought it as well to break to him that you saw great difficulties in the way of complete autonomy. I said that you feared that, without the control of the

European Powers, complete autonomy would either lead in the end to a worse Turkish rule than ever, or to anarchy, but that you also thought that interference on their part would be necessary to make Lord Derby's proposals work; and that in fact, without more harmonious action on their part than could reasonably be expected, you did not seem sanguine of any satisfactory. results, as you placed little or no value on Turkish promises of reform.'

Mr. Gladstone wrote to Lord Frederick that he had heard with much pleasure this report of Hartington's opinions. But he was 'exceedingly sorry that he should have dined, if he did dine, with those Turkish Ministers who, whatever their personal guilt or otherwise may be, are at this moment the symbols and representatives of horrible iniquity.'

History, alas! records not whether Hartington dined with the Symbols.

## IV

Lord Hartington broke his long silence on the Eastern question by a speech at Keighley in Yorkshire, on the 3rd November, which satisfied moderate-minded Liberals. It was to the effect that he could neither unreservedly support, nor yet condemn, the policy of the Government. There had been, he thought, some errors in their conduct of the business, but he believed that the objects which they had in view were such as the nation would approve. The root of the mischief was the incapacity of the Turks for good administration. There seemed to be no hope of a cure of this defect. There was therefore, he thought, ground for some degree of external interference.

Mr. Gladstone was in advance of his time in his faith that down-trodden Bulgarian peasants could be formed into a fairly civilised State, and hold their own without either anarchy or foreign control.   Even he could not foresee that, in thirty years, Bulgaria would become, by its own strength, an entirely independent State, under a new southern Czar, well-armed, sufficiently strong to be both a danger to the possessors of the city on the Bosphorus, and a barrier against Hellenic ambition.   This is one of the most unexpected and remarkable events in modern history.

Lord Beaconsfield's tone at Aylesbury in September and at the Guildhall in November, had aroused furious suspicion of his intentions among those who hated the Turks more than they feared the Russians.   Arrangements were made for a 'National Conference' at St. James's Hall to protest against any support to the Turk.   Lord Hartington declined an invitation in a reasoned letter to the Duke of Westminster.   In less formal terms he wrote to Lord Granville :—

CHATSWORTH, CHESTERFIELD,
*November* 26, 1876.

MY DEAR GRANVILLE,—I am very sorry that you could not come, and still more that you have been laid up.

I heard first on Thursday from Freddy (my brother), about the proposed Conference.  Mundella had written to him pressing him strongly to give his name and to get my father's.   I wrote to him that I saw no use in it; that the names of the promoters did not appear to be generally of much weight;   that such a Conference would be almost sure to get principally into the hands of men of extreme opinions, who would make speeches under no sense of responsibility whatever ;  and that, if it was true, as alleged, that there is a strong feeling of indignation against Lord Beaconsfield's speech, it appeared to me that public meetings (though I did not wish to recommend them at present) were a more legitimate and effectual mode of expressing it.

I wrote on Friday to Adam (to Scotland) asking him what he had heard about it, and expressing the same opinions. I suppose that he will have got my letter by this time. I am sorry that he seems inclined to give it any countenance, and I am glad that you told him to keep us out of the question.

I feel tolerably sure that it will be a failure, whatever encouragement Adam may give it. I object to the terms of the circular. The provinces of Bosnia, Herzegovina, and Bulgaria are not *Christian*. None of them are more than partially so, and Bosnia is more than half Mussulman. And I do not see why, at this moment when a Conference is going to meet, ostensibly to see what *can* be done, any moderate man is to pledge himself to the 'release of the provinces from the direct rule of the Porte,' as the only remedy. I see no great harm, if it is a failure, so long as the moderate men in the party are not mixed up in it. They cannot talk more nonsense than has already been talked at the meetings; but why should we encourage any respectable member of the party to go and listen to, and be in some sense perhaps, committed by the speeches of men like Freeman, Canon Liddon, Jenkins, Maxse, Lyulph Stanley, &c., &c., and innumerable parsons?[1] The number of the latter on the list is quite enough for me. I am afraid that the tendency of anything of this kind is to drive our best men, or at all events the Whigs, to the side of the Government. Something of this kind was the result of Gladstone's speeches, and this Conference, if supposed to be with our assent, will, I am afraid, be worse.—Yours,

HARTINGTON.

*P.S.*—Have you heard anything lately from Mr. G., and in what frame of mind is he? I am in daily dread of seeing his name in the Conference list.

[1] Lord Hartington would have felt no sympathy with the Rev. Mr. Spurgeon, who at this epoch was offering public prayers for the cure of the 'extraordinary folly of Her Majesty's Government.'

This was the Conference of 9th December, at which Canon Liddon sagely said that it would please the Russians were England to occupy the Turkish provinces 'with 50,000 or 80,000 or 100,000 men,' and Professor Freeman uttered his famous sentence, 'Perish the interests of England, perish our dominion in India, sooner than that we should strike one blow, or speak one word, on behalf of the wrong against the right!' It was the saying of a man whom Napoleon would have called an *idéologue.* In the tangled affairs of this world moral right and wrong are not so easily discerned. No Englishmen desire that injustice should be done, but that our dominion in India should perish would be the greatest injustice of all. The real question was whether the integrity of the Turkish Empire as it then stood was important to the existence of that dominion. Time has answered that question in the negative, but this has been due to events which could not, in 1876, have been easily predicted.

The following letter shows the view which Lord Hartington took of these proceedings, and of the question of the day :—

HOLKAM, NORFOLK,
*December 18, 1876.*

MY DEAR GRANVILLE,—Many thanks for your letter, which was extremely interesting and acceptable. Only I should be glad to know a little more of your own opinions about the state of things. I am rather surprised you think the Conference was a success. My impression was that it was much what I expected, and, therefore, rather the reverse. Numbers were, of course, satisfactory, but there could not be much difficulty about that, and there is no doubt that, in the North especially, there exists a very strong anti-Turk feeling. With the exception of Gladstone, I do not see that they obtained the adherence, or at all events the active support, of any men of much weight.

The speeches were perhaps, with a few exceptions, more moderate than might have been expected. But nothing was said, even by Gladstone, to repudiate the extravagances of Freeman, Fawcett, and one or two others, and the whole thing seems to me to be more or less discredited by them. But putting the extravagances out of the question, I do not recollect anything that was said that was either new or useful. All the anti-Turk abuse was warmed up again, a good deal of unnecessary confidence in Russia expressed, and all the difficulties carefully ignored.

What is the practical result of it all ? If it was intended as a demonstration that the country would not stand Lord Beaconsfield's pro-Turk speeches and policy, I think that it has been a failure. I have not, of course, seen many people, but the few moderate Liberals I have met disapprove altogether of the Conference, and are rather more inclined than they were before to support the Government.

The Stafford House Committee seems to be a foolish business; but it is the natural result of the Conference. Gladstone *might* be supported in the country at a general election, though I doubt it; but I feel certain that the Whigs and moderate Liberals in the House are a good deal disgusted, and I am much afraid that, if he goes on much farther, nothing can prevent a break up of the party.

My brother (Freddy) is at Hawarden, and I am going to write to him to try and find out what Gladstone's ideas are. I shall let him know that I regret his proceedings, as mildly as I can.

I suppose it is of no use to try to consider what our course should be until we know something of the result of the Conference, and the policy of the Government. The accounts look as if the Turks were going to make it comparatively easy for the Government; for, if they refuse all concessions, there will be no temptation to back them up, and to involve us in any obligations towards them. But I don't feel the slightest confidence in Russia, and I think that it would be a mistake to base our policy in any degree on Russian assurances. If Russia should occupy the

Provinces, I doubt whether, under certain circumstances, the Government would be wrong in taking some steps for the protection of Constantinople and the Bosphorus; and this would certainly be a material though indirect assistance to Turkey, and would, I suppose, be objected to by Gladstone and the pro-Christians. Austria, I should think, if encouraged by us, would be inclined to take the same line, *i.e.* might apply a strong pressure on Russia to leave the Provinces after the reason for the occupation has ceased.

It seems to me that in some shape or other this question is sure to come up for us. If the Turks are reasonable and the Russians exacting, the case will be stronger for taking precautions; but are we in any case to look on at Russia establishing a footing in Turkey, and more or less threatening Constantinople, without any security but the Emperor's assurances?

The danger with the present Government seems to be that they may encourage the Turks, and lead them to expect that we shall do more than this. I should not have objected to a protest, however strong, that we will not fight to maintain the Turkish Empire; but the Conference people appear to be so anxious to get rid of the Turks, and so confident in the good intentions of Russia, that they don't care to look at what may follow the destruction of the Turkish Government.

I have only just come here, so these are not heretical opinions which I have imbibed here.—Yours very truly,

HARTINGTON.

Lord Hartington during these years, in his speeches in the country and in Parliament, fully discharged the duties of criticism of the Ministerial policy, so far as criticism could be based upon well-ascertained facts and published papers, and was not injurious to the national interest. His view throughout was that the Government had erred in refusing to accept the overtures of co-operation made by the Berlin Memorandum, and in the subsequent communications from the Russian Government, and he condemned the menacing tone of Lord Beaconsfield's speeches. Admitting the desirability from the point of view of our own interests of a strong barrier between Russia and the Straits, the Government would, he thought, have attained this object by an active co-operation in compelling the Turks to concede effective guarantees for provincial liberties. Action of this kind might have prevented both the Servian-Turco and the Russian-Turco war. He thought that there was a time, about September 1876, before Russia had mobilised her armies, when 'Europe might have intervened, and intervened with force, without bringing about a war.' By refusing to co-operate with Russia the Government had left Russia and Turkey face to face, had made almost certain a war dangerous to our interests, and had ceded to Russia the position of sole protector of the Christians.

Lord Hartington criticised a policy which was surely open to criticism, but he was throughout these transactions hostile to any attempts to tie the hands of men who were responsible, and who possessed the fullest information, by an agitation in the country, or by passing in Parliament resolutions binding future conduct. Nor could he agree that the treatment of the Christian subjects of the Porte was, for an English statesman, the dominant or, at any rate, the only, consideration. He must have agreed with the words used by Lord Beaconsfield in the House of Lords on the 8th February 1877 in attacking this view :—

'Surely some of the elements of the distribution of power in the world are involved. It is a question in which is involved the existence of Empires. . . . It is only by bringing our minds, free from all passion, to a calm and sagacious consideration of this subject, and viewing it as statesmen, that we can secure the interests of this country, which are too often forgotten in declamatory views of circumstances with which we have to deal practically. It is in this way only that we can secure an amelioration in the condition of the population of the Ottoman Empire.'

Lord Hartington, always suspicious of the poetical, disliked the exaggerated language of Tory speakers about British Empire, and British interests, and British prestige. He disliked still more the perpetual attack made by Gladstonian speakers upon the doctrine that British statesmen must be guided by British interests. He must have heard with disapproval the assault made by Mr. Gladstone upon the British Ambassador at Constantinople, on the 27th March 1877, for his immorality in considering 'what will be the bearing of this or that measure on British interests.' 'What is to be the consequence to civilisation and humanity?' 'What,' asked the orator, 'is to be the consequence to public order, if British interests are to be the rule for British agents all over the world, and are to be for them the measure of right or wrong?'[1]

For all these reasons the passionate agitation led in letters and speeches by Mr. Gladstone during the autumn of 1876, and actively supplied with fuel for its flames from Nonconformist pulpits and Radical platforms, was distasteful to Lord Hartington. He felt also that it made his position as official Liberal leader difficult. The following letter to him from Lord Spencer shows the position

[1] Lord Beaconsfield once commented on the platitude that 'the greatest of British interests is peace.' He said: 'We do not want to be informed that the cardinal virtues are British interests. We possess and endeavour to exercise them, but they have not the peculiar character which the British interests that we refer to possess' (17th January 1878).

at the time, and it is a just and kindly appreciation also of
Mr. Gladstone's character :—

*Lord Spencer to Lord Hartington,* 16th November 1876.

'I do not wonder at your feelings of difficulty as regards
Gladstone ; you express them with your usual calmness
and good temper, and I cannot but admit that you have
much reason to feel anxious as to what may happen when
Parliament meets.

'I have not, however, any fear about it, for I am convinced that Gladstone is thoroughly loyal and true to you,
and, that being the case, your own character and influence
will prevent your losing the control of the party which
every day is placing more and more confidence in you.

'It is useless to try and gauge Mr. Gladstone's conduct
by any ordinary tests.   He is governed by the most intense
impulsiveness and enthusiasm, and when once his indignation is roused, he cannot be guided by the prudence
which would no doubt better become the position of a
retired Premier.

'He carried his indignation, I quite agree, too far ; but
I should be disposed to say that his throwing himself into
the spontaneous movement of protest against Turkish incapacity had the effect of preventing Turkey placing reliance
on the support of England, and possibly did more to
prevent immediate war between Turkey and Russia than
anything else.

'No doubt he went on too far, and I think his letter
to Stansfeld and his last war with the *Pall Mall Gazette*
exceedingly injudicious.

'But Gladstone, altogether judicious, when once
launched in a movement without the check of colleagues,
would not be Gladstone as he exists.

'One must take him with all his faults, but I am drifting
away from what I wanted to say, and that is that, just as I
am convinced of his loyalty to you, so am I sure that he
never for a moment took up this question with a view to
taking office or of supplanting you.

‘I quite agree with you as to the responsibility attaching to such conduct; had the movement gone on, Gladstone would almost have been forced, if the country backed his view and turned out the Government, to have taken office, and, if you would not agree with him, he must have had the lead again.

‘All that would have been hard on you, and considering the impossibility of Mr. Gladstone acting as an ordinary follower from his abilities and influence, it is no doubt wrong on his part to commence a crusade of this sort without consultation with you.

‘Could not, at a proper moment, this be pointed out to him? and could he not see the force of the difficulties which he creates for you?

‘All this arises from the incongruity of Mr. Gladstone's position. It would have been easier for every one had he when he retired from leadership retired from Parliament too, but I suppose it is too much to expect of any one to give up the enormous power and influence which he so marvellously possesses; he must think on some occasion or another this power ought to be applied for the public service, and in his own mind (which is a queer mixture of modesty and self-will) he no doubt argues that he is supporting by his efforts the party of which you are leader.

‘The crisis, as far as he goes, seems over for the present, and the public and all of us will gradually learn that Gladstone does not intend to lead again, whatever excitement he chooses to throw himself into.

‘All this will in the end strengthen your position, as the party will look to you for the sound and steady good sense which is required to solve political difficulties, and extricate them from the popular turmoil in which Mr. Gladstone loves to mix, and which probably in its way is necessary to carry great measures and effect a change of policy.

‘The nation will soon see that Mr. Gladstone does not enter into these affairs with selfish motives or a wish to become leader again.

‘I make these remarks not that I believe you suspect

Gladstone of ulterior and selfish views, but because that line has been widely taken by the public.

'Ever since we left office Mr. Gladstone's position has made yours exceedingly difficult, but you have steadily and constantly gained ground, and your position of leader is much stronger than it was when you began or even than it was last year.

'I am very much inclined to think that Mr. Gladstone's late excitement and movement, and the firm and sensible line you have taken will more than ever rally to you our party, who no doubt on this question are much divided.

'What you say as to possibly having to get some explanation with Gladstone and Granville as to the future is, I think, quite right, and no doubt opportunities for this will occur.

'Before January, Mr. G. will probably be upon some new trail.'

Lord Hartington had to deal on the 23rd March 1877 with a motion by Henry Fawcett which contained a declaration of anti-Turkish policy. He said that if the motion were pushed to a division he should vote against it. Every one knew that the Government did not propose to enforce by coercion upon Turkey the demands which had been made. 'We know that they are not prepared to resort to coercion themselves, neither are they prepared to sanction the use of coercion on the part of others.' If his friends 'thought that policy was open to challenge— and I must say that it appears to me a very grave question whether the policy is, or is not, open to challenge,'—they should have raised the question earlier. Until the negotiations with the Powers [1] were completed he was unwilling 'to fetter myself as to a judgment which I may, or may not, be called upon to give, upon the whole of the transactions of Government, by any declaration of policy.'

---

[1] Those which resulted in the Protocol signed in London on 31st March.

He thought it to be the duty of a leader of Opposition to credit the Government of the day with good motives and common sense, and not to hamper its action by ill-informed speeches or votes in Parliament. In foreign affairs he thought that an Opposition should try to give as much, and not as little, support as it could to the men who were conducting the national business. It was in this spirit that he met the party crisis caused by Mr. Gladstone's famous ' Resolutions ' of May 1877.

Mr. Gladstone's action had rapidly developed.[1] At the beginning of March he had ready for the press a new pamphlet entitled *Lessons in Massacre*. He wrote to say that he was 'restrained' from publishing until he knew that Granville and Hartington ' actually declined a Parliamentary movement, which will make my duty clear.' Lord Granville sent on this ultimatum to Lord Hartington, who wrote to his former chief.

DEVONSHIRE HOUSE, PICCADILLY, W.
*3rd March* 1877.

MY DEAR MR. GLADSTONE,—You asked me yesterday whether I thought that Granville intended his note to you of last Tuesday to be final.

I certainly understood from him that he so considered it ; but, of course, any new circumstances might induce him to change his opinion.

So far as I am aware there are no such circumstances. From conversation with Adam and others, I am as strongly persuaded as ever that there exists on our side of the House no disposition to raise, at the present time, any definite issue relating to the Eastern Question, and further,

---

[1] Mr. Forster wrote on 29th January to Lord Hartington that he could not understand ' what Gladstone is at. His late speeches begin and go on as if they were to end with a statement that he would coerce Turkey, and actually end merely with a statement that he does not consider the Treaties bind us to support the Turks. It looks as if Freeman and Liddon had worked him up to high excitement, and that he wishes to do something, yet hesitates to go in for war.'

that, if it were considered necessary to raise such an issue, the Bulgarian case would not be considered the best ground on which to raise it. I understood from you at the Speaker's that you are quite clear as to what your own course in the matter should be ; and it would not occur to me to have the presumption to express an opinion on that subject. But, as I believe that Granville, in writing to you the other day, said that, in his opinion, objections which he had indicated to your publishing a pamphlet no longer existed, I should like to guard myself from any, even the slightest, responsibility for such an opinion. The probable effect of either a motion or a pamphlet from you on the Bulgarian case would be the revival of the feeling of horror and detestation of the Turkish Government, which existed last autumn. I do not see at this moment what evil this is intended to avert, or what good it is to effect. I see no danger of our going to war *for Turkey*. On the other hand, there seems to be no prospect of securing collective European action to enforce the Conference proposals.

A renewed agitation might tend to lead Russia to act alone. In such a case it would be the duty of our Government, with other European Governments, to watch, and prevent Russia turning the opportunity to her sole advantage ; and I should be sorry to see a state of public opinion, in which horror of the crimes of the Turkish Government would overpower every other consideration.— I remain, yours sincerely,             HARTINGTON.

The pamphlet was forthwith published. It had but a small sale for a work from that pen, and the author admitted that it 'produced no great impression.' The soil was, perhaps, a little exhausted. The war began on the 12th April, and, in England, party passion shot up to fever level. Mr. Gladstone's 'heroic intensity had for the time taken him beyond the region of pain and pleasure,' says his biographer, and, one might add, beyond that of human loyalty and wisdom. He believed that he was guided by a higher loyalty and a diviner wisdom, and his conduct certainly had the great merit of courage. On the 27th April, as he notes in his Journal, he took his decision, 'a severe one in face of my not having a single approver in the upper official circle.' He gave notice of five Resolutions to be moved in the House of Commons. The pith of these Resolutions was, to use Lord Morley's summary, 'first, an expression of complaint against the Porte; second, a declaration that, in the absence of guarantees on behalf of the subject populations, the Porte had lost all claim to support, moral or material; third, a desire that British influence should be employed on behalf of local liberty and self-government in the disturbed Provinces; fourth, this influence to be addressed to promoting the concert of the Powers in exacting from the Porte such changes as they might deem to be necessary for humanity and justice; fifth, an address to the Crown accordingly.' This bold action caused intense excitement in the political world. The Resolutions not only challenged the fundamental policy of the Cabinet, but also, it was clear, the principle upon which Lord Hartington and his friends were acting, the patriotic acceptance, that is to say, with any necessary criticism, of a national policy in a difficult foreign question, when that policy had once been adopted by the Government. There was joy in Tory circles. A Whig colleague wrote to Lord Hartington :—

'I saw Lady Bradford last night.[1] She could not conceal her exultation at Gladstone's motion. Small blame to her. I heard also from a pretty safe philo-Turk source that the Civil War in the Cabinet is in full swing, and

[1] Lady Bradford was Lord Beaconsfield's great friend.

Salisbury, Carnarvon, Derby and Northcote are against Dizzy and his followers. My informant saw as clearly as we do that Gladstone will give Dizzy a decisive advantage over his peaceful colleagues. The thing really in its mischievous egoism and folly is past endurance.'

The same colleague wrote on the 30th April to Lord Hartington :—

'There never was a leader of a party who has been placed in a more incessant series of awkward and disagreeable situations than it has been your lot to encounter. The patient temper and courage you have shown have won for you, and increased every day, the esteem and confidence of your friends.'

Obviously a split was impending. The Radicals, led by Mr. Chamberlain and Sir Charles Dilke, hailed the Resolutions with fervour ; the Whig leaders could not possibly support them without loss of honour. They decided to take the manliest course, that of themselves opposing them, by moving the 'previous question.' At the last moment Mr. Gladstone partly gave way before this strong action. He consented to drop the last three Resolutions, and restrict himself to the two first, which were of a negative character, and did not involve the positive policy of coercing the Turks. Then Lord Hartington wrote to Sir Stafford Northcote to say that the previous question would not be moved that afternoon from the Liberal side of the House. Sir H. Drummond Wolff accordingly moved the amendment that 'this House is unwilling to embarrass Her Majesty's Government in the maintenance of peace and the prote ion of British interests.'

Mr. Gladstone said that :—

'To the whole of these Resolutions (though he would

not move them) 'I, as an individual, steadfastly adhere. I ask no sanction from my noble friend near me, nor anything except that for which he votes. . . . I really know not on what grounds he is not willing to accompany me in the whole of these Resolutions. I would thankfully accept his aid, as I would the aid of the Government, for I think the union of the English people in this grave matter is an object of the highest importance.'

Lord Hartington, in his speech in this debate, claimed that the two surviving Resolutions did not go beyond the policy declared by the Government itself. They asserted that the policy laid down in the despatch of September 21st, and supported by Lord Salisbury at the Conference, 'is a reality and not a sham.' He added :—

'I do not do Lord Derby or Her Majesty's Government the injustice of supposing that their policy was taken up merely in deference to popular clamour, or even to that of humanitarian and sentimental agitation. I believe that if that policy was adopted by Her Majesty's Government, it was because they believed that it was a policy not only in accordance with right and justice, but was also a policy demanded by the true and real interests of England. But though most of us approved the tendency of that policy, some of us thought that it might have been worked out in a more active manner.'

This was a very different thing from saying, as Mr. Gladstone did, 'I know no chapter in our foreign policy so deplorable as that of the last eighteen months.' Even if it could be assured that the Tory leader desired a war at all costs—rather an absurd supposition—Lord Hartington, as a man of sense and honour, felt able to place a fair trust in a Cabinet which included men like Derby, Carnarvon, Salisbury, Stafford Northcote, and

Michael Hicks Beach. The real danger was that the attempt to dictate by popular agitation a policy to the Government might kindle feelings of resentment which would make the Cabinet and the Tory party incline too much to counsels of the opposite kind. Lord Hartington once said that the Government had made every mistake at the beginning of this question, and Mr. Gladstone at the end of it. The story of this episode may be closed with a letter which Lord Hartington wrote to. Lord Granville on the 25th May. Lord Granville replied, a few days later, that he had sent it on to Mr. Gladstone, but that it had elicited no response.

CHATSWORTH, CHESTERFIELD,<br>
May 25, 1877.

MY DEAR GRANVILLE,—I have seen a letter from Mr. Gladstone to Freddy, in which there are one or two things which cause me to apprehend very seriously the renewal of recent difficulties; and I think that we ought to have some explanation, and, if possible, an understanding.

Mr. G. says that he has never been able to comprehend the cause of the late split; and under those circumstances it seems to me very likely that it will occur again.

He also says that, if at Birmingham they attempt to make him a leader, he will be obliged to abound in the opposite sense.

Now the explanation of recent divisions appears to me very simple and to be just this: that upon the Eastern Question Mr. G. has taken the lead, and is looked upon by a large portion of the party as their leader. Whether if you, I, or others were out of the way, he could unite the party upon the subject, is not the question. While we remain responsible for the management of the party in Parliament, Mr. G. cannot expect that we should entirely subordinate our own opinions and judgment to his, and, unless we do, it seems inevitable that one section of the party will follow his lead, and the other ours.

The cause for wonder seems to me not that the split has recently occurred, but that it has not occurred before. When Fawcett gave notice of his Resolution, it was thought inopportune not only by us, but by almost all the men below the gangway. Steps were taken (not by my instigation) to prevent its being brought forward. But Mr. Gladstone appeared on the scene, announced his intention of speaking on the Resolution, and immediately the Notices which stood in the way were withdrawn, and the Resolution came on. Mr. Gladstone, it is true, although he had encouraged Fawcett to bring on his motion, declined to support him, and Fawcett, showing unusual moderation, offered to withdraw it. But the split was on the point of taking place then.

As to the recent Resolutions, I fail to see how the split could have been avoided. We adhered to our original judgment—not to challenge the House to a decision on a definite issue; Mr. G. sent us a minimum, which he was prepared to accept if moved by us. We adhered to our decision; Mr. G. then took the lead into his own hands, and submitted his own policy to the House. Unless we were prepared to follow instead of lead, how was it possible that we should accept.

As to the recent Resolutions, I need not go over their history, but I fail to see how the split could have been avoided, *unless* we were prepared to follow instead of to lead. Mr. G. may think that the compromise come to at last might have been adopted at the beginning; but I think that, unsatisfactory as it was, it could only have been accepted by us after the protest on behalf of our independence, which was made by our announced intention of voting for the previous question on the Resolutions taken as a whole.

I have no right or wish to complain that upon a question in which he takes so deep an interest, Mr. G.

should assume the position which he is entitled, if he chooses, to assume upon all questions, the position of leader of the Liberal party.   But I think that we have some right to ask Mr. G. to look at the facts as they exist, and not to be surprised at divisions in the party, which under the circumstances are inevitable.

He does not cease to be the leader of the party by merely saying that he will not be the leader. If, as he has done since the autumn, he takes the lead, he *is* the leader, and all that he can do is to disclaim (for I do not think that he can really divest himself of it) the responsibility which naturally attends upon leadership.

I think that you will best be able to put this before Mr. G., but in some way or other it seems to me essential that there should be some understanding before it becomes necessary to take any fresh action.—Yours,

HARTINGTON.

The visit to Birmingham, referred to in this letter, was to attend the Conference organised by the Birmingham Liberal Association. ‘I believe,’ wrote Lord Hartington to Mr. John Fell (18th May 1877), his supporter in North Lancashire, ‘that Mr. Gladstone's own intention is to take advantage of the opportunity to enforce his views on the Eastern Question upon the country, but it is quite clear that his enthusiasm upon this subject is being made use of by others for the purpose of advancing their own extreme views upon questions of home policy.’

### V

The war between Turk and Russian was fiercely waged, with varying success, in Asia and in Europe throughout the rest of the year 1877.  By the end of January 1878 the Russians, after immense losses, had prevailed in both areas of conflict, and their European Army was close to Constantinople.

Lord Beaconsfield, in his speech at the Guildhall, on 9th November 1877, had declared that if British interests 'were assailed or menaced, the existing "conditional neutrality" must cease.' He had added :—

'Cosmopolitan critics, men who are the friends of every country but their own, have denounced this policy as a selfish policy. My Lord Mayor, it is as selfish as patriotism. But it is the policy of Her Majesty's Government. It is the policy which they adopted from the first. It is the policy which they have maintained, and it continues to be their policy to believe that it is their duty to protect British interests abroad.'

On the other side, Mr. Gladstone, in a speech at Oxford a little later, said :—

'My purpose has been . . . to the best of my power, for the last eighteen months, day and night, week by week, month by month, to counterwork as well as I could what I believe to be the purpose of Lord Beaconsfield.'[1]

And John Bright, in a letter of 29th December to the *Times*, said :—

'I do not think we shall have war, for the country is for peace, and the Government has no ally. The Administration may not be a wise one, but it must bend to circumstances. It has, as a Government, no interest in a war, for a war would soon destroy it.'

---

[1] One day in November 1877 the writer, then a Cambridge undergraduate, went over to Oxford to attend (as a guest of the present Sir Cecil Spring Rice) a dinner of the Palmerston Club. Mr. Gladstone was there, and several other leaders of the Liberal party. Mr. Gladstone, after speaking mellifluously of Oxford, and comparing disadvantageously the Liberalism of Palmerston with the Toryism of Canning, said, 'Now I must speak here, as everywhere, of the subject that lies nearest to my heart,' and plunged, thundering, into the Eastern Question. At the end of the proceedings a man of about twenty-five, in proposing a vote of thanks to the Chairman, said with cool emphasis that there was another side to the Eastern Question which must not be forgotten, that of the interests of the British Empire. I was struck by this boldness, and inquired who this speaker was. I was told that he was 'Alfred Milner, of Balliol.'

The Russian Government therefore had notice that English Liberals would do all they could to hinder and impede the action of the British Government, and it was very necessary for the latter to show, by deeds as well as words, that the fixed policy of the nation was not disturbed by these discordant voices.

The Queen's Speech at the opening of Parliament, on 17th January 1878, reiterated the position of 'conditional neutrality' laid down in Lord Derby's despatch of the 6th May. So far, the conditions on which that neutrality was founded had not been infringed, but, should hostilities be prolonged, some measures of precaution might become necessary. On the 23rd of January the Cabinet decided to send the Fleet from Besika Bay to the mouth of the Dardanelles, and Lord Carnarvon resigned office by way of protest. On the 25th January the Russian Ambassador communicated to Lord Derby the terms of the treaty which the Russians had exacted from the Turks at San Stefano, by which, among other things, autonomy was given to Bulgaria. The British Government at once took up the position that the Treaty could not be recognised until it had been submitted to the Powers of Europe in Conference. This position was unassailable, because the Treaty of San Stefano modified the Treaty of Paris 1856, and the Treaty of London 1871 had laid down the principle that no treaty could be altered without the consent of all the parties to it. It was the same ground as that taken, with less success, by Sir Edward Grey in 1909, on the occasion of the transformation by Austria of her occupation of Bosnia and Herzegovina into full annexation.

On the 28th January the Government asked the House of Commons for a vote of £6,000,000, in order that they might go into the Council of Europe strong and prepared. Mr. Gladstone assailed this proposal with arguments of the

kind dear to those who love hollow, sonorous phrases.
He spoke of the 'clash of arms'—

'It is really,' he said, 'an attempt to associate arms with
negotiations. Now permit me to say that such an attempt,
by whomsoever made, is radically bad. . . . This vote is
entirely at variance with the principle of taking from war
as much as we can, and giving to peace as much as we
can. It is a step backwards; a step towards violence and
barbarism, instead of towards reason ; a step in the opposite direction to that in which we have been endeavouring
to march, and it ought to be viewed with the utmost aver-
sion by all who are in favour of peaceful methods.'

A few days later came the news that the Russians, as a
reply to the move of the Fleet, had advanced their forces
nearer to Constantinople, and the excitement in London
became intense. On the 13th February the Fleet, under
orders from London, passed through the Dardanelles, and
anchored in the Bosphorus. The 9th February was the
day on which the debate on the Vote was to be concluded.
On the 30th January Lord Hartington had received sound
advice from the Speaker, Mr. Brand, who wrote that—
'Your position as leader of the Opposition, in view of the
Eastern Question, becomes more and more difficult. You
have had always a formidable opponent in Lord Beaconsfield, and a dangerous ally in Gladstone.' Beaconsfield
would 'take a good opportunity to dissolve.' The Speaker
advised that Hartington should, while criticising, give
the Government support, casting responsibility on them,
and asking them in return that they should take the House
into their confidence. This was, in effect, the line taken
by Lord Hartington in his speech of the 8th February. It
drew from the Chancellor of the Exchequer an expression
of thanks 'for the general tone and spirit' of his observations. He had already laid down his views very clearly in

the following letter to Lord Granville, which was, no doubt, intended for communication to Mr. Gladstone and other leading men.    Lord Granville was always the central post-office for Liberal intercommunications on delicate occasions.

DEVONSHIRE HOUSE, PICCADILLY, W.,
*Jan. 29, 1878.*

MY DEAR GRANVILLE,—I am sorry to say that after considering the matter as well as I can, I have come to the conclusion that, not only am I unable to move an amendment negativing the Vote, but also I could not vote for it.

I have only time now to state in the shortest and most imperfect manner my reasons for this conclusion, but they are mainly these :—

1. I should look upon a Vote of Want of Confidence in the Government at this moment, if it could be carried, as a very serious evil.    It is impossible that we could form a Government with the present Parliament, and a Dissolution in the course of the next few weeks would utterly paralyse the influence of the country at a critical time.

2. I am not able to condemn altogether the general policy of the Government since the outbreak of the war. I accept the policy of conditional neutrality, and I accept the conditions as well as the neutrality.

Faults may be found in details, but it seems to me that they have not departed from a strict neutrality till the conditions were nearly touched ; and they have succeeded in convincing the Turks that for them, or for the maintenance of their Empire, they were not prepared to fight.

3. I think that it is not unreasonable that we should place ourselves in a state of moderate preparation in anticipation of the possible events of the next few weeks.    It does not appear to me a question of going armed into a Conference. It is rather a question of looking on at two armed Powers treating separately on matters concerning our interests. The other two Powers most closely concerned, Germany

and Austria, have, from the circumstances of their position, the means of intervening with effect whenever they please. I cannot think it wrong that we should be placed in a position to use whatever power we may possess without delay.

If you should consider it necessary, I would come and discuss these points, but I see no advantage in doing so. I am aware that I disagree with almost the whole of my late colleagues, and also the great majority of the party. I might very probably be silenced in argument, but I do not think that my opinion could be changed.

A compromise, by which a resolution might be agreed to which would not directly negative the Vote, would, I think, be unsatisfactory. I do not believe that the majority of the party will now be satisfied with anything short of a direct negation.

And I feel that there is a difference between myself and the majority of the party, which, if not now, must shortly make itself felt.

They, I believe, virtually hold that no English interests in the Black Sea are involved for which we ought to fight. I, on the contrary, think that circumstances may arise in which it would be our duty to fight.

My own opinion is that the best course would be that I should, in whatever way may be thought most desirable, resign the leadership, and leave my colleagues to take their own course.

I do trust that Mr. Gladstone may find it in his power to resume the leadership, at all events until this crisis is over. He must be aware that it is he who has formed and guided the opinion of the Liberal party throughout these transactions, and I think that he ought to be at the head.

I cannot conceal from myself that I have not been able in this question to lead, but have rather followed a long way behind.—Yours very truly,

HARTINGTON.

P.S.—I feel that you have reason to complain that I have not earlier communicated these conclusions to you.

I have really no excuse to offer, except that it was not until I seriously considered how I could meet the wishes of the party in opposing the Vote that I found how considerable were the differences between my own opinions and those which I know are held by the majority.

On February 9th, Lord Hartington's secretary, Mr. Reginald Brett, wrote in his journal :—

'These two weeks have been anxious and troublesome ones, especially for Lord Hartington. Not only has he had the usual responsibility of an Opposition Leader, but the additional difficulty of managing a refractory, undisciplined party, and soothing the furious outbursts of Mr. Gladstone. A less calm, less self-controlled, vainer man than he would have given up long ago, and most assuredly last week. He sticks to his guns with difficulty, grudgingly, but still valiantly.'

On this same day, 9th February 1878, took place the division upon the vote of £6,000,000, and the Government carried it by a majority of 328 to 124. About 20 Liberals voted with the Government. Lord Hartington and a number of other Liberals did not vote. Mr. Gladstone voted in the minority.

The final crisis of the Eastern Question now came on. The Russians had announced that they would submit the Treaty of San Stefano to the European Congress, that other Powers might raise questions on it if they pleased, but that Russia reserved the liberty of accepting, or not accepting, the discussion of such questions. The British Government insisted that the Treaty must be submitted without reservations.

On the 27th March the Prime Minister, now rapidly failing in body but undaunted in spirit, sent this note to his Secretary for War :—

'Rest assured that the critical time has arrived, when we must declare the emergency.

'We are drifting into war. If we are bold and determined we shall secure peace and dictate its conditions to Europe.

'I shall put before the Cabinet to-day my views, which are, at least, well matured, and if they are adopted we shall be acknowledged to be not unequal to the trying situation. On you I mainly count. We have to maintain the Empire and secure peace. I think we can do both.'[1]

His proposals were adopted by the Cabinet, at the cost of the loss of Lord Derby, who had already resigned when the Fleet was moved to the Dardanelles, but had withdrawn his resignation.[2] The Reserves were called out, and a strong body of native troops was ordered from India to Malta.

For a few days war seemed almost certain. The Government issued from the *impasse* by an arrangement with Russia. They agreed to the San Stefano Treaty, with the modification that Bulgaria was to be severed into two portions, the Russians on their side retreating from their position as to the Congress procedure. Sir Stafford Northcote wrote on the 5th April to Lord Hartington to assure him on the word of the Prime Minister that the Government were 'earnestly desirous of peace and of a true European concert.' Lord Hartington was asked to restrain the ardour of his party as much as possible while delicate negotiations were in progress. On the 9th April there was a debate upon Sir Wilfrid Lawson's amendment regretting the calling out of the Reserves. Lord Hartington expressed his view that, on such an occasion, occasions of differences between one side of the House and the other

---

[1] *Memoir of Lord Cranbrook*, vol. ii. p. 54.

[2] Lord Derby explained to the House of Lords that he had resigned not only because of the decision to call out the Reserves, but because of other schemes.

ought not to be multiplied. If common ground could be found between the Government and the Opposition, 'in that agreement and in that concord would be found the surest and the most hopeful prospect of peace.' He said :—

'There is a danger of the Government, by the language which they hold, rendering any acceptance of modifications of the Treaty by Russia impossible. There is another danger — lest, by the language held by a party in this country, the Russian Government may be encouraged to believe that they will be supported in any refusal to entertain demands, however just.'

The Lawson amendment against calling out the Reserves was defeated by 319 to 64 (9th April 1878). Again Lord Hartington did not vote ; some twenty Liberals voted for the Government ; and Mr. Gladstone voted in the minority. Lord Granville told him next day that the proceedings had been one of the heaviest blows to party discipline that he remembered.[1]

In May there was much discussion as to the legality of the action of the Government in bringing 7000 Indian troops to Malta without first obtaining sanction from Parliament. Did the word 'kingdom' in the Bill of Rights, 1689, mean these Islands only, or did it cover prophetically the not then acquired oversea dominions of the Crown ? Lord Cairns and Lord Selborne each argued his party brief for two hours by the clock of the House of Lords. In the Commons Mr. Gladstone sustained a joust against the law officers which showed how magnificent an advocate he would have made had his lot been cast in the Courts of Law, just as, had he followed

---

[1] This was when Lord Granville met Mr. Gladstone in Regent Street, in the rain, with his hat turned the wrong way. *Life of Lord Granville*, vol. ii. p. 176.

his first impulse and taken orders, he would have been the most irresistible of preachers. Lord Hartington stated lucidly the finest old Whig doctrine, but declined to vote against the money grant demanded by the Government. The object of the movement of Indian troops to Malta was, he pointed out, 'to show to the whole world that you have power to move and dispose the forces of your Indian Empire for the purposes of European policy.'[1]

Beaconsfield, as Bismarck said, led his country gallantly to the brink of war. He achieved his object, the assertion of the right of England to have a leading voice in the settlement of the Eastern Question. Well-informed men knew that even if England had not interfered, the Russians would have found it difficult to annex, even if they desired to annex, Constantinople. The alliance between Germany and Austria was not declared till 1879, but these Powers had long been acting in concert.[2] It was of more importance to Austria than to England that the gate to the Black Sea should remain in the hands of a weak Power. Nor had the Austrians and Magyars any desire to see a large and strong Bulgarian State, a grateful client of Russia, rising to their south. At the crisis in March 1878, the Austrian Government, though not very decidedly, were prepared to co-operate if necessary with England. No doubt the Statesmen who directed the course of the Central Powers preferred that England should bear the brunt of the diplomatic collision with Russia at the end of the war. If England had joined in coercing the Sultan in 1876, the war might probably have been avoided, but, in that case, the settlement would probably have been less definite, complete, and lasting. The war showed also that

---

[1] Lord Beaconsfield said on one occasion to the Russian Ambassador, 'Well, if you force us to do it, we can bring 100,000 men from India.'

[2] Mr. Abraham Hayward in a letter to Lord Hartington quoted the very best authority on these points.

there was more vitality and possible 'future' in the Turks, notwithstanding the rottenness of their Government, than had been supposed. Lord Beaconsfield said finely in his Guildhall speech of 1877, 'The independence of Turkey was a subject of ridicule a year ago. . . . It is not doubted now. It has been proved by half a million of warriors who have devoted their lives to their country without pay and without reward.'

It was not borne in mind by those who insisted that England ought to assist in coercing the Turks that the Ruler of India could not, in a quarrel between the Czar and Sultan, act without regard to the feelings of the Mahomedan population subject to the Empire. Englishmen, far away in their island, are too apt to forget the existence of India. They assail the rule of men of one race over men of others, or they condemn in unmeasured terms any system of government which does not rest, for all purposes, upon the elective choice of the people governed, without remembering that they are condemning principles upon which are founded the government of the British Empire, with the exception of the self-governing dominions.[1]

The Government had made not only an arrangement with Russia, but a convention with Turkey. The effect of this was that England guaranteed the Asiatic dominions of Turkey against foreign aggression ; that Turkey undertook, *pro formâ*, to carry out certain reforms there ; that England was to occupy and administer the island of Cyprus. The Congress met at Berlin on the 13th June 1878, and lasted for a month. Lord Beaconsfield, with Lord Salisbury, represented England, and rose to the culminating point of

---

[1] This has been true even of English Conservatives. Madame de Staël said, 'The Tories of England are the Whigs of Europe.' England established her own empire while resisting, by supporting national movements, the rise of any other empire.

his own romantic ambition. The son of the Jewish book-
man sat as a protagonist in the great Council of Europe.
He said in the House of Lords (18th July) that by the
modifications made in the Treaty of San Stefano, 'the
menace to European independence has been removed,
and the threatened injury to the British Empire has been
averted.' The new Bulgaria no longer severed Constantinople from Macedonia and Thrace by descending to the
shores of the Ægean. The Balkans were to be the Turkish
frontier, with a limited Turkish authority in the province to
the south of the mountains.[1] Austria had been invited to
occupy Bosnia and Herzegovina, 'and not to leave it till
she had deeply laid the foundations of tranquillity and
order.' In Asia, Kars and Batoum were to go to Russia.

The settlement satisfied the average Englishman. The
Bulgarians were to be free, and therefore, presumably,
happy; at any rate, they were off his conscience. Nor had
the rich gone empty away. A picturesque addition had
been made to the British Empire in the shape of the island
beloved by Aphrodite, at the cost of a vague guarantee
which threatened no credible demands upon his purse ;
above all, his country had played a distinguished part at
Berlin, and the business was over. Lord Beaconsfield was
extremely popular on his return, bringing, as he said,
'Peace with honour.' Had he then dissolved he would
have won, it was thought, the General Election. The
Liberals were, however, in duty bound to perform a piece
of retrospective criticism, and to exhibit as best they could
the vanity of all this glory achieved by their opponents.

On July 29th Lord Hartington moved Resolutions expressing regret that the Greek claims had not been met at
Berlin, that by the Asiatic guarantee the military liabilities
of this country had been extended, that the Government

---

[1] This arrangement only endured for a few years.

had entered into responsibilities for administrative reforms in Asia Minor which they could not fulfil, and that these engagements had been entered into and responsibilities incurred (horrible to say) ' without the previous knowledge of Parliament.' The affair was a sham fight, but it allowed Lord Hartington to make an excellent historical *résumé* of the whole history. His real mind was in this sentence: ' I believe that the future of the inhabitants of what remains of the dominions of Turkey will ultimately be determined by internal and natural causes rather than by causes which are external and artificial, and I rejoice that a temporary solution has been arrived at which will leave scope for those natural causes to work, and will not replace the military domination of Turkey by the military domination of Russia or the Slav over unwilling races.'

Mr. Gladstone had described as an ' insane covenant' the arrangement as to Asia Minor and Cyprus made with the Turks. Lord Beaconsfield, in the ' Peace with Honour' speech had, in revenge, contrasted ' a body of English gentlemen, honoured by the favour of their sovereign and the confidence of their fellow-subjects, managing your affairs for five years, I hope with prudence, and not altogether without success,' with ' a sophistical rhetorician, inebriated with the exuberance of his own verbosity, and gifted with an egotistical imagination,' and so forth. Lord Hartington solemnly read out the whole opprobrious passage, to the amusement of the Conservatives, and then, while admitting that a statesman whose policy had been called insane might have some fair retort, he said that ' the Prime Minister was offering somewhat of an insult to the Sovereign of whom my right honourable friend was for no inconsiderable time the chief adviser, to the Privy Council, which he has led, to the people of this country, whose confidence at one time he possessed, and the confidence of a large portion of whom he still commands.' Not altogether a happy way of putting the case. A day or two later the Prime Minister, at Oxford, excused himself for his caricature portrait by saying that Mr. Gladstone had described him as a 'dangerous and even a devilish character.' Mr. Gladstone wrote to ask for exact and specific references, which could not be produced, and so the incident was closed.[1] But if a man is truly convinced that his cause is that of heaven, what can he think of those who actively pursue a policy opposed to his own ?

This final debate aroused small interest. Neither Parliament nor the public can be excited over the discussion of accomplished and unalterable facts at the end of July.

Lord Hartington retired to Holker Hall, and attended the annual sale there of a famous breed of 'shorthorns.' He wrote on September 20th to Lord Granville :—

'I am not shooting partridges, but I do not think that I am improving my mind. I have seen much of the shorthorn world, who do not appear to me to be wiser than other people.

'I saw Odo Russell the other day, who came with the F. Hanleys to the sale. He seems to expect that peace will shortly be patched up in the East ; says that the Austrians would have had no trouble if they had entered Bosnia at once, and that Bismarck told them so. He does not seem to believe in the permanence of the settlement, and would not be surprised to see the Turkish Empire in Europe collapse very suddenly. He thinks that if Austria

---

[1] An amusing story, told by Mr. George Russell in one of his books of recollections, shows that Mr. Gladstone did descry something diabolical in his rival. It is the tale about the Royal Academy dinner, and how Mr. Gladstone said it was 'devilish' of Lord Beaconsfield to have criticised in private the pictures which he praised in public. If Mr. Gladstone had been the orator, he would have convinced himself, *ad hoc*, that the pictures were as good as he described them.

and England do not settle between them what is to take
its place, the Russians will.   Dizzy and Schouvaloff appear
to have made the most impression on him at Berlin.

'What is the meaning of Bismarck's outbreak against
Gortschakoff ?   O. Russell did not seem to have any clear
explanation to give about it.   Mr. Gladstone's American
article is rather annoying.   What is the good of telling
people that the Americans are going to beat us, and that
he rather likes it ? '

Now a new great affair of imperial policy began to stir
the public mind.

## CHAPTER X

### THE AFGHAN WAR AND SOUTH AFRICA

LORD LYTTON succeeded in April 1876 to Lord Northbrook as Viceroy of India. Sher Ali sat on the uneasy throne of the Afghans, which he had captured after five years of dynastic war, in 1868. The Russians, continuing their great advance across Asia, had annexed Tashkend in 1865, Samarcand in 1868, and the Khanate of Khiva in 1873. This brought their outposts to the banks of the Oxus, and within little more than 300 miles in that direction from the Afghan frontier. Sher Ali, alarmed by the advance of the Northern Power, turned towards the English. He came down to Umballa for a conference with Lord Mayo in 1869, when the Liberals were in office and the Duke of Argyll was Secretary of State for India.

The Amir asked the Viceroy virtually for a full defensive alliance, support to his dynasty, and a fixed annual subsidy. He received only a general assurance of friendship, and of undefined material support to be given at the free discretion of the Indian Government as to times and occasions. He was informed that any assistance was given for the purpose of 'establishing a just and merciful as well as a strong government in Afghanistan,' and that the continuance of the support must always depend upon the pleasure of the Government of India. In fact, the British Government treated Sher Ali rather as a proud and virtuous patron might treat a not very necessary dependent of bad character. The Duke of Argyll even thought that the Viceroy had not made it sufficiently clear to the Amir that our support depended upon the goodness and justness of his internal administration, and intimated his opinion in a moral and disapproving despatch.[1] The Secretary of State maintained this attitude in 1873. In that year Sher Ali, still more alarmed by the rapid Russian advances, sent his chief Minister, Syud Nur Mahomed Shah, to Simla to confer with Lord Northbrook.

This Envoy said that whatever specific assurances the Russians might give, and however often these might be repeated, the people of Afghanistan could place no confidence in them and would never rest satisfied until they were assured of the aid of the British Government. He asked, as Sher Ali had asked at Umballa, not only for a guarantee against foreign aggression and for unlimited supplies of arms and money, but also for a promise to support the succession of the Amir's chosen son. He asked also for an assurance that there should be no interference with the internal affairs of his country.

The Viceroy telegraphed home (24th July 1873) to ask leave to give to the Amir, who was 'alarmed at Russian progress, and dissatisfied with general assurance,' an undertaking that the Government would help the Amir with money, arms, and troops, if necessary, to repel an unprovoked invasion if he unreservedly accepted our advice in foreign affairs. But the Duke of Argyll replied that the Amir was to be told that the Cabinet did 'not at all share his alarm,' and considered 'that there was no cause for it,' and would maintain their 'settled policy in favour of

---

[1] 'There are conditions,' wrote the Duke, 'under which it would not be for the credit of the British Government to support the Amir either by money or by arms. If he succeeds in establishing a government which is strong, but notoriously cruel and oppressive, H.M.G. ought to be free to withhold all assistance from him.' (See C. 2190 of 1878–79, despatch of 14th May 1869.)

Afghanistan.' The Viceroy was, therefore, only in a position to renew general assurances of support so long as the Amir should conduct internal government with justice, and follow British guidance as to foreign relations. On the other hand, the Amir was told that the Government of India thought it highly desirable that British officers should be sent to certain places on the further borders of Afghanistan to examine and report at Kabul to the Amir regarding measures necessary for the security of the frontier. This suggestion was made in pursuance of an old policy of the Indian Foreign Office. The right to send British officers into Afghanistan, to see that the military subsidy given to the Amir was properly expended, was one of the stipulations in Lord Dalhousie's treaty with Dost Mohammed in 1857, and more than one Viceroy had since then expressed the opinion that the step ought to be taken. The Afghan Envoy to Simla raised objections of a general character—that there was a strong party in Kabul opposed to more intimate relations; that British officers might observe things in the Amir's governments which would displease the Indian Government; that his country-men, who were 'deplorably ignorant,' had an idea that British officers were always the fore-runners of annexation. Lord Northbrook did not press the demand. The condition that the Amir should govern with justice may have seemed (and with reason) still more ominous to the Afghan.

Sir Frederick Roberts, in a letter of 22nd November 1879, reported the following statement as having been made to him, in substance, by the Amir Yakub.[1]

'In 1869 my father (Sher Ali) was fully prepared to throw in his lot with you. He had suffered many reverses before making himself secure on the throne of Afghanistan; and he had come to the conclusion that his best chance of

[1] *Afghanistan*, 1880   No. 1, p. 170.

holding what he had won lay in an alliance with the British Government.  He did not receive from Lord Mayo as large a supply of arms and ammunition as he had hoped, but nevertheless he returned to Kabul fairly satisfied, and so he remained until the visit of Nur Muhammed Shah to India in 1873.  This visit brought matters to a head.'

The diaries received from Nur Muhammed Shah during his stay in India, and the report which he brought back on his return, convinced my father that he could no longer hope to obtain from the British Government all the aid that he wanted ; and from that time he began to turn his attention to the thoughts of a Russian alliance.  You know how that ended.'

Yakub, who had spent the last years in prison, was certainly not in his father's secrets, but on the whole evidence the impression seems to be a true one.

Meanwhile the Russian advance continued.  In the autumn of 1875 General Kauffman annexed Khokand, the Bosnian insurrection broke out, and the aspect of affairs in South-east Europe became menacing.  It had been known before Lord Northbrook left India that communications, not then thought by the Indian Government to be very important, were passing between the Amir and the Russian authorities in Turkestan.  It was known that, after September 1875, a succession of Russian agents visited Kabul and transacted business with the Amir.  The Tory Government, soon after their accession to power, entered upon a definite policy.

Lord Salisbury, now at the India Office, returning to the idea suggested, but not insisted upon, by Lord North-brook in 1873, instructed that Viceroy in a despatch sent in January 1875, to enter into negotiations with the Amir with a view to the establishment of a British officer at Herat.  This would, he said, not only be a means of obtaining reliable information, but also would be an ' indication of English solicitude for the safety of our allies, and may so tend to discourage counsels dangerous to the peace of Asia.' The Indian Government replied in June in a well-reasoned despatch. They gave every reason for thinking that the Amir would not willingly consent to this step, or would refuse assent. If he assented unwillingly it would be difficult for an officer at Herat to obtain information, and there would be risk to his safety. If the Amir refused assent, the refusal must either be calmly accepted, which would impair the influence of the Indian Government at Kabul, or it must be resented, and this would change relations with the Afghans, and probably throw them into the arms of Russia. It would be wise to wait till an advance of the Russians to Merv should make the Afghans approach us again for aid to which new conditions might be attached.

Lord Salisbury then sent a second despatch, 19th November 1875, insisting on his policy, and instructing the Viceroy that, as a first step, the Amir should be asked to receive a temporary embassy at Kabul, which need not be publicly connected with the establishment of a permanent mission within his dominions. After replying in a despatch renewing the objections, making some alternative suggestions, and asking further instructions, Lord Northbrook left India at the beginning of 1876, having completed the term of his government. His successor, Lord Lytton, had been fully instructed to carry out the new policy. He was to ask the Amir to receive a special mission in connection with the assumption by the Queen of the Imperial title, and, 'if the language and demeanour of the Amir be such as to promise no satisfactory result of the negotiations thus opened, His Highness should be distinctly reminded that he is isolating himself, at his own peril, from the friendship

and protection it is his interest to seek and deserve.'[1]
The Amir was to be given, in return for concessions,
those specific and definite pledges of defence against
Russia, and support to his dynasty, which he had failed to
obtain in the days of Lord Mayo and Lord Northbrook.
The essence of the policy was that, in consequence of
the state of the great Asiatic rivalry, it was necessary that
the Amir should be brought more definitely into the
position of a protected ally.

Lord Salisbury said in his despatch to Lord Lytton,
after referring to the Russian advances, that the Government—

'cannot view with complete indifference the probable
influence of the situation upon the uncertain character
of an oriental chief whose ill-defined dominions are
brought within a steadily narrowing circle, between the
conflicting pressures of two great military empires, one of
which expostulates and remains passive, whilst the other
apologises and continues to move forwards."

If Lord Salisbury did not sufficiently appreciate the
practical difficulties so clear to men in India, perhaps, on
the other hand, men of the Lawrence school did not
sufficiently allow that changes in the general Asiatic
position had made an assertion of power necessary, if we
were to retain Afghanistan within our sphere of influence.

Lord Lytton began proceedings in May 1876 by asking
the Amir to receive Sir Lewis Pelly, on a special mission
at Kabul, or elsewhere in Afghanistan. The Amir de-
murred, and a second letter was addressed to him by Lord
Lytton, of a reassuring character as to the objects of the
mission, but warning him that, if he rejected the 'hand of
friendship,' Afghanistan must be regarded as 'a State which
has voluntarily separated itself from the alliance and sup-

[1] Lord Salisbury's despatch to Lord Lytton of 28th February 1876.

port of the British Government' (8th July 1876). Further communications took place, and Lord Lytton practically offered to grant all the requests which had been denied to the Amir at the Simla Conference of 1873, and which, had they then been granted fully, and unqualified by moral conditions, might, perhaps, have secured Sher Ali as a firm ally. In return for these concessions Lord Lytton demanded complete control over the Amir's foreign relations, the right to send British officers to Herat or elsewhere on the frontier, and the reception by the Amir of special British missions, whenever requested. If the British Government had now, in 1876, given to Sher Ali a full alliance and regular subsidy without the condition as to British officers, the ally would probably have been secured and the war avoided. These negotiations led to the conference at Peshawar, early in 1877, between Sir Lewis Pelly and Syud Nur Mahomed.

Sir Lewis Pelly defined the new arrangement offered as 'a treaty of defensive and offensive alliance, and one tending to strengthen and secure the Amir's dynasty and power by the public recognition and support of the British Government provided that the Amir should agree to the conditions which are absolutely necessary to enable the Viceroy to carry out the obligations undertaken.' The Afghan Envoy was determined not to admit the British *sine quâ non* condition that British officers should be stationed on the Herat frontier, and he gave some sound reasons, only too well justified by later events.

'The people of Afghanistan,' he said, 'have a dread of this proposal, and it is firmly fixed in their minds that, if Englishmen or other Europeans once set foot in their country, it will sooner or later pass out of their hands. In no way can they be reassured on this point and it is impossible to remove this opinion from their minds, for they adduce many proofs in support of it. Therefore, since the opinions of the people are such, the residence of Englishmen in the midst of these hill-tribes is difficult, nay, impossible, because the whole army and subjects of the Government are of these mountain people.'

In case, he added, the Sahibs were killed, there would be 'eternal reproach and bitterness against Afghanistan, and friendship with the English Government would be exchanged for enmity.' These arguments he repeated day by day,[1] and he also referred to certain grievances of the Amir, such as the concession to Persia in the matter of the Seistan boundary, and the protest which the Indian Government had made as to his imprisonment of his son Yakub, 'that undutiful son and ill-starred wretch,' as his father once called him. The conference broke down, and Lord Lytton wrote a strong letter for communication to the Amir in which he summed up the history of the matter, withdrew all offers of material assistance, and repudiated all liabilities or obligations on the part of the Indian Government towards the Amir or his dynasty. Syud Nur Mahomed died at Peshawar before he could answer the letter, and so the conference came to an end. On April 2, 1877, Sir Lewis Pelly left Peshawar and, about the same time, the native agent of the Indian Government was withdrawn from Kabul. Certain military dispositions were also made on the frontiers, and an attitude towards the Amir 'of the most complete indifference and unbroken reserve' was adopted.[2] In other words, there was a hostile suspension of all relations. The Amir now began to receive more openly the overtures which came from beyond the Oxus River. At the critical moment, in the spring of 1878, when war between England and Russia seemed imminent, the Russian Government authorised an

---

[1] C. 2190 of 1878-79.    [2] Lord Lytton's words to Major Cavagnari.

open and formal mission to Kabul. It was a strategic move in the great game, and Lord Beaconsfield said in conversation, as a correspondent told Lord Hartington, that, in their place, he should have done the same thing. The Amir received notice of the intended visit, was alarmed, and begged to be excused it, but the Russians insisted upon coming. The mission left Samarcand on the 14th June, the day of meeting of the Congress at Berlin, and reached Kabul on July 22nd. The European crisis was over, and in August the Russian Government assured the British that the Afghan negotiations had been stopped. Meanwhile, General Stoletoff had been ostentatiously received at Kabul. He remained there till September, 'stringing,' as the Amir wrote, 'the pearls of friendly sentiment on the thread of statement.' In fact he negotiated a complete alliance. Some of his staff were there almost to the end of the year.

Thus the Amir had formally refused to receive a British mission in 1876, and had as formally received a Russian mission in 1878, and that at a time when, as he well knew, a war between England and Russia was threatening. Apart from questions of previous policy, and taking all things as they stood in the summer of 1878, the Indian Government was clearly bound to demand, in the sight of Asia, at least as favourable treatment as that which had been accorded to the Russians. Notice was therefore given to the Amir, with Lord Salisbury's sanction, that a British mission would be sent, and he was requested in civil terms to receive it. No answer was returned, either yes or no.[1]

---

[1] The distractions of Sher Ali were increased by the death of his favourite son and recognised heir, on 17th August. He wrote : ' In consequence of the attack of grief and affliction which has befallen me by the decree of God, great distraction has seized the mind of this supplicant at God's threshold. The officers of the British Government ought therefore to have observed patience, and stayed at such a time.'

The mission, under Sir Neville Chamberlain, left Peshawar on 21st September, and was stopped by Afghan officers at Ali Musjid. Major Cavagnari met the Afghan Sirdar, Faiz Mahomed Khan, under some trees by the river. At the close of a politely but unyieldingly conducted interview, Cavagnari said to the Sirdar, 'We are both servants, you of the Amir, I of the British Government. It is of no use for us to discuss these matters. I only came to get a straight answer from you. Will you oppose the passage of the mission by force?' The Afghan said, 'Yes, I will, and you may take it as kindness, and because I remember friendship, that I do not fire upon you for what you have done already.' 'You have had a straight answer,' he added as they parted. So they shook hands, and mounted their horses, and went their several ways. War was now inevitable. On the 20th November an Anglo-Indian army, to the immense delight of all in it, crossed the border line, and, after some fighting, commanded the road to Kabul. Another force, under Sir Donald Stewart, advancing by the line of the Khojak, entered Kandahar on the 9th January and sent out cavalry as far as the Helmund River. Sher Ali had made extensive preparations. He had raised and equipped a standing army of about 60,000 men. He had 300 guns, an arsenal, and great stores of ammunition.[1] He did not, however, know how to use his force, relied entirely on the aid which he expected from his faithless Russian friends, and, receiving none, fled into Turkestan where, on the 21st February 1879, as Yakub, his son, wrote to Lord Lytton, he 'obeyed the call of the Summoner, and, throwing off the dress of existence, hastened to the region of Divine Mercy.' The dying Sher

[1] General Roberts's Report to the Government of India, 22nd November 1879, C. 2457 of 1880.

Ali must have thought himself the most unfortunate or the most ill-used of princes. He had asked the English for a complete alliance against the Russians, and had been refused it, and told to govern with justice; he had then accepted the alliance thrust upon him by the Russians; he had then been attacked by the English, and abandoned by the Russians.[1]

Yakub, released from prison, was recognised as Amir, and—to anticipate this history a little—entered in the summer of 1879 into the Treaty of Gundamak, which closed the first chapter of the second Afghan War. It has not been possible, in the space at disposal, to give a detailed account of the complex events which led to the Afghan War, but enough has been said to show that the situation was difficult throughout, and that a wise statesman would have been slow to commit himself to a condemnation of the action of the Government.

## II

Lord Hartington, being in Opposition, had to await the publication of papers by the Government before he could form a well-based opinion. He had, however, the advantage of the advice and information which Lord Northbrook, the Liberal ex-Viceroy, who had returned from India at the beginning of 1876, could supply. Lord Northbrook believed that the Amir, although discontented between 1873 and 1878, was by no means hopelessly alienated, and that he still feared and hated the Russians, even more than he did the English. In a memorandum written in November 1878 and sent to Lord Hartington

[1] The position of Afghanistan and the probable feelings of an Amir are admirably described by the late Sir Alfred Lyall in a poem included in his volume *Verses written in India.*

and others, Lord Northbrook said : 'The real history of the transaction is, that the Amir wished for an unconditional guarantee of protection, and, although I wished to give him, and did give him a guarantee with reasonable conditions attached to it, I did not wish to give him an unconditional guarantee.'

Lord Northbrook, in 1878, while admitting that the negotiation of 1873 had not improved the situation, attributed the complete alienation and hostility of the Amir to the policy of active demands upon him adopted by Lord Salisbury and Lord Lytton.  On the other side it was maintained that the Gladstone Government, in 1869 and 1873, by its general tone of conditional and indefinite support, and menacing morality, had driven the Amir to believe that he could hope for no effective assistance from India, and might even have something to fear from that quarter, and must therefore make terms with the Russians. This error, it was alleged, brought about that condition of affairs when stronger measures were necessary.  This is a view of the matter which General Roberts's report of his conversation in the autumn of 1879 with the Afghan prince, Yakub, already quoted, went far to confirm, but this conversation was yet to come.  Hartington's own view of the question in the autumn of 1878 is shown in the following letter.  It is a good example of his way of dealing with a question when he was not in possession of the full facts requisite for the formation of a definite judgment.

Studley Royal, Ripon,<br>
October 15, 1878.

Dear Granville,—Ripon, Northbrook, and I had a long talk yesterday on Afghan affairs, and I think you may like to know the result.

1. We think that, whatever the engagements may be into which the Russians entered with us, our conduct

to them, and especially our bringing over Indian troops, perhaps warranted their conduct, both in sending a mission to Cabul, and in moving troops to their southern frontier in Central Asia, and if they had any inkling of what seems to have been contemplated at one time of some move on our part against them in Asia, it became almost a defensive measure. At any rate we shall get some explanation from them, true or false, with which we must be content.

2. Whether the Ameer can have been warranted or excusable in his conduct towards us, depends in a great degree on what we do not at present know. At the time of Sir Lewis Pelly's negotiation, Lord Lytton wrote to the Ameer and I believe had some answer. What Lord Lytton said we don't know, nor what passed with Sir L. Pelly. But the result was a failure altogether, and we went so far as to recall our native agent from Cabul. This rather looks like a disclaimer on our part of having anything more to do with the Ameer, depriving ourselves of any means of communication with him. Now if Lord Lytton told him that we could no longer look on him as a friend, and that we should consider any expectation of such aid from us as he might have entertained to be at an end—there is a good deal to be said for him. We certainly brought the rebuff on ourselves—but even in taking notice of it, he may be entitled to more consideration than if he had wantonly treated us as he has done, and we should be reasonable in what we require.

That his conduct can be altogether passed by we none of us think.

But in order to form an opinion of the Ameer's conduct we want certain information.

1. Correspondence between Lord Salisbury and Lord Northbrook in 1875–1876 as to sending a mission to Cabul.

2. And, above all, Lord Lytton's letter to the Ameer and all the correspondence to which it led at the time of Sir L. Pelly's negotiation, together with an account of that negotiation, and its results.

We think that the least that we should require would be an apology for the treatment of our officers and the reception of our mission at Cabul, as he chose to receive one from Russia.

We hope and trust that this may be attained without further action. If such action should become necessary, the best course would probably be the occupation of Candahar, which would not be difficult, and might bring the Ameer to reason. It is impossible, however, to say from hence what may be the most advisable in a military point of view.

We think, however, that it would not be safe to undertake any operations beyond our frontier without an addition of about 10,000 European troops, and we think further that the greater part, if not the whole, of the expenses should be borne by this country.

One thing under any circumstances we should declare against, and that is the conducting operations with a view to the *permanent* occupation of the country.

I understand that Salisbury is against this, but the objections to it, as you know, are almost insuperable. On this point perhaps the same silence need not be preserved during the recess as certainly should be preserved as to the conduct to be pursued ; and the objection to any extension of our Indian frontier should be insisted upon.—Yours ever,

H.

Lord Granville was doubtful whether silence was not, as yet, the best course for the Liberal leaders. He wrote (4th November 1878) :—

‘I am of opinion that, although your silence will be found fault with, it is the best course for yourself and the *chose publique*. But I should not like you to follow exclusively my advice. There is no doubt our temperaments tally too much on this point for us to be the best advisers of one another.’

Lord Beaconsfield, by his speech at the Guildhall, added

fuel to the rising flame of Radical indignation, for he intimated that one result of the proceedings would be the acquisition of a 'scientific frontier.' Lord Hartington was not much perturbed. He wrote to Lord Granville on 13th November 1878 :—

'I thought Lord Beaconsfield's speech moderate in tone, though the Indian part appeared to be a mis-statement of the case; and the rectification of the frontier will enrage Lords Grey, Lawrence, &c. I do not think it was judicious to acknowledge that our object is a better frontier; but, even on this point, I scarcely think that, without more materials for information, we are in a position absolutely to condemn the policy. The frontier tribes do not appear to be exactly subject to the Ameer. They constantly give us trouble, and we have to punish them severely. The Ameer is unfriendly, and some military authorities say that positions in the hands of these tribes may be used by him or by Russia through him to endanger our safety. I am not prepared to say that respect for the independence of robber tribes of this character ought absolutely to bar us from occupying such posts as the military authorities may decide are essential to our safety. But we seem to be getting on better terms with Russia, and there appears to be a sort of idea that the quarrel with the Ameer will be patched up. I don't think it would be wise to abuse them too much for a policy which we don't know, and which may be going to be successful.'

Parliament was summoned specially to approve of the war. Lord Hartington addressed the following letter to Mr. Gladstone :—

RIDDLESWORTH HALL, THETFORD,
*28th November* 1878.

MY DEAR MR. GLADSTONE,—As we shall not have an opportunity of meeting before you speak at Greenwich, I think that it may be desirable that, for the sake of avoid-

ing any possible future misunderstanding, I should write
you a line or two with reference to our probable course of
conduct next week. I suppose that there will be little
difference of opinion among us, as to the impolicy of
the conduct of the Government in much of their proceedings with regard to Afghanistan, nor as to the un-
fairness of Cranbrook's· statement. Northbrook's paper,
if supported, as I suppose it will be, by the despatches,
seems to prove these two points; and they may now, or
at some future time, be proper subjects for a motion of
censure.

But Northbrook suspends his judgment as to the
justification and necessity for the war, in the actual circumstances; and I suppose that we shall be agreed
that a final opinion on this ought not to be pronounced,
pending the publication of the despatches. But I should
be disposed to go rather further, and to say that, whether
the Government can produce a sufficient justification or
not, our action in Parliament ought not to take the form
of direct opposition to the war, or to giving the Government the means of continuing it. This is, of course, only
my own opinion, and I shall be quite ready to discuss the
question if necessary next week. My object in writing is
simply to let you know that I hold this opinion, and to
suggest to you, if you can do so consistently with your own
opinions, to abstain on Saturday from any declaration
which would make it impossible or difficult for us to
act accordingly.

I shall be in London on Monday at latest, and probably Granville will summon us shortly.—I remain, yours
sincerely,                            HARTINGTON.

It would have been as easy to arrest the course of the
Thames in flood as that of Mr. Gladstone borne away on
a new tide of righteousness and passion. His speech at
Greenwich on 30th November was a most violent denunciation of the Afghan War. There was much about
'covenants.' 'The Amir was under no covenant not to

receive a Russian mission; we were under a covenant with him not to send a British mission. Russia was under a covenant with us to exercise no influence in Afghanistan.' This therefore was *the* covenant which we ought to have enforced, by a war against Russia, if necessary. 'Anything so painful and so grievous has not come under my notice.' The war was not only an error but a sin. 'The question is whether this war is just or unjust. So far as I have been able to collect the evidence it is unjust. It fills me with the greatest possible alarm, lest it should be proved to be grossly and totally unjust. If so we shall come under the stroke of the everlasting law that suffering shall follow sin.' It was this constant use of Heaven's own artillery which irritated men who differed from Mr. Gladstone with regard to the expediency of political actions.

A few days later, in Parliament, he said that the first Afghan War must have left 'on the minds of the people of Afghanistan most painful traces. How could they look with friendly eyes on those who had inflicted such miseries on them without a cause?' But by wise Liberal Governments and Viceroys during the last twenty-five years, 'every effort has been made to efface those painful memories.'

'I remember,' he went on, 'a description by one of our modern poets of a great battlefield during the Punic Wars in which he observed that for the moment nature was laid waste and nothing but tokens of carnage were left on the ground, but, day by day and hour by hour, she began her kindly task, and removed one by one and put out of sight those hideous tokens, and restored the scene to order, to beauty, and to peace. It was such a process that the Viceroys of India had been carrying on for years in Afghanistan,' &c.

The eloquence was remote from the facts. The

Afghans were a people delighting in war from generation
to generation.  Both the Afghan Wars probably gave an
even fiercer joy to the clansmen than they did to the
Anglo-Indian combatants.  Their bards in their ballads
claimed victory rather than bewailed defeat.  Lepel
Griffin, in a letter from Kabul in 1880, said that the war
had enriched rather than impoverished Afghanistan, a
natural result of the invasion of a poor country by a
host bringing countless rupees contributed by Indian
peasants, and that never had he 'seen in India so
prosperous-looking a peasantry as that round Kabul.'
Mr. Gladstone (10th December 1878) predicted that other
Governments and other Viceroys would undo 'this evil
work on which you are now engaged.  It cannot be
undone in a moment, although the torch of a madman
may burn down in a night an edifice which it has taken
the genius, the labour, and the lavish prodigality of ages
to erect.'[1]

It is a far cry from this splendid imagery to the dubious
relations between Kabul and Simla existing before Lord
Lytton's advent, as depicted by the unromancing pen of
Lord Northbrook.

Lord Beaconsfield, speaking in the Lords, saw in the
opposition to the war—

'that principle of peace at any price which a certain
party in this country upholds. . . . That doctrine has
done more mischief than any I can recall that have
been afloat in this century.  It has occasioned more war
than the most ruthless conquerors.  It has disturbed and
nearly destroyed that political equilibrium so necessary
to the liberties of nations and the welfare of the world.
It has dimmed occasionally, for the moment, even the

---

[1] Mr. Gladstone may have had in mind York Minster, which was so
destroyed by a lunatic in his time, not with a torch indeed, but a box of matches.

majesty of England, and, my lords, I trust that you will brand to-night these deleterious dogmas with the reprobation of the Peers of England.'

Hartington, standing as usual half-way between the Gladstonian and Disraelian positions, made two speeches in the House of Commons. In the first, on 5th December 1878, he admitted that the Government had a right to enter upon the war without previous sanction of Parliament, and that it was 'due to the safety of our soldiers, to the interests of the Empire, and mercy to the enemy that it should be carried on with vigour.' He and those with whom he acted had not, he said, the slightest intention of impeding supplies, or of opposing any measure which might be necessary for the vigorous prosecution of the war. Passing to the merits of the policy, he stated, fully and fairly, the case of the Government. If, he added, the attitude of the Amir had been correctly described, 'it went a long way towards establishing the painful necessity for the war.' He then stated the opposite case, viz. that, in their relations with Kabul, the Government of India had better have left well, or even ill, alone. Lord Hartington said that the best authorities in India had condemned Lord Lytton's insistence upon a conference as unwise and dangerous, and that Lord Lytton had frightened the Amir into thinking that a partition of his country was intended. 'Lord Lytton having repudiated the relations between his Government and the Amir, was it,' he asked, 'to be wondered at that the Amir should seek the support of his next most powerful neighbour?' Lord Hartington did not deny, like Mr. Gladstone, that, after the reception of the Russian mission, the Government were justified in requiring the reception of a British mission, but he thought that, if more delay had been allowed, an arrangement could have been made. The Government, he suggested,

were in search of a 'scientific frontier,' and were not sorry
to find a pretext for war. 'If their object was to cultivate
friendly relations with the Amir, and to secure in him a
friendly ally instead of a sullen enemy, I must say that
they have mismanaged the negotiations as negotiations
never before were mismanaged.' He admitted the gravity
of the considerations involved with advance of Russia in
Asia, but thought that the situation would not be met by
hasty and ill-considered measures in the way of extending our frontiers. We should, he thought, have
dealt directly with Russia in this matter, and not with
the Afghans.'

This statesmanlike and reasonable treatment of the
case deeply disappointed fiery Radicals and strong party
men. Lord Hartington was not allowed to leave the
matter there. He was obliged to speak again, a week later,
on a vote of censure, and, yielding to party pressure and
alarmed Whips, spoke more like a partisan than was his
wont. He now expressed the opinion that Lord Lytton
should 'be recalled because he appears to be the incar-
nation and the embodiment of an Indian policy which is
everything an Indian policy should not be.' A few weeks
later he wrote to Lord Granville: 'Gladstone's violence
almost makes me a Jingo again.' In a debate at the
end of the session upon the Treaty of Gundamak, Lord
Hartington raised the question whether 'a policy has not
been embarked upon which will necessarily lead us a great
deal further than either the Government at home or the
Indian Government at present desire to go.' Our sphere
of operations and of responsibility had now been advanced
by the guarantees given to the new Amir beyond the natural
boundary of the mountain wall 'into a district where we
find no natural boundary at all, and no possible limit to
the extension of our responsibilities and relations until

that takes place which is so often spoken of, the meeting of the Sepoy and the Cossack.'

The Treaty of Gundamak, providing by one of its articles for the reception of a permanent British Resident at Kabul, with the right to station other officers on the further frontiers, had been made in May 1879, the British forces were being gradually withdrawn, and all seemed to be well. On the 19th July Sir Louis Cavagnari parted with General Roberts on the crest of the Shutargardan Pass, and five days later entered Kabul, where he met with a full and brilliant State reception. He had three other Englishmen on his staff, and an escort of some seventy of the 'Guides.' On August 5th some mutinous regiments, clamouring for arrears of pay, arrived from Herat, and on September 3rd the Residency buildings were attacked by these and other soldiers and the Kabul mob, and the British officers and most of their escort were slain after a gallant, desperate resistance. The officials at Simla woke on the morning of the 5th to hear of this tragedy, and on the 6th it was in the London newspapers.

The retiring British forces were turned back towards Kabul, and the war began anew. The policy of sending a British Envoy to Kabul had led to disaster. Superficially at any rate, it seemed that the policy of Lord Salisbury and Lord Lytton had failed. Certainly the mutinous soldiers and fanatics at Kabul contributed their share to the fall of the Beaconsfield Government.

Lord Granville wrote to Lord Hartington (20th September 1879) that the event was 'exactly what old Lawrence told me at Walmer last year would happen.'[1] He wrote also that he had 'seen Gladstone and talked about the Cavagnari affair.'

[1] The ex-Viceroy, Lord Lawrence, who was strongly opposed to the whole of the Lytton Afghan policy.

' . . . He was so triumphant about the varnish being all off Dizzy, that I could not help asking him what he thought would be the effect of much alarm, much blood spilt, and a complete victory. All the same, I do not feel as sure as I did that the Government will have a majority at the distant day on which the election will take place.'

Such were the echoes, in political England, of that hopeless fight of four Englishmen and their faithful frontier ' Guides,' to the death, at remote Kabul.

### III

Under the impulse dominant in London a forward policy was pursued in South Africa as it was in India. In 1877 Sir Theophilus Shepstone, acting under discretionary powers given by Lord Carnarvon, proclaimed the annexation of the Transvaal territory, then in the hands of a Boer Republic, which had fallen into an anarchical and insolvent condition, and was in danger from the growing power of the Zulu army. The territory was treated purely as a Crown Colony, and no steps were taken to establish self-governing institutions to replace the Volksraad. Almost immediately it appeared that the Boer farmers were strongly opposed to the annexation and the new form of government. Sir Bartle Frere, an Anglo-Indian of strong character, had landed at Cape Town as High Commissioner and Governor of Cape Colony about the time when the annexation was completed, and had to deal with the situation, which became very threatening by 1879. He met the Boer leaders in conference in a camp of armed men. They demanded restoration of independence; he assured them that it could never be given.

Mr. Gladstone in his Midlothian campaign denounced

the annexation as one of the crimes, or sins, of the Government. It was the 'invasion of a free people.' He said at Peebles on 30th March 1880, with regard to the Transvaal and to Cyprus, 'If those acquisitions were as valuable as they are valueless, I would repudiate them, because they are obtained by means dishonourable to the character of our country.' But on 21st May, when he had become Prime Minister, the Queen's Speech announced that the Transvaal annexation was to be maintained. On January 21, 1881, he explained to the House of Commons that 'repudiate,' at Peebles, meant 'disapprove,' and that 'to disapprove of the annexation of a country is one thing; to abandon that annexation is another.' The Boers, unaccustomed to subtle distinctions, did not understand that to 'repudiate' meant to 'disapprove.' They claimed reversal of annexation, and, when it was refused, rose successfully in arms. Mr. Forster was inclined to support the annexation mainly because he thought that in this way only could the black natives be protected from cruelties and virtual slavery at the hands of the Dutch farmers.[1] Lord Hartington expressed his view in a speech made in Parliament on 5th February 1880. In his view the annexation was not a crime, but probably an error. It was clear, he said, that 'the annexation was a measure adopted by the Government and sanctioned by this House under wrong impressions and under incorrect information.' It appeared that the majority of the Boers were 'bitterly against it instead of for it.' As to the plea that we saved the natives from serf-like treatment

---

[1] Mr. Forster wrote (1st January 1880): 'Once the Queen's sovereignty is declared over the territory we have not to deal with the Boers only, but with the English inhabitants and also the natives. The Queen has now probably more than ten Transvaal black subjects to one white, and has no business to hand them over to slavery or war, but Gladstone has always been consistent in ignoring the nigger, or in only acknowledging him to make a slave of him.'

by annexation, he observed that we ourselves had been obliged to ' adopt almost precisely the same line of policy which was adopted by the Boers.'[1]   He did not, therefore, think that the question should be regarded as finally settled.   ' If it was necessary for the peace of South Africa that the Transvaal should devolve upon us, by all means let that be proved, but if, on the other hand, we find that it would be more honourable to restore the former government, no false sense of our dignity being involved ought to stand in the way.   Our true dignity would be best consulted by acknowledging that we have made a mistake, if indeed it is found that a mistake has been made.'

By the light of subsequent events it seems to be true that the first annexation of the Transvaal, or the way in which it was effected, was an error.   Unfortunately the error was rectified in a way which led, through calamities and sufferings which might have been avoided, to the destined union of South Africa, which might have been reached by a smoother road.   From the point of view of that time, however, the Conservative Government cannot be seriously blamed for sanctioning the annexation upon the information before them, nor the Liberal Government, in 1880, for not immediately reversing the step.   Both were, perhaps, to blame for not taking steps to inaugurate some kind of self-government, especially the Liberals, who had denounced the annexation, but the time allowed by the Boers was short, official meditations proceed slowly, and statesmen in England were pre-occupied with the close of one Ministry and the beginning of another.

In the case of the Zulu War in 1879, Sir Bartle Frere

---

[1] This was a phenomenon which recurred both in the case of natives and Asiatics after the second annexation, between 1900 and the grant of self-government in 1906.

took upon himself more responsibility than met with the
approval of Downing Street, but probably, sooner or later, it
would have been necessary to crush the military strength
of the Zulus. One of the chief assailants of the South
African policy was Mr. Chamberlain. He said, ' in 1806 we
took final possession of Cape Colony, a most unfortunate
acquisition as it turned out.' He spoke of the constantly
fruitless efforts on the part of the British Government to control the action of their servants in the Colony, who were, he
said, quoting Sir William Molesworth, ' possessed with an
insane desire for worthless empire.' He traced the period
from 1806 to 1879, and showed that there had been a succession of wars and annexations. Once again, he said, with the
advent of Sir Bartle Frere, we were in the midst of a war
cycle. Not for some years to come did Mr. Chamberlain
emancipate himself from this kind of view of imperial policy.
More or less he retained it throughout the Government of
1880-1885, of which he was a member. He had been
brought up in the strictest doctrine of Nonconformist
Radicalism, and he spent half his political life in escaping
from bad traditions. Not till 1886 did he find his road to
Damascus.

Lord Hartington treated the subject of the Zulu War with
his usual caution. Amid the clamour which arose after the
destruction of a British battalion by the Zulus, he said, ' I
entirely agree as to the responsibility which attaches to the
Government in this matter, and I cannot conceive anything
more disastrous than that the House of Commons should
attempt in any way to regulate the conduct of a campaign for which it does not possess the requisite military
knowledge.' [1]

In his speech on the Address at the opening of Parliament in 1880, he referred to the condition of Europe, and

---

[1] House of Commons, 14th March 1879.

said that he did not consider it desirable that we should join 'in this race of enormous armaments.'   But, he added—

'if, in the threatening state of affairs, the Government were to come down and say that in their opinion, the naval power and superiority of this nation ought to be maintained, I, for one, should hesitate in criticising such a statement and opposing those demands.   I say that our position is such, and the state of Europe is such, that we ought to concentrate our resources and limit, instead of extending, our responsibilities.   But this is not the course which we have pursued.   In every quarter of the world we have undertaken fresh responsibilities.'

*L'homme propose mais Dieu dispose.*   The speaker was to be a member of a Liberal Government which added to our responsibilities not only Egypt, but widely extended areas of influence both in East and West Africa,[1] and, in that Government, he was to be the strongest advocate of a forward imperial policy.   The destiny of the Empire prevails over the will of the most reluctant, and the reason of the most cautious, of statesmen.

[1] The annexation of Burmah took place just after the end of this Administration, but the events which led up to it were all within the period.

.

# CHAPTER XI

## PARNELLISM, RADICALISM, AND TORYISM

WHILE Disraeli was Prime Minister and Hartington led the Opposition the stage was occupied chiefly by external affairs.   Internal events pregnant with future history were the swift rise of Nationalism in Ireland and that of Radicalism in the larger island.   Charles Stewart Parnell, a young squire of a not very old Anglo-Irish family, entered Parliament in 1875.   He was even worse educated than most of his class, had been 'sent down' from Cambridge University for misconduct, had no inborn power of speech, financially was hardly solvent.   In two years, by the time he was thirty-one, he had driven Isaac Butt, a veteran of seventy-six, broken in spirit and soon to die, out of the chairmanship of the 'Home Rule Confederation,' and, by substituting open war against the English for courteous diplomacy, had all the ardent Nationalists behind him. Youth defeated Age.   It was a fitting Nemesis that the death-blow to Parnell's own political career should have been given, thirteen years later, by the reluctant hand of a still more venerable warrior.

During the session of 1877 Parnell, at the head of a small guerilla band, developed those tactics of obstruction which were to change the whole procedure, and, in the end, seriously to affect the character, of the House of Commons.   It became gradually obvious that these Irish were treating politics, not as a game with recognised rules, but as a war in which every advantage should be taken. The prophecy of Grattan seemed at last to be coming true, that, if the Union were carried through, Ireland would send a hundred rebels to Parliament.

In Ireland, as in England, the wet seasons at the end of this decade, and the fall of prices, gave rise to difficulties in paying rent. Irish members, in April 1877, supported a motion in favour of legal limitation of rents. Hartington said that the motion either meant nothing at all, or it meant valued rents, and a 'principle which involved valued rents appeared to him to conflict altogether with the freedom of contract.' He was not convinced by anything that he had heard that 'the prosperity of Ireland would be advanced or improved by the adoption of an altogether new and untried system instead of that which had been found to work, on the whole, in a satisfactory way.' He would be averse to inquiry by a Commission, if it should lead the Irish people to believe that it was intended as a prelude to legislation on new principles for the purpose of establishing fixity of tenure and valuation of rents. The days of free contract in Irish tenancies were, however, almost ended. The parliamentary and agrarian movements were now in line, and directed by the same minds. This did not happen in the days before the elections of 1874, when the Irish members of Parliament were mostly landlords. There were evictions on the estates of some more hard-hearted, or more hard-pressed, landowners, and there were acts of retaliation. The highway murder of the Earl of Leitrim, together with his secretary and his car-driver, in April 1878, was an event of sinister omen.

Mr. Gladstone made, in the autumn of 1877, his first and last visit to Ireland, and stayed there for three weeks. He wrote some impressions to Lord Granville, who sent on the letter to Lord Hartington. 'I am afraid,' replied the latter, 'that the renewed interest which his visit has given him in Irish politics will not make our lives more comfortable. 'As to Local Government,' he added :—

'I have not the remotest idea what Mr. Gladstone's views about it are ; and I should doubt very much whether he goes further than I should like to go, or than the average Liberal would like to go, if he saw his way. I should like to see County Boards take the place of the Government and Parliament to a great extent in Sanitary, Police, Educational matters, Inspection of Mines and Factories, perhaps to some extent Railway Legislation, and many other matters. But I don't see how this can be done except very gradually ; and I have no idea that anything of this sort would in the least satisfy the Home Rulers. Of course, I should want Parliament to remain supreme, and only to delegate its powers, whereas the Home Rulers want it to give up all its powers in relation to Irish domestic questions. However, it would be most interesting to know what Mr. Gladstone's views on Local Government are, and what bearing he thinks they would have on the Home Rule question. After we were beaten on the Irish University Bill, I put the whole question, which I always detested, entirely out of my head ; and I should have great difficulty in getting it in again.'

These ideas of reform were of value, because Lord Hartington arrived at them through his practical experience as Chief Secretary during three years of Irish history. But any advance upon lines of this kind was thrown back for years by the development upon quite other lines of the Nationalist movement, led by Parnell, and nourished by the agrarian discontent due to a bad land system, the wet seasons, the cheapening of transport from America, the relative scarcity of gold, and the great fall of prices for food-stuffs of all kinds. The Irish distress was aggravated by the incidence of taxation, arranged by the economic reforms of Peel and Gladstone upon a basis which was, no doubt, for the time, convenient to middle-class and manufacturing interests in England, but was most disastrous to the small peasant farmers in Ireland.[1]

## II

The lowering of the franchise in 1867 increased, not only the power of extreme men in Ireland, but also that of the 'radical' wing of the Liberal army in England and Scotland. John Bright was already regarded as a Radical of obsolete type. The rising leader of the newer radicalism was Mr. Chamberlain, a man of clear mind and strong will, who had made his mark and trained himself in the local politics and administration of Birmingham, and had entered the House of Commons in mid-life. He was, above all things, a practical fighter, and initiated in 1877 a scheme of reorganising the Liberal party in the constituencies. Hitherto the choice of candidates and management of electoral affairs had been in the hands of quite independent and self-nominated local committees, who corresponded when necessary with the party Whips, but formed no part of any larger association or federation. Mr. Chamberlain's plan was twofold. He proposed the formation of large local associations on a representative

[1] See Report of the Royal Commission on the Financial Relations between Great Britain and Ireland, 1896, especially pages 10 and 11. The Commission, though disagreeing in certain other respects, unanimously agreed upon this (*inter alia*) viz., that 'the increase of taxation laid upon Ireland between 1853 and 1860 was not justified by the then existing circumstances.' This taxation was initiated, and in the main carried out, by Mr. Gladstone, as Chancellor of the Exchequer. It placed a crushing load on Ireland. The Report of the Majority of the Commission also pointed out the injury done to Ireland by the post-Peel policy of admitting all foreign food products free of toll to the British markets, and raising indirect taxation almost entirely from tobacco, tea, spirits, and beer, so largely consumed by a poor, rural population.

basis in each constituency, and the subsequent federation of these associations in a central organisation. In the autumn of 1877 he asked Lord Hartington to confer by a speech his blessing on the scheme. Hartington sent a guarded reply. To Lord Granville he wrote on 23rd November 1877 :—

'I do not feel at all certain that we ought to give in our adhesion to this federation scheme. The Birmingham plan is perhaps the only one on which the Liberal party can be sufficiently organised in a great constituency ; and I do not know whether there is much or any objection to its being extended to others. But it is almost certain to put the management into the hands of the most advanced men, because they are the most active. And when we come to a federation of these associations, it seems to me that it will come before long to placing the chief control and direction of the party in the hands of these men, to the exclusion of the more moderate and easy-going Liberals. There is a good deal of the American caucus system about it, which I think is not much liked here ; and though we have all been preaching organisation, I think we may sacrifice too much to it.'

Mr. Chamberlain, with whom there has ever been short interval between thought and deed, proceeded with his scheme. Many local associations on the new model were established, especially in the Midlands round Birmingham. At the end of the following year he asked Lord Hartington, as leader of the party, to address a meeting of representatives of these associations at Leeds. The following letters are of some interest :—

*Mr. Chamberlain to Lord Hartington, 22nd December 1878.*

'I am very much obliged to you for the full expression of your views in reference to the Leeds invitation, and

I clearly appreciate the difficulties which you feel with regard to its acceptance.

'I quite agree with you that the first object of all Liberals at this moment should be to unite the party in order to put a stop to the reckless foreign policy of the Government.

'There are many home questions on which it is possible that I may desire to go farther than you, but these must wait their proper time, and for the present I am perfectly content that they should remain in the background. When the occasion comes for their discussion, I hope that room may be found for common action and that our views will not be so far divergent as to prevent this.

'Meanwhile it is true that many Liberals, in some cases from want of information and in others from settled conviction, are opposed to our organisation. It is also true that it has not always succeeded in practice, and it is not pretended by its promoters that it is equally suited for every constituency.

'The fault however, as we maintain, lies in defective practice and not in the principle of the association, which is, in theory at all events, the broadest which has ever been attempted in connection with the Liberal party.

'Its avowed object is to unite every shade of Liberal opinion in a thoroughly representative organisation, and we claim to be judged by our object and not to be condemned because in some exceptional instances it has not been attained.

'In any case the system, good or bad, has been voluntarily adopted in more than a hundred constituencies. In almost all these places it forms at the present time the only Liberal organisation ; and I doubt whether it would be possible to get together by any means a more influential representation of a great body of Liberal opinion than is likely to be gathered at the Leeds meeting.

'Can the leader of the Liberal party afford to ignore altogether so large a section of it ? If he does, the organisation will necessarily tend more and more to separate from official Liberalism and to form a party within the party. On the other hand, your recognition of it as one of the forces under your command cannot give offence to any reasonable Liberal, while your presence at Leeds and a speech by you mainly directed against the foreign policy of the Government would, I am convinced, strengthen your position in the country, and materially increase the enthusiasm of the party in the large towns and boroughs, especially in the manufacturing districts.

'The points in reference to the federation on which I thought you would be inclined to dwell are, first :—That while experience has shown that the organisation has been eminently successful in uniting the party in many places in which it has been voluntarily adopted, there may also be other constituencies to which it is unsuited ; and which being already united under an organisation which meets their requirements would be unwise to make any change ; and secondly :—That the strength and success of all such organisations must depend upon the fidelity with which its leading principles are adopted, namely, that it should be thoroughly representative of all sections of the party, and that, with a view to this, no Shibboleth in the shape of a formal programme should be required, but that member-ship should be extended to all who accept the name of Liberals.

' If you were to take this line, all I should venture to ask of you would be that you should make it understood that these opinions are not criticisms directed against the association, but axioms already accepted by its promoters ; although in some instances they have been lost sight of by those who have professed to adopt the system. . . .'

*Lord Hartington to Mr. Chamberlain, 29th December* 1878.

'I am exceedingly obliged to you for the kind and courteous tone of your letter ; and I entirely join with you in the hope that differences of opinion upon some domestic questions may not prevent common action in the future.

'Your letter has not, however, removed the difficulties which I felt as to accepting the Leeds invitation ; and

they are probably such as could not be removed by correspondence. The more I consider the matter, the more
I feel that the relation of the Birmingham organisation to
the Liberal party is a question which is so important, and
will probably become so much more important, that I
should not be justified in thus publicly connecting myself
with it, unless I were prepared to state rather fully my
views with regard to it, and as to what are, in my opinion,
its defects as well as its merits. How or when this should
be done, I do not at present see very clearly; but I am
sure that the Leeds meeting would not be a convenient
opportunity.

'There is one point to which I think I did not sufficiently
advert in my last letter, but which appears to me of much
importance. The plan may have its advantages or disadvantages as applied to particular constituencies. But
I understand that it aims at much more than a merely
local organisation, and that the Leeds meeting will in fact
be an assembly of delegates from federated Associations
with the object of taking common action on certain
political questions. The party is still, I am bound to
confess, so deplorably deficient in anything in the nature
of an effective organisation either for electoral or other
political purposes, that I am very far from complaining
that the active and energetic men with whom you are
associated should have made this effort to supply the want.

'But, at the same time, I am not convinced that the
system is one which can ever be applied successfully to the
whole party; and it is certain that it at present represents
one section only of the party which I endeavour to lead as
a whole in the House of Commons. For this reason I
think that it would be unwise for me openly to connect
myself with your association, until I am convinced that
no more general organisation is practicable.

'I am sorry that, after full reflection, I have been unable to comply with the wish which you have, I am sure
with the general interests of the party in view, so kindly
expressed.'

Mr. Chamberlain's 'new model' was, no doubt, suited to modern conditions, so far as regards the local associations for choice and election of candidates in large towns. It is a question whether either the National Liberal Federation, or the corresponding organisation on the Conservative side, has served any purpose more formidable than that of distributing literature, periodically bringing active local politicians together to hear a leader speak, and giving an appearance of party unity which is often fallacious. Englishmen are incapable of sustained interest in a body which has no definite powers or functions.[1]

Towards the end of the session of 1879 Lord Hartington had 'a row with Chamberlain and the Radicals,' as he called it in a letter to Lord Granville. The cause was the question of physical punishments in the army. Chamberlain and Parnell were in alliance on this question, and Hartington was in some degree opposed to their wishes. It was on this occasion that Mr. Chamberlain described Lord Hartington as 'lately the leader of the Liberal party but now of a section only.'

### III

On the 31st January 1879 Lord Hartington was compelled to deliver an address before the University of Edinburgh, on his inauguration as Lord Rector. He chose for his theme the influence of University education in preparing young men to take part in the political life of

---

[1] Mr. A. L. Lowell, the American author of the book called *The Government of England*, published in 1908, concludes an excellent study of this subject by saying (vol. i. p. 570): 'Both the National Liberal Federation and the National Union of Conservative Associations have been sources of anxiety to the party leaders, but, for the time at least, both have been made harmless. The process in both cases has not been the same, although the results are not unlike. Both are shams, but with this difference, that the Conservative organisation is a transparent, the Liberal an opaque, sham.'

the nation.   Recent events, he said, had indicated the great share in the government of the world exercised by the people of these islands.

'While the vastness of that share excites in different minds different emotions; whilst various opinions are held as to the responsibilities undertaken, and the means of meeting them; as to the advantages conferred upon our own people and those with whom we are connected; as to the expediency of extending and strengthening on the one hand, or, on the other, of diminishing and loosening the ties which bind us to different communities, no one can for a moment doubt that it is the duty of a courageous and intelligent people to look boldly in the face the extent and nature of those responsibilities, together with the means at their disposal for undertaking them.'

He referred to the school of Scottish thinkers, Adam Smith, James Mackintosh, Dugald Stewart, who had done so much to formulate the accepted political doctrine, and warned his hearers that, in the faithless South, attacks were beginning to be made against the first principles upon which that fabric rested.

'Certainly, at this moment there are not wanting signs that principles which we imagined had been settled for us—one nearly two hundred years ago, the other more recently, but not less conclusively, about the middle of this century—are not yet quite safe from the dangers of reactionary onslaught.'

The older doctrine in peril was that, dating from 1688, of government by party leaders as opposed to government by the Crown; the younger doctrine was that of Free Trade, against the principles of which, he said, 'whispers have begun to circulate.'

'What,' he asked, 'would be the feelings and reflections of those early political reformers in Scotland, to whom I have referred, if they could learn that now, in the latter days of the nineteenth century, doubts are openly expressed of the merits of their system? that we are invited to go back to first principles, and discover by what combination the rival principles of force and opinion can be brought into harmony; that we are told that party government is an excrescence due to the unnatural conduct of former sovereigns which constituted a temporary eclipse of the Crown; that, in fact, the representative element has already nearly disappeared, and that by the Reform Act of 1832 the sovereign was once more brought into direct personal contact with his subjects in a government resting almost entirely on opinion; and finally that it can be proved from reason and experience that a House of Commons elected on the principle of numerical representation is utterly un-qualified for the functions which its flatterers would thrust upon it, those functions being not only to decide on the direction of its internal interests, but to originate and control the course of foreign policy. When such doctrines as these can be gravely put forward, it seems to me that the future may have in store for us issues to be decided not less momentous than any which may have had to be decided by our forefathers.'

These doctrines had recently been set forth in an article called 'The Crown and the Constitution,' published in the *Quarterly Review*. It alleged, in the words quoted by Lord Hartington, that the House of Commons was incapable of forming a sound judgment on foreign policy, and illustrated this position by reference to recent history. It contained other views opposed to Whig principles, such as 'there is a perpetual gravitation of the Crown and the People towards each other, tending to close up the breach that was made in the royal authority by the Revolution.' ... 'Strong monarchs have always been popular in England,' and so forth. The article was in reply to an ably written pamphlet by 'Verax,' which imputed as an accusation to the age those tendencies vindicated and eulogised by the *Quarterly* Reviewer. 'Verax' had assailed the lately published third volume of Theodore Martin's *Life of the Prince Consort*, both because its revelations disclosed anti-Russian feelings at Court, and because the entire work, in his opinion, seemed 'intended to enshrine a courtly theory of the Constitution, to exalt the prerogatives of the Crown, to debase the position of the Cabinet, and to familiarise us with the interference of an autocratic will in counsels of men who have hitherto been regarded as responsible, not to the Queen, but to the nation.' The danger in that particular quarter was slight indeed, but in London, and in the English Universities, and in Germany, a strong tide of historical and political thought was certainly flowing in a direction opposite to that taken by former Scottish philosophy. Thomas Carlyle was no longer a solitary voice crying in the wilderness. Froude and Maine, Seeley and Mommsen, influenced the younger political thought, and, in a more popular way, the novels of Disraeli had done much to undermine the orthodox Whig tradition. Imitating the old Tory-Radical Cobbett without acknowledgment, he dared to deride the cause for which 'Hampden died on the field and Sydney on the scaffold,' as being that of the government of England by a Whig oligarchy. His idea was that, if much were done to improve the material condition of the working classes, they, on their side, might support those leaders who were in favour of a strong imperial policy, and were opposed to the views and ideals, so powerful between 1830 and 1867, of the nonconformist and individualistic part of the middle classes. It was upon these grounds that he persuaded his party to accept the extension of the franchise in 1867. After his death Lord Randolph Churchill became the recognised exponent of 'Tory democracy.' These tendencies coincided with the growing idea, due to closer identification through extended suffrage of the House with the People, that the Commons were, not a ruling assembly but, a body of delegates who could only act in large matters upon special 'mandates' given to them by the electorate, and with the view also that the business of the House of Lords was to see that the House of Commons did not act without, or go beyond, such mandates. Sidonia, in Disraeli's novel, says to the young Coningsby, instructing him in the wisdom of this world :—

'The tendency of advanced civilisation is in truth to pure Monarchy. Monarchy is indeed a government which requires a high degree of civilisation for its full development. It needs the support of free laws and manners, and of a widely diffused intelligence. Your House of Commons, that has absorbed all other powers in the State, will in all probability fall more rapidly than it rose. Public opinion has a more direct, a more comprehensive, a more efficient organ for its utterance than a body of men sectionally chosen. The printing-press absorbs in a great degree the duties of the Sovereign, the Priest, the Parliament ; it controls, it educates, it discusses. That public opinion, when it acts, would appear in the form of one who has no class interest.'

And Coningsby, retailing the Sidonian wisdom, as though his own, to his college friend, says :—

'Parliamentary representation was the device of a ruder age, to which it was admirably adapted, when there was a leading class in the community, but it exhibits many signs of desuetude. It is controlled by a system of representation, more vigorous and comprehensive, which absorbs its duties and fulfils them more efficiently, and in which discussion is pursued on fairer terms, and often with more depth and information. . . . If we are forced to revolutions, let us propose to our consideration the idea of a free monarchy, established on fundamental laws, itself the apex of a vast pile of municipal and local government, ruling an educated people, represented by a free and intellectual Press.'

If ever we were '*forced to revolutions*,' the gate would, indeed, be open to all ideas, and this, among others, would certainly be worth consideration.

# CHAPTER XII

## THE ELECTIONS OF 1880 AND THEIR RESULT

IN the autumn of 1879 the House of Commons was nearly six years old, and a dissolution was evidently close at hand. Neither Hartington nor Granville expected more than a moderate gain of seats; Harcourt was more sanguine. It was a great autumn for oratory in provincial centres. Lord Hartington spoke at Newcastle in September, and in October he invaded Lancashire, and spoke at Liverpool and Manchester. Harcourt had written to him, 'you must give up Newmarket and all your favourite sins, and give yourself up entirely to your Manchester speech.' He accepted an invitation to stay, on this occasion, with Lord Derby at Knowsley. This was taken as a sign that the ex-Foreign Secretary of the Tories had joined the Liberal party. 'In my belief,' wrote Harcourt, 'his open adhesion is the gain of half Lancashire.' Lord Hartington felt pleased neither with his own speeches nor with the situation. He wrote to Lord Granville from Devonshire House on 28th October :—

'Thanks for your letter. I have never looked at the report of my Friday speech ; but it was not a success at the time. It was exceedingly dull, and the audience showed that they thought so ; though they behaved very well. It was too long, and not well got up ; and having a bad cold, I soon got tired, and missed almost all the points I intended to make. How I did hate it ; and I never felt so utterly and completely wretched as I did, for a day or two before. It gets worse and worse every day. I hope I shall have no more for the present; but they want me to speak at one or two places to my Lancashire constituents in December. I shall have to try to find some excuse. I doubt whether these demonstrations do the least good. After all this fuss and enthusiasm, the result is that we have no candidate in North-west, South-east, or South-west Lancashire. Harcourt is by way of being satisfied; but I think less enthusiastic than he was. . . .

'Forster will ask you your opinion as to Gladstone's intentions as to taking office; thinks that it would now not be impossible for me to get on as leader, with Gladstone in office as Chancellor of the Exchequer; and that it would strengthen us at the elections if he would say that he would return.

'Finance would, of course, give him a special and complete occupation for a time, and the anomaly of the position might not be so glaring at first; but I cannot conceive any arrangement of the sort lasting; or indeed any arrangement where Gladstone would be in the House and not leader. I don't suppose it is of any use talking to him about it?'

Lord Granville, ever-consoling, replied that he did not believe in his kinsman's disparaging account of his own speech. He had advised him, he added, years ago, to attend innumerable charity dinners for the benefit of his elocution, and could conceive nothing better for finishing the immense improvement in his speaking than 'a political stump in Lancashire. It is almost as good as taking lessons from Coquelin.' Mr. Gladstone had been visiting Sir Walter James at Betteshanger in East Kent on his return from the Continent, and had called at Walmer Castle. On his way through Paris he had been 'interviewed' by a *Gaulois* newspaper man, and, said Lord Granville—

'he brought the *Gaulois* with him marked in pencil, and gave me an account of several trifling mistakes made in the statement. When he got to the bit about the resumption of office, he said what had passed was that the interviewer had asked him whether he should come back to power. He answered "No." "But your countrymen will force you to do so," to which he responded by a gesture which he repeated to me, and which looked like "Alors comme alors." I have not liked to argue with you on a hypothetical case, but it appears to me impossible that you should form a Government without making an earnest attempt to combine all that is really strong in the party. It would be fatal if Gladstone could say, "I was not asked to join" or "I was asked, but in such a manner as showed there was no wish to have me." It is impossible to say whether he would accept or refuse a subordinate place. If he refused, others could not resent it. If he accepted, I believe you exaggerate the impossibility of working together.

'The case of Government is different from Opposition.

'If the Government was once formed Gladstone would lose much of his popularity and weight with the advanced party, and you would retain yours with the rest of the House. If he chose to lose his importance by coming to the Lords (which I do not believe) I should not object to his being first or second.

'I have sometimes asked myself the question whether, if I were you I should press him *beforehand* to take your place. It would put you on velvet if he refused, as it is certain he would do. But the objection is that it would be an illusory offer, and an offer to do what would not be for the good of the party.' [1]

Lord Granville, in his retreat in unimpressionable Kent, did not realise the amazing hold which Gladstone had obtained over the more sentimental or imaginative people of North England, Wales, and Scotland. His magic had evoked a spirit which, unless he were capable of a high act of renunciation, would restore the sceptre to his grasp. This was made abundantly clear by the results of his

[1] This letter has already been published in the *Life of Lord Granville*, vol. ii. p. 182.

northern campaign at the end of November and the beginning of December.  Lord Morley has described it with the
hand of a master.  His eloquence was inspired by a
passionate detestation of Disraeli and all his works.  He
threw in everything, as soldiers say : the support of Turkey,
the 'slaughter of thousands of Zulus defending their
homes,' the 'invasion of a free people' in the Transvaal,
the disregard of 'the sanctity of life in the hill villages of
Afghanistan,' and above all the imperial doctrines and 'the
policy of denying to others the rights that we claim for
ourselves.'  He blew into a burning flame the ever-
smouldering Scottish sense of righteousness, which
strangely co-exists with that Scottish spirit of acquisition
so close-allied with Powers of Darkness.  The attack was
terrific, and, no doubt, did much to destroy the Government.  At the end of it Lord Beaconsfield wrote to Gathorne
Hardy from the calm retirement of Hughenden : 'It certainly is a relief that the drenching rhetoric has at length
ceased—but I have never read a word of it.  "Satis
eloquentiae sapientiae parum."'  Whether or not Gladstone had overthrown the Tories by this campaign, he
had certainly thereby resumed the virtual leadership of the
main host of the Liberals, and Hartington was convinced
that it was useless and mischievous any longer to divide
the form of power from the substance.  He wrote to Lord
Granville from Sandringham on 2nd December :—

> 'I wish I could have seen you sooner, and must try to
> find time to write my sentiments to you.  I think that it is
> quite clear that after the Scotch campaign, and the effect
> it has had in the country and on the party, it is absolutely
> necessary that the offer which you once suggested I
> should make to Gladstone should be made without much
> delay.
> 'The only difficulty is the form and way in which it

should be made, and I am inclined to think that it should be by an absolute and irrevocable resignation, so that he might not anticipate me by offering to retire himself, which of course would be fatal to me and everybody at the present moment.

'I need not say that I am not influenced in this by any hints and advice here, though I have a message from Forster on the subject.'

Lord Granville replied that, in his opinion, an absolute resignation would be injurious to the prospects of the party. 'Your resignation would throw much cold water upon the party, and would be used with tremendous effect by the Tories and by the lukewarm Liberals.' He thought that it would be difficult to throw upon Gladstone the whole responsibility, or to avoid the appearance of hostility and of some pique and jealousy. But, Lord Granville added, 'Your position in any case is a great one, whatever you may think.'

Lord Hartington replied on the 7th December :—

'Possibly it would be a mistake to begin with an irrevocable resignation. What is essential is to start with a fixed determination to meet the refusal, which would probably be Mr. Gladstone's answer, by resignation.

'But it is possible that he might not absolutely refuse. The arguments seem so strong that I do not see how he could refuse to consider them.

'I should either write to him directly or (which I should prefer) through you, something to the following effect. The near approach of a General Election makes it necessary to consider what is to happen in the possible event of the Government being placed in a minority. Would it be possible for either you or me to form a Government, in which I should be the Leader of the House of Commons? I do not think that it would. It is clear that a great majority of the party will not be satisfied unless Mr. Gladstone is the next Liberal premier and leader of the House; and it is natural that it should be so. His eloquence and abilities, as well as his position in the country and in the House, and his popularity, point to him as pre-eminently the leader of the Liberal party. Nothing could have overcome this settled conviction on the part of the majority of the party, except the certainty that his health would not allow his undertaking the labour, or that he had definitely abandoned politics for other pursuits. With this conviction in the minds of a majority of the party, my position would be an impossible one. He knows himself the difficulties of leading the Liberal party. They would be enormously increased if, in every case when things went wrong, many would honestly think, and many would maliciously say, that it would have been different if Mr. Gladstone had been the leader; and if it were impossible to contradict them.

'Mr. Gladstone has done, and would no doubt continue to do, much to prevent this feeling. But it has nevertheless existed, and has sometimes made my position very difficult. I feel that the difficulties of leading the House would be much greater than those of leading the Opposition, and the consequences of failure would be much more serious. In short, there is not room for argument about the proposition that the man who leads the Liberal party out of doors ought to lead it in Parliament.

'The remarkable feeling which has been excited by his late speeches is to a great extent the expression of this conviction in the mind of the party. If we are convinced, as I think that we must be, that Mr. Gladstone is the only possible Prime Minister, it seems to me that it is only fair to the Queen, to the country, to the party, and to myself, that this should be acknowledged at once. Nothing can be gained by continuing an arrangement which we know to be an artificial one, and which must break down when exposed to the test of the responsibility which the Opposition ought always to have in view.

'I think that something of this kind would do to begin with. The real difficulty is what is to be done in answer to a refusal; and it is with regard to this contingency that I think I ought to be prepared to insist on my resignation, whatever course he may take. It might then be necessary to speak a little more plainly, and to point out that he must bear the responsibility of his own actions; that he has almost continually since his resignation chosen to act in most important matters as the leader of the party out of doors; that he has done so more conspicuously than ever during the last few weeks; that such a course renders my position intolerable, of which I do not complain, but only point out in order to show that if he refuses to resume the nominal position, which he now occupies virtually, the responsibility of leaving the party without leadership does not rest with me, but with the man who has created the position. But I hope this may be unnecessary.'

Sir William Harcourt wrote (15th December 1879) to Lord Hartington that he was much alarmed by the prospect.

'All I can say is that I hope most earnestly you will not flinch from the position you have filled at times when others shrank from the heat and burthen of the day. We have stuck to you, and I hope you will stick to us. For my part, my sentiments on this subject are unaltered.'

It was decided at a meeting of Liberal leaders, held at Devonshire House on the 16th December, that no formal communication should be made to Mr. Gladstone at present. The meeting was no doubt influenced by the expert opinion of the Liberal 'Whip,' Mr. Adam. He thought that, although, if Gladstone remained in Parliament, there could be no Liberal Government except with him as Prime Minister, yet it would be better that the election should be fought under the leadership of Hartington, for, he wrote, 'those who follow Mr. Gladstone will all join him in following Hartington, whereas there are many who call themselves moderate Liberals, but who would not move a finger to support Mr. Gladstone.' This has always been the strength of the Whig minority in the Liberal party, that nothing in their fundamental principles prevents them from withdrawing their support, if the Radicals move too fast.

Mr. Gladstone, in a letter of the 29th November to Mr. Bright,[1] had given strong and really convincing reasons why he should resist any popular call for his resumption of leadership. They were, shortly, that his health and strength (at the age of seventy) would be unequal to the strain, that the work to be done was formidable; that a Liberal Government under himself 'would be the object from the first of an amount and kind of hostility such as materially to prejudice its acts and weaken, or, in given circumstances, neutralise its power for good; that he was bound by honour to render a loyal allegiance to Granville as leader of the party, and to Hartington as leader in the Commons; that it would be odious to him to force himself, or to be forced, upon the Queen. Gladstone wrote this letter in the midst of his Midlothian campaign. In a letter to Lord Wolverton on the 18th December he made it clear that his renunciation was not absolute, and that the question of leadership must be considered 'in connection with what may appear at the dissolution to be the sense of the country.'[2] After the dissolution, on March 14, 1880, Mr. Gladstone wrote to Lord Acton, 'a clear answer from the nation, a clear answer in the right

---

[1] Given in the *Life of Gladstone*, vol. ii. p. 599.
[2] *Life of Gladstone*, vol. ii. pp. 603, 608.

sense, and a decisive accession of the Liberal party to power without me, this is what I hope and pray.' If the voice of the people is the voice of God, the prayer was answered in the negative. A month after this letter was written the writer was being forced by the weight of opinion in the Liberal party, and, perhaps, by the larger power of national expectation, upon the service of a most reluctant Sovereign. To have refused to obey so great an impelling force he must have possessed the magnanimity, and real preference for private over public life, of a George Washington. Those virtues were not among the great qualities of Gladstone. He had persuaded himself that he wished to retire and 'faire son salut,' but, at bottom, he never did. For he who wills the end wills the means, and, if he does not take the means, he does not really will the end. The means in Gladstone's case would have been to retire from the House of Commons. But he had sub-consciously the will to rule by no means finally 'mortified.' Hartington, who had a real distaste for leadership, was forced to undertake it in 1875, because Gladstone then had persuaded himself that he no longer desired to lead. He was deprived of the rewarding honour, to which no man can be absolutely indifferent, that of being First Minister, because Gladstone had recovered from his illusion. In public, as in private life, there are troubles to be undergone by those who are attached by bonds to the company of 'genius.' [1]

---

[1] Some of Mr. Gladstone's most ardent followers anticipated a different course of events. Mr. Mundella wrote to Lord Hartington, 15th January 1880, that he had 'seen Morley, whose admiration and respect for Mr. Gladstone is unbounded, but he is looking forward to his playing the part of Nestor of the party, and giving to the next Liberal Government the sort of assistance which the late Marquis of Lansdowne gave to the Government with which he was associated in his later life.' Lord Morley in his *Life* indicates a certain regret that Mr. Gladstone did not choose such a course. But the rôle of Nestor was the last which Mr. Gladstone was qualified to fill. He was rather Achilles.

II

Lord Beaconsfield went to the country, in March 1880, upon the challenge sounded in his letter to the Duke of Marlborough, then Lord-Lieutenant in Ireland.

'A portion of the population,' he said, 'is endeavouring to sever the Constitutional tie which unites it to Great Britain in the bond which has favoured the prosperity of both. . . .

'The strength of this nation depends on the unity of feeling which should pervade the United Kingdom and its widespread dependencies. . . .

'There are some who challenge the expediency of the imperial character of this realm.  Having attempted, and failed, to enfeeble our Colonies by their policy of decomposition, they may, perhaps, now recognise in the disintegration of the United Kingdom a mode which will not only accomplish, but precipitate their purpose.'

To many men at the time it seemed that Lord Beaconsfield took too seriously the new Irish Nationalist movement, and the inclination of some English Radicals to meet and support it.

Mr. Gladstone, in his answering manifesto, said that this reference to Ireland was untrue and unnecessary, and that the real disintegrators of the United Kingdom were those who had resisted Liberal measures intended to remedy Irish grievances.  He declared, later, at Edinburgh that in Ireland there was 'an absence of crime and outrage, with a general feeling of comfort and satisfaction, such as was unknown in the previous history of that country.'  This was not saying much.  One passage is worthy of citation :—

'I see the efficiency of Parliament interfered with, not only by obstruction from Irish members, but even more gravely by the enormous weight that is placed upon the time and the minds of those whom you send to represent you. We have got an over-weighted Parliament, and if Ireland or any other portion of the country is desirous and able so to arrange its affairs that, by taking the local part, or some local part of its transactions off the hands of Parliament it can liberate and strengthen Parliament for imperial concerns, I say I will not only accord a reluctant assent, but I will give a zealous support to any such scheme. One limit only I know to the extension of local self-government. It is this. Nothing can be done, in my opinion, by any wise statesman or right-minded Briton to weaken or compromise the authority of the Imperial Parliament, because the Imperial Parliament must be supreme in these three kingdoms. And nothing that creates a doubt upon that supremacy can be tolerated by an intelligent and patriotic man. But, subject to that limitation, if we can make arrangements under which Ireland, Scotland, Wales, portions of England can deal with questions of local and special interest to themselves more efficiently than Parliament now can, that I say will be the attainment of a great national good.'

These not untrue observations were taken by most men at that time to be a polite way of saying, without prejudice to Liberal principles, that desirable as self-government might be, it was not in this case practicable, except upon the most modest scale.

Lord Hartington had already re-stated his own view in the speech which he made at Newcastle on 19th September 1879. Parnell had said that obstruction in the House of Commons, as practised by some of the Irish members in late sessions, was only necessary as against a strong Tory Government, and that there were ' *other ways of bringing the Whigs to reason.*' Lord Hartington said :—

'If he means that we shall be ready to purchase his support by concessions which we think fatal to the integrity of the Empire, I can only repeat now, in the last year of this Parliament, what I said in its first session—that I believe that those statesmen who should be so rash and foolish as to offer any concession of this description would thereby condemn themselves to lasting exclusion from office.'

In his election address, issued three days after Lord Beaconsfield's manifesto, Lord Hartington said that the Prime Minister had exaggerated the Irish danger, but he added :—

'I believe the demand to be impracticable, and considering that any concession, or appearance of concession, in this direction would be mischievous in its effects to the prosperity of Ireland as well as to that of England and Scotland, I have consistently opposed it, in office and in Opposition, and I shall continue to oppose it.'

It was clear that Lord Hartington's position in this matter was that rather of Lord Beaconsfield than that of Mr. Gladstone.

Lord Hartington had accepted an invitation to stand at this General Election for North-East Lancashire, the division lying next to that which he had lost in 1868.  His adversary was Mr. Farrer Ecroyd, an early advocate of the ' fair-trade ' doctrines.  He won the seat on the 9th April by a good majority.  His old division of the Radnor Boroughs also returned him unopposed by way of compliment, and in case of a mishap in Lancashire.  He represented North-East Lancashire, and, from 1885, the Rossendale division carved out of it, until he ceased to sit in the House of Commons in 1891.

Lord Hartington fought the election with vigour, and made over twenty speeches.[1]  In one of these he spoke

---

[1] Lord Hartington consented ' with reluctance ' to publish a volume containing this series of speeches, compiled and revised by his friend Sir Ughtred Kay Shuttleworth in 1880.

with chivalrous generosity of Lord Beaconsfield. The passage deserves to be quoted as an example of a good spirit in politics. He said :—

" It may be said that Lord Beaconsfield is ambitious. I should like to know what man who has attained to the position to which he has attained in the political life of his country is not actuated by motives of ambition. No one can, certainly, attribute any mean or unworthy motive to Lord Beaconsfield. We may disagree with his politics, but we must admire the genius which the man has shown under the disadvantages that he has laboured under. I firmly believe that Lord Beaconsfield has had in view what he believes to be the greatness of his country and the power of the Sovereign whom he serves. . . . But while I don't want to make any personal attack upon Lord Beaconsfield, and while I cannot help admiring his career, I believe that the policy which he has advocated was a dangerous and mischievous policy. Lord Beaconsfield has told us that he considers popular government by means of representative institutions to be a popular fallacy. He has told us that in his opinion it is by statesmen and by sovereigns and not by the people that the world is governed, and he has not admitted into his political theory the inter-vention of representative assemblies. That accounts for the manner in which Parliament has been treated during the period of Lord Beaconsfield's ascendancy. His ways are not our ways, and his politics are not our politics. But that does not make it necessary for us to blame the man. If we have to blame anybody it is the party which sup-ported those principles and those doctrines. The Conser-vative party have made a compact with Lord Beaconsfield. He gave to them his great talents and his great abilities. He cheered, and supported, and helped them, and organised them during the period of their adversity, and finally he brought them back to office. In return for that they sur-rendered their opinions and adopted his policy. If there is anything in that bargain—and I think there is something in that bargain—of which either party ought to be ashamed, it is not Lord Beaconsfield who is to blame, but the Tory party, who have supported him in their desire for place and power, and who, in order to secure the discomfiture of their enemies, have adopted principles unknown to their party in former times, principles which have never been adopted under any former Tory leader.'

Lord Hartington was perhaps, like the hero of Scott's *Waverley*, a little fascinated by the spell of the more romantic opinion, but held, all the same, by education, instinct, and common sense to the broad and beaten track. In another of these speeches, that made at Haslingden on March 30th, Lord Hartington made some characteristic remarks worth quoting because they illustrate his personal history. He said that his opponent, Mr. Ecroyd, had declared—

'that he was a member of the Liberal party and a supporter of mine at the time that Lord Palmerston was the leader of the Liberal party, but that when Mr. Gladstone became the leader of the party, and when I chose to ally myself with a man like Mr. Gladstone instead of with a man like Lord Palmerston, he was entitled to reconsider his opinion, and select the party with which he would act. I may observe, as some mitigation of my conduct in the matter, that I could not very well serve under Lord Palmerston after Lord Palmerston was dead, and as to serving under a man *like* Lord Palmerston, I am not endowed with the power of creating political leaders, and it would have been difficult for me to have constructed from any materials which were at my command a political leader exactly like Lord Palmerston. But I have served under and with Lord Granville, who was a member of Lord Palmerston's Government, as was also indeed Mr. Gladstone, and I do not know where I was to find a political leader who would more truthfully embody or more faithfully carry out the policy which I believe to have been that of Lord Palmer-

ston than Earl Granville. I am of opinion that the views
of Lord Granville are essentially the same as those of
Lord Palmerston, and I cannot see that it would be consistent with my public duty to have suddenly abandoned
the Liberal Government and party, because I could not
have as leader either Lord Palmerston or a man exactly
like him.'

In the same speech, Lord Hartington renewed his
pledges against Home Rule. He said :—

'On the very first occasion when this subject was
brought forward in the late Parliament, I, and other of
my friends spoke as strongly and firmly as we could, and
used what we supposed to be the most convincing arguments upon the subject. I protested that I would never
be a party to the legislative separation of England and
Ireland. I said that I believed—and I believe it fully now
—that it would be fatal to all hopes the Liberal party
might ever have of getting a majority, and of regaining
power in this country if they were to show any complicity
with those who agitated for the separation of Ireland from
the Empire. I have repeated that on every occasion when
I have had an opportunity of speaking on the subject.
There is not a Home Ruler in the House, there is not
a Home Ruler in the country, who is under the slightest
misapprehension as to what my views upon that subject
are, and at no time, neither at the beginning nor in
the middle of Parliament, nor when it was approaching
its conclusion—when the Irish vote might have been some
use to us—have we made the slightest concession in the
direction of granting those demands of the Home Rulers
which we considered impracticable.'

It must have been a sanguine man who ever thought
Lord Hartington could be persuaded to go back upon
declarations like these.

Mr. Gladstone also made long and numerous speeches
in Scotland, and Sir William Harcourt bore himself like

a valiant man-at-arms in England. When the turmoil was over the results well rewarded the efforts of the Liberal leaders.

### III

The General Election of 1880 sent to Parliament about 347 Liberals, 240 Conservatives, and 65 Irish Nationalists of varying shades. Ireland still retained 13 Liberals and 25 Tories. The Liberals, therefore, had a majority of 42 over Conservatives and Nationalists combined, and not upon many questions was such combination probable. The Conservatives had a large majority in the still un-reformed rural constituencies, and they carried the City of London, ever since faithful to the cause, by a two to one majority, and some of the smaller boroughs. As the results came pouring in, Mr. Gladstone felt much elated and assured of the victory of goodness under Divine Providence. In the *Memoir* of Lady John Russell there is a picture of him joyfully repeating the old Hebrew psalms of triumph, like Cromwell after Worcester or Dunbar.

Speculation now began as to the succession to the office of Prime Minister. The *Times*, which, on the whole, had supported the Beaconsfield Government, spread a large sail to the Liberal breeze, and showed remarkable and ostentatious acquaintance with the views and intentions of Mr. Gladstone. On 12th April this journal anticipated that Lord Granville, to whom, it said, Mr. Gladstone had 'resigned his trust' in 1875, would be Prime Minister, with Lord Hartington as Foreign Secretary, Mr. Childers Chancellor of the Exchequer, and Mr. Gladstone a Minister without portfolio.[1] A day or two later the *Times* intimated that

[1] Mr. Gladstone, in the Memorandum of April 23, given in his *Life*, vol. ii. p. 622, said that the Queen had acted wrongly in offering the Government to Lord Hartington and not to Lord Granville, to whom he 'had resigned his trust.' As

Mr. Gladstone, under pressure by the other Liberal leaders, might be persuaded, after all, to be Prime Minister, though he would only retain that office for a year or two. This conviction grew daily from one leading article to another. The leading Liberal organ, the *Daily News*, expressed similar views, with an equal air of inspiration.

On the 10th April, Lord Wolverton, ex-Whip, spent an evening with Mr. Gladstone at Hawarden Castle. Mr. Gladstone entered that night in his diary : ' He (Wolverton) threatens a request from Granville and Hartington. Again I am stunned, but God will provide.'[1] On the 14th Lord Hartington wrote a letter to his father, which shows that he was not devoid of a wish to be Prime Minister. He said :—

' I don't think Wolverton's report about Mr. Gladstone very satisfactory. He seemed at first anxious to be out of active politics at present, but, after talking about the great majority, and how much was to be done, seemed half to wish to be back again. He is quite decided that he can take no place except the first, and would no doubt take that if it was pressed upon him. In fact, as Granville says, " he really wishes to be Prime Minister," though I suppose he would not admit it. As I don't think it likely to be pressed upon him, it does look a very hopeful prospect for me.'

So late as the 18th April Sir William Harcourt was still urging the Whig leader to try his fortune. He wrote :—

' I saw Brett yesterday, and I daresay he will report to you the substance of our conversation.

' In fact, I have nothing to say that at all differs from what I urged on former occasions. I have been desirous

a matter of fact, there was a perfect accord and understanding between Lord Granville and Lord Hartington. Lord Granville never seems to have had any desire to be Prime Minister, and did wish Hartington to have the post.

[1] *Life of Gladstone*, vol. ii. p. 616.

not to force my opinions upon you. But at this critical moment I cannot refrain from expressing my earnest hope that you will not shrink from the great opportunity which now legitimately falls to you. Every year of your lead of the party has strengthened your hold upon it and your influence with it. I am confident it is more powerful than you are yourself disposed to believe, and that the noisy talk of which we hear so much by no means represents the true sentiments of the most influential sections of the party. I feel sure that you have only to face the obstacles in your path in order easily to overcome them. And you will find plenty of loyal friends to stand by you in the day of trial.

'The notion that any one has had more to do with the great victories of the election than yourself I consider entirely unfounded. The effect which your address to your constituents in contrast to Beaconsfield's letter had upon the mass of moderate opinion has, in my judgment, been a far more potent element of success than all the oratory in the world. And those who rallied to you in reliance upon your wisdom and moderation have a right to expect that you would not deliver them over into other hands.

'I consider that the battle was fought under your banner, and that you have no right in the hour of victory to lower the flag.

'Forgive my saying so much, but after our intimate political relations now for six years, I felt at this moment I could not say less. . . .'

Lord Beaconsfield resigned office on the 21st April, and on the same evening Lord Hartington opened the following letter, not, it may be believed, without some natural emotion :—

'The Queen has this evening received Lord Beaconsfield's resignation, which she has felt herself compelled to accept.

'Under these circumstances the Queen turns to Lord

Hartington as Leader of the Opposition, and would wish to see him here at a quarter to three to-morrow—when she will ask him to undertake to form a Government.'

Lord Hartington, on the 22nd, saw the Queen at Windsor and advised her to summon Mr. Gladstone. On the evening of the same day, at the Queen's request, he visited Mr. Gladstone in order to ascertain definitely whether it was, as he had told the Queen, the fact that Mr. Gladstone would accept no post in the Government except that of First Minister. Mr. Gladstone replied in the affirmative, and added that, if a Government were formed without him, he would support it from outside, subject to unforeseen contingencies.[1] Lord Hartington did not think it desirable to communicate to Mr. Gladstone how great was the Queen's reluctance. On the following day the Queen saw Lord Hartington and Lord Granville together. They returned from Windsor to Carlton Terrace and conveyed to Mr. Gladstone the Queen's command that he should go to Windsor. The Queen, 'natural under effort,' as Mr. Gladstone described it, asked him to form a Government, warning him also that he would have to 'bear the consequences' of his previous sayings.[2]

Among the papers at Devonshire House are two memoranda by Lord Hartington. The first of them was docketed by him at a later time, in 1893, 'Notes apparently written before first audience with the Queen and probably in substance repeated to her,' and is as follows :—

'The principal difficulty, and a very great difficulty, is the position of Mr. Gladstone.

---

[1] A very full and vivid account of Mr. Gladstone's interviews with (1) Lord Hartington; (2) Lord Hartington and Lord Granville; (3) the Queen, written at the time by Mr. Gladstone himself, is given in Lord Morley's *Life*. On each occasion Mr. Gladstone evidently did almost all the talking, especially on the first.

[2] *Life of Gladstone*, vol. ii. p. 628.

'No strong Liberal Government could be formed which did not receive the support of Mr. Gladstone.

'Circumstances had prevented him from retiring, as he had intended, from public life.     He had, in fact, taken an extremely active part in public affairs during the last three years, and he possessed an influence in the country as great, or greater than, he had ever possessed.

'I have no reason to suppose that Mr. Gladstone would consent to accept any subordinate place in a Cabinet.  He must therefore be outside the Cabinet either as a confidential but irresponsible adviser, or as a friendly but independent critic.  The first position would be obviously an unconstitutional and dangerous one.  In the second, whatever might be Mr. Gladstone's desire to assist the new Government, it would be his duty to form an independent opinion on their policy and their measures.  He would be exposed to constant pressure from the more extreme section of the party, and from all those who must be disappointed in the selection of offices.  It would inevitably happen, sooner or later, that he would be obliged to criticise adversely, or even to oppose, our policy or measures, and I could not conceal from myself that opposition from him would be almost certainly fatal to the Government.

'If the Government should fall from such a cause, Mr. Gladstone would then become the only possible Minister, and would from the nature of the case be called to power, relying on the support of the more advanced section of the party, whereas, at the present time, if called on by Her Majesty to form a Government it would be necessary for him to obtain the support of as large a number as possible of its more moderate members.

'In addition to these difficulties which would exist if Mr. Gladstone were outside the Cabinet, there would be some very strong reasons why he should be Prime Minister.

'There was no statesman whose experience or abilities could be compared with his.     There was no one whose loyalty and personal devotion to Her Majesty were more undoubted. If Her Majesty had ever been led to believe that he had been wanting in these respects, she had been entirely misinformed. When most warmly engaged in opposition to the measures of the Government, and carrying that opposition to a length which Her Majesty might have thought extreme, I could personally speak of the profound and evidently sincere feelings of respect and personal devotion to the Queen which he had always entertained.

'The questions with which the next Government would have to deal were questions as to which little or no difference of opinion existed among us, as to principles, but as to which there would be very great difficulties in detail. Mr. Gladstone, so far as I am aware, entertains no extreme ideas of violent or sudden changes. The redistribution of parliamentary representation, the reform of the land laws and of local government, both of them subjects with which the present Government proposed to deal, and some financial questions, are all subjects in which Mr. Gladstone's power of legislative arrangement and mastery over detail would be of immense advantage. He would be by far the most competent man to deal with such questions, and, to revert to the other branch of the question, he would be by far the most dangerous and formidable critic, if they were dealt with by any one else.

'As to the fact of Mr. Gladstone having resigned, and my having acted as leader of the Opposition in the House of Commons for five years—no one would doubt that a great mistake had been made by Mr. Gladstone in his resignation. Perhaps also a mistake had been made by myself in not earlier recognising the fact of his virtual return to the position of leadership, and retiring from a false position. I might have something to say in justification, but I am ready to take on myself any blame to which I may be open for my conduct in this respect.

'But the fact that mistakes had been committed did not alter the situation at the present time. *Facts are stronger than words*, and it is not the written resignation of Mr. Gladstone but his actual presence and influence in political life that have to be considered. The spirit of the Constitution is that the ablest and most powerful member of the Opposition should be called on to take the position of the retiring Government. That person is Mr. Gladstone. In or out of the Government he must exercise, so long as he continues in political life, the greatest influence in Parliament, and the strongest and most satisfactory Government would be formed by recognising that fact and by connecting the responsibility with the power.'

The second of these memoranda was docketed by the Duke of Devonshire in 1893 as 'Notes before second audience with the Queen.' This memorandum, showing how strong, at his first audience, Lord Hartington had found the Queen's objection to be, cannot properly be given as a whole, but some extracts are necessary. With regard to his interview with Mr. Gladstone, he notes, after explaining what he did *not* tell Mr. Gladstone :—

'I confined myself to informing him that H.M. had insisted strongly on the responsibility which she considered to rest on the ostensible leader of the Opposition to form a Government; and I asked him for a distinct intimation as to his disposition to accept any subordinate position in a Government which might be formed by Lord Granville or by myself. His answer as I anticipated was one distinctly and definitely declining any such position. He also took the opportunity of defining what his attitude towards a Government under Lord Granville or myself would be; and whilst expressing his willingness to support and his belief that he would be able to support such a Government, he allowed me plainly to understand that such support would be an independent and discriminating support. He referred to and justified his conduct and that of his friends in 1855 after separating from the

Government of Lord Palmerston, and thus clearly intimated that his support would only be given while our policy was in accordance with his own views.

'I discussed more fully with Lord Granville what H.M. had said to me, both before and after my interview with Mr. Gladstone, and I regret to say that what has passed only strengthens us in the opinion which I expressed yesterday that it is impossible for either of us to form an Administration which would command the confidence of the majority of the House of Commons. We felt that we could only do so on the condition that Mr. Gladstone formed a part of that Administration, or that he had voluntarily declined to return to office as Prime Minister. We had now ascertained with certainty that he declined the first position, and H.M. refused to offer him the other. We felt more strongly than ever that we should not be doing our duty to H.M. in attempting to form an Administration which would divide our party from the outset, and which could have no chance of permanence. . . .'

At the end of this memorandum Lord Hartington wrote :—

'I felt as strongly as it was possible to feel the responsibility which I had taken in assuming the leadership of the party during the last Parliament. I felt, as I said yesterday, that I might have committed a mistake in remaining so long in what had become somewhat a false position.

'But, after all, Lord Granville's position as leader in the House of Lords was not affected by any mistake which I had made in this respect; and Lord Granville entirely concurred with me in the advice which I had given.

'We felt that we were bound to serve H.M. unless we could propose to her an arrangement which on general grounds and, on the whole, was a better one. We had proposed what we believed under the circumstances was a better arrangement than our own service.

'If from any cause over which we had no control that arrangement became impossible, we were bound to serve if H.M. required it. But, if I might speak very plainly, the only obstacle to that better arrangement were H.M.'s personal feelings founded on circumstances which I believed were capable of explanation. H.M. had never allowed her personal feelings to interfere with the discharge of her constitutional duties, and I trusted that she would in this case be able to follow the same course.'

Lord Hartington's conduct in this matter was loyal and correct.[1] He wrote to his father on 23rd April, after his second interview with Mr. Gladstone :—

'I have just come back from Windsor for the second time, and I am happy to say that my troubles are ended, and that the Queen has decided to send for Mr. Gladstone, and that he is ready to form a Government. I had a long talk with her yesterday, and of course she wished me to accept it ; but I told her that it was impossible unless Mr. Gladstone would consent to take a place in it ; or unless he voluntarily declined to be Prime Minister. She did not like it, and made a good deal of resistance, and made me see Mr. Gladstone and find out positively whether he would not join the Government.

'I found her much more amenable this morning, and she gave way without much difficulty.

'I am very glad that it is settled ; for I have been awfully worried, and whatever place I have it will be almost rest after the leadership. I believe Mr. Gladstone wants me to take the India Office, but it is not settled.'

One or two letters addressed to Lord Hartington at this

---

[1] Sir Algernon West, once Mr. Gladstone's private secretary, says, in his *Recollections*, vol. ii. p. 103, that first Lord Granville and then Lord Hartington were sent for to Windsor. 'The former realised at once that the only man the country wanted was Mr. Gladstone ; the latter, *after a vain attempt to form a Cabinet*, declined the task.' This statement is untrue and should not have been made. It may have been the impression existing in the Gladstonian 'entourage.'

conjuncture are of interest. The Prince of Wales wrote on the 23rd April:—

'Much as I regret that you should have found it unadvisable to form a Government at the Queen's wish, I am glad to hear that Mr. Gladstone has been sent for, as I know it is what you so much wished. It gives me the greatest possible pleasure to hear that your interview with the Queen was satisfactory, and I hope all will soon be arranged to the mutual satisfaction of everybody.'

Lord Suffolk wrote—

'to congratulate an old friend on what appears very fair ground for congratulation, viz., that you have raised yourself to the position of being offered, and declining with thanks, the Prime Ministership of England. . . . I'll wish you what at this moment would probably be the best thing for you, a couple of pleasant days at Newmarket, and a successful plunge on one of your own horses.'

Sir John Rose, the Canadian, his old fellow-traveller in the United States, reminded him of Abraham Lincoln's prophecy, nearly twenty years earlier,[1] and said,—

'the high tone which has marked every word you uttered will have an enormous influence in elevating the standard of political sentiment and conduct, not for the present only, but will be pointed to in after years as an example of what a leader should be, both in the hour of adversity and that of triumph.'

A strongly individual thinker, Mr. Auberon Herbert, wrote to express his regret that Lord Hartington was not to be Prime Minister—

'not because I agree in all your opinions, but because I believe that you will not allow yourself to be pushed in directions where you have not the inclination to go, a virtue which is conspicuous by its absence in political life.

[1] See *ante*, p. 43.

Nothing could have been more justly said.

Lord Hartington accepted the India Office, especially important at the moment because of Afghan affairs. Mr. Gladstone himself took the Treasury. Lord Granville went to the Foreign Office, Sir William Harcourt did not, after all, refuse the Home Office, Lord Northbrook went to the Admiralty, Mr. Childers to the War Office, Lord Kimberley to the Colonial Office, Mr. Forster became Chief Secretary for Ireland, Lord Selborne was Lord Chancellor. The Duke of Argyll, Lord Spencer, and John Bright were also members of the Cabinet. Mr. Gladstone had not dreamt of admitting the newer Radicalism into that conclave. He was compelled to do so because Mr. Chamberlain and Sir Charles Dilke informed him that neither would accept any office unless one were made a Cabinet Minister. Mr. Chamberlain was reluctantly selected and was sent to the Board of Trade, an appointment productive of many results thereafter. The parliamentary undersecretaryship of the India Office was offered to Lord Rosebery, but he did not wish at that time to begin an official career. Had he so wished there was no post, he wrote to Lord Hartington, which he should have liked so much. 'I should have liked my chief above all ; and an official pitted against Salisbury, Cranbrook, and Lytton in the House of Lords could not have been disgraced, while he might have earned distinction.'

An acute observer at the time said that the new Cabinet was three-fourths Whig and one-fourth Radical, but that the Liberal party in the country was three-fourths Radical and one-fourth Whig, and that this fact would give to the Radical minority in the Cabinet a moral strength out of all proportion to their number there. Mr. Gladstone himself, with regard to many questions of internal policy, was by no means a Radical, but rather a Liberal-Conservative, and upon some questions almost more Tory than the younger Conservatives. It was fortunate for the stability of institutions that a man with his immense power over popular emotions should, while controlling the Liberal party, have been Conservative at heart. Except with regard to Irish and foreign policy there was never any serious difference between his views and those of Lord Hartington.

The new Government contained a larger proportion of men of individual distinction, and certainly far more oratorical power, than did its predecessor. Its weakness was that common to all Liberal Governments, the want of essential unity in feeling and opinion. But it was a lovely April, that of 1880; there was a feeling that the period of wars and rumours of wars had passed away, like the long cold winter; and a cheerful and sanguine spirit was abroad in the land. The gay daffodils filling the baskets of the flower-girls in the London streets seemed to symbolise a happier age to come.

# CHAPTER XIII

## MR. GLADSTONE AND LORD HARTINGTON

THE social world in these islands is diversified as the landscape, and the Central Committee which conducts our affairs has corresponding contrasts, especially when Liberal Governments are in power. The Cabinet of 1880 contained striking contrasts, but none greater than that between the Prime Minister and the Secretary of State for India who, in absences of his chief, led the House of Commons. One was descended through English magnates, employed for three hundred years in the business of State or County, in sports and pleasures, and in the administration of great landed estates, and marrying women of like breeding; the other through a line of Scottish yeomen and men of commerce. One was of the fair complexion and phlegmatic or moist Anglo-Saxon temperament, with light-coloured eyes and hair, hands and feet small, body tall, but not relatively broad, brow high in proportion to width, the bulk of head not large, the movements slow and inexpressive. The other was of the dark complexion, perhaps from his strain of Celtic blood, of dry-fiery temperament, eyes large and powerful, black and bright, the head monumentally big and developed, the brow broad, but relatively low, the chest strong and wide, motions and gestures restless, rapid, and varying.[1] If the human may be illustrated

[1] There is a good physical description of Mr. Gladstone in his sixtieth year in the *Memoir* of Mr. Bigelow, the American journalist and diplomatist. Lecky's physical description in the 1898 edition of *Democracy and Liberty* is also good. Pictures and photographs (as well as the memory of the present writer) show the truth of the above description, especially a series of admirable photographs made

from the animal world, one of these men might be said to belong to the slow and sagacious elephant type, while the other rather had the fierce, swift, and intense nature of the leonine species. Suppose this leonine temperament to be, as Gladstone's was, under the sway of a strong religious creed, supporting a code of gentle and pacific ethics, the result will be singular, because as a rule this is not the 'anima naturaliter Christiana.' The natural fierceness, forbidden to take personal objectives, may pass into support of religious or political principles. 'The fierceness of man shalt Thou turn to Thy praise.'

The education of the two was also strongly contrasted. Hartington, like Bismarck, was reared in the wholesome and un-idea'd life of the countryside, amid the more mundane youth of a calm-minded and scientifically inclined University, and under the influence of a few hereditarily accepted doctrines. He can hardly be said to have had intellectual interests outside of politics. His chief had spent his most susceptible age in the disturbed, morbid, and questioning atmosphere of which Oxford was the radiating centre in the 'thirties' and 'forties,' and had gradually worked his way from High Toryism into Liberalism. Something from the dream-like, or ghostly, ecclesiastical region of thought still inspired him and invaded his political visions. Even in Scotland Gladstone was famous for the intense seriousness with which he treated all subjects, great and small, and the true English (and therefore Cavendish) way of looking at things was beyond his apprehension. Lord Hartington once said, 'Whenever

by Mrs. Frederic Myers. Mr. A. Liddell, in a recent book of recollections, notices the curiously different effects produced by Gladstone's full face and profile, and also the surprising heat of his hand. Boehm, the sculptor, who had modelled from Mr. Gladstone, told Mr. Lecky that Mr. Gladstone's head gave him the impression of an eagle, especially something in the expanding and contracting action of those formidable and wonderful eyes.

I said anything in the Cabinet which I meant to be humorous Mr. Gladstone took it seriously.'

Lord Hartington was faithful and loyal, but he was tenacious, and proudly tenacious, of a few strong convictions, and resisted as much and as long as he could the sacrifice of that which he conceived to be the public interest to the passions or interests of party. The drama of his political life is the long and slow conflict, ending in a decisive severance, between his inherited instinct of duty to the Liberal party and his strong regard to national interests. On one question, that of the Legislative Union, he stood like a rock from the beginning of his career to its end; the mass of the Liberal party streamed past him and away from him. At a later date, on another question and in another party, he was again abandoned by the stream of change.

Gladstone's mind was not rock-like, but of the liquid order. It was highly sensitive to outside forces and influences; like a river, it was in perpetual change and motion. If Hartington's soul had been embodied in a Roman noble of the time of the Antonines, it is inconceivable that he should have become a Christian; if Gladstone had been then incarnate he could hardly have escaped from that mighty influence and stream of tendency. This fluidity and impressionability was the cause why colleague after colleague found it to be so difficult to work with him.[1] One day he seemed to have taken up a final position upon some question; a little later some alien influence had supervened; the position was abandoned, and the essential Gladstone was elsewhere, leaving perhaps the colleague committed by speech to a view which, for

---

[1] It was also perhaps the reason why he failed to maintain his hold on three very different constituencies consecutively, and why it weakened at last even in Midlothian. The electors, carried away at first, even at Greenwich in Kent, by the power of eloquence, came dimly to feel that he was not quite what they had imagined.

his leader, no longer existed. Did he, at any given moment, know exactly what his own opinions were? There seems to have been an unusually powerful 'subliminal self' moving along from point to point like a strong under-stream, with eddies and back-currents on the surface. At a much earlier time Archbishop Whately had put this in another way when he said that Gladstone's mind was 'full of *cul de sacs* leading to the midst of a thicket, or the brink of a precipice, without his being aware of it.'

The first Earl of Selborne was not only Mr. Gladstone's colleague through two Administrations, but also an old ally in ecclesiastical matters. His *Memorials*[1] contain a close and admirable study of this wonderful being, from which it may be permitted to quote a passage :—

'He was a man of complex nature, emotional, vivid in all phases of thought and feeling. In all men there are some extraordinary elements, but in most men one or other of the opposing elements prevails ; or, if it does not, there is a corresponding loss of energy. All the contradictory elements in him seemed to move *together*, with equal or almost equal power. Free from the lower forms of self-seeking, he was too much occupied with his own thoughts to give much attention to those of other people. His opinions on some subjects of great moment were in a constant process of flux and decomposition ; and yet he was impatient of opposition to whatever might be the attitude of his mind for the time being. There was in his thoughts about many things, and in his language with all its glitter, an involution and indistinctness which made his footing less secure than it seemed, and his guidance less safe. With great appearance of tenacity at any given moment, his mind was apt to be moving indirectly down an inclined plane. It was not his habit to look all round a question, or to take in with patience both sides of an argument ; when not a partisan he was generally an

[1] *Memorials*, vol. ii. p. 348.

antagonist. He had no consistent or settled respect for law. He had a propensity towards intellectual subtlety and casuistry which was apt to mislead him as to the proportions of things, and he was not a good judge of men, &c.'

The whole of Lord Selborne's analysis is worthy of careful study. It agrees with impressions formed by other good observers. Perhaps the most complete study of Gladstone's character is that given by Lecky in the introduction to the 1898 edition of *Democracy and Liberty*. He cites the remarks of several good observers at different times, leading to much the same conclusions about this strange and remarkable man. Gladstone had, perhaps, in an eminent degree the characteristic which Shakespeare reveals in his profound saying, 'Thought is the slave of Life.' Had Gladstone in his composition too much of the 'eternal masculine,' insufficiently balanced by that other element which makes for settled order and law? 'Man,' says Goethe, 'strives towards freedom, woman towards moral order.' It is a dividing line which passes through the universe, and all that therein is, and, among other effects, gives their distinctive character to men and nations. It is a difference in composition which divides the Greek and the Celt from the Roman and the English.

Perhaps the secret of his fascination to varying natures, the secret also of a certain weakness in character, and of the difficulty which plain men of simple and united intellect had in understanding him, was that Gladstone was, more than most men, of a double nature. As Cromwell, who also blended Saxon with Celtic blood, doubled in a strange and eternally perplexing manner the character of a religious enthusiast and that of a level-headed English country gentleman, so Gladstone doubled the circumspect, calculating, Lowland Scot character, which came out so strongly in his political minor tactics, with a second and fiery self difficult to define. That indistinctness of expression noted by Lord Selborne was a striking feature in him, as it was also in Oliver Cromwell.[1] He expressed himself darkly because he did not think clearly. With so complex a nature he could not, perhaps, think clearly, ' Magnam rem puta unum hominem agere ; praeter sapientem nemo unum agit ; multiformes sumus.' True in some degree of all men, this saying of Seneca was especially true of Gladstone. His multiform mind in action was like a strong, half-smothered fire, burning a slow way, with clouds of smoke, through the fuel. Consequently his meanings were seldom understood. When, in 1845, he wrote to Sir Robert Peel resigning because of the grant to Maynooth, Sir Robert wrote to Sir James Graham, ' I really have great difficulty sometimes in apprehending what Gladstone means.' Sir James replied, ' It is always difficult through the haze of words to catch a distant glimpse of Gladstone's meaning.'[2] The influence of the Oxford movement was bad for an impressionable mind like his. Oxford was then a hot-bed of subtle distinctions and ' views,' where men were engaged, not so much in ascertaining facts, as in proving them to be what they wished them to be. Many a fine intellect, it has been said, was killed or damaged for life in those spiritual battles.

Hartington, on the other hand, as Lord Granville once told him, resembled the French philosophic writer Joubert, ' who says that his head is so constructed that it can take in very little of what is not perfectly clear.' He was, as the French say, of a *caractère très uni*, or, as we say, ' all of

----

[1] There is a curious description of Cromwell by a contemporary, who listened to him for an hour in private conversation, and went away without having understood his meaning in the least degree, although the hearer possessed a good ordinary understanding.

[2] *Life of Sir James Graham*, vol. ii. p. 2.

a piece,' *unum hominem*, and had even more difficulty than most men in comprehending the meanings of his illustrious and ambiguous chief. Towards the end of their connection he abandoned the attempt in confessed despair.

Gladstone, more like a Greek than a Roman, was of the artistic temperament. He had a great faculty for the rapid transaction of business. But, had fortune led him to the mimic stage, he would have been one of the greatest actors of the world. To see him move, or hear him speak, was to be reminded of the finest acting. The great actor is not the man who simulates a passion which he does not feel, but one in whom the expression of passion can, for the time being, evoke the passion itself. Every motion, gesture, and inflexion of voice was appropriate and telling. The whole combination riveted and never wearied the attention, for there was no monotony. He delighted in his audience, and his audience in him. Orator and audience exchanged inspiration. He was probably one of those who draw actual physical vitality from a crowd instead of losing it to the crowd. His power lay less in the substance than in the manner of his speeches. His force was in his personality, almost in his physical qualities. He was not an original thinker like Bolingbroke, Burke, Disraeli, or Salisbury. When he used the pen instead of speech his style was dull and uninspiring, and neither arrests nor holds the attention. But he undoubtedly had that which Fitzjames Stephen once described as 'a good hold upon commonplaces and a facility in applying them'; and he had also within him a burning fire, of which the absence in subsequent leaders gives a sense of something sadly lacking to those who remember those days.

Lord Hartington, on the contrary, was not a good actor, not indeed an actor at all. His speeches only

succeeded, so far as they did succeed, because of the
weight and sincerity of his character. His word was
known to be one with himself; he was, as the saying is,
'as good as his word.' He was averse to speaking, nor
was he flattered by the applause of the crowd. Had he
evoked any loud applause, he would probably have felt
like the Greek aristocrat who, hearing plaudits, turned to
a friend near him and asked, 'Have I said anything very
foolish?' Not to him would have been applicable the
lines which Johnson wrote in his prologue for Garrick:—

> 'Ah! let not censure deem our fate our choice;
> The stage but echoes back the public voice;
> The drama's laws the drama's patrons give;
> And we, who live to please, must please to live.'

Cartoonists and descriptive parliamentary reporters
were never weary of depicting Hartington as somnolent,
bored, and lethargic, and, no doubt, he had to contend
by force of will and sense of duty against a strong and
inherited tendency in those directions. And, although
he was by no means disposed to defer to the opinions of
other men, however illustrious, when he had slowly made
his way to his own conclusions, he was modest, to the
verge of complete diffidence, as to his own intellectual
and oratorical powers. He thought his own speeches extremely dull. The legend was that he yawned in the middle
of his maiden speech in the House of Commons, displaying
at once his coolness and his ennui. 'You yawned in the
middle of your speech,' said a friend to him, according
to one version. 'Did I? Well, I suppose it *was* very
dull,' replied Hartington. To Lord Wolmer, urging him
to accept an invitation to speak at a great city, he once
said, 'Are you sure they want to hear me? Why on earth
should they care to hear me?' He had no desire to impress upon others an image of that which he would like

to appear to be. He needed not the advice given by the Roman poet :—

> 'Nequidquam populo bibulas donaveris aures ;
> Respue quod non es.' [1]

He was never deceived by imagination either as to himself or as to other men, or into taking phrases for things. Lord Hartington, in a word, had in a high degree the character produced by the ordinary breeding and training of an English gentleman, with its merits and defects. If all statesmen were of this kind no great or rapid domestic changes would be effected ; if none were, the far more important foreign and imperial affairs of the nation would be badly administered.

Like all men, or women, of intense vitality and self-concentrated personality, Gladstone was hated and adored. To hosts of his contemporaries he appeared to be a 'warrior of God,' a hero of the purest type. Some, on the contrary, almost believed him to be satanically inspired. Others, like Carlyle, held him to be a mere rhetorician. To many he came in 'questionable shape,' leaving them doubtful whether they admired or condemned him. Some, like Tennyson, solved the difficulty by saying, 'I love Mr. Gladstone as a man, but hate his politics.' The best opinion was, perhaps, that he was a mighty force working, possibly, on the whole, towards ideal good, but that he was in the highest degree an unsafe and dangerous steersman in British imperial affairs.

Certainly his name was more glorious than that of any other English statesman of his time. He was known throughout Europe and America as, in a different sphere, Byron was known, compared with Wordsworth, Shelley,

---

[1] 'Not to the people give your thirsty ears ;
Reject the character which is not yours.'
—Persius, *Satire IV.*

and the rest. The idea of him resembled that held of Garibaldi, not that held of Bismarck, who was indeed his immortal and magnificent anti-type. Gladstone was famous as the protagonist of nationalities 'struggling to be free' (as he said of the Soudanese) and to live their own lives. Though rather touchingly loyal to the Crown, he was by nature a rebel. His ardent and fiery mind could not endure that one man, or nation, should rule another without full and explicit consent. It was this which brought him into collision with every manifestation of the opposing idea— whether Austria, or Rome, or Islam in Turkey, or British Imperialism. He was a citizen and a statesman at the centre of a great Empire, embracing a vast population most of which is not self-governing, but is ultimately controlled, with or without its consent, as the case may be, from the offices in Whitehall. When therefore he was in Opposition, he was violently opposed to the Government's policy in imperial matters. When he was Prime Minister, he was the victim of a contradiction between his beliefs and feelings on the one side and, on the other, his duties and the necessities of the case. He pledged himself in Opposition to principles which, when in power, he could not, or could only in a small degree, carry into practice. Born to be chief in a small, free, self-contained State, like an old Greek or Italian Republic, he found himself adviser to the Head of an Empire greater, more varied, and largely as much controlled from the centre as that of Trajan. This contradiction not only weakened his conduct of affairs, but impaired the sincerity and lucidity of his thought, and made his actions, when they were in accordance with reason, out of harmony with his words. His life was a compromise between holding power in the concrete and condemning it in the abstract. Here was the great opposition between him and

Hartington, culminating over the Irish question. To Gladstone, bred among books and intellectual controversies, Liberty was, after he had rejected his first high Tory views, the essential; order and strong government were of secondary importance. To Hartington, bred amid the realities of country life, and in the sound and sane tradition of a territorial aristocracy, order and strong government were the essential things, the foundation of all else. Degrees of liberty, self-government, and so forth, were advantages to be given to those capable of using them rightly.

Lord Hartington was neither hated nor adored by his countrymen, but, more than any statesman of his time, he was trusted by them. His strength lay in calm reason undisturbed by ambition, or by theories, or by vanity, or by storms of passion; in a quiet but real patriotism and desire for the public good; and in a fair, sincere, loyal, and honourable character. Akin in type to men like George Washington, or the first Duke of Wellington, he possessed that which Napoleon describes as the 'foremost quality in a general,' viz., 'a cool head which receives just impressions of things, which is never confused, nor allows itself to be dazzled or intoxicated by good or bad news.' His judgment was better than Palmerston's, and he was far less ambitious of power and office, but, like that Minister, he embodied very completely the normal English temperament. For this reason, and because it was felt that he was not dominated by party emotion, and was under no temptation ｜to adapt his principles to his personal ambition, and that he weighed every question honestly on its merits, he exercised throughout his career, and increasingly as it lengthened, a very remarkable influence over that central body of moderate political opinion which so often turns the scale on critical occasions. Had he become Prime Minister in 1880, not only would imperial affairs have been conducted with more credit to England, but bitterness in politics would have been far less than, in fact, it was during the following years. The Queen was right in her choice. Hartington, though far less brilliant, would have been a safer Prime Minister than either Gladstone or Disraeli. His judgment was swayed neither by sentimental idealities nor by a romantic imagination.

Pascal says of Montaigne, speaking, of course, of action in the intellectual sphere :—

'Il met toutes choses dans un doute universel et si général que ce doute s'emporte soi-même, c'est-à-dire s'il doute, et doutant même de cette dernière proposition, son incertitude roule sur elle-même dans un cercle perpétuel et sans repos, s'opposant également à ceux qui disent que tout est incertain, et à ceux qui disent que tout ne l'est pas, parce qu'il ne veut rien assurer.'

Some statesmen, in all times and countries, brought by virtue of birth or intellectual power to a high position, have suffered in various degree from this perpetual doubt, this inability to make and abide by a full and final decision. Those are frequently the men of most charming disposition and of finest intellect. It is the character of King Charles I. as opposed to that of Cromwell. It is, in Shakespeare, the character of Hamlet, Richard II., Henry VI., perhaps of Macbeth, as contrasted with that of Laertes, Othello, Bolingbroke, Octavius Cæsar. Neither Gladstone nor Hartington was at all of the cast of mind ascribed by Pascal to Montaigne. Each could arrive at and act upon strong and tenaciously held decisions. Gladstone said on the occasion of the Kilmainham Treaty, with the heroic touch, 'Followed or not followed, I must go on.' Hartington's 'won't' was stronger than his 'will.' His strength lay rather in his power, in the last resort, to refuse to follow, or be driven, against his convictions. But Gladstone arrived at his decisions less by process of reasoning, or of innate sagacity, than by that of emotional impulse, gathering under impressions and influences from without, and culminating in a mighty wave within him, while Hartington arrived at his by cool, slow reasoning combined with the action of instinct or sagacity, derived, one would say, from a long line of ancestors engaged in large affairs of a public nature. He was never satisfied until, by passing and turning arguments over and over, he felt himself upon sure ground, and had formed a resolution by which he could abide. And if to be original means that a man thinks things out for himself, and does not accept thoughts or phrases ready-made by others, then Hartington may be said to have had a mind of original power. The character of every man is his destiny, nor are men to be blamed because they are what they are, but it is for a prudent nation to consider to what type of statesman it can most safely entrust those issues of foreign and imperial policy which are more vital now than our domestic or provincial questions, because they touch the very foundations of a commonwealth whose property consists largely in foreign investments, and whose actual means of subsistence are mainly derived from beyond the oceans.

Lord Hartington began his new term of administration in a mood neither joyous nor sanguine. Lord Northbrook noted in his diary on April 24th that he had seen Hartington, 'who seemed to be rather concerned as to whether he might not be blamed for throwing up the lead (though he wanted to do so before) after having "fought the election." . . . Could not exactly make out whether Hartington was satisfied or not.'[1] Perhaps Hartington

[1] Bernard Mallet's *Life of Lord Northbrook*, p. 151.

himself could not 'exactly' make this out. Lord Houghton talked with him on April 29 at a party at Lady
Cork's. Speaking of Lord Ripon's appointment to India,
Hartington said, 'I should like to change places with
him.'[1] Certainly, if he had gone to India, he would have
had a happier time for the next five years and he would
have made an ideal Viceroy. Strong, calm, deliberate,
self-contained, and afraid of no man, he possessed the
qualities needed at the centre of the official organisation
which maintains our Empire in the East. He was also
well suited for the post which he actually received in
the Cabinet of 1880. Lord Northbrook, an expert judge
on this point, told a friend that 'no man on either side
had finer qualities for the work of the India Office than
Hartington.'

---

[1] *Life of Lord Houghton*, vol. ii. p. 387.

# CHAPTER XIV

## THE INDIA OFFICE

THE new Government, as a whole, entered cheerfully on its career in the naturally hopeful days of April. The Afghan War had passed successfully through the second of its three stages, there was for the moment no other war on any of the far extended frontiers of the Empire, and the elections had caused a brief lull in the growing agrarian disorder of Ireland.

The settlement of the Afghan policy was the first large question before the new Cabinet. The treaty of Gundamak, made with Yakub, son and successor of Sher Ali, in the summer of 1879, had included British control of Afghan foreign relations and defence of the country against foreign aggression, the right of the Indian Government to place a British Resident at Kabul, and power to send British officers to places on the Afghan frontier, the restoration to the Amir of all Afghan territory, except the Kurum, Pishin, and Sibi valleys, and an annual subsidy to the Amir. This arrangement broke down when Cavagnari was slain. General Roberts, at the head of the avenging force, about 6000 strong, entered Kabul after some severe fighting on the way, on the 12th October, only five weeks after the massacre. Yakub sought refuge in the English camp, abdicated, and was deported to India in November 1879, and the Afghan throne was without an occupant. The military executions of men on somewhat dim evidence supposed guilty of the attack on the Residency, and the burning of villages round Kabul which followed, exasperated the tribesmen, and probably prolonged the war.[1] Early in December 1879 the Afghans gathered in great numbers, drove in the British outposts, in fighting which, on one day at least, very nearly ended in a bad disaster, recaptured the city of Kabul, and surrounded our force in the fortified cantonment of Sherpur. They made their grand assault on 23rd December, were repelled with great loss and dispersed. On the 19th April Sir Donald Stewart, marching from Kandahar, with over 7000 men, in order to make a display of our strength before the evacuation of the country, defeated another strong tribal gathering near Ghazni.

Lord Lytton, in a despatch of 7th July 1879, two months before the death of Cavagnari, had explained that the Government of India had refrained from occupying Kabul, because they had wished not to 'shake to pieces all the independent materials of government in Afghanistan,' and not to place themselves in a position 'from which we could not withdraw without surrendering to anarchy a State which it was our object to consolidate in the manner most conducive to peaceable and friendly relations with it.' But this position was precisely that which now appeared to exist for the consideration of the new Viceroy and Lord Hartington. Yakub was deposed; there was no Amir with whom to deal; and to keep an army at Kabul was

---

[1] Colonel Macgregor wrote in his diary of 28th November 1879 : ' I do not think this burning of villages a good plan. It exasperates the Afghans and does not funk them. To me it is especially repugnant, as it reminds me of the days when they used to do the same with the Highlanders.' On 31st December 1879 the Colonel wrote: 'There is no doubt a very strong feeling of hostility against us which all this indiscriminate hanging and burning of villages intensifies. In fact we have not got a single friend in the country.' (*Life of Sir Charles Macgregor*, vol. ii. p. 171.) Macgregors have a long memory. About the year 1600 the Scottish Privy Council ' denounced letters of fire and sword' for the space of three years against ' the wicked Clan Macgregor so long continuing in blood, slaughter, and robbery.' This decree was obtained and executed by the Campbells. Scotland was then much like Afghanistan, as Afghanistan will, perhaps, some day be much like Scotland.

difficult and costly. Lord Lytton's Government, with
sanction from London, had decided that, whoever might
become Amir, they would no longer insist upon a British
Resident at Kabul, but instead, as an alternative mode of
maintaining influence, or 'material guarantee,' would make
Kandahar and its province, which by the Gundamak treaty
had been left with the Amir, a distinct state under British
protection, military occupation, and control. The head-
ship of this future state was publicly promised by Colonel
St. John, the political Resident, on behalf of the Viceroy,
in the presence of a large assembly, on 1st April 1880, to
Sirdar Sher Ali Khan, who had for some time been the
'Wali,' or Governor, of Kandahar.

As to the Amir-ship, Lord Lytton had been through Lepel
Griffin at Kabul in communication with Abdurrahman Khan.
This prince was a nephew of the late Amir, Sher Ali; he
had been chased out of the country, in the civil wars, by
his uncle; and had spent the last eleven years as an exile in
Russian Turkestan. His name was popular; he could raise,
it was believed, the fighting clansmen of Kohistan and the
great men of the north country. It was thought that, if
some weaker claimant were placed on the throne, Abdurrahman, with or without the aid of his Russian patrons, would
soon overthrow him, and so create an embarrassing situation. Native envoys were sent to Khanabad to sound the
intentions of the exiled prince. Another pretender was
Ayub, a son of the Amir Sher Ali, and brother of the
unsuccessful Yakub. He was then in possession of Herat.
Such was the position when Lord Hartington took up
his duties at the India Office, at the end of April 1880,
and Lord Ripon was appointed to succeed Lord Lytton,
who cabled his resignation on the fall of the Beaconsfield
Administration.

The new Government were more or less committed, by

the declarations made before the elections, to reverse the decision of their predecessors as to Kandahar. The Queen communicated to Lord Hartington her earnest hope that no sudden change of policy would follow on Lord Ripon's arrival in India.[1] Such a change would be 'most disastrous and would give rise to serious troubles.' Lord Hartington assured her Majesty that he had no intention of proposing any sudden turn of the wheel without full consultation with Lord Ripon, his advisers in the department, and his colleagues in the Cabinet. Lord Lytton in a despatch had treated the separation of Kandahar as an accomplished fact which could not be reversed. Lord Hartington, in his long despatch of 21st May, declined to take this view. He said, after a terse description of the existing position, in a paragraph which sounds like his own writing :—

'It appears that, as the result of two successful campaigns, of the employment of an enormous force and the expenditure of large sums of money, all that has yet been accomplished is the disintegration of the State which it was desired to see strong, friendly, and independent, the assumption of fresh and unwelcome liabilities in regard to one of its provinces, and a condition of anarchy throughout the remainder of the country.'

The Government, the despatch continued, fully recognised that a too hasty withdrawal, either from Kabul or Kandahar, would probably lead to a prolonged civil war, and that the indispensable preliminary to withdrawal was the dispersion of any considerable hostile force in the field. It was, however, their desire that Afghan territory should be evacuated so soon as it appeared 'possible to entertain the hope that the prospect of a stable government has been secured.' The despatch stated the arguments for

[1] Sir H. Ponsonby to Lord Hartington, 29th April 1880.

and against Lord Lytton's scheme of dividing Afghanistan into two independent provinces, and expressed the view that, since no Amir at Kabul could acquiesce in the loss of this fertile and important province, such a policy would involve the necessity of giving permanent military support to the ruler of Kandahar, 'a liability to which Her Majesty's Government would entertain the greatest objection.'

Lord Lytton's Government had weakened their own position as to the retention of Kandahar by the reasons given in their despatch of 7th July 1879 for their decision, at that time, to withdraw from its occupation. They had then written :—

'Kandahar is now easily accessible from our advanced position in Pishin, and can, at any time, be occupied without difficulty, but the permanent occupation of it (involving the maintenance of long lines of communication) would have considerably increased our military expenditure without strengthening our military position.' . . . 'It is, however, mainly on political grounds that the retention of Kandahar was excluded from the conditions of the Treaty of Gundamak. Such a condition would have been extremely painful to the Amir, and detrimental to the strength and credit of his Government. Without Kandahar it would be difficult for the central authority at Kabul to maintain any effective hold upon Herat ; and the foreign occupation of so important a city, in the interior of his dominions, would have been inconsistent with those relations of friendship and mutual confidence which the treaty was designed to establish between the British Government and the Amir of Afghanistan.'

The question was whether the failure to establish a permanent British Resident at Kabul did, as Lord Lytton considered, destroy the force of these considerations.

Lord Ripon reached Simla at the critical moment in

the negotiations with Abdurrahman which had been commenced by Lord Lytton.   That prince had maintained a
mystery as to his intentions as dark as that of General
Monk when he marched from Edinburgh to London in the
autumn of 1659, and, in the middle of June, it was still
doubtful whether he came as friend or foe to the English.
Messages of enigmatic import to the Afghans were intercepted.   Lepel Griffin thought that his action was intended
to force the Indian Government to restore Kandahar, and
otherwise offer good terms.   Abdurrahman's main idea
seems to have been to appear to the Afghans as a victorious claimant owing nothing to foreign assistance, and
at the same time to keep on good terms with the English,
and get what he could out of them, yet to do nothing to
irritate the Russians, whose salt, as he said, he had eaten
during his years of exile.   The diary kept by Colonel Macgregor shows vividly the doubts and uncertainties among
the leading soldiers and 'politicals' at Kabul.   Some
thought that we ought to annex the country, that the
Afghans would soon accept our control as well as the
Sikhs had done after the conquest of the Punjab, and
that Kabul, especially as it seemed after winter was
over, and spring came lovely with roses, would be the
pleasantest hot weather station in Asia.   Early in June
Donald Stewart and Lepel Griffin thought that we ought
to break with Abdurrahman, and recall Yakub.   Lord
Ripon's private letters to Lord Hartington show that for
a moment he doubted whether this might not become a
disagreeable necessity, but he did not depart in public
from the fixed policy.   Abdurrahman, as he slowly approached Kabul, made it sufficiently clear at last that his
intentions were not hostile.   The British authorities recognised his assumption of the throne at a durbar held
in Kabul on the 22nd of July, and final preparations

were made for withdrawing the army. A few days later came startling news from the South. Ayub Khan had been advancing from Herat towards Kandahar, and, when he reached the Helmund River, had a considerable strength of horse and foot, and thirty guns. On the 27th July he encountered and utterly routed a weak Anglo-Indian brigade under Burrows at Maiwand, a village about forty miles west of Kandahar. Many of the native troops were slain, and most of a British half battalion, and all the transport, treasure, and ammunition was lost, though four guns were saved.[1] The remains of the brigade fell back to Kandahar, and Ayub besieged that city.

When the Queen heard of this disaster she telegraphed to Lord Hartington : ' The honour and name of the Empire as well as its safety must be maintained. We *cannot* be defeated. The danger would be incalculable.' The defeat was avenged, and Kandahar relieved with decision and promptitude. General Roberts, with 10,000 combatants, the pick of the Kabul force, marched 318 miles to Kandahar in twenty-three days, defeated Ayub, and captured all his guns. The rest of the troops at Kabul were sent down to India, and Abdurrahman was left there in sole possession.

The victory at Kandahar was on the 1st September. Soon afterwards the larger part of the Kabul-Kandahar field force marched for India. Sir Frederick Roberts, one October day, as he rode down the Bolan Pass, crossing and recrossing the river, heard ' the martial beat of drums and the plaintive music of the pipes,' as the band of each corps which he passed played ' Auld lang

---

[1] Out of 2734 officers and men engaged on the British side at Maiwand, 1039 were killed in the fight and flight. Hanna, in his history of the war, estimates Ayub's force at above 6000 infantry and 4000 cavalry, besides at least 15,000 irregulars, mostly the self-devoted fanatics called 'Ghazis.' The Afghan guns were effectively used on the occasion.

syne' to salute him, and saw, with the sad pleasure which
accompanies an end to stirring times, ' Riflemen and Gurkas,
Highlanders and Sikhs, guns and horses, camels and mules,
with the endless following of an Indian army, winding
through the narrow gorges or over the interminable
boulders,' like the dissolving phantasmagoria of a dream.[1]

These events strengthened the views of those who were
already opposed to complete retirement from Kandahar.
Among these were the majority of the Viceroy's Council,
most of the soldiers, and many civilians.  Their arguments
were based partly upon military and political reasons for
holding Kandahar, partly upon grounds of honour and
consistency, in view of the fact that Lord Lytton had
publicly pledged the Indian Government to uphold the
Wali, Sher Ali, as the ruler of a province independent of
Kabul.  Lord Ripon, at first, thought that the second of
these arguments was conclusive.  He wrote to Lord
Hartington on the 6th July 1880, before Maiwand: 'It
seems to me that we are bound by Lytton's engagement
to see Sher Ali through the present crisis, and that, being
now in possession of the districts of Sibi and Pishin, it
will be sound policy to keep them.'  Subsequent events
showed the weakness of the Wali's position and the difficulty of supporting him.  It was also clear that Abdurrahman would not be content without the restoration of
Kandahar, and might have a difficulty in maintaining himself
on his throne if he consented to its surrender.  Lord
Hartington, at the end of July, had given full discretion
to Lord Ripon to reconsider the engagement with the Wali,
Sher Ali, and, if he thought good, to offer Kandahar to Abdurrahman.  Lord Ripon wrote on the 1st August to Lord
Hartington that events had convinced him that the Wali
was a ' mere man of straw, and that his chance of con-

[1] *Forty-one Years in India*, by Lord Roberts, vol. ii. p. 373.

solidating his power within a reasonable time is of the smallest.' He appeared to have no hold on the country, and to depend entirely on the British troops. Lord Ripon felt that we should maintain our agreements with scrupulous faith, but that these engagements were made on the supposition, now disproved, that Sher Ali had a substantial position of his own in the country. But Lord Ripon showed his intellectual honesty by adding that, from the point of view of ease, the transfer of Kandahar to Abdurrahman was so seductive, that he felt bound to allow time for ripening of consideration.

The Viceroy, in a telegram of 6th September, had put the question which had to be finally decided, ' Do you wish for complete withdrawal from Kandahar, and its reunion with the rest of Afghanistan ? ' He was himself in favour of these measures, but said that they would encounter great opposition in India. He doubted whether he could get a majority of his Council to assent. One of the strongest opponents of this policy in England was the Queen. Sir Henry Ponsonby conveyed her views to Lord Hartington on the 23rd September.[1] Lord Hartington, in reply, said that he could not refrain from giving to Lord Ripon the assurance that his views were shared by the Government at home. He added that, ' unless Kandahar is to be permanently annexed, a policy to which the present Government have always declared themselves to be strongly opposed, and which had never been adopted by their predecessors, the present time may probably offer a more favourable opportunity for retirement, without the possibility of our motives being misunderstood, than is likely to recur.' He assured the Queen that he did not advocate ' a hasty or undignified withdrawal,' but he added :—

---

[1] The reasons against evacuation given in this letter correspond very nearly with those given by Lord Lytton in his speech of Jan. 10, 1881, referred to later.

'If complete tranquillity can be restored, and if the government can be handed over with something like the general acquiescence of the people to Abdurrahman, there would appear to be a better prospect of the restoration of a strong and friendly kingdom of Afghanistan than has existed since the disturbance of our relations with the late Amir.'

A subsequent letter from Sir Henry Ponsonby shows that the Queen's mind was under an impression which was not quite just, certainly not in the case of Lord Hartington, or Lord Northbrook, or Lord Ripon.

BALMORAL, *September* 8, 1880.

MY DEAR HARTINGTON, — The Queen has received your letter and telegram respecting the retirement from Kandahar.

Her Majesty is glad to find that you do not advocate the immediate retreat of the army and the abandonment of our positions, but that you intend to ascertain if complete tranquillity can be restored and if the government can be handed over with the acquiescence of the people to Abdurrahman.

In the meanwhile the Queen wishes to know the opinions of the officers of the army on the line of frontier which it is advisable to secure, and whether they consider we shall be protected if we abandon the advantages we now possess in holding Kandahar. What does Napier of Magdala say upon this question? What are Sir Donald Stewart's and Sir Frederick Roberts's opinions? Has Sir Frederick Haines, or Sir E. Johnson, written anything about the frontier?

To give up Kandahar solely because the members of the present Government, when in opposition, and unaware of all the real causes of war, were unfavourable to the policy of their predecessors would be a most deplorable course to follow and would lead to inevitable confusion and disaster.

The Queen is willing to admit that, notwithstanding the strong arguments in favour of its retention, it may still be desirable to hand it over to the ruler of Kabul, but her Majesty wishes to be convinced of this by the opinions of competent military commanders, and not to accept as final a decision that is only based on political and party expediency.—Yours very truly,

HENRY PONSONBY.

The Queen, three days later, gave way and sanctioned the decisive telegram to Lord Ripon authorising the withdrawal from Kandahar.

Early in October, Alfred Lyall, the Foreign Secretary, visited Kandahar, and, on his return, fully confirmed the impression that the Wali, Sher Ali, could not hold his own as ruler of that province. He found him depressed, and full of fears for his personal safety, and brought back a written expression of his desire to place himself at the disposal of the Viceroy, and to retire to India.[1] This difficulty, on the point of honour and pledges, was therefore removed.

On the 11th November 1880 Lord Hartington addressed an important despatch to the Viceroy stating fully the view and policy of the Imperial Government. The arguments, military and political, which had been advanced in favour of a permanent British occupation of Kandahar were fairly stated and fully answered. The main issue was whether the military occupation of Kandahar was made advisable by the advance of the Russian power.

[1] An interesting Report of this visit is given in C. 2865 of 1881. Alfred Lyall had also visited Kabul early in 1880. He was Foreign Secretary throughout these transactions from 1878 till 1881, and both Lord Lytton and Lord Ripon expressed strongly their sense of the value of his services. He was made a K.C.B. in 1881, was Lieutenant-Governor of the North-West Provinces and Oude, 1882 to 1887, Member of the Secretary of State for India's Council 1888–1902, and died 10th April 1911, after a most distinguished career in India and at home.

'The question,' ran the despatch, 'is one on which those who are responsible for the government of India must form their own judgment upon two absolutely conflicting lines of policy, between which there is no room for compromise. It is not contended that there is now, more than in the past, anything in our relations with the tribes on our frontier, or the more powerful tribes which inhabit Kandahar and the surrounding province, which makes it necessary for us to establish a military post or a military protectorate at Kandahar. It is as a measure of defence against some power far more formidable than any Afghan race that the extension of our military frontier is recommended, and it is both as to the existence of such a danger and as to the expediency of this mode of resisting it, if it does exist, that it is deprecated.'

The question was examined upon these lines, and reasons were given for holding that the balance of expediency was against a costly occupation which might probably lead to further responsibilities and entanglements in a dangerous country. Reference was made to the declarations made at the opening of the war that the British Government had no quarrel with the Afghan people—'Nothing but the most imperative necessity of self-preservation would justify them, after such declarations, in the annexation, against the will of the people, of Afghan territory'—and there was no doubt that 'the mass of the inhabitants of the territory which it would be necessary to annex would be bitterly opposed to the loss of their independence, and to the government of a Power alien in race and religion.' The despatch also said that—

'the moral effect of a scrupulous adherence to declarations which have been made, and a striking and convincing proof given to the people and princes of India that the British Government have no desire for further annexation of territory, could not fail to produce a most salutary effect in removing the apprehensions and strengthening the attachment of our native allies throughout India and on our frontiers.'

If the advance of a foreign Power made it necessary at some future time to occupy Kandahar, this step would then be taken in the defence and with the goodwill of the Afghan people.

'Whatever strategic advantages may be looked for from the occupation of Kandahar, they must be immensely increased by its occupation with the assent and goodwill of the Afghan people, as a measure needful, not only for the defence of our own dominions, but for the protection of their independence. If the Afghans have ever been disposed to look with more friendship upon either their Russian or Persian than their British neighbour, it is not an unnatural result of the fear for the loss of their freedom which our past policy has been calculated to inspire. There is nothing in the character of the Afghan people which would lead to the belief that they would welcome invasion or subjection by any power whatever, and it appears to Her Majesty's Government not unreasonable to hope that a policy of complete withdrawal from interference in their internal affairs, adopted after the signal vindication of our military superiority, will, if publicly announced and steadily adhered to, have the effect of converting their semi-civilised but brave tribes into useful allies of the British power.'

Lord Hartington then expressed his opinion in favour of the restoration of Kandahar to the ruler of the rest of Afghanistan, if he was able sufficiently to establish his position. In any case it was essential that—

'as in the case of Kabul, having assisted in the establishment of that form of government which appears to offer the best prospects of permanence, and to be most in con-

formity with the wishes of the people, the Government of
India should make it clearly understood that the future
ruler should be left to rely on his own resources, and that
it is not their intention to interfere further in the internal
affairs of Afghanistan in a manner which would involve the
employment of her Majesty's forces beyond the frontier.'

The concluding paragraph of this deciding despatch
ran as follows :—

'The mission of Mr. Lyall to Kandahar, and the information which your Excellency has at your disposal, will enable
you to form a more accurate judgment on the details of
the policy to be adopted than can possibly be in my power.
These, as well as the time for the final withdrawal of the
troops from Afghan territory, Her Majesty's Government
leave with confidence to the decision of your Excellency
in Council ; but I have felt it my duty to place on record
in the plainest and strongest terms the opinions which
they entertain on the important question at issue, and the
expression of the disapprobation with which they would
view any measure involving the permanent occupation of
Kandahar by British troops.'

The Queen thought that the circumstances of the time
did not justify this finality of decision, and on the 17th
November wrote to Lord Hartington from Balmoral :—

'The Queen returns these letters, and wishes to observe
that the reason she was so very anxious to prevent the very
strong expressions at the end of the despatch to Lord
Ripon was because circumstances alter, and any positive
declarations of opinion may prevent our doing what becomes necessary and would seriously hamper our action.
*Not* doing so beforehand does in no way prevent our taking
the decision, should this be found to be the *right* one. But
nothing is worse than making declarations which we cannot
abide by without detriment to the interests of the Empire.

'How often, in the heat of opposition, in the desire to

injure the Government, are assertions made and promises held out at public meetings and on the hustings, which are frequently afterwards found to be *most inconvenient* and *detrimental!*

'The Queen thinks Lord Hartington will not deny that he and his colleagues have experienced this themselves.

'The Queen looked at the Proclamation of the year 1858, and sends an extract from it, by which he will see that the expressions are not of a nature to preclude annexation if it is absolutely necessary. "We do not desire," is the expression used, and *rightly*. But we may be *obliged* to do what we do not desire.' [1]

Lord Hartington had not himself been wholly convinced in the earlier autumn of 1880. He felt, as he told a colleague in conversation, that the arguments for annexing Kandahar were not easy to answer if the question were argued upon strategical grounds alone, putting aside the question of moral right and wrong. It must be remembered that the great mass of military opinion was in favour of retention, and that General Roberts himself, while strongly contending that the rest of Afghanistan should be left as much to itself as possible, had maintained that the military occupation of Kandahar was of 'vital importance.' [2] Lord Northbrook was of the opposite opinion. Events on the whole, dictated the best line to pursue, and statesmen wisely followed it.

A further despatch from Lord Hartington to the Viceroy, dated 3rd December 1880, stated what were to be the future relations with the Amir, practically those of the days of Lord Northbrook—viz., assurance of support

---

[1] The Queen's Indian Proclamation of the 1st November 1858, runs, on this point, ' We desire no extension of our present territorial possessions, and while we will permit no aggression upon our Dominions or our rights to be attempted with impunity, we shall sanction no encroachment on those of others,' &c.

[2] Letter of General Roberts to Indian Government of 29th May 1880.   C. 2840 of 1881.

against unprovoked foreign attack, some assistance with money and arms, and maintenance of a native agent at Kabul.[1] One paragraph in this despatch bears strongly the impress of Lord Hartington's mind.

'Her Majesty's Government are not disposed to take an exaggerated view of the advantage to British interests of the recognition of Sirdar Abdul Rahman Khan as the Amir of Kabul, nor to anticipate in too sanguine a spirit the course which events may take in Northern Afghanistan. But they consider that there are reasonable grounds for expecting satisfactory results from the policy which has been pursued. Peace has, at any rate, been restored at Kabul, and the greater portion of the British army operating beyond your north-western frontier has been enabled to return to India. It is not to be expected that the Amir should establish undisputed authority over the country without difficulty, delay, and perhaps disturbance. But Her Majesty's Government entertain the hope that the ability of Abdul Rahman, and the countenance which has been accorded to him by the Government of India, may, in course of time, ensure his success as a ruler, and enable him to maintain and strengthen, as time goes on, peaceful and amicable relations between the two Governments.'

In a private letter to the Viceroy, Lord Hartington put the idea more tersely. 'If there must be a period of anarchy there must.'

The decision for withdrawal from Kandahar having been taken, two alternative courses were open. The Indian Government might withdraw its authority to the old line of the 'Sind frontier,' or it might make Quettah the advanced military station and retain the previously ceded Sibi and Pishin districts. This would give a very strong position both for defence and offence on the road to Kandahar, and so to Herat.

[1] C. 2840 of 1881.

This second policy was strongly and almost unanimously approved in India, both by those who were against, and those who were for, withdrawal from Kandahar. It proved, in the end, to be the compromise which reconciled the former to that decision. Lord Ripon, from an early date, strongly urged the adoption of this policy, basing his opinion upon that of his civil and military advisers, especially Alfred Lyall and Robert Sandeman, the man so well known for his work in Beluchistan. The difficulty lay at home, in the House of Commons, and perhaps in the Cabinet. The Liberals were shackled by their previous declarations against any acquisition of Afghan territory, and against the 'scientific frontier' policy, and Lord Hartington was therefore wisely slow in formally assenting to the retention of these districts. He wrote to Mr. Gladstone, on the 19th September 1880, that 'it would be a strong measure to direct Ripon absolutely to override his Council on this question, and, looking at the difficulties both in India and at home, I think it will be best to give him a good deal of discretion.'

The Viceroy wrote vigorous private letters to the Secretary of State urging the retention of these districts. 'I think,' he wrote on 1st November, under the erroneous impression that a final negative had been adopted, 'I think that you are entirely wrong, but I am prepared to carry out your policy, though I shall, of course, have no responsibility for its results. You may, however, rely upon my doing my best to render it successful.'

As late as 3rd December 1880, Lord Hartington expressed in a despatch the continued objections of the Government to a permanent retention of Sibi and Pishin. But the movements of Ayub in Southern Afghanistan soon made it possible to postpone *sine die* our withdrawal from these districts, which had, in fact, been added to the dominions of the Crown by the Treaty of Gundamak. This was done in Lord Hartington's despatch of April 29, 1881. The Radicals were pleased by the final withdrawal from Kandahar; they had forgotten their declarations against the annexation of any Afghan territory whatsoever, and were now away upon other trails.

Afghan policy was discussed in Parliament at the opening of the session of 1881. The Queen's Speech announced the intention to withdraw the remaining troops as soon as the condition of the country should permit. Lord Lytton made, in the House of Lords, a fine defence of his policy. He represented the possession of Kandahar as a 'material guarantee' made necessary by the break down of the plan for a 'moral guarantee' in the presence of a Resident at Kabul. It would, he said, effectually secure India's only vulnerable frontier against both attack and intrigue, and would lay open the whole of Afghanistan to our arms in case of need. It would enable us to bring by railway the trade of Central Asia to Calcutta and Kurrachi. Lord Hartington, he said, had, in reply to a deputation, given some countenance to the idea that it was immoral to annex Kandahar unless the Kandaharis desired annexation. 'But,' said Lord Lytton, 'the noble marquis is a statesman whose mind is not swayed by impulsive sentiment, and I earnestly hope that he will not allow his calm and manly judgment to be confused by a mere word.'

Lord Hartington's argument in the House of Commons (25th March 1881) rested chiefly on the ground that it would not be sound policy to spend a large annual sum and lock up a large force in a position lying so far from our frontier, and surrounded by a population which had proved its passion for a wild kind of independence. No Amir who acquiesced in the loss of Kandahar could have a sure tenure of the throne. It was perfectly true that our withdrawal might be, and in all probability would be, followed by some fighting for the throne after the wont of the Afghans; but it was absurd that objection on this humanitarian ground should be taken by the Tories, who had entered on the war and broken up the existing system. A phrase in a despatch of General Roberts had been quoted: 'The less the Afghans see of us the less they will dislike us.' Lord Hartington enlarged on this theme. He said:—

'It may not be very flattering to our vanity, but there is one thing which Sir Frederick Roberts has recognised, and which I think it would be better for us to recognise, and that is that the Afghans do not like us. The more they see of us the less they like us, and Sir Frederick Roberts acknowledges frankly the fact that no ruler appointed by us, who is acting as our agent, or who owes his authority to our military assistance, has any chance of maintaining his position when we withdraw.'

We had not, he pointed out, imposed the rule of Abdurrahman upon the Afghans, but had merely recognised him, and told him that on a certain day the troops would leave Kabul. As to the alleged influence which we should retain by holding Kandahar, it would, Lord Hartington maintained, be limited to the ground in actual military occupation. It would be an influence generating not friendliness but the bitterest hostility. 'It is an influence which unites the tribes as nothing else can unite them, and of a bitterness which brings down upon us from time to time the whole fighting power of Afghanistan, and induces them to invite the assistance of Russia or of any other Power.' He gave as an instance the December rising round Kabul, 'where everything appeared to be quiet, when all of a sudden, with scarcely a day's preparation, the whole countryside was swarming with armed men, of whose existence we previously knew nothing.'

In fact, our position in Afghanistan was like that of
Napoleon in Spain when he tried to subjugate a country
where ardent religion was commingled with wild freedom
under the deluding appearance of an absolute Government.[1]
Lord Hartington also said, 'We go away now because we
do not want Kandahar, and because we have no right to be
there, but, if we go back, we shall do so with the assent
and goodwill of the Afghan people to defend them against
some other Power.'    Thus he endorsed the old Indian
policy—to keep Afghanistan intact, as a prickly hedge,
with the prickliest side, so far as possible, turned away
from India.    Mr. Gladstone once told a friend that, in
his opinion, this was the most powerful speech that
Hartington ever made.    That acute observer, the author
of 'Essence of Parliament' in *Punch*, wrote in his
report :—

'Hartington came up (not exactly smiling) at half-
past eleven, and hammered away for an hour and a half.
Every blow a nail in the coffin of Lytton's glittering
policy.  Tremendous slogger—Hartington.  Not that you
see much upheaval of the hammer.  But there is no
mistaking when it comes down, and no resisting its
successive blows.  Hartington speaks as if he were himself convinced.  A little detail this—hardly worth men-
tioning—but goes a long way with the House.'

The American democratic leader, Mr. Bryan, in later
days, after hearing the leading English speakers, said that
he thought Hartington the most effective of them all, and
that the way in which he laid down his argument was
like 'the driving in of piles.'

The Queen, fortified by the knowledge that most of

---

[1] A distinguished soldier, returned from Afghanistan, told the Viceroy that
what we occupied was the ground held by our troops, and half the range of
a Martini rifle beyond.

the military, and some of the civil, opinion in India was against retirement, and that Ayub was once more becoming a danger, still desired to protract the provisional occupation. Lord Hartington had written to her on 6th February a long statement of the position. In conclusion he said that he felt—

'more than ever convinced of the expediency of adhering to the intentions which the Government have announced with regard to this question. The difficulty of obtaining supplies for the Army of Occupation, the restless and unsettled condition of the country, and of the tribes, through which communications must pass, the dissatisfaction caused both to British and native troops by the service, and the heavy expenditure involved, are considerations which more than counterbalance the military advantages of this post, advanced as it is almost 400 miles from the frontier of India.'[1]

These were reasons of a real order. Lord Hartington said in another letter that to stay at Kandahar would be 'to double our stake.' It would have been difficult for the Conservatives, for reasons connected with the credit of their general policy, to give up Kandahar, but there is this advantage in the system of government by alternating parties, that it enables a modification of policy to be made without loss of personal consistency or mortification of pride.[2] The remaining troops were withdrawn in April 1881. This was the end of the whole affair. As Lord Ripon wrote to Lord Hartington, a

---

[1] Query. Was Kandahar more than 300 miles from the nearest points of the old frontier?

[2] An instance of this was the grant of full self-government to the Transvaal in 1906. The Conservatives made, in the war and annexation, the necessary assertion of power, the Liberals afterwards, without surrendering the substantial gain, secured the credit of extreme generosity. Mediæval Popes, when they wished to change their policy, had to call in the aid of a 'Vision.' In England the thing is done by a change of Government.

certain good had come out of the evil of Maiwand ; we were able to retire under the impression of Roberts's victory at Kandahar, the most complete success of the war.

A victory gained by Ayub over Abdurrahman's troops near the field of Maiwand in July 1881, and his transient occupation of Kandahar, gave some alarm, but this disturbance passed away like a sudden storm.  Abdurrahman dispersed his rival, and secured himself solidly.  With the aid of our fixed annual subsidy he made himself less dependent than Amirs of old on the allegiance and goodwill of chiefs and clansmen, and ruled the land with the strong hand, using those methods by which Louis XI. controlled fifteenth-century France.  No further attempt was made by the Liberal Government, as in 1869 and 1873, to make the grant of aid depend upon the morality or humanity of the Amir's administration, as to which grim tales were told.  That which had been arrived at, and still subsists, was the full alliance and constant support for which Sher Ali had asked in 1869 and 1873, without *either* the moral condition of just internal government insisted upon by the Duke of Argyll, *or* the material condition of the admission of British officers, suggested in 1873 by Lord Northbrook, and demanded in 1876 by Lord Salisbury with, in the end, such disastrous results. Experience had guided men to the true road.  So ended this epilogue to the Eastern policy of Lord Beaconsfield. The last speech of that statesman was made in the debate upon this question.  After saying that he did not think the possession of Kandahar absolutely essential, he added :—

'My lords, the key to India is not Merv, or Herat, or Kandahar.  The key of India is London.  The majesty of sovereignty, the spirit and vigour of your Parliaments, the inexhaustible resources of a free and ingenious and determined people—these are the keys of India.'

This was rather a retreat, under the covering fire of eloquence, from the Lytton position. The speech was made on the 3rd March 1881, and the Earl of Beaconsfield died on the 18th April in his house in Curzon Street. Lord Salisbury said of him in the House of Lords that 'zeal for the greatness of England was the passion of his life.' Lord Beaconsfield, he said, had always treated questions of interior policy 'as of secondary interest compared with this one great question—how the country to which he belonged might be made united and strong.'

Lord Hartington, in moving a vote of thanks to the army of Afghanistan in the House of Commons on the 5th May 1881, gave an admirably summarised history of the operations. He described the rapid march of Roberts on Kabul in the autumn of 1879, the fighting in December round Kabul, Sir Donald Stewart's march from Kandahar to Kabul, and his action near Ghazni in April 1880, Ayub's victory over Burrows at Maiwand and the investment of Kandahar, the relieving march of Roberts from Kabul and his defeat of Ayub, a romantically interesting series of events. He eulogised severally the chief commanders in fitting terms. During the occupation of the country, he said, as well as during the operations, 'the troops were constantly in contact, and frequently in collision, with an active, brave, and sometimes treacherous enemy, especially on the lines of communications, and when employed in the dangerous duty of securing supplies.' 'It is unrecorded service of this kind,' he added, 'that is a better test than is furnished by more conspicuous operations of the true quality of the men.' He spoke also of 'the unfailing discipline, the high spirits, and the cheerful endurance which have been conspicuously evinced by the whole force during this prolonged and trying service. They exhibited the most soldierly qualities, and rarely, if ever, has a war been conducted with such a strict regard to the principles of humanity and honour, and with such a total absence of excess of any kind.'

The speech is a good model of dignified, compressed, and unrhetorical eulogy.

A few days later there was a little scene in the House of Commons, which cannot be better described than in a second quotation from the inimitable writer of *Punch's* ' Essence of Parliament ' :—

' Lord George Hamilton succeeded in probing beneath the thick covering of imperturbability which Lord Harting-ton usually wears. It takes a good deal to do this, and Lord George did a good deal. Went back to old questions of delay in producing papers before debate on Afghanistan. Once before question raised on Conservative benches, and plain intimation given of suspicion that Lord Hartington had deliberately kept the minutes back for party purposes. His lordship flared up then with such blazing wrath that the Opposition protested with one voice that they had meant nothing. Lord George, forgetful of this lesson, mildly insinuates the old scandal. Lord Hartington down upon him in a twinkling. Takes him between his teeth and shakes him as a mastiff might shake a terrier. . . . The Government should pay some one to "rile" Hartington from time to time. Very good when he is roused.'[1]

The Afghan War, resulting in the destruction of the temporary Russian influence, the substitution of Abdur-rahman the nephew for Sher Ali the uncle, the permanent transfer to British rule of Quettah and the Sibi and Pishin districts, and the reminder given to the Afghans that we

---

[1] The minutes in question were those by two members of the Viceroy's Council adverse to the views of the Government, and had been delayed in transmission by a mistake due to the suicide of a high Post-Office official at Bombay.

could march to Kabul or Kandahar when we chose, had cost, excluding expenditure on frontier railways, about £20,000,000. It was generally felt that the war was so far connected with European and general policy that the whole cost ought not to fall upon Indian revenues. Mr. Gladstone, indeed, denouncing the war in 1878, had declared that the Indian people ought not to be charged with any part of its cost, because they had had nothing to do with it.

'They are wholly guiltless,' said the orator, 'and have washed their hands in innocence so far as that war was concerned. Can I bring myself to vote that the expense of this struggle, which is wholly our own act, shall be placed on India? I say No, and I will go freely into any assembly of Englishmen, and tell them I say No, and appeal to them whether they will not say No also. Nay, I am persuaded that when they thoroughly understand the facts of the case, they will say distinctly that those who make the war should pay for the war.'

Mr. Gladstone in faithful charge of the British Treasury was not the same man as Mr. Gladstone denouncing a Beaconsfieldian policy, and endeavouring to awaken the fears, and excite the repugnance, of the British taxpayer. He now went no further than to consent that the Imperial Government should contribute £5,000,000, or about one quarter of the total cost.

Lord Hartington, throughout this great affair of the settlement after the Afghan War, manifested his rather uncommon gift of deliberation, in the true sense of that word, the power, that is, of fairly and fully appreciating and weighing opposite motives or reasons, without throwing into the scale personal feeling, until the balance issues in the right decision. It is the quality which would have made him an excellent Prime Minister.

## II

The forward Russian movement in Central Asia had not ceased during these events in Afghanistan. Their forces had occupied Khokand in 1876, and each subsequent year saw some new advance across the Turcoman Steppe. Skobeleff, after long preparations and gradual approaches, inflicted a crushing blow on the Tekke Turcomans at Geok Tepe in January 1881, and, by the end of that year, the whole territory of the Akhal Turcomans had become part of the Russian Empire. It was obvious that the next step would be the occupation of the Merv district, a fertile territory only 250 miles due north of the city of Herat, and a centre of routes. The advance of the Russians, since 1868, had been accompanied at each stage by protests, under the form of requests for explanations, addressed from London to St. Petersburg, and by vague assurances given in return. The Russian Government had fully admitted that Afghan territory, in normal times, lay outside their sphere of action, but it was clear that they would admit no limit to possible annexations short of the Afghan frontier. The history of this question illustrates the law that when two civilised empires are separated by an uncivilised region, their advance cannot cease until their frontiers, or at any rate their effective spheres of influence, meet one another. During Lord Hartington's tenure of the India Office there was some discussion of a proposal that the shadowy sovereignty of Persia over the Atek strip of territory lying between the Russian advanced posts and the north-western frontier of Afghanistan, should, by assistance from India, be converted into effective occupation. This, it was suggested, "might give Russia what she has so long desired, namely, a quiet and settled frontier in the

Turcoman country, while interposing a comparatively civilised State between the territories of the Czar and our own uncivilised allies and dependents.'[1] By this means, it was thought, the danger of collision between Cossacks and Afghans might be avoided. Lord Hartington, with his usual sagacity, disbelieved in the scheme, and Lord Ripon wrote that he had no faith in the idea of 'galvanising Persia, and making her an effective barrier against Russia.' M. de Giers at St. Petersburg and the Russian Ambassador in London at once gave it to be understood that their Government would object to the effective occupation of the Atek region by Persia. They claimed the right to occupy or control the whole region to the north of the frontiers of Afghanistan and of Persia proper. As the Russians had full power to enforce this view there was not much more to be said. Lord Hartington, in the October of 1882, was in favour of a definite treaty with Russia. It would, he wrote to Lord Granville—

'at least mark what we consider essential, and what we do not. We have long been indicating our dissatisfaction at the Russian advances in Central Asia and deprecating their continuance; but Russia knows perfectly well that we should do nothing to stop her. There is a risk that our language about Afghanistan may be supposed to mean nothing more. If we had a treaty, or even if we proposed a treaty, Russia would know that interference in Afghanistan would be a serious matter, and, as regards us, of a character quite different from her Central Asian enterprises, and this would give some chance of her putting a check on her officers.'

This advice corresponded with that which had been given in a 'Note' made by Sir Alfred Lyall, the wisest Englishman then in India, when he retired from the

[1] Lord Hartington's official despatch to Lord Granville, 21st February 1882.

Indian Foreign Secretaryship in the autumn of 1881. Lord Hartington showed, in adopting this view, his own good judgment and foresight. The policy of a definite treaty with Russia was initiated in practice by Lord Lansdowne, after the Russian-Japanese War, before he left the Foreign Office in 1905, and it has, since then, been carried into effect by Sir Edward Grey.[1] This has, in fact, become the corner-stone of our Asiatic policy, and has materially strengthened our amicable relations with Russia in Europe.

## III

The internal relations of the British Empire, close in the case of India and of the Crown Colonies and Protectorates, loose in the case of the self-governing Dominions, are maintained by a few men who have hitherto, as a rule, been more or less of the same aristocratic class and training, corresponding with each other across the world. The centre of the whole network is in a single stately block of buildings in Whitehall. Part of this correspondence consists of official despatches and telegrams intended for publication, more or less edited, if necessary. Side by side with this official correspondence, and often preparing for it, or explaining it, with regard to parliamentary or other necessities of each case, runs the continuous private correspondence of Secretaries of State with Viceroys, Colonial Governors, Ambassadors, and in this correspondence lies the finer nerve system of

---

[1] The Anglo-Russian Agreement, signed 31st August 1907, draws lines demarcating Russian and British spheres of influence through the middle of Persia to the point where Russian, Persian, and Afghan territory meet. By it also Russia recognises Afghanistan as outside the Russian sphere, and agrees to act in all political relations with Afghanistan through the British Government, and to send no agents into Afghanistan. Great Britain agrees, *per contra*, not to annex or occupy any part of Afghanistan and assures to Russia equality of commercial conditions in that country.

empire. In this way it has hitherto been found possible to combine publicity and democracy at home with efficient imperial administration.

The private correspondence between Lord Ripon and Lord Hartington is large, and it shows with what harmony these two men of sense and courage worked together. On the whole, however, it belongs rather to the Life of the Viceroy than to that of the Secretary of State. Only those questions are properly included in the Life of the latter which, like the close of the Afghan War, were matters of political controversy at home, and, except the final Afghan settlement, no Indian question attracted much attention in England during his control of the India Office. One question, however, may be mentioned as to which there was temporary divergence between the policy of the Home Government and the view of the Government of India. When the Egyptian troubles came to a head in the summer of 1882, the Indian Government were directed to send a strong military contingent to Egypt. The force was despatched promptly, and took part in the victory at Tel el Kebir, and in the occupation of Cairo. Lord Ripon had been under the impression that the whole cost of this force would, as on the occasion in 1878 when Indian troops were sent to Malta, be defrayed by the Imperial Treasury. When he heard of the decision of the Cabinet that the whole cost should be borne by India, he and his Council strongly protested. In a long letter to Lord Hartington the Viceroy contended that the course adopted was neither just nor wise. India, he said, had nothing to do with the Khedive, or the Bondholders, or the shares in the Suez Canal; her interest was simply to keep the Canal open and unimpeded. But from a military point of view the Cape Route was almost as valuable as the Red Sea Route, and from a commercial

point of view the interest of India was very small compared with that of England, whose trade, not only to India,
but to the Far East, and to the colonies of the South Pacific
Ocean, passed through the Canal.   Indian finance was re-
covering slowly and with difficulty from the drain caused
by war and famine, and it was not a moment to impose
new burdens.   Lord Ripon gave these and other cogent
reasons in a frank and able private letter, and the objections were afterwards embodied in a formal despatch from
the Governor-General in Council to the Secretary of State,
dated the 4th August 1882.

There was a debate in the House of Commons on July
31, 1882, upon a resolution moved by the Government
authorising the employment of Indian troops outside of
India, and implying that the whole cost would fall upon
Indian revenues.   Lord Hartington cited several precedents for the employment of Indian troops beyond the
sea, and said that it was 'impossible to separate the interest
of the people and the interest of the Government of India.'
He said that the Government of India were, in fact, interested in the suppression of a military adventurer in
Egypt, who proclaimed himself a hero of the Mahommedan world.   He said also that it was important that
we should be able to proclaim to the world that we could
trust our Mahommedan and Hindu troops, and that they
were not merely a garrison of India, but 'form part of
the forces of the Crown, and are able to support the
policy of this country, at any rate in all cases in which
the interests of India are concerned.'   This was precisely
the ground upon which Lord Beaconsfield had brought
the Indian troops to Malta in 1878, and a subsequent
Conservative speaker twitted Lord Hartington with defending in office a policy to which he had objected in
Opposition.   'I never objected to the Indian troops being

brought to Malta,' interrupted Lord Hartington. At any rate, continued his critic, the noble lord was then the leader of a party who objected. Tory speakers summoned up from their tomb Mr. Gladstone's objection of 1878 to placing upon the Indian taxpayers any portion of the cost of a war of which these fellow-subjects had 'washed their hands in innocence,' and cited his general condemnation of any use of Indian troops in our wars beyond the seas at India's cost, which he had compared to a fraud perpetrated by a guardian upon his ward.[1] A concession was, in the end, made to the Government of India, and the charge to the Indian revenue was reduced to £500,000, estimated to be a seventh part of the whole cost of the Egyptian Campaign of 1882.

This chapter of Lord Hartington's official life may fitly be closed by a letter which he received from Lord Ripon when his tenure of the India Office came to an end in December 1882.

GOVERNMENT HOUSE, CALCUTTA,<br>19th December 1882.

MY DEAR HARTINGTON,—It seems very strange to me that after more than two years of such close intercourse our official connection should have come to an end, and that I am now writing to you, not as the head of the India Office, but as the friend and associate of many years of political warfare ; but I cannot take leave of you as Secretary of State for India without thanking you very much for the uniform kindness and frequent forbearance with which you have acted towards me in that capacity. I am afraid that with my eager temperament, and with my very deep and keen interest in my work, and my strong sense of what England ought to do and might do for India, I have often given you a great deal of trouble, and have been not seldom unduly pertinacious in pressing my opinions, and

---

[1] He said this in an article in the *Nineteenth Century* in June 1878.

needlessly strong in my defence of them. I have chafed, I know, at what seemed to me to be the unnecessary delays and the petty intrusions of the India Office, and I fear that I have not always made as much allowance as I ought for the difficulties of your position and the heavy burden of your extra-official work; but you will, I hope, forgive me for all my failings in these respects; and, for my own part, I shall retain in my memory nothing but the recollection of your unvarying patience, courtesy, and friendship. I have spoken my mind with great, possibly sometimes with too great freedom; but I held it to be my duty to tell you what I really thought, and I hope that I have said and done nothing to forfeit your confidence or esteem. My task has not been an easy one, but I have tried to do my duty to the best of my ability, and so far as I know myself I have had no other object. . . . —Good-bye, yours very sincerely,

RIPON.

It may be said, in concluding this very important chapter of the political life of Lord Hartington, that his steady and clear-headed administration during his tenure of the Indian Secretaryship of State, through a most critical and difficult period of India's foreign complications, is memorable, because it laid down upon solid foundations the principles which have since been followed and developed in dealing with the external relations of our Indian Empire—that is to say, friendship with the rulers of Afghanistan, abstention from interference in the internal affairs of that country, and a definite understanding with Russia upon Asiatic questions.

# CHAPTER XV

## IRISH AFFAIRS

Fʀᴏᴍ the sincerities and veracities of Eastern war and statecraft it is necessary to turn back to the internal politics of these islands. The Secretary of State for India usually lives with his thoughts far from England, high above the dust and clamour of the conflict below, but Lord Hartington, being in the Commons, and also second in command of the Liberal party, was forced to take part in these combats. The battle over Irish affairs, which filled so much of the first three years of this Ministry, touched him nearly both as a former Irish Chief Secretary, and as the son of a great Irish landowner. The things at issue were the authority of the law, and the conditions of land tenure. The direct responsibility for Irish government rested upon Mr. Forster, a man of veracity, sincerity, honesty, and courage, but, perhaps, as a defect of some of his qualities, deficient in that cool and slightly cynical judgment which is so necessary in administration. It is one feature of Irish history that while, for a hundred years after the Union, the country was governed much, in essence, on the lines of a Crown Colony, the heads of the Executive have not been men with lifelong official training, like the governors of such colonies, but members of Parliament, usually with no official training, and with strong political principles. This hybrid system was bound to produce unsatisfactory results.

That it has worked at all has been due to the fact that the Englishmen sent over to govern Ireland have, like Lord Hartington himself, usually belonged to the governing class, Whig or Tory, trained in the administration or tradition of large estates. Mr. Forster's training was that of a member of the Society of Friends, a partner in a Yorkshire wool factory, a Liberal member of Parliament, and for some years a Minister of Education. He was sent over to face one of the wildest storms in modern Irish history. The murder of Lord Montmorres and other crimes in the autumn of 1880, and the inauguration of a cruelly enforced system of social excommunication in the case of Captain Boycott, enriching the language with a word, recalled English attention to the affairs of Ireland. The new Government allowed the existing 'Coercion Act,' that of 1875, to lapse. In the summer of 1880 they brought in a bill giving compensation, on certain conditions, to evicted tenants, which might, or might not, have done some good. The House of Lords rejected the bill, an error, since the responsible Government stated that, in their opinion, it was necessary to meet the special agrarian distress.

Disorder in Ireland became fiercer, and Mr. Forster asked for new and drastic powers. He demanded a wide extension of the preventive principle of the Westmeath Act, passed while Lord Hartington was Chief Secretary in 1871. This would enable the Irish Executive, unfettered by restrictions of ' Habeas Corpus,' to arrest and detain in prison without trial, and so long as might seem necessary, men known or suspected to be implicated in crime, or to be promoters of agrarian disorder. This proposal met with strong opposition from the Radical section of the Cabinet. By way of temporary compromise legal procedure of an ordinary kind was set in motion at Dublin against Parnell and other leaders of the Land League. The proceedings dragged along slowly, and at last the jury were unable to agree upon a verdict.

Lord Bessborough's Commission had been appointed in 1880 to inquire into the Irish land question, but though its work was, for a Royal Commission, so rapid that Tories accused its recommendations of being pre-ordained, it did not report till early in 1881. The Cabinet in the autumn of 1880 were divided upon the question whether an Act giving the new powers desired by the Irish Government should be introduced as soon as Parliament met, or whether it should be delayed until a Bill dealing with the land question could also be introduced. In November Mr. Forster threatened resignation unless Parliament were at once convened to grant the powers desired. Lord Hartington supported him by the following letter to the Prime Minister :—

DEVONSHIRE HOUSE, PICCADILLY, W.,
*November* 19, 1880.

MY DEAR MR. GLADSTONE,—Forster has just left me, and has, I believe, gone on to tell you the decision he has come to.

I do not think that you can be in any doubt as to my position in regard to this matter ; but I think it may be right that I should say to you before the Cabinet, that I do not see how it would be possible for me to remain in the Government, if Forster is forced to leave it by the refusal of the Cabinet to grant the additional powers he asks for.

I hope you will excuse this curt and bald communication, but there is no time for explanation, and I thought it more fair to you that there should be no possibility of your being taken by surprise in the Cabinet.—Yours sincerely,

HARTINGTON.

On the evening of the same day, November 19th, Mr. Reginald Brett, now Viscount Esher, then private secretary

to Lord Hartington, made the following entry in a journal
which he kept :—

'To-day has been full of excitement. A Cabinet
Council was held to decide the fate of the Ministry.
Forster came back from Ireland with a proposal to call
Parliament together for the purpose of passing a Coercion
Bill, and suspending the Habeas Corpus Act. Bright and
Chamberlain objected strongly, and would, if Forster's
view had been adopted, have resigned. This would not
so much have mattered, but Mr. Gladstone was himself
inclined to resign with them.

'This was the state of affairs on Wednesday—that is,
two days ago. Yesterday Forster and Lord Spencer came
to the India Office, and at six o'clock Forster left, having
settled to maintain his demand, and to resign if it was not
conceded to him. Lord Hartington, who for the last five
years has invariably—out of some high feeling of obligation
to Forster which does not exist, or desire not to triumph
over him—supported him through all his difficulties, determined once more to see him through a peril, and agreed
with Lord Spencer and others to resign if Forster was
forced out of the Cabinet. It looked this morning as if not
only the Cabinet but the Liberal party must break up, and
I suppose this consummation has never been so nearly
approached before. However, to-day Forster has gone off
to Ireland to see what still can be done to keep things as
they are.

'Meanwhile a supposed arrangement has been come to
which means merely that the storm has passed over for the
present.'

Mr. Forster made the mistake of sending in an ultimatum before he was finally determined to act upon it.
He wavered. On the 23rd November he wrote to Mr.
Gladstone : 'If I insist further on Parliament meeting
on December 2nd, I suppose one of two results must
happen, either Bright and Chamberlain will leave the

Cabinet, or I shall have to do so myself, with or without those who agree with me.'[1] This was a fact which had for some days been evident. Forster wrote on 24th November that he had consulted the Dublin officials, and that they thought that a break up of the Government would do more harm in Ireland than the postpone-·ment of a Coercion Bill to January; so he was inclined to wait. It was surely more a question for statesmen than for officials. Forster, with all his high qualities, lacked, perhaps, that last and rare touch of decision which makes the leader of men.

Mr. Gladstone, master in this art, succeeded in holding together those whose first object it was to maintain order and protect life, and those whose first object it was to disestablish Irish landowners. There was compromise. Parliament was to be summoned, not in the autumn, but earlier than usual after Christmas, and promises were to be made in the Queen's Speech both of coercion and of land reform, so that every one might be pleased. Coercion was to have a slight precedence. The affair showed the difficulty of government by a Cabinet so heterogeneously composed. Lord Hartington was low in spirits, and said to his secretary that 'this attempt to govern by a combination of Whigs and Radicals is to ride two horses.' His secretary replied that everybody knew this. 'It is an attempt rather to drive two horses, one a sluggard and the other a runaway. It is a difficult job, and there is the credit of attempting and succeeding.'

On the 4th December Lord Hartington received a letter from the Lord-Lieutenant depicting in the gloomiest colours the anarchy in Ireland. 'I am so convinced,' Lord Cowper wrote, 'that to bring in what are called remedial measures before a Coercion Bill will be so demoralising and at the

[1] *Life of W. E. Forster*, vol. ii. p. 270.

same time would so utterly fail in pacifying the country that I could not under such circumstances remain as Lord-Lieutenant. In fact, unless a Coercion Bill is brought in when Parliament meets, my intention is to resign.'

Lord Hartington disliked the principles of the proposed land legislation almost as much as the Radicals of the Cabinet disliked coercion. Mr. Gladstone knew at the beginning of December 1880 what would be the main recommendations of the Royal Commission, and he informed Lord Granville and Lord Hartington.[1] The latter replied in the following letter :—

INDIA OFFICE,<br>
December 9, 1880.

MY DEAR MR. GLADSTONE,—I return the letters received through Granville.

The proposals of the Commissioners, judging of them by your description, seem to be alarming. Perhaps I look at the question from a landlord's point of view; but the ' confiscation of the rights of property' seems to me even more serious than a heavy charge on the English Exchequer. I doubt whether it would be just, or possible, to require from the landlords any further considerable sacrifice of the rights which the law has hitherto given them without some compensation in the shape either of money, or at least of increased security for the enjoyment of the rights which remain to them. I suppose that the advocates of the three F's would say that the tenants would be satisfied, and that the landlords might feel secure of getting their fixed rents. But what certainty is there of this, and why should there not be another agitation and strike against the payment of any rent at all, enforced by

---

[1] Mr. John Morley, who was then editor of the influential *Pall Mall Gazette*, called, he says, on Mr. Gladstone ' one morning, early in 1881.' '" You have heard," I said, " that the Bessborough Commission are to report for the three F's?" " I have not heard," he said, " it is incredible." '—*Life of Gladstone*, vol. iii. p. 56.

This is a fine;.bold way of dealing with the Press, and may be commended to private secretaries of Ministers.

the same methods? Would it be possible that the State should be guaranteed against loss in the purchase of land by making the instalments a charge on the rates?—Yours sincerely,                                    HARTINGTON.

How keenly Lord Hartington felt the hesitation of the Government to take coercive action the following letter, dated December 14, 1880, to Lord Granville shows :—

'Two letters received this morning which are pleasant reading.[1]

'I do not believe there was ever a shadow of disturbance at Lismore in the worst times previously. I have a good mind to go to Lismore, and take my chance of being shot. It would be better than staying here, and not daring to look any one in the face, which is my case now.

'I have given up my Lancashire meeting, as I literally do not know what can be said for the Government.

'And all for this precious remedial measure, which, it seems probable, will be laughed out of the House.'

A week later took place the following exchange of letters between Lord Hartington and Mr. Gladstone :—

INDIA OFFICE,
*December* 19, 1880.

MY DEAR MR. GLADSTONE,—I am sorry to have to add anything to your labours at this anxious time, especially when what I have to say is of a personal character; but I will put as shortly as I can what I think I cannot any longer leave unsaid.

You know, I think, that I have been an unwilling party to what I must consider the most unfortunate recent decisions of the Cabinet in regard to Ireland; but you cannot know fully the pain, and, I must add, humiliation with which I see their results daily developing themselves.

It is not on this, however, which I wish to dwell now.

---

[1] The letters were from the Agent at Lismore giving an account of some outrages.

I have consented to remain in the Government and I must take my share of the responsibility. But when I reflect on the whole of our Irish policy, I find that there has not been (with one exception) a single important measure on which I have been in agreement with the Cabinet.

I was opposed to the decision not to renew the Peace Preservation Act; I strongly objected to the Compensation for Disturbance Bill; I was in favour of calling Parliament together in November to grant the Irish Government the powers they deemed necessary for maintaining order, and was, as you know, prepared to resign on that question if Forster had remained firm; and I again supported Forster's last appeal on Monday last. The only measure which I can recollect, of which I have approved, was that of the prosecution of the Land League. But that proposal was made at the end of a Cabinet summoned for other business, and was scarcely explained to us. I, and I imagine others, supposed that Parnell and his associates would be charged before a magistrate, and brought to trial within a short time. Had I supposed that the prosecutions must be so conducted that months must elapse before the trials, I do not think that I should have approved of a proceeding which has placed some obstacle in the way of more summary measures.

My object in going over this story is not to complain of the conduct of my colleagues. It is, I hope, of a more practical character. Every Minister must, I think, at some time have felt the extreme difficulty of forming a decision as to the exact amount of difference of opinion which justifies him in leaving a Government. The particular occasion or decision does not often seem adequately to justify such a step. But the time must come when further concession becomes impossible. I hope that there may not be in the future occasions of so much difference. But if it should be otherwise, I think that I am entitled to point out to you that in my case, such a difference would not be an isolated one, but the culminating point of a long series of differences.

I do not wish to anticipate our future course, but it is only fair to you that I should say that I hold that our coercion measure will have to be strong in proportion to the delay in introducing it, and to the aggravated condition of Ireland which that delay has brought about. I apprehend also that the country will by that time be, and in fact now is, in a state which will not admit of any further delay, or concession to obstruction. I do not mean to say that fair debate ought not to be permitted, but I do think that obstruction will have to be sharply dealt with.

As to the Land question, I entirely admit the moderation with which you propose to approach it, though I think that your proposals go nearer than you intend to some which you disapprove. In some respects I should perhaps be prepared to go further than you are, and I hope in a few days to be able to make some suggestions on the subject. But I have no confidence in the good effect at this time of any proposals which we may be able to make. I think that we have throughout been too sanguine in our estimate of the fairness and sense of justice of the Irish people. We have been too confident in our ability to govern without the use of force, and by the power of conciliation and justice; and I fear that we have at last been led into a most disastrous error by weak concessions to some of our colleagues in (as I consider) their sentimental and illogical objections to the use of force proved to be necessary, unless accompanied by conciliation which we know could have no immediate effect.

It is quite unnecessary that you should take the trouble to reply to this unless you should wish to do so.—Yours sincerely,　　　　　　　　　　　　HARTINGTON.

Mr. Gladstone replied on the following day :—

HAWARDEN CASTLE, CHESTER,
*20th December* 1880.

MY DEAR HARTINGTON,—There are one or two things I may as well say on your letter, especially as they need not be polemical.

1. When the prosecution of the chief Land Leaguers was proposed, there was no positive decision, for it was started by English influences, and pressed on the Irish Government. That Government adopted the present mode of procedure in lieu of the one you anticipated or preferred, because, among other reasons, it was greatly more expeditious.

2. So far as I know, you had not urged any difficulties in regard to the less or greater stringency of coercion. I am adverse generally to meddling with the press; which I think has not been mentioned. But, as we have to coerce, the first consideration is to do it effectually; and you will find I have already communicated with the Speaker on the means of expediting its progress through the House of Commons.

3. I am not more sanguine perhaps than you as to the immediate effect in Ireland of any land measures we can propose; nor at all disposed to mix them with the measures of repression on the principle of *pari passu*. What I think is requisite is that, in setting out upon the repressive operation, we should in the main know our own minds as to land, and should make known authentically the basis on which we mean to proceed.

4. I will not go back upon the past decisions to which you refer. To me they appear to have involved considerations of great difficulty, upon which men, thoroughly allied in political principles, might not unnaturally differ. From this I own that I rather except this—not renewal but—revival of the Arms' Act, which, after the late Government had virtually dropped renewal, would, I believe, have been not only useless in Ireland (from incompleteness) but a very serious parliamentary error.—I remain, sincerely yours,                    W. GLADSTONE.

Lord Hartington, in the debate on the Address (11th January 1881), ended his speech with a powerful peroration. He said :—

'Hon. members opposite have wisely appealed to the

attachment which all parties in this House feel to our constitutional liberties and to the forms which guard them. But, attached as we are to those forms, I trust that we are not yet altogether the slaves of form. I trust that, in respecting and vindicating the forms of our Constitution, we are not indifferent to that which is a yet more precious thing, the substance. I have had before, and I fear we may have again, to point out in this House how, in the sacred names of freedom of debate and liberty of discussion, the forms of the House have been abused until, for the great majority of hon. members, there is little freedom of debate, and no freedom of action, remaining. And so it is in Ireland at this moment. Under the forms of constitutional liberty the substance is disappearing. It is not, as described by some, a condition of anarchy. A law does prevail, but it is not the law of the land. For the law of the land has been substituted the law of the Land League ; for the Judge and the Magistrate has been substituted an irresponsible Committee ; for the police constable and the sheriff's officer, for those who work in the service of the law in the full light of the day—have been substituted the midnight assassin and the ruffian who invades the humble cottage, disguised, at midnight. From this tyranny there are thousands at this moment suffering, and it is for them, and not for the landlord class alone—it is for hundreds of thousands who desire to gain honestly their living, but cannot do so except in fear of their very lives, that we ask you to give us, not permanent but temporary, measures to restore the substance of liberty, though it may be by a temporary abridgment of some of its forms.'

He spoke *con amore*, and with the eloquence of long restrained indignation, and, for once, was satisfied with a speech which he had made. He wrote to his father :—

' My speech the other night was wonderfully successful ; and I am quite astonished at it. I had no idea that I was going to make a better speech than usual ; and although I felt that it went off well, I had no idea that such a fuss would be made about it. I was afraid at first that I had been rather too strong, and that some of the Radicals would have been disgusted, and that we might lose some votes, but I hear that they are generally pleased, and that even those who intended to vote against us have come round. I ought never to make another speech again, for I shall never make so successful a one.'

The Home Rule question also entered into the early debates of this session. Mr. Gladstone, in a speech on 16th February, said that the wise way of meeting the Irish demand, that Irish affairs should be under Irish control, was to ask, 'What are the provisions which you propose to make for the supremacy of Parliament? That has been my course, and that is the course in which I intend to persevere. I am bound to say that I have not yet received an answer.' He was not, he said, prepared to give anything to Ireland which could not also, if Scotland desired it, be given to Scotland. Lord Hartington, on the following day, said that he had read the Prime Minister's 'speech with some anxiety.'

The Life and Property Protection Act passed through all its stages by Easter 1881. Furiously resisted by the Irish party, it was only carried over the barrier by a *coup d'état* of the Speaker, powers for overriding obstruction not yet having been developed. Next came the Land Bill. It comprised the 'three F's,' viz. 'fair rent,' 'fixity of tenure,' 'free sale.' Rents were to be judicially fixed; the tenants were secured against eviction so long as they paid them; and they were enabled to sell their right of occupation. The innovation was certainly startling, but it was probably a necessary intermediate step to the transfer by assisted purchase of the whole right in the land from landlord to tenant, and the creation in Ireland

of a class of small freeholders. It is a political axiom
that the same policy applied to different conditions
produces different results. Like much else, the English
system of land tenure had broken down when applied
to Ireland. Mr. Gladstone was at his greatest in carrying
through, with labour, courage, and skilful strategy, this
large and complicated piece of social legislation. It was,
perhaps, the most far-reaching accomplishment of his
career. It cost him the alliance of the Duke of Argyll,
who had been an uneasy colleague from the beginning.
On the 21st February the Duke wrote a long letter to Lord
Hartington, and said that the more he looked at the
measure 'the more monstrous all its provisions appear to
be.' At the beginning of April he resigned office. The
Bill was almost as distasteful to the heir of the Cavendishes as it was to the fiery chief of the Campbells. He
wrote on the 6th April :—

INDIA OFFICE, *April* 6, 1881.

MY DEAR MR. GLADSTONE,—Thanks for the letters.
Argyll told me on Monday that he could not remain. I
could not say anything against his decision, for his objections to the Bill have always been stronger than mine ;
and I find it a hard morsel to swallow.

But, as I have swallowed it, I will not trouble you with
my difficulties. I will only express a hope—

1. That we shall adhere in the main to the limitations
of the Bill which have been adopted, and,

2. That I shall not be asked to take part in its defence
more than can be helped.

I shall, of course, be attacked, and have to defend
myself as well as I can, and incidentally defend the Bill ;
but its active support may, I think, best be left to the
members of the Government who do not share my objections.—Yours sincerely,                HARTINGTON.

Lord Hartington, in the House of Commons (19th May

1881), rested his support of the Land Bill mainly on the fact that 'it is too little to say that we are within a measurable distance of civil war,' the same ground as that on which the Duke of Wellington justified 'Catholic Emancipation.' He said, however, that there was nothing very alarming about the 'three F's,' which formed at that moment 'the basis of the management of a great many of the best estates in Ireland.' The Act of 1870 had been found to be 'practically inadequate,' and this Bill was intended to 'supplement that Act by other and more direct provisions intended to secure to the tenant his equitable and customary rights.'[1]

On 3rd June there was a sharp encounter in the House between Parnell and Hartington. The Irish leader told the Government that if they used further their new coercion powers, murder and trouble would be the result, and said that, if they withdrew their troops and police from the disturbed regions, and left these to the bishops and priests, order would be better kept. Lord Hartington said, at the end of a powerful reply :—

'Whatever may be the fate of our efforts to improve the law, we hold now, as we have always done, that it is our duty to carry out the existing law as it stands, and not to surrender the powers, ordinary or extraordinary, which Parliament has confided to us, into the hands of the Land League or any other body.'

After the Land Act had been passed, Mr. Gladstone was disposed, for a time, to support strongly the Irish Executive in their attempt to re-establish order. His speech at Leeds on 8th October 1881 assailed Parnell for his endeavour 'to

---

[1] In a speech made on the 9th March in the following year, 1882, Lord Hartington had occasion to refer to the Land Act of 1881, and said, 'That Act is the law of the land, for good or for evil.' Hearing Tory cheers, he repeated, 'It is law, and I am not going to be drawn by the cheers of hon. gentlemen opposite into a discussion whether it is for good or evil."

arrest the operation of the Land Act,' and contained the famous passage :—

' If it shall appear that there is still to be fought a final conflict in Ireland between law on the one side and sheer lawlessness on the other ; if the law, purged from defect and from any taint of injustice, is still to be repelled and refused, and the first conditions of political society to remain unfulfilled, then I say, gentlemen, without hesitation, the resources of civilisation against its enemies are not yet exhausted.'

Four days later the Cabinet, after long discussion, decided that Mr. Parnell should be arrested and imprisoned under the powers of the new Act. It was a true and bold stroke of State. On the following day the man was imprisoned in Kilmainham who, in Mr. Gladstone's words, had ' made himself beyond all others prominent in the attempt to destroy the authority of the law, and to substitute what would end in being nothing more or less than anarchical oppression exercised upon the people of Ireland.' That winter the Irish Government had about a thousand suspected men in prison without trial, but the country was still the scene of violent disorder. The Lord Mayor of London appealed for funds to support an association formed in Ireland for supplying labour, or otherwise assisting landlords and farmers who were ' boycotted.' Mr. Forster favoured this step, and wished the Duke of Devonshire and Lord Hartington to subscribe. Mr. Gladstone thought it would be unwise that any member of the Government should assist. Lord Hartington replied :—

INDIA OFFICE, *December* 12, 1881.

MY DEAR MR. GLADSTONE,—I have received your letter of the 11th, and Forster has sent me the correspondence between you and himself on the subject of the Lord Mayor's movement, which I have read with some regret.

The Irish Government have not *participated* in the action of the Property Defence Association because, as I understand, their operations have been such as could not be initiated by Government, but could only be undertaken by landlords themselves, or, under present circumstances, by a private association coming to the assistance of individuals. But I understood Forster to say that the Government had in all cases given to the agents of the association protection when necessary when carrying on their operations. Therefore the Irish Government, while not *participating* (because it could not), approves of the objects of the Association.

Then why should we not approve of an English Association to aid the legitimate Irish Association?

The one argument is that it is undesirable for England to interfere in an Irish class struggle. I altogether dissent from this description of what is going on in Ireland. It seems to assume that the merits of the struggle are equally balanced, while the fact is that one class is trying to obtain some portion of its legal rights, and the other is setting all legal obligations at defiance.

The funds of the Irish Association are failing, not necessarily from want of union and of vigour on the part of Irish landlords, but from want of rents. What can be more legitimate than that those in England who are interested in the defence of the rights of property should help those who are carrying on the struggle in Ireland? My own inclination would be strongly to subscribe, and to advise others to subscribe, to the Lord Mayor's fund. But the question is whether, after the rather No than Aye answer which has been given, it would embarrass the Government if I and perhaps some other of the more Whig section were to subscribe, and the others hold aloof. I feel convinced that if we abstain, and maintain the rather No than Aye attitude, the movement will assume the character of a demonstration against the supposed inactivity of the Government, and that this will be joined in by many Liberals.

I have seen Northbrook this morning, who concurs generally in what I have said, and would subscribe, if it would not be considered objectionable.—I remain, yours sincerely,                                HARTINGTON.

Lord Hartington wrote a letter to Lord Granville on 11th April 1882, which is of interest as showing his mind at this point of time :—

*April 11th, 1882.*

'. . . I am glad that Mr. Gladstone is prepared for strong measures about crime.  But I anticipate very great difficulties, the greatest of which at present seems to me to be the temper of the Opposition.  They are in such a state of irritation and fear of Gladstone that I believe they will oppose almost anything we propose.  It is a very serious thing to have to deal with such a state of things as exists in Ireland in the face of two Oppositions like the Irish and the regular one.  And the worst of it is that I believe there is very little real difference between us and the Opposition now on Irish questions.  They have accepted the Land Act, for I believe that even the Lords' Committee have not seriously attempted to break down the rent clauses; and there is no difference in principle between us about the extension of the purchase clauses.  It seems to me that, in such an alarming condition of Ireland as Mr. Gladstone described last Tuesday, some effort ought to be made to unite the two great parties in an Irish policy and to establish a sort of truce on all other questions till the Irish difficulty is settled.  I don't believe that any real sacrifice of importance would have to be made ; for though we go on talking about local government, and about the county franchise and redistribution of seats, and though Chamberlain thinks that we are on the eve of great political changes, I do not believe that one of them will be made while the Irish difficulty lasts.  It is not easy to see how such a union of parties could be brought about ; but it is possible that a conciliatory reception of Smith's motion about the purchase clauses would give an opening.  One indispensable concession would be the bare majority in the cloture resolution. I think that we shall very likely have to give way about it; but, if it were announced at once as a concession, it would have a great effect. I am all for the bare majority in principle, and I think we shall have it some day; but it is not indispensable for the present emergency, and I have no doubt that the Opposition do really dread it as the instrument with which some terrible changes are going to be forced on them, as soon as our hands are free. Of course it would be a sacrifice to make such a concession now after what we have said; but my position is that the Irish difficulty is almost insuperable in the present state of parties, that a temporary union between the two parties on the Irish question would have a great moral effect in Ireland, and that such a union cannot be effected without some sacrifice.

'Of course the Radicals would be a difficulty; but would they desert Mr. Gladstone?'

Lord Granville replied, in his usual humorous vein, that 'one fatal objection to your idea of union with the Conservatives would be the impossibility of our finding capital with which to buy them, unless we tossed Gladstone into the scales, which neither you nor I are prepared to do.'

Lord Hartington wrote to him again four days later—

'Mr. Gladstone's letter is most depressing; but I like anything better than his cheerful and rose-coloured moods. I saw Spencer on Friday. Neither he nor Forster seem to like the Lord-Justices idea better than Mr. Gladstone does, and I admit that there is much to be said against it; but I still think that there is something to be said for it, in competition with the plan of the substitution of Spencer for Cowper.[1] Is Ireland to be governed from London, or in Ireland? If Forster remains as Chief Secretary and as the Minister mainly responsible, the Lord-Lieutenant you want

---

[1] This suggestion was that the 'Lord Justices' in Ireland should discharge the duties of the Lord-Lieutenant, this post thus being put into commission.

is a man who will work hard, but who will work, in the main, under Forster's orders. If Spencer goes, it will be for something more than this, and I am afraid there will be two centres of government not always in complete accord. Lord-Justices would be Forster's ministers, dividing the executive duties under his orders, and at the same time forming a council whom he could consult.

'Spencer, however, seems ready to go. I have told him that I think he ought to have a very clear understanding with Forster before he decides. Of course the latter would continue to have a voice, perhaps the chief voice, in matters of policy and legislation, though Spencer remaining in the Cabinet would also have his voice. But in executive action it would have to be understood that Spencer should be supreme and responsible, and that Forster, at all events when he is in London, should interfere as little as possible in executive work.

'I don't know what Lord Russell's plan was. I confess that I do not much like the idea of it. The four provinces have no real existence, and are only geographical expressions. To give representative bodies in them larger powers than could be exercised by county boroughs would, I think, be a long step towards Home Rule and a representative body for all Ireland.'

Mr. Gladstone's mind had for some time been travelling in a direction quite opposed to that of a 'temporary union between the two parties' for the purpose of resisting the Nationalist political and agrarian movement. In February 1882 he had declared in the House of Commons that he would not say at what decision the House might arrive as to Home Rule, provided that 'a plan were to be laid before it under which purely Irish matters could be clearly and definitely separated from what are purely Imperial matters.' On 12th April he wrote to Mr. Forster the remarkable letter quoted in Lord Morley's *Life*, in which he said that, after the settlement of the agrarian question, the next step must be 'to relieve Great Britain from the enormous weight of the government of Ireland unaided by the people, and from the hopeless position in which we stand while we give a Parliamentary representation, hardly effective for anything but mischief, without the local institutions of self-government which it presupposes, and on which alone it can have a sound and healthy basis.'

About this time Mr. Chamberlain had entered into those negotiations with Parnell through the medium of Captain O'Shea which soon led to the release of the State prisoners at Kilmainham.[1]   The terms of the 'understanding,' which its enemies called the 'Kilmainham Treaty,' were virtually that the Government, on its side, should release the three prisoners and bring in a measure dealing with the question of arrears of rent, and that Parnell, on his side, should co-operate to the best of his power in discouraging further disorder.   Parnell also threw in a hope that he would be able to co-operate in a more general way with the Liberal party in future.   'This,' wrote Mr. Gladstone to Mr. Forster on 30th April, 'is a *hors d'œuvre* which we had no right to expect, and, I rather think, have no right at present to accept.   I may be far wide of the mark, but I can scarcely wonder at O'Shea's saying "the thing is done." . . . On the whole, Parnell's letter is, I think, the most extraordinary I ever read.   I cannot help feeling indebted to O'Shea.'[2]

[1] Mr. O'Donnell, in his *History of the Irish Parliamentary Party*, alleges that Mrs. O'Shea had negotiated the treaty directly with Mr. Gladstone at the same time.

[2] Parnell's letter ran: 'If the arrears question be settled upon the lines indicated by us, I have every confidence—a confidence shared by my colleagues— that the exertions which we should be able to make strenuously and unremittingly would be effective in stopping outrages and intimidation of all kinds. . . . The accomplishment of the programme I have sketched out to you would, in my judg- ment, be regarded by the country as a practical settlement of the land question, and would, I feel, soon enable us to co-operate cordially for the future with the Liberal party in forwarding Liberal principles and measures of general reform,

In asserting in the House of Commons on the 2nd May that the release of the prisoners was an 'act done without any negotiation, promise, or engagement whatsoever,' Mr. Gladstone made one of those fine mental distinctions with which he from time to time perplexed the blunter English mind.

It was part of the scheme put forward by Mr. Gladstone, in his Memorandum circulated before the decisive Cabinet of 2nd May 1882, that Parliament should not be asked to renew the 'Life and Property Protection Act' of 1881, but that the ordinary law should be strengthened in Ireland. All the Ministers agreed to this course.[1] But Forster and the rest of the Cabinet disagreed as to the point of time at which the Kilmainham prisoners should be released. Mr. Forster, in his speech of 4th May 1882, held firmly to the position that the release should not be made unless at least one of three conditions should be satisfied. *Either* Ireland should be in a sufficiently tranquillised condition, *or* Parnell and his friends should give a *public* undertaking that they would in no way approve of intimidation, as a principle of action, *or* a fresh Act strengthening the law should be not only promised, or introduced, but actually passed. He wrote on the morning of the 2nd May, 'Either the release is conditional or it is not.

and the Government, at the end of this session, would from the state of the country feel themselves thoroughly justified in dispensing with further coercive measures.'

O'Shea, in his interview of 30th April with Mr. Forster, told him that he could supplement Parnell's letter by stating ' that the conspiracy which has been used to get up boycotting and outrages will be used to put them down, and that there will be a *union* with the Liberal party.' O'Shea also mentioned Sheridan as an agent of disorder who might organise order in the west. The revelation seemed calculated to make Mr. Forster, at least, resign rather than assent to the proposition.—*Life of W. E. Forster*, vol. ii. p. 436.

[1] As a consequence, the prisoners in Kilmainham would, in any case, have been released in September 1882, the date at which the Act under which they were imprisoned without trial expired.

If unconditional, I think it is, at the present moment, a surrender to the law-breakers. If conditional, I think it is a disgraceful compromise.' [1] But Mr. Gladstone had made his decision. That same morning he wrote to Forster: 'I have no choice; followed or not followed, I must go on.' There spoke the true leader of men. To resist him one must be enrolled in the opposing host, or else possess great strength and courage of one's own.

Mr. Forster resigned his office, and on the 4th May came one of the most thrilling scenes in the long and tempestuous existence of the House of Commons. Parnell, straight from Kilmainham, entering amid the triumphant shouts of his followers, turned to face the fallen Minister whose will had been the cause of his imprisonment. The Prime Minister now went nearer the true facts of the case than he had gone two days earlier. The release, he said, was due to the belief of the Government, founded upon certain information, that the imprisoned members would, on regaining their freedom, and if the arrears question were settled, 'find themselves in a condition to range themselves on the side of what I should call law and order and individual freedom in Ireland.' This dim and inadequate statement was far too strong for Parnell, who could not let his followers suppose that he had bought release by promises or pledges to support the English Government. After he had icily spoken little indeed was left of the promise.

Lord Hartington took in this debate the different ground that, whether those gentlemen so ranged themselves or not, the Irish Government was now in a sufficiently strong position to be able to afford their release. The Government had, he said, arrested the three Irish members—

'because we believed that they were the active leaders in an organisation, the object of which was to intimidate

[1] *Life of W. E. Forster*, vol. ii. p. 441.

persons in the discharge of their duties, and in the exercise of their rights. We believed that the organisation, of which these hon. members were the leaders, was one so formidable that we could not be responsible for the peace of the country and the execution of the law, if we did not, at that time, exercise in their regard the arbitrary powers conferred upon us by the Coercion Acts.'

These powers, he said, had been exercised with effect, and—

'the organised resistance to the law, the organised refusal to pay rents, and the organised attempt to dictate what the amount of such rents should be, has to a great extent failed owing to the action which we took under the Act. . . . We are asked why do we think now that we are able to release the leaders of this agitation? It is because we have reasonable grounds for believing, as we had reasonable grounds in October for believing the reverse, that those leaders will not now, or if they wished, cannot, act in a manner to obstruct the execution of the law.'

He added that the Government were acting upon all the information they had, both that supplied by the Irish Government as to the improved state of things in Ireland, and also information as to the intention and disposition of the recent political prisoners. He said :—

'When the moment arrived when we could no longer say that their continued detention was required for the safety of the country, at that moment we were not only justified, but absolutely compelled, to agree to their release.'

Upon no other ground could a statesman, who had assented to their imprisonment, properly assent to the release. Vague and private assurances given by a deeply committed rebel could not be more than a slight and incidental consideration. Lord Hartington noted his impressions of what had taken place, so far as regards the negotiations, in a memorandum written at the end of 1882. He wrote :—

'My recollection of the communications which took place is that they were mainly for the purpose of ascertaining the intentions of Parnell and his colleagues at the time ; what course he would probably pursue if he were released ; and, consequently, whether it would be safe to release him or not. I do not think that the first communication from O'Shea could have been disregarded. Parnell had at that time no public or official means of communication open to him. But, although the first letter indicated, if it were confirmed, a great change in Parnell's sentiments, it was scarcely possible to act upon it without taking some steps to ascertain how far it did really represent his opinions, and what course of conduct he was likely to pursue if released. It is probably the case that these further steps did assume something of the character of a negotiation, and that, although there was no pledge, there was an understanding that an Arrears Bill would be brought in based on certain principles.'

Years later, at the time of the 'Parnell Commission,' Mr. Gladstone said that members of the Cabinet of 1882 could not have supposed Parnell and his friends to have been guilty of any kind of complicity with crime, or they would not have consented to their release. Lord Hartington replied that he had consented to the release, not because he thought them to be innocent, but because he believed the law to have been so far reasserted in Ireland that they could be released without much danger.

Lord Cowper, before these events, had wished to resign the Lord-Lieutenancy of Ireland, and the Prime Minister had desired to replace him by Lord Spencer, who had held the post in the last Liberal Administration. Lord Spencer being a member of the Cabinet, this plan, had Mr. Forster remained, would have involved the consequence that both Lord-Lieutenant and Chief Secretary would have been Cabinet Ministers. Lord Spencer was doubtful. His chief difficulty, as he wrote to Lord Hartington on the 12th April, was that it might be difficult to work with Mr. Forster, who had held a practical monopoly of power in Ireland for two years. Mr. Forster, on his side, wrote (13th April) that what was wanted was an Administrator who would be at Dublin Castle all day. He himself could do the work when he was in Ireland, but when he was attending Parliament the work was not done. Lord Cowper definitely resigned with Mr. Forster. Lord Spencer then accepted the Lord-Lieutenancy, and Lord Frederick Cavendish, then Financial Secretary to the Treasury, accepted the succession to Mr. Forster.[1] They crossed together to Dublin on the night of 5th May, the day following the memorable debate in the House of Commons. The official houses of the Viceroy, the Chief Secretary, and the Permanent Under-Secretary are in the Phœnix Park, and lie about a mile down a straight, broad road leading from the gate which opens into the town. Lord Frederick Cavendish spent the afternoon at the Castle offices in Dublin transacting business, and discussing the provisions of the coming Crimes Bill, and, towards seven o'clock, followed Lord Spencer, who had ridden homewards an hour earlier. It was a fine May evening, and there were still people walking and bicycling in the Park. Inside the gate of the Park Lord Frederick overtook Mr. Burke, the Permanent Under-Secretary, who was walking homewards from the gate, and dismissed his car in order to walk with him. By a curious chance the detectives who usually

---

[1] Sir Algernon West asserts in his *Recollections*, vol. ii. p. 149, that, before asking Lord Frederick, Mr. Gladstone asked Lord Hartington to take Forster's post, and was refused. This is not the fact. Lord Hartington was not asked, and did not refuse.

followed Mr. Burke failed on this occasion to do so. The
two were near to the Chief Secretary's Lodge, lying ahead
of them, and almost opposite to the Viceroy's Lodge, on
their right, when they came to a car standing by the path,
and four men on the grass near it. These were comrades
in that gang who, having failed in almost successful
attempts to murder Forster, were determined at least to
murder Burke. Lord Frederick was not known to them.
He was killed while vainly endeavouring to defend his
companion. How the news came that night to London,
and spread among the dismayed guests at the Admiralty
evening party, has been told in other books.[1] Lord Hartington was at the party. The host, Lord Northbrook,
had the news from Sir William Harcourt. He took Lord
Hartington, Lady Louisa Egerton, and Admiral Egerton to
his study, and told it to them there.

This crime made immense impression on the mind of
England. It was one of those tragic events which, by
superior reality, reveal the pettiness of much of ordinary
political strife, and purify the passions for at least a time.
The crime cleared the air, like a disastrous storm, and
made possible the beginning of better relations between the
English and the Irish. The cruel death of a blameless man
full of good-will was a lesson in the results of national
hatred and passion. It was felt on both sides of the
Channel that there was much to forgive, and to be forgiven.
Lady Frederick Cavendish believed, and rightly, that her
husband had died for Ireland. She accepted the dreadful
blow with a courage worthy of the race of which she
came, the race whose name she bore, and the religion
to which she belonged. Lord Hartington wrote on
the 7th May to Lord Granville, 'She is quite extra-

[1] See Lives of Mr. Gladstone and Mr. Forster and Lord Northbrook, and
Sir Algernon West's *Recollections*.

ordinary, and I have talked to her for a long time this morning about him, when she was perfectly calm. She has not a shadow of doubt on her mind about his being right to go, and most anxious that no one should be blamed for it.' Of the Duke, his father, he wrote :—

'His grief is at times terrible; but he recovers, and talks of him and of the crisis quite calmly. Eddy tells me that he has not uttered a word of reproach against any one. He says that he does not think that any one persuaded him to go, and that he had quite made up his mind that, if he was thought fit for the post, he could not refuse. I think he is much touched by all the sympathy which I have been able to report to him.'

In the sad and solemn meeting of the House of Commons on 8th May, Mr. Gladstone, after deploring the death of Mr. Burke, said very finely :—

'But, sir, the hand of the assassin has come nearer home; and, though I feel it difficult to say a word, yet I must say that one of the very noblest hearts in England has ceased to beat, and has ceased at the very moment when it was just devoted to the service of Ireland, full of love for that country, full of hope for her future, full of capacity to render her service.'

Mr. Forster said :—

'I knew and respected Lord Frederick Cavendish. I knew his worth, his spotless integrity, his remarkable industry, his great courage, and his unselfishness. I was more aware than many members of this House of those qualities because I have been brought more in contact with him; but I was also more aware of his possession, to an extraordinary extent, of a sound judgment; and when I heard of his appointment as Chief Secretary I thought it was the best appointment that could be made, considering, not only his patriotism, his unswerving impartiality, his integrity, his administrative power, but especially this faculty of judgment.'

Lord Granville said in the House of Lords :—

'My Lords, I have known intimately for many years Lord Frederick Cavendish, and I have never known a higher or finer nature. He was absolutely without personal vanity, without any love of display; but his great ability, his knowledge, and his industry only required a difficult position in order to show the nature of which he was made. He was reluctant to leave the Office which he filled so well; but, like a soldier, he obeyed without one moment's hesitation the call of duty to a place of enormous difficulty. He has suffered a miserable death, but one glorious to himself, dying as he did in the service of his country. That death has left a noble woman desolate, and may we all join in her most courageous prayer, that God may influence the results of this fearful crime in a manner contrary to the hopes and expectations of its perpetrators, and that it may result in the eventual good of Ireland.'

Lord Frederick Cavendish, in the words engraved on the fine monument in the ancient church of Cartmel, near Holker Hall, 'died in the service of his country and in defence of his friend,' nor could man have nobler epitaph.

The death of the brother of Lord Hartington and the nephew, by marriage, of Mr. Gladstone, was the loss of a link between them. Lord Frederick had often done much to prevent, or to remove, or to soften misunderstandings between these strangely assorted leaders. The succession to the Chief Secretaryship was offered to Sir Charles Dilke, who declined to accept it unless he could also have a seat in the Cabinet. The honour, therefore, of accepting a post full of difficulty and attended by personal danger, fell to Mr. George Trevelyan.

Mr. Gladstone achieved the belief that the events of

April and May 1882 had completely changed, as by
religious conversion, the character and views of the
Irish leader.[1] The following letters show that indirect
communications between the Prime Minister and Parnell
continued from time to time.

### Lord Hartington to Lord Granville

'INDIA OFFICE, *October 11th*, 1882.

'I send you back the letters. I suppose that Mr. Gladstone's letter does not really commit him to anything.
But I think that it is extremely to be regretted that such
proposals should have been answered in such a tone.

'I sincerely hope that the correspondence will not
be continued either by Mr. Gladstone, Trevelyan, or
Grosvenor.

'If there is to be a Bill next Session amending the
Land Act, there might be a necessity for communication as to its details with the leaders of the Irish party.
But it has never yet been decided that there is to be
any such Bill, and I should most deeply regret the
necessity.

'But as to anything like a negotiation embracing procedure and Land Legislation, or assurances intended
to influence Parnell's conduct on the Cloture Resolution,
it seems to me absolutely inadmissible. I have the
most painful recollections of the communications of
last Session. But there was this to be said for them,

---

[1] In the correspondence there is a letter from a certain clergyman to Lord
Hartington at a later date, in which the writer says that he heard Mr. Gladstone
state this theory at a small dinner party. Mr. O'Donnell, in his *History of the Irish
Parliamentary Party*, states that after the Phœnix Park murder, 'Mrs. O'Shea,
who had already negotiated the Kilmainham Treaty, invited Mr. Gladstone to
see her again in this terrible hour, and, before he should form any resolution, to
hear what she had to say. . . . From her lips, from her tearful appeals, from her
high courage, and exhortations not to yield to the awful blow, the Premier
gathered the elements of a fresh determination to stand by the other party to the
treaty. Mrs. O'Shea finally convinced Mr. Gladstone that this crime was a
horror and a loathing to Parnell as much as to himself.'

What a good subject for a painter of historical scenes !

that it was impossible to communicate otherwise than indirectly with men who were in prison, and who had no public means of expressing their opinions or intentions.

As to the further communications which took place during the debates on the Prevention of Crimes Bill, my recollection is that the Cabinet emphatically disapproved of them. I see *no* necessity for *any* communications now. I hope there will be no new Land Bill, but if there is, I protest against its being used to influence Parnell's vote on Cloture. I also object to the sort of encouragement which has been given to Parnell's monstrous proposition about the Committee which is to discuss Irish Bills.'

### Lord Hartington to Mr. Gladstone.

'INDIA OFFICE, 14*th October* 1882.

'Granville sent me, by your desire, the correspondence between you and himself on Mrs. O'Shea's letter. In returning the correspondence to Granville, I sent him some observations which were only intended for his private perusal; but I find from another letter that he wishes me to give you my opinion on the subject. I do not know whether the draft reply to Mrs. O'Shea was sent or not; but I confess that I most earnestly hope that it was not. I think that the expediency of entering into further private communications with Parnell through O'Shea is open to the greatest doubt; and I go further than Granville in deprecating any such communications even through Trevelyan or Grosvenor.

'It seems to me that, embarrassing as were the first communications of this character, there was sufficient reason for them in the fact that, when Parnell and his friends were in prison, no public mode of expressing their opinions and intentions, either in Parliament or elsewhere, was open to them. But when, in the course of the debates on the Prevention of Crime Bill, some private communications were renewed, or were supposed to be renewed, my impression was that the Cabinet expressed a very strong opinion against their continuance. I venture to think that there exists now no sufficient reason for any communication with Parnell, other than across the floor of the House, either as to procedure or as to amendment of the Land Act; and I sincerely hope that no legislation on the latter subject may be necessary in the next session. It further appeared to me that some of Parnell's suggestions were of so objectionable a character, that I should regret even a simple acknowledgment of them without a protest.'

Mr. Gladstone in his reply put the other side of the case.

### Mr. Gladstone to Lord Hartington.

'HAWARDEN CASTLE, CHESTER,
'18th October 1882.

'The reply to Mrs. O'Shea is gone, with modifications, and with a paragraph proposing that any further communication, should there be such, should come through another channel.

'My recollection about the Cabinet is that there was informal conversation about it, but not any decision of any kind; much less that no communication should at any time be held with Parnell except across the table.

'In my opinion, as a general rule, every member of Parliament is entitled to make communications to the Government, at any time, and even though he be in avowed opposition to it. The exceptions to this rule, if any, would, I think, have to be founded on very definite grounds—I hold advisedly that this is a *right* of members of Parliament as such, and not a mere matter of policy. I cannot help thinking you may be inclined to allow some force to the consideration of the character with which a member of Parliament as such is invested.

'I think with you it would be very advantageous if Parliament could let Irish land lie fallow for a season. I should be glad, however, if circumstances were to allow of the passing of a good measure for local government in Ireland next year.'

If Mr. Barry O'Brien, the biographer of Mr. Parnell, and Mr. F. H. O'Donnell, the author of the *History of the Irish Parliamentary Party*, both of whom knew well the interior affairs of that connection, are correct in their statements, Mr. Gladstone continued to be in occasional communication with Parnell through Mrs. O'Shea until the end of the year 1885. After that time communications were, naturally, open and official, and were carried on, when necessary, through Mr. Morley and others, until Mr. Gladstone's denunciation of Parnell as an immoral man with whom he could no longer co-operate politically, in consequence of the O'Shea divorce case.[1]

Mr. Gladstone was consistent, and quite justified from his own point of view. He was continuing upon the lines of the new departure of April, which involved an attempt to carry out a working alliance between the Liberals and the Irish Nationalists. It was, on this basis, reasonable to consult the Irish leaders as to Irish legislation. Lord Hartington, never having made the 'new departure' in the same sense, still stood on the shore which his leader had quitted. As to the O'Sheas, they were no doubt an undesirable channel, but, assuming that there were to be communications, Parnell was the last man who would have agreed to carry them on through the medium of officials belonging to the Whig connection. The incident is interesting, and necessary to mention, because it shows how wide the divergence of feeling upon the Irish question already was between Mr. Gladstone and Lord Hartington.

[1] Mr. Barry O'Brien quotes, to corroborate his own statement on this point, that made to him by Mr. Chamberlain in an interview. I am not aware that the publication of this book elicited any denial.

Mr. F. H. O'Donnell says of Mrs. O'Shea that ' the most important and delicate negotiations had passed through her fine and tactful hands.' He is speaking of those between Gladstone and Parnell.—*A History of the Irish Parliamentary Party* (Longmans, 1910), vol. ii. p. 160.

# CHAPTER XVI

## EGYPT

THE Irish storm had not yet altogether subsided into more tranquil gloom, and some rural crimes of peculiar ferocity illumined with pale flashes the summer of 1882. But English attention was now called away from the waste Atlantic shores to the Mediterranean region.

Ismail Pasha, Khedive of Egypt, fifth in succession from Mehemet Ali (the Viceroy who made himself, save for a nominal suzerainty, independent of Constantinople), fell into the hands of European investors and concessionaires, accumulated a magnificent public debt, mostly incurred to meet foolish expenditure, sorely plundered his people, under the name of taxation, in order to raise money to meet coupons, and came at last beneath the control of the French and British Governments, who maintained the rights of their respective money-lenders. The financial 'dual control' was established in 1876. At the end of 1878, after a European commission of inquiry, there appeared to be a prospect of fiscal reform. Nubar Pasha formed a Ministry, in which Sir Rivers Wilson was Minister of Finance, and M. de Bligniéres of Public Works. In February 1879 there was an army demonstration at Cairo which caused the fall of Nubar. In April, the Khedive dismissed the European Ministers, and formed a purely Egyptian Government under Chérif Pasha, announcing also his determination to establish a truly free and representative assembly. The European Powers brought pressure to bear at Constantinople, with the result that Ismail was deposed and exiled from Egypt, and Prince Tewfik was installed as Khedive. In September 1879, Riaz Pasha replaced Chérif as Prime Minister, and, as Egypt was bankrupt, a Commission of Liquidation under Sir Rivers Wilson was constituted in the spring of 1880. Sir Evelyn Baring was at this time the British Controller-General of Finance until June 1880, when he was appointed by Lord Hartington to be Financial Member of Council in India, and for a space left the valley of the Nile. He was succeeded there by Sir Auckland Colvin.

The military movement headed by Colonel Ahmed Arábi became threatening early in the year 1881. There were mutinous proceedings at Cairo in February, and the colonels gained their object, the dismissal of the Minister of War. In September there was a more serious mutiny. Arábi marched 2500 men and 18 guns to the square before the Palace, and demanded the dismissal of the Ministry, the convocation of a Parliament, and an increase in the strength of the army. This mutiny, again, was successful. A new Ministry was formed under Chérif Pasha, with the consent of the British and French Governments. Chérif was the leader of that which Sir Auckland Colvin described, in a despatch of 26th December 1881, as 'an Egyptian national movement' of a liberal character. Sir Auckland thought that it was 'essentially the growth of the popular spirit,' that it was 'directed to the good of the country,' and that it 'would be most impolitic to thwart it.' He advised that it should be canalised within strict limits, and that 'neither the Government nor the Chamber should be allowed to forget that the Powers have assumed a direct financial control and mean to maintain it.'

Four days after this despatch reached the Foreign Office, Lord Granville took the step which Lord Cromer

deems an error, the acceptance of Gambetta's Anglo-
French Joint Note intimating the determination of the
two Powers to support the Khedive's Government 'by
their united efforts against all cause of complication,
internal or external, which might menace the order of
things established in Egypt.'[1]  Lord Cromer's comment is
that the Joint Note was issued 'without any sufficient
reason' at the moment when there was some hope that
the national party, the healthy element, might predominate
over the military party, the dangerous element.  The Note
operated like a candle in a mine.  'In an instant the two
elements combined with an explosion.'  This was the result
of another chemical combination, that of the cool Lord
Granville with the fiery Gambetta.  Events now rushed
forward towards the bombardment of Alexandria and the
battle of Tel-el-Kebir.  The Chérif Ministry fell in February,
and Arábi became Minister of War.  In France, Gambetta
resigned, and was succeeded by the timid, or pacific,
Freycinet.  The final result of this change was that England was left to carry out alone the armed intervention
which the initiative of France had made necessary.  Arábi
was now dictator in Egypt, and the country was falling
into a state of anarchy.  In May, the French Government
proposed that an Anglo-French squadron should be sent
to Alexandria, and admitted as a possibility the occupation
of Egypt by Turkish troops, an alternative which the
British Government preferred to an Anglo-French occupation.  The British Government desired, and the French

---

[1] Lord Cromer's *Modern Egypt*, vol. i. p. 223.  The acceptance was on
January 6, 1882.  Chérif Pasha told Sir E. Malet on 9th January that the Joint
Note was regarded (1) as encouraging the Khedive to place himself in antagonism
to reform, (2) as unfavourable to the new Chamber, (3) as indicating a desire to
loosen the tie to the Porte, (4) as containing a menace of intervention which
nothing in the present state of Egypt justified.  (Sir E. Malet to Lord Granville,
10th January 1882.)

Government did not desire, that other Powers should be represented navally before Alexandria, and, diplomatically, in the sanction given to a Turkish occupation. Lord Granville, however, agreed to the French proposal. At the end of May, the two Powers demanded from the Khedive that his Ministry should resign, and that Arábi should leave Egypt. The Ministers resigned, but Arábi did not retire, and, on the contrary, was reinstated as Minister. The British fleet, commanded by Lord Alcester, arrived at the end of May before Alexandria. On 11th June there was a Moslem riot in that city, and some fifty Europeans were murdered.

The French had proposed a conference of the great Powers at Constantinople. It met on 23rd June, Lord Dufferin representing the British Government. Meanwhile the military party in possession of Alexandria were raising batteries which commanded the fleet, the massacre was unavenged, and opinion in England was becoming impatient. In the Cabinet itself there was the usual conflict of opinion between those who desired to take strong action and those who did not. Lord Hartington's letters show on which side he stood in this matter. On the 27th of May he wrote :—

‘ I wonder whether any human being (out of Downing Street) would believe that not a word has been said in the Cabinet about Egypt for a fortnight, and I suppose will not be for another week, if then.’

When M. de Freycinet made the dilatory proposal of a conference of the Powers, Lord Hartington wrote (30th May), ‘ The French seem to be behaving worse than badly.’ He thought the proposal was ‘ nothing less than a breach of faith with us, and practically a desertion of the Khedive, who will inevitably be killed before the English and French troops can possibly intervene. . . . What is the use of such allies? They have brought us into the fearful mess we are in. I believe it would be easier to deal with the Turks and the whole of the remaining European Powers than with them alone.'

The two following extracts are also illuminating :—

*Lord Hartington to Lord Granville, 14th June 1882.*

'I am getting very unhappy about Egypt. It is a fort-night to-day since we agreed to the conference, and we seem to be scarcely any nearer to its assembling, or to the adoption of any measures for restoring order, and all the time the state of things is getting worse and more dis-creditable to us.'

The French do not seem even yet to intend to ask the Turks to send troops. 'They seem to look on the confer-ence as the main object, whereas it is now nothing but the means towards affecting the main object, viz. the despatch of a Turkish force.' 'It seems to me that, if we are to wait till we can get all Europe to move together, we shall never move at all. Could we not tell the French that, if they will not join us in asking the Turks to send troops at once under conditions to be settled at the conference, we must ask them ourselves? And we might tell the Turks at the same time that, if they continue to make difficulties about the conference, or about the conditions of the employment of their troops, we shall be compelled to resort to a joint occupation by English and French.'

*Lord Hartington to Lord Granville, 20th June 1882.*

'The Government is, in my opinion, in more imminent danger of being broken up than it has ever yet been. I heard from Northbrook last night that he had had a con-versation with Kimberley, who, he understood, agreed with our views. . . . I don't think that any of us wish to be unreasonable as to the time when the final declaration of our policy should be made. The essential points are that we cannot accept the present position in Egypt even if sanctioned by the conference, that we are ready for a joint French and English intervention if the Turks refuse, and (for myself) an English one if the French refuse.'

It was agreed at the Cabinet of 21st June, as a compromise between the rival views, that the War Office and Admiralty should consider what would be the best means of protecting the Suez Canal, should occasion arise. Two battalions were also to be sent to the Mediterranean stations. On July the 8th Lord Granville wrote to Lord Hartington :—

'Gladstone admitted to me yesterday for the first time that we were bound to protect the Suez Canal, but neither he nor Bright would agree at present to any advance on the agreement of the other day.'

This 'agreement' was, no doubt, that under which instructions were sent, on 3rd July, to Lord Alcester to prevent by force, if necessary, the continuance of work on the land - batteries at Alexandria. The French Government declined to take part in action at Alexandria on the ground, or pretext, that they could not make war without the consent of their Chamber, and their squadron left those waters. Lord Alcester, after demanding surrender of the forts, bombarded them on 11th July. On the 12th, the Egyptian garrison evacuated Alexandria, leaving the town on fire, and under pillage by the mob, until a force of marines were landed from the fleet. On the evening of the 11th, Lord Hartington wrote the following note to Lord Granville :—

*Lord Hartington to Lord Granville, 11th July.*

'I am afraid that there is no chance of a Cabinet, or of getting Mr. Gladstone to pay any attention to Egypt while the Arrears Bill is going on.

'But the next move may be very important, and we ought to be ready for it.

'The action at Alexandria may settle Arábi, but we cannot reckon on it. If it does not, it has probably increased the divergence between us and Turkey and France. After all that has happened lately there can scarcely be much use in keeping up any longer the fiction of any special alliance between us and France.

'Bismarck seems to be the only man who can help us, if he chooses. He will probably rather admire our vigour, especially if we push on our preparations. Can't we tell him that if the Turks decline, as they probably will, we are quite ready to act, either alone or with other Powers, and get him to make a proposal to the conference?'

The Government were blamed for not having had at hand some military force which might have landed on the evening of the bombardment, and saved Alexandria from a costly night of fire and plunder. The reason given by Mr. Gladstone to the House of Commons on 22nd July was that to land a force would have involved 'the assumption of authority upon the Egyptian question,' and would have been 'grossly disloyal in the face of Europe and the conference.' As Lord Cromer remarks, 'It is difficult to conceive the frame of mind of any one who considers that firing several thousand shot and shell into Egyptian forts did not involve an 'assumption of authority,' whereas landing some men to prevent a populous city from being burnt to the ground did involve such an assumption.'[1] Public interests suffered through these Egyptian events from the fact that Mr. Gladstone was acting, unwillingly and perforce, on behalf of British 'interests,' and in opposition to the fundamentally anti-imperial principles which he had laid down in his attacks on Disraeli. There were consequently throughout weak and disastrous compromises

[1] *Modern Egypt*, vol. ii. p. 298.

between the 'Aye' and the 'No' of action. Arábi was
now more defiant than ever, the anarchy of Egypt more
complete, and a few days showed that much larger steps
were necessary. On 22nd July Lord Hartington wrote to
Lord Granville :—

'I am very sorry that Mr. Gladstone does not feel able
to go as far as you proposed in the note which you showed
me. It seems to me that what will be needed above all
things on Monday will be a very clear statement of the
objects we have in view in sending the force to the
Mediterranean. I think that Parliament will feel that there
is something to be condoned in the delay which has led to
such disastrous consequences in Egypt, and that it has a
right to expect a pledge from us that the resources which
are to be placed at our disposal will be used in any way
that may be necessary to repair them.'

The force of public opinion now ran with irresistible
force, and carried down the stream the reluctant Prime
Minister. On 22nd July, Mr. Gladstone stated in the House
of Commons that, if the co-operation of the European
Powers could not be obtained, the work of restoring order
in Egypt would be 'undertaken by the single power of
England.' A grant of £2,300,000 was made by the House
of Commons, 15,000 troops were sent to the Mediterranean,
and an order was cabled to India for the despatch of
5000 more. Sir Garnet Wolseley was placed in command.
The campaign was short and decisive. The victory at
Tel-el-Kebir was won at dawn on the 13th September, and,
late next day, the English and Indian cavalry under Sir
Drury Lowe rode into Cairo, preventing by this swift and
daring movement the chance that Cairo might share the
fate of Alexandria after the bombardment. It was one of
the great moments of history.

Egypt, though statesmen at home neither knew nor

desired it, had virtually become one of the protected States within the British Empire. Never has there been a more striking instance of the prevalence of destiny over the intentions of men than this result achieved by the unwilling hands of Gladstone. His belief, or, rather, his self-justification, at the time, was that his Government were merely repressing a military tyranny 'incompatible with the growth and existence of freedom.' He observed that the reigns of Cromwell and Napoleon 'had done nothing for English or French freedom.'[1] He said, 'We have carried out this war from a love of peace, and, I may say, on the principle of peace.'[2] These convenient theories liberalised armed intervention, and distinguished it, to Mr. Gladstone's apparent satisfaction, from Disraelian imperialism. John Bright saw the thing in a different light, and thought that the real origin and cause of this use of force was to protect the road to India and the interests of bond-holders. He resigned his place in the Cabinet. To hold one is, perhaps, an impossible position for a genuine member of the excellent Society of Friends. But the instinct of the nation cordially supported Mr. Gladstone in a reluctant policy which, had it been carried out by Lord Beaconsfield, he would certainly have denounced. 'Where,' sadly wrote one all too consistent Nonconformist minister to a Radical paper, 'where are those unions, conferences, Liberal hundreds, leaders of the masses, and eminent philanthropists, who denounced the Tory wars? Not one of them, or scarcely one, has a word to say, or speech to make, or sermon to preach.'

[1] House of Commons, 22nd July 1882.
[2] Speech at Penmaenmawr, 3rd October 1882.

# CHAPTER XVII

## INTERNAL POLITICS—1882-1883

AT the moment when all available power of attention should have been concentrated upon Egypt, the Cabinet suffered from some difference of opinion with regard to the measure for dealing with arrears of rent in Ireland. On the 9th July, two days before the action at Alexandria, one of his Cabinet colleagues wrote to Lord Hartington :—

'From an expression you let fall at the Cabinet, I see that you have formed the opinion that the end of the Government is at hand on the Arrears Bill. I agree in that opinion, and it is an event I do not at all deprecate, nor would do anything to avert. The only justification for the Arrears Bill is that it would pacify Ireland. But from all I hear it will do nothing of the kind. . . . The *couleur de rose* view in which Gladstone persists in looking at the state of Ireland is most disastrous. In my judgment it incapacitates the Government from doing what is necessary to restore peace there. . . . In my opinion the sooner the end comes the better, for this Government is not fit to govern Ireland.'

If Mr. Gladstone saw Ireland through glasses too much the colour of the rose, some of his colleagues saw it through glasses too much darkened. The failure of the English land system, as applied to Ireland, was a fact. Destiny drove the Liberals to begin, and the Conservatives to complete, its destruction. War and revolution are nature's attempt to rectify a diseased condition of things, and the business of the statesman is to canalise natural forces, and to guide a nation smoothly down its predestined course. This was achieved in the case of Ireland when Lord Salisbury's Government strongly maintained order *and* passed the Land Purchase Acts.

One effect of the tragedy of May was that the new measure strengthening the power of the law in Ireland passed rapidly through the House of Commons. It had become evident, however, that there must be some change in procedure adapted to the changed conditions of the time. The unlimited right of speech had to be curtailed. Apart from the Irish, this step would, before long, have become necessary in consequence of the vast increase of business transacted in an assembly which has to deal with increasing imperial affairs, and at the same time with the rapidly increasing sphere of legislation in three very distinct kingdoms; in consequence also of the widened representation of different social classes, and the importation into Parliament of a much larger number than formerly of ambitious and energetic men, whose position depends, not on social status, but on their power to make themselves heard and noticed. Lord Hartington, on 20th March 1882, defended the proposal to introduce the principle of 'closure.' He did so on the ground that the 'time of the House belongs not to every individual member of the House, but to the House itself.' Those who claimed unlimited right of speech really claimed, he said, the appropriation of something which was not theirs, the time of the House, which might be better employed. Conservative opponents replied that the closure was an invasion of the power and freedom of the House of Commons, and would, in the end, lead to the autocracy of the Prime Minister. This view no doubt was largely true, but the stream of change was too strong to be resisted. The old House of Commons consisted of gentlemen of varying views but no very deep-lying divisions, who played at politics as at cricket, observing the rules. The Irish and Radical movements, deriving power from the great extensions of the franchise in 1867 and 1884, turned the game into something more nearly resembling a war—war, as Lord Salisbury once observed, 'with the gloves on'—and civil wars in all ages and countries have led towards the greatly increased power of the central executive.

The limitation of the right of speech was regarded as a disagreeable necessity by the older parliamentarians, Mr. Gladstone for one. The following letter shows the view taken by Lord Hartington, and his feeling at this time as to the relation between the two main parties :—

BALMORAL CASTLE, October 7, 1882.

MY DEAR MR. GLADSTONE,—I had some talk with Granville in London the other day about the autumn session and about Procedure, and he urged me to write to you fully my views on these subjects. I have since received a copy of your letter to him of the 2nd, which seems to be in some degree an answer to his report of our conversation.

I confess that I am extremely anxious about the prospects of the autumn session, and I apprehend that, if it is not very carefully managed, it will not only be productive of no good results, but will leave us in a worse position as regards obstruction and the powerlessness of Parliament than it finds us.

The necessary shortness of the session is one considerable danger. We know by experience that the time of an ordinary session is quite insufficient for the work which the Government proposes to do ; but, at its commencement, the time looks almost unlimited, and the prospect of opposing by mere delay a measure which the Government brings forward and pushes on with all its might does not at first appear to be very hopeful. But the duration of the autumn session is absolutely limited to six or seven weeks; it is not likely that discussion on Egypt or Ireland can be excluded; and, with the experience which has lately been acquired, it will be easy enough for a strong and resolute Opposition to defeat by delay any of the Procedure Rules to which they are strongly opposed. And what is worse is that the resistance aimed at one or two specially obnoxious Rules will possibly be fatal to the whole series. I think that there can be no doubt that a great part of the Opposition do honestly dread and dislike the Cloture by the bare majority, and that the remainder see in it a good subject for a party fight. Is there any reason to think that, under such circumstances, they will only offer to it a moderate resistance, and that, having made their protest, they will submit to the decision of the majority? On the contrary, I think there is every reason to believe that, having the power, as I am firmly convinced they have, to defeat it by delay, they will use it.

At all events, I feel tolerably certain that, if you do carry the Cloture by the bare majority, it will be at the expense of the other important Rules about Supply and Standing Committees. If you get rid of Cloture by some compromise, there may be time to discuss these, and come to some experimental arrangement about them; but a contest such as I anticipate on Cloture, *pur et simple*, will leave no time for any other debatable question.

Is this worth while? I retain the opinion that the bare majority is the right principle; but I think that it is far more a question of logical accuracy than of practical importance. It will never be possible in practice to enforce the Cloture on the regular Opposition. The practical evil with which this Rule is intended to deal is obstruction by small minorities, and for this purpose, and for all cases of which we have had experience, the two-thirds would do just as well as the bare majority. We cannot expect in one short session to make a complete and perfect reform of our procedure, involving so many important changes in the former practice. The essential thing is to establish the principle that *a* majority may, under certain circumstances, put a stop to debate. When once the principle has been established, it will be pushed as far as may be necessary, and if ever a large majority abuses its privileges as small ones have recently done, the rule will be extended so as to meet the case.

I think it is impossible to contend that this is a question of principle of so much importance as to justify the certain waste of a great deal of time, and the possible wreck of the whole reform of procedure. We may have very good explanations to give for withdrawing the offer of the compromise made in May, but the country will never understand that what we ourselves *proposed* in May is so inadmissible in October that the whole power of the majority must be exercised to force it on the minority at the risk of the loss of the session.

The reform of procedure is admitted to be a subject which ought, if possible, to be dealt with by communication and consultation between the leaders of the two great parties. We made some attempt last February to deal with it in this way, but it was not successful, and perhaps it was not made in a way which was very likely to succeed. I think that, owing to want of time, our proposals were made known to the Opposition just before the meeting of Parliament, and rather as settled intentions of the Government than as subjects for consultation and discussion. The frequent interruptions and fragmentary character of the debates made it rather difficult to ascertain what was the exact position towards the Rules which was taken up by the Opposition ; but, though they have never said as much, I think there is little doubt that the leaders would either willingly accept, or be compelled by public opinion to accept, the two-thirds majority as a fair compromise. This brings me to other considerations, which I find it difficult to describe, but which have more influence with me than any of the preceding ones.

During this autumn there has been, I think, for the first time for the last five or six years, some intermission in the intensity and bitterness of party spirit. There is no use in going back to the times of the late Government, but I suppose it may be admitted that, though it may have been justified by the end in view, the extreme violence of the attacks on the late Government must sometimes have had an unfortunate effect on the policy of the country. Certainly during the existence of this Government I think it is impossible to estimate the mischief which has been done. The constant and hostile cross-questioning and partial discussions arising from this temper during the Egyptian difficulties were a great embarrassment, and, over and over again, nearly upset the whole policy. But it is in Ireland where I think that the violence of party spirit has done the most harm. I have always thought that the position which Parnell and his party have been able to assume in the House of Commons, and the impunity with which he has been able to defy and sometimes insult the House of Commons, have had a great deal to do with the collapse of order in Ireland. It would never have been possible for them to have obtained this position but for the intensity of the party conflicts, in which both the great constitutional parties seemed to hate and distrust each other a great deal more than the open and avowed enemies of order and of the Constitution.

Whether it will last or not, no one can tell, but there does seem to be a sort of lull at the present moment; and the great successes in Egypt, and the signs of improvement in Ireland, ought to have some effect in improving the temper of both sides. If we do not go out of our way to irritate the Opposition, and if we can avoid, as I think we might, any very burning question next session, I should hope for a considerable diminution of the bitterness of feeling between the two parties. But, if the session of 1883 opens in the middle of a violent and

unsettled party fight about procedure, I see no prospect
of a session more satisfactory than the two last, and
every prospect of the Irish party being able to do more
mischief, and undo any improvement which has taken
place.

If all this should happen, I cannot think that we shall
be altogether free from responsibility. We shall not have
gone one inch in the direction of conciliation. We are
insisting on a point, on which the Opposition have nailed
their colours to the mast, and we have not; which they
consider, or say that they consider, of the first importance,
and *we avowedly do not*; on which their party is unanimous,
and ours is not.

I am aware that in your letter to Granville you suggest
another concession which you think we might make, and
which might be accepted in a spirit of conciliation. However acceptable it might be in regard to the other rules, I
am afraid that it will not be accepted as any concession in
regard to the Closing power. Granville's objection appears
to me conclusive. The experience of one session may
prove that the Rule is intolerable, but, on the other hand,
it cannot possibly prove that in another session, under
totally different circumstances, it will be tolerable. Besides,
if you are going to make the new Rules experimental, does
not this concession point to the adoption of the other?
Is it not more reasonable to try as an experiment whether
the *milder* rule is sufficient than whether the more severe
rule is intolerable? But my great objection is that I do
not think that the Opposition will accept it as a compromise, and I admit that I am almost as anxious to
avoid a quarrel as to have a good cause if we cannot
avoid one.

I am heartily ashamed of the length of this letter,
but having been asked to write *fully*, I have been
unable to make it shorter; and indeed I am afraid
that I have omitted a good deal of what I ought to
have urged.

I do not think that I ever had a stronger opinion on

a question which is one more of policy than of principle than I have on this.—Yours sincerely,

HARTINGTON.

Mr. Gladstone said in his reply (October 9, 1882) :—

'I do not think the length of your letter requires any apology. It is useful to have all the points raised in a difficult matter. I had better say at once that it contains much in which I cannot follow you, but there would be little advantage in my enumerating the points one by one, and arguing upon them. The more so, as the matters in which we are agreed are fundamentals; and especially there is the fact that we both take a very serious view of the matter.

'Indeed I go beyond you in this that I think there is one very grave element in the case which you do not mention. It is this, that a large part, probably the majority, of the Conservative party are not agreed with us as to our aim. We want a drastic reform of procedure, with a view both to a diminution of the aggregate labours of the House of Commons and especially to a more rapid and extensive transaction of legislative business. This is exactly what they do *not* want. The noble function which they assign to the House of Lords, of retarding the hasty proceedings of the House of Commons, is at present, more conveniently and safely for them, performed by the state of procedure in the House of Commons itself ; and this advantage I do not think they will lightly surrender.

'I was, as you know, originally of the opinion that the closing power was not worth all the squabbling it would cost ; but I gave way to you and to the Cabinet generally. I still hold the same opinions, but I have now to consider together with the *plus* quantity of value in the closing power, the *minus* quantity on the other side of the equation, which is practically the same thing, namely, the difficulty and discredit of retirement from a ground which we have actually taken up—which we have fought for many nights—and to which I believe the large majority of our friends attach, like our foes, a vast, though as I think, an exaggerated importance.'

The rest of Mr. Gladstone's letter dealt with details not now of interest, but it is worth noting that he thought that 'a closing power, such as we propose, could not possibly be used with effect in an unjust or harsh manner against a large minority, *i.e.* a regular Opposition.'

Mr. Gladstone, when he assumed power in 1880, told the Queen and others that it was his intention to hold it only for a year or two. He proposed to set right the misdoings of his predecessor in foreign and Indian policy, and then to retire. This intention, to which he frequently referred, was a cause of weakness to the Government by reason of the uncertainties to which it gave rise. It was, however, a powerful means of retaining Lord Hartington in the Cabinet, who felt that, if he himself resigned, the leadership might in a few months pass into the hands of a Radical successor. In November 1882 the following letters passed between Mr. Gladstone and Lord Hartington :—

*Lord Hartington to Mr. Gladstone.*

'SANDRINGHAM, *Nov.* 12, 1882.

'Granville showed me his letter of October 28th which he had written to you with reference to yours to Spencer, a copy of which you had sent to him and me.

'It seemed to me at that time unnecessary to add anything to what he had said, partly because the contingency on which your intentions were based, viz., the passing of the Procedure Rules appeared to be still uncertain, partly because I agreed with him that the question of your retirement was one which it was rather for us to decline to discuss, than to discuss.

'But your letter of the 11th, which Granville has sent to

me, makes it necessary that I should at least say a word before you take any further step, or proceed to any further discussion on the subject.

'As to your reasons for retirement, I will only say, that without venturing to dispute any opinion which you have formed, which rests on your own feelings and your sense of your own powers, I am convinced that there does not at this moment exist in the party any man possessing a fraction of those mental powers which you consider so necessary to future constructive legislation.

'But as to the effect of your retirement upon the party, I feel bound to state my own clear and distinct opinion. I think the leadership of the House of Commons, in its present temper, an impossibility for any one but yourself. The advanced section which forms the strength, if not the majority of the party, would require stronger measures from any successor than it would from you—measures in which I should certainly not be prepared to lead them. And if any other leader should attempt the task, I do not think that the tie—already strained—which unites the moderate section with the party would hold for a moment.

'My letters of last month on Procedure and other matters must have proved to you how unfit, and how indisposed I am to take charge of such legislation, especially in regard to Ireland, as I conceive you anticipate as necessary, and which certainly the advanced party have been led to expect; and I more than doubt whether I should be justified in attempting to resume the leadership in the House of Commons under such circumstances.

'It would be no sacrifice to me to see it placed in the hands of others who would not feel the same difficulties, but I cannot pretend to think that such an arrangement would have any prospect of success or permanence. For these and many other reasons which I need not enter into now, I cannot feel a doubt in my own mind that your retirement would lead to the speedy, if not the immediate dissolution of the Government and of the present Liberal majority.'

*Mr. Gladstone to Lord Hartington.*

'10 DOWNING STREET,
'WHITEHALL, *Nov.* 13, 1882.

'I thank you very much for your letter. There is no hurry. In no case should I do anything in a hurry: there is much to consider; I am bound to visit Mid-Lothian: this must of course be after the prorogation. I look to a preliminary conversation with Granville; and I will then communicate with you further. My idea generally is that there is no *great* question immediately or soon to come on, probably none for this Parliament, on which Whigs and Radicals could not put up their horses together. I think Ireland is the sorest place, but this is not markedly a question of division between our sections.'

Sir William Harcourt, on 10th December, wrote to Lord Hartington that he had had a visit, in the New Forest, from Mr. Gladstone :—

'I spoke to him very strongly about the position in which the Cabinet and the party would be on his departure, and the impossibility of holding the various sections together without the authority of his name. He constantly observed, "What you say is exactly what Hartington told me." . . . His view of his own situation is that, though he was equal to the regular House of Commons work, and even to administration generally, his brain powers (as he phrased it) would not enable him to face the great measures of construction which are before the Liberal party.'

The upshot of all this was that Mr. Gladstone consented to go on, giving up, however, the work of Chancellor of the Exchequer which, since 1880, he had combined with that of Prime Minister. Mr. Childers went from the War Office to the Treasury, Lord Hartington consented to take the War Office, and was succeeded at the India Office by Lord Kimberley. Some of his friends thought that Lord Hartington, as next in succession to the Prime Ministership, should have claimed the Chancellorship of the Exchequer. The War Office, one wrote to him, was a difficult and thankless post, not higher in dignity than the India Office, and to 'step into the old shoes of Mr. Childers,' on his promotion to the office usually held by the first or second man in the Government, was something of a descent. It was not, however, in Lord Hartington's character to make difficulties about matters of this kind. The War Office, at any rate, was not inferior in hierarchic dignity to the India Office. Some other changes were made, and Lord Derby and Sir Charles Dilke entered the Cabinet. This rearrangement was completed by Christmas 1882.

One of Lord Hartington's last acts at the India Office was to appoint a successor to the permanent Under-Secretary, Sir Louis Mallet, the very able representative of a family distinguished in the annals of our Civil Service. The following letter from Sir Louis is of interest :—

INDIA OFFICE,
*29th November* 1882.

DEAR LORD HARTINGTON,—I have latterly often felt that the time could not be distant, when I should be compelled, by the increasing difficulty of passing the winter in London, to retire from my present office, and recent experience has satisfied me, very reluctantly, that it will be better that I should do so in the course of the coming year.

Independently of this decisive consideration, I am inclined to think that the best precedents of the service are not in favour of the retention of offices such as mine much beyond the age which Parliament has assigned as the appropriate limit. In the present case, at all events, the very heavy and unintermittent work of this department requires the unimpaired energy, and perhaps the more sanguine temper of a man in the full vigour of life.

Much as I shall regret the close of our official connection, upon which I shall always look back with pleasure, there is no one to whom I would so willingly resign my office, because I have entire confidence in the choice which you would desire to make of my successor, a question in which, I may perhaps be excused for saying, I feel great anxiety.

The Under-Secretaryship in the three political offices, Foreign, Colonial, and Indian, are certainly among the most important appointments which a Government has to make—for, although obscure and subordinate, the holders have at least much power, both of causing and of preventing mischief.

As regards India, it is, I am convinced, more and more to be desired, with a view to the inevitable tendencies of things—that whoever fills my office, should possess the habits of thought and of political training engendered by contact with English public life—and that he should be in sympathy with the best forms of liberal opinions.

At the centre of a vast administration, composed of powerful services, the India Office is the connecting link between two systems of government—the Parliamentary and the Autocratic, which are always liable to be brought into dangerous collision—and the Under-Secretary is the one permanent official whose especial function it should be to resist and restrain the influences of the bureaucratic spirit which always animates and pervades, more or less, Anglo-Indian counsels, and to endeavour to throw light on the dark places in Indian government.

It is also very important that he should have a general knowledge of economic and financial principles, or he will be of little use in unravelling the intricate threads of the various complex problems of Indian administration.

The man of all others for the post would have been Baring, and I have reason to know that he would have liked it, but he cannot cut short his Indian work, and unless some unforeseen accident occurs in the course of the next six months, I fear that it will be impossible to make my resignation coincident with the term of his present office.

This is not, however, a matter for me to decide, I can

only leave it in your hands, convinced as I am that you will understand the strong interest which I feel in the selection which may be made.

Always, dear Lord Hartington, sincerely yours,

LOUIS MALLET.

Lord Hartington, with Mr. Gladstone's approval, chose Mr. Arthur Godley, who had worked on the Prime Minister's staff, to succeed to Sir Louis Mallet, and a long and distinguished service has proved that no better choice could have been made.[1] He had occurred, as the best man for the post, independently to the minds of Lord Northbrook, Lord Granville, and Sir Louis Mallet, a rare proof of pre-ordination.

II

During the winter of 1882–83 the Liberal party was distracted by divisions of opinion as to that local government or administrative decentralisation in Ireland which, it was vaguely conceived, was an approaching question. The Queen's Speech at the opening of the session of 1881 had stated that a measure would be submitted to Parliament 'for the establishment of County Councils in Ireland founded upon the representative principle, and framed with the double aim of confirming popular control over expenditure, and of supplying a yet more serious want by extending the formation of habits of local self-government.'

This proposal sounds innocuous enough at the present day, and Irish County Councils were, in fact, established by Lord Salisbury's Government in 1898. But in 1881 most of Ireland was in a rebellious and disorderly condition, the Land Act had not been passed, and the conditions in which the elective principle could be with any safety introduced into local administration were absent. Elective County

---

[1] Afterward Sir Arthur Godley, and now Lord Kilbracken.

Councils had not at that date been instituted even in England and Scotland.

The ministerial manifesto, called the Speech from the Throne, is annually composed in 10 Downing Street by the Prime Minister and his secretaries, out of contributions suggested by different departments, almost at the last moment, and the Cabinet do not hear it as a whole until immediately before Parliament opens. This proceeding gives a certain power to the Prime Minister, if he likes to use it. The paragraph about Irish County Councils seems to have been inserted without Lord Hartington's previous knowledge or approval. Mr. Gladstone, however, in 1883, laid much stress upon it as indicating that extension of local government was, *pari passu* with coercive measures, the policy agreed to by the Cabinet. In the recess of 1882–83 the Liberal leaders had spoken on this subject with diverse voices. Mr. Gladstone, in a letter to M. Clémenceau, had said, ' What I hope and desire, what I labour for and have at heart, is to decentralise authority in Ireland. We have disestablished the Church, we have relieved the tenant class of many grievances, and are now going to produce a state of things which will make the humblest Irishman realise that he is a governing agency, and that the government is to be carried on by him and for him.'[1] His son, Mr. Herbert Gladstone, in a speech at Leeds, had strongly attacked the system of Irish government, and avowed himself to be an advocate of the widest possible measures of local self-government, and Mr. Chamberlain had said :—

'So long as Ireland is without any institution of local government worthy of the name, so long the seeds of

---

[1] Lord Salisbury, who was averse to any cant, said that he did 'not much like the idea of the humblest Irishman as a "governing agency."' What would Carlyle have said?

discontent and disloyalty will remain, only to burst forth
into luxurious growth at the first favourable season.'

Lord Hartington, on the other hand, said, in a speech
at Bacup in January 1883 :—

'It is supposed by some that by changes in the system
of local self-government we can restore contentment to
Ireland. It would be madness, in my opinion, to give
Ireland more extended self-government unless we can
receive from the Irish people some assurance that this
boon would not be used for the purposes of agitation.'

Lord Salisbury, in the House of Lords, at the opening of the session of 1883, said that there had been a
'regular tournament between the various members of the
Government in which Lord Hartington had challenged all
comers.' He added, 'It is not for me to reconcile these
divergent opinions ; it is enough to say that Mr. Chamberlain's and Mr. Gladstone's views are regarded by Lord
Hartington as madness.' In the House of Commons Lord
Randolph Churchill said—

'the noble Marquis is more closely connected with Ireland
than almost any man in this House. He is connected with
that country by the vast estates which are the appanage of
his house ; he is connected with it by a long and prosperous administration of its affairs ; and he is connected
with it by the bitter memory of an irreparable loss. The
noble Marquis is one of the few, perhaps the only, statesman in whom the people of this country are prepared to
repose a large and generous measure of confidence.'

Would the noble Marquis, therefore, he asked, say
whether Mr. Herbert Gladstone's utterances were simply
the expression of personal views, or whether they reflected
the tendency of Liberal legislation ? Lord Hartington,
thus appealed to, answered that Mr. Herbert Glad-

stone's speech contained much with which he could not
agree, but that no Government could be responsible for
the opinions of one of its members, especially one not in
the Cabinet. There might be room for improvements in
the Irish executive system, but, he added :—

'I am certainly of opinion, whatever changes it may be
desirable to make, that this is not a time, that the state of
political feeling in Ireland is not such, as would make it
desirable that the Executive Government of Ireland should
be relieved of any of the responsibilities which now lie on
them, or be deprived of any of the powers they now exercise for the maintenance of public order, and for the
repression and detection of crime.'

On the following day Mr. Chamberlain made the start-
ling speech, so famous at the time, in which he compared
Ireland under English rule to Poland under Russian.
Thus the difference between the Whig position and the
Radical was brought clean-cut before the public view.

The men who were directly responsible for Irish
government certainly thought that the condition of Ireland was not one in which administrative powers could be
weakened. The Phœnix Park murderers were not tried
and convicted till June 1883. They had been discovered
through informers. Lord Spencer then wrote to Lord
Hartington that even these criminals met with sympathy.
He said :—

'The fact is that anything which is a movement against
Anglo-Saxon rule enlists sympathy among certain classes
here. The men engaged in those crimes were enthusiasts
in politics and perfectly reckless as to consequences. This
shows a frightfully demoralised state of society, and nothing
but stern execution of the law can bring men so influenced
to their senses.'

In a letter of 16th January Lord Spencer told Lord

Hartington that Mr. Gladstone 'seems bent on a Local Government Bill for Ireland going as far as Provincial Councils.' The Chief Secretary, Mr. Trevelyan, wrote to express his admiration for, and complete concurrence with, Hartington's Bacup speech. 'The right policy,' he said, 'seems to be to go our own way, to appeal to the law-abiding party in the country, whether it is large or small, and, above everything, to say what one really believes and thinks about Ireland, and not what it is the fashion to think that one ought to think.' The following correspondence shows the positions now held by Mr. Gladstone and by Lord Hartington. Mr. Gladstone was taking rest on the Riviera; Lord Granville, as usual, mediated.

*Extract from letter from Mr. Gladstone to Lord Granville, 22nd January 1883.*

'To-day I have been a good deal distressed by a passage as reported in Hartington's very strong and able speech, for which I am at a loss to account, so far does it travel out into the open, and so awkward are the intimations it seems to convey. I felt that I could not do otherwise than telegraph to you in cipher on the subject. But I used words intended to show that, while I thought an immediate notification needful, I was far from wishing to hasten a reply, and desired to leave altogether in your hands the modes of touching a delicate matter. Pray use the widest discrimination. I console myself with thinking it is hardly possible that Hartington *can* have meant to say what nevertheless both *Times* and *Daily News* make him seem to say, namely, that we recede from, or throw into abeyance, the declarations we have constantly made about our desire to extend local government, properly so called, to Ireland, on the first opportunity which the state of business in Parliament would permit. We announced our intention to do this at the very moment when we were preparing to suspend the *Habeas Corpus* Act.

'Since that time we have seen our position in Ireland immensely strengthened, and the leader of the agitation has even thought it wise, and has dared, to pursue a somewhat conciliatory course.

'Many of his coadjutors are still as vicious, it may be, as ever, but how can we say, for instance, to the Ulster men, you shall remain with shortened liberties, and without local government, because Biggar and Co. are hostile to British connection?

'There has also come prominently into view a new and powerful set of motives which, in my deliberate judgment, require us, for the sake of the United Kingdom even *more* than for the sake of Ireland, to push forward this question.

'Under the present highly centralised system of government, every demand which can be started on behalf of a poor and ill-organised country comes directly on the British Government and Treasury; if refused, it becomes at once a head of grievance, if granted, not only a new drain, but a certain source of political complication and embarrassment.

'The peasant proprietary—the winter distress—the state of the labourers—the loans to farmers—the promotion of public works—the encouragement of fisheries—the promotion of emigration—each and every one of these questions has a sting, and the sting can only be taken out of it by our treating it in correspondence with a popular and responsible *Irish* body—competent to act for its own part of the country.

'Every consideration, which prompted our pledges, prompts the recognition of them, and their extension rather than curtailment. The Irish Government have in preparation a Local Government Bill.

'Such a Bill may even be an economy of time.

'By no other means that I can see shall we be able to ward off most critical and questionable discussions on questions of the class I have mentioned.

'The argument that we cannot yet trust Irishmen with popular local institutions is the mischievous argument by which the Conservative Opposition to the Melbourne Government ruined, and finally crippled, the reform of Municipal Corporations in Ireland.

'By acting on principles diametrically opposite, we have broken down to thirty-five or forty what would have been a party, in this Parliament, of sixty-five Home Rulers, and have thus arrested (or at the very best have postponed) the perilous crisis, which no man has yet looked in the face: the crisis which will arise when a large and united majority of Irish members demand some fundamental change in the legislative relations of the two countries.

'I can ill convey to you how clear are my thoughts, or how earnest my convictions, on this important subject. Do not hurry any reply, if you find the reply difficult.'[1]

*Lord Hartington to Lord Granville, 25th January* 1883.

'I am very sorry that my speech should have caused so much disturbance to Mr. Gladstone, and I fear that I cannot say anything reassuring. My reason for forestalling the discussions in the Cabinet was that other members of the Government, Chamberlain for instance, and Herbert Gladstone, had spoken very strongly in the sense of advocating a large change in the local government of Ireland, and that it appeared to me that the Cabinet might, to a certain extent, become committed to a policy which it had never discussed, and to which I felt the strongest objection.

'Till I read Mr. Gladstone's letter I confess that I had forgotten that the subject of Irish Local Government had ever been mentioned in a Queen's Speech by the present Government. How the paragraph referred to by Mr. Gladstone could have found its way there I cannot in the least remember. So far as I know, no Bill was ever proposed by the Irish Government. No discussion upon it ever took place in the Cabinet, and I can recollect no reference to, or explanation of, the paragraph in debates.

[1] This letter is printed in Lord Morley's *Life of Gladstone*, vol. iii. p. 553.

'But the pledge which was then given might have been an extremely harmless one. It might have committed us and I should suppose, in the opinion of the Irish Government, did commit us, to nothing more than the alterations in the grand jury laws which had been in slightly different shapes proposed by Liberal and Conservative Governments. I should not think it wise in the present state of Ireland to introduce any repetition of such measures, which would satisfy nobody, would disgust a few, and would, if carried, only effect some slight alterations in the mode of managing county roads, bridges, buildings, and a few other small matters, and would at the same time enable a few more seditious resolutions to be passed by constituted public bodies. But no measure of this character would in the slightest degree fulfil the expectations which have been held out by Chamberlain, or accomplish the objects indicated by Mr. Gladstone. I have not the slightest conception of the bodies which it is proposed to create, or of the powers which it is proposed to confer upon them; and I cannot imagine that the Cabinet should have agreed to such a revolution in the system of Irish government, as is pointed to in the letter, with only a week for consideration before the measure was announced in the Queen's Speech. But whatever the plan may be I see no prospect of my being able to support it. I think that Ireland requires a strong government, and I am opposed to taking away any of the powers of the executive, and placing them in the hands of the enemies of the Government. The difficulties of the Government are increased by the action of every popular institution in the country, from the Irish representatives in Parliament to the town commissioner of a small village. The attempt to rely on juries selected from the body of the people had to be abandoned. I cannot think that this is the time for creating new and powerful bodies which will certainly use every power you confer upon them for the embarrassment of the Government, and the further destruction of the property of the landlords.'

*Extract from letter from Lord Hartington to Lord Granville,*
*30th January* 1883.

' I cannot imagine what you consider Mr. Gladstone's
weighty arguments. They seem to me to be dreams. Do
you really believe in the creation in Ireland of local representative bodies, which are going to relieve the Government
and Parliament of the responsibility of dealing with
questions of peasant proprietors, emigration, relief of
distress, &c., &c. ? '

*Mr. Gladstone to Lord Hartington, February* 3, 1883.

' I have read your letter to Granville in which your view
on the formidable difference lately developed is exhibited
with your usual force and frankness.

' Formidable it is, in my mind, for your contention cuts
deep down into my elementary and fixed ideas; it seems
to me to revive in principle the opposition offered in
1836–8 to the establishment of elective municipalities in
Ireland, and indeed to be hard to reconcile with the policy
as a whole which has been pursued towards Ireland in and
since 1829.

' However, I hope the suggestion I have made for the
speech may be thought suitable to give us time, and time,
which is a great teacher, may disclose much and alter
much between this date and Easter.

' You do not deal with the considerations stated by me
in my letter to Granville of January 22nd, and I need not
now refer to them, but I will notice one or two matters
suggested by your letter to him.

' It is highly probable that there was no discussion in
the Cabinet on the paragraph of January 1881, but this
could only be because all were agreed.

' It was only when the session of that year was considerably advanced that Forster abandoned the idea of
bringing in his Bill.

' We did not omit the subject in 1882, but while announcing positively a measure for England and Wales, we announced that it would apply financially to Scotland, but that the case of Ireland (and this was essential in regard to finance) would be reserved for a separate consideration.

'This fell short of an absolute promise for the session of 1882, but neither was it, nor was it taken to be, a retreat from the ground taken in 1881, and it seems hardly compatible with the policy recently announced by you, at least it would have been pushing reticence very far, if we had used such words with such a policy in our minds. Nor was such a policy, I believe, even mooted in the Cabinet.

'Accordingly, when challenged on the subject in the course of the session, I, without doubt or question, referred to the state of business as the reason why we had not redeemed the pledge of 1881, and expressed my hopes of its early redemption. I have no words before me, but I believe I have not overstated the general effect.

'Owing probably to the circumstances of the time preceding my departure, I do not know the precise point up to which Chamberlain may have gone in a recent speech. But I looked at my son Herbert's words, and I do not think he used any words which went beyond his just liberty or, viewing his position, could tend to commit or hamper the Government.

'If, however, I understand rightly Forster's language, he contemplates as impending a measure of Local Government for Ireland ; and his voice is an important one in the matter.

'I had a long conversation with Argyll last night. His general tone is unaltered ; but not only did he seem to have no idea of withholding local government from Ireland, but he even glanced quite spontaneously at the idea of some kind of Irish legislature as a thing which might have to be entertained.

'Lorne is a person sufficiently conservative, but a short time ago he wrote me a remarkable letter, in which, from his Canadian experience, he recommended a *large* allowance of local government to Ireland.

'In my opinion one of the most vitally important objects we have attained since we took office has been splitting the Home Rule party, and reducing it for all practical purposes from (say) sixty-five to forty. What will the section now with us say if we make such an announcement as you seemed to shadow forth? Indeed, I am not very sure what our Ulster men would say.

'I admit that the pledges of the Government have touched County Government only, and that my leaning to provincial assemblies (or some combination of counties) is an ulterior development. I am told that this was Lord Russell's plan.[1] I can readily believe it, for, regarding the scheme as Conservative, I incline to consider this form of it the most Conservative. Whether any special power of control ought to be reserved is a matter open, I think, to consideration, on which I could not at once say aye or no.

'These remarks are made by way of clearing the ground; but what I hope for is a breathing time, during which none of us should in any respect commit himself in advance of what has been said or done.'

Could Mr. Gladstone rightly claim the credit of 'splitting' the Home Rule party, or was not this rather a natural first effect of the extreme policy of Parnell?

The result of the division of opinion in the Cabinet was that the question of local self-government in Ireland was postponed for the present, and that of extension of the franchise and redistribution of seats was taken in hand. Since 1867, Parliament had discussed almost annually the question whether men living in rural districts should be allowed to vote, like those in towns, upon the qualification of living in a rate-paying tenement. The step, it was admitted, was inevitable; the question

---

[1] In a letter to the *Times*, in 1872, on the subject of congestion of business in Parliament, Earl Russell said that the 'local wants of Ireland and Scotland' might be better met 'if the four provinces of Ireland and the Highlands and Lowlands of Scotland each had an elected representative Assembly.' Perhaps this plan would have been better than that of County Councils in Scotland and Ireland.

had been whether the future voter was as yet sufficiently educated to vote with discretion. It was a great change in the balance of power. To the existing 3,000,000 of voters in the United Kingdom nearly 2,000,000 more would be added, that is, about 1,300,000 in England and Wales, 200,000 in Scotland, and 400,000 in Ireland.

Lord Hartington's attitude was that of reluctant acceptance. Mr. Goschen had alleged, in the debate of 29th July 1877, that 'in all legislative assemblies where numbers, and numbers alone, have been allowed to prevail, the doctrines of political economy have never been able to take root, but have in many cases been discarded and treated with contempt,' and had suggested that already these doctrines were threatened, on the one side by the ever-smouldering Tory Protectionist inclinations, on the other by the growing Radical-Socialist tendency to interfere in the relations between capital and labour, and to undermine self-help by State action. Had not, Mr. Goschen asked, Lord Beaconsfield already denounced the orthodox doctrine at Glasgow, and told his followers that they should no longer 'gnaw the dry bones of political economy'? Lord Hartington, on that occasion, made the inadequate reply that political economy was not much more regarded in the days before the extension of the franchise in 1867. The Tories, he said, had sacrificed the Corn Laws rather under pressure of necessity than following the dictates of economic reason, and the Factory Acts which offended so much against the pure doctrine of *laissez-faire* had been passed by Parliaments elected on the restricted basis, and even by Conservative Governments. But Mr. Goschen was right. It was most natural that doctrines of free international trade and of non-interference by the State in internal industrial questions, should commend themselves to the flourishing and world-monopolising English and Scottish traders and manufacturers of the 'fifties' and 'sixties,' but, as population increased at home and competition abroad, and foreign statesmen adopted, on improved and thought-out lines, and with visible success, our own discarded national policy, it was no less natural that these beliefs should begin to wane. Franchise extension ,diminished the influence of finer reasoning. The obvious and immediate consequence, not the less obvious and more distant, sways minds accustomed to judge by instinct, and, possibly, instinct may be more akin to practical wisdom than are the paradoxical reasonings of abstract economists. Pascal thought that popular instinct arrives 'at right conclusions for wrong reasons.[1]

Extension of franchise involves rearrangement of electoral areas, so that reasonable proportion may be kept between populations and representation in Parliament. From a tactical point of view extension of the franchise is a simple operation; redistribution of seats is one of extreme difficulty, magnitude, and danger. Mr. Gladstone doubted whether his physical strength was sufficient to allow him to carry both measures in a single session. Lord Granville, in August 1883, reported to Lord Harting-ton that, in conversation, Mr. Gladstone had said that 'his mind was equal to small measures but not to complicated ones.' He thought that a beginning might be made by franchise without redistribution. Lord Granville had asked whether Mr. Gladstone could not leave details to younger men, reserving to himself general control. Mr. Gladstone replied 'that a peer could do this, and Lord Palmerston had done it, but that it was

---

[1] Pascal, however, had in mind an almost uneducated people. Semi-education spoils the justness of instinct. The abstract political economists flourished exceedingly during the mid fifty years of the nineteenth century and became text-books.

impossible for him.' He asked, 'with apparent sincerity,' added Lord Granville, 'whether I thought that he ought to resign before beginning half a session.' If, on the other hand, extension of the franchise were carried through, and redistribution were postponed to another year, a general election might intervene, with new electors and the existing areas. This, it was thought, would result in an extremely Radical House of Commons, and this House might create equal electoral districts, in most of which the wealthier minority might be totally submerged in the mass of electors. If the existing Parliament passed both measures it would be practicable to guard to some extent against this danger by preserving some of the small boroughs, and pursuing a certain policy in demarcating the boundaries of the rest. Lord Hartington, in the autumn of 1883, was, for this reason, in favour of passing both measures in the same session, and, if it were necessary for this purpose, adjourning the whole legislation until 1885. He was opposed also to any extension, at present, of the electoral change to Ireland. Evidently the 400,000 new Irish electors would be under clerical and Nationalist control, in favour of agrarian revolution, and, for the most part, ill-educated and illiterate.

Mr. Chamberlain, on the other hand, strongly advocated immediate extension of franchise to the whole United Kingdom, and postponement to another session of redistribution. Hence came a new crisis in the life of this Cabinet. On October 24th Lord Hartington wrote to Mr. Gladstone :—

'The equalisation of the Franchise in the present Parliament presses, I think, mainly on account of the pledges which we have given ; not much for any other reason. The point which seems to me to have been omitted in such discussion as has as yet taken place, is what will be the effect of the measure in Ireland, in either of the forms referred to in your letter. The con-

dition of Ireland has become so much more critical since
our pledges were given that I do not think that any
measure which would add another to the difficulties of
Irish government ought to be adopted merely because it
was promised under different circumstances.  The separation of the two measures of Suffrage and Redistribution
is, I think, very questionable.  It seems to me almost
certain to postpone the latter to another Parliament; and,
if that Parliament should happen to be elected by the new
voters in the old constituencies, I do not see how it is
possible to form any estimate of the probable result.'

At the end of November Mr. Chamberlain and Lord
Hartington made in the country speeches expressing diametrically opposite views upon this important question of
procedure, and the divergence was, of course, seized upon
by the writers for the Press.  Lord Hartington then wrote
to the Prime Minister :—

Chatsworth, Chesterfield,<br>
December 2, 1883.

My dear Mr. Gladstone,—I am afraid that my
speech at Manchester, and the comments which have, not
unreasonably, been called forth by the marked difference
of its tone from that of Chamberlain's speech on the
previous day, will compel me to come to some earlier
understanding as to my position in regard to the Reform
question than I had previously thought would be necessary.

I had intended to have avoided if possible any reference
to the subject which would have finally committed me,
but Chamberlain's speech, which I read a very short time
before I spoke, seemed to make it necessary for me to
put in some protest, if I was unwilling to be definitely
bound to the policy which had been decided on in the
Cabinet, but which I thought was not as yet to have been
announced.

However, my speech has now been made, and the
conclusions drawn from it as to my attitude about Reform

are, on the whole, sufficiently accurate. There seems to be now no alternative for me between abandoning the position which I have publicly, perhaps prematurely, taken up, and sooner or later separating myself from the Government.

I do not think it is possible for me to take the former course without so weakening my position in the country as to prevent my being of any further service to the Government. And, even if this premature disclosure of my opinions had not taken place, I do not think that I could have been a party to a simple Franchise Bill for England and Scotland; more especially to one which will reduce the franchise in Ireland without providing any security whatever for the representation of the loyal minority in the northern, and perhaps some other, constituencies.

I will not in this letter discuss the other alternative, although it seems to me to be the inevitable one. I would rather wait to hear your opinion on what I have already written, and I feel some hope that, unfortunate as are the differences which exist between my colleagues and myself, and unfounded as you believe my objections to be, you will be inclined to agree with me that, after what has taken place, it would not be for the credit of the Government, or for my own, that I should now, even if it were possible, recede from the position which I have taken up.—I remain, yours sincerely,     HARTINGTON.

At the same time Lord Hartington wrote to Lord Granville :—

'I have not at all made up my mind that I will agree to a single-barrelled Reform Bill. I am terribly sick of office, and seldom find myself in real agreement with my colleagues. I think that the state of Ireland is a reason for delaying rather than hastening a Franchise Bill, which will probably permanently strengthen Parnell. I also think that the arguments in favour of dealing completely with the question, or not at all, are very strong. And I see a great probability that, having passed a

Franchise Bill next session, you and I will be left in another session to deal with Redistribution under the most unfavourable possible conditions.'

The last sentence referred to the ever-impending retirement of Mr. Gladstone. To this Lord Granville replied :—

'Your resignation would be received with applause in some quarters, but it appears to me to be an immense responsibility to break up the Government, to turn Gladstone prematurely out of office, and to destroy the cohesion of the Liberal party. The effect upon the position of the aristocracy, and the richer classes, and the best interests of the country may be very great.'

The strain endured all through December. Lord Hartington remained strongly entrenched at Chatsworth, except for one visit to Kimbolton Castle. The Duke, his father, agreed with his views. His defensive position was strong because, as Lord Granville wrote on 19th December to Mr. Gladstone, 'if he is not convinced as to his public duty, there is no other temptation for him. He dislikes office, still more his present office, and, above all, he dreads the brilliant success which some time will fall to him.' The weak point in the position lay in a question which Lord Granville put to Lord Hartington, 'What are you going to do if you give up politics?   Nothing but horse-racing'?

Lord Granville doubted whether, if Lord Hartington resigned, the Government could go on, notwithstanding Mr. Gladstone's great hold on the country. The moderate Liberals in the House of Commons, he thought, were strong enough to hold the balance. He told Lord Hartington on the 23rd that Mr. Gladstone was most anxious to arrange matters, but considered it impossible to postpone the Franchise until it could be introduced together with Redistribution. 'He has mentioned more than once that he has a right, if you force him to resign, to call upon you to form a Government, with a pledge from him of support. I believe him to be ready to promise to attempt himself the solution of both branches of reform.' This letter elicited the following sulky reply, written from Kimbolton Castle, on Christmas Day :—

'I got your letter this morning which makes me slightly indignant.

'What right can Mr. Gladstone have to say that I force him to resign when, with the exception of myself, he has the whole Cabinet with him, and as far as he can tell the whole party. And if my assent is necessary, and my single dissent forces him to resign, don't you think that my assent should have been obtained before, instead of after, the policy was settled ?

'Of course, nothing can prevent his resigning if he chooses to do so, and putting the responsibility on me; and of course he knows that I could not form a Government under those circumstances.

'There will be a very edifying public squabble; but I do not know that I should very much care.

'Nothing in the least controversial has yet passed between Mr. Gladstone and me.'

The difficulty at last was settled upon the basis of a pledge given by Mr. Gladstone that, in introducing the Franchise Bill, he would indicate the lines upon which Redistribution would be proposed, and would remain in office an additional session for the purpose of carrying through Redistribution. The following letters show the course taken by the affair :—

*Lord Hartington to Mr. Gladstone.*

'WAR OFFICE, *December* 27, 1883.

'I have seen Harcourt to-day and had a long talk with him on the subject which you discussed with him at Hawarden.

'I gather from what he has told me, as well as from
some letters of Granville's, that you would be disposed to
consider the possibility of remaining in office for the
purpose of carrying through the Redistribution as well
as the Franchise Bill. Although this does not in itself
remove my difficulties, I can assure you that I feel very
grateful to you for your willingness to relieve me of a
responsibility which I certainly do not feel competent
to bear.

'I have endeavoured to put into the form of a short
memorandum the main objections which I feel to the
course which I understand the Cabinet intend to take ; a
copy of which I enclose. From what Harcourt has told me,
I should not despair of the possibility of our being able
to come to some understanding, and of your being able
to make some such statement on the subject of Redistribution, as regards England and Scotland, as would
enable me to acquiesce in the introduction of a simple
Franchise Bill, although I cannot think that this is the
best course. But as regards Ireland, I am afraid that
the difficulties are greater ; and I do not at present see
any mode in which it is possible to reconcile the opinions
held by yourself and the Cabinet, with the strong repugnance which I feel to a policy which, as I think, will have
the effect of strengthening the party of rebellion, and of
discouraging, if not crushing, the remaining supporters
of order in Ireland. I have endeavoured to make my
memorandum as short as possible, which has perhaps
given to it a more dogmatic and less argumentative character than I should have wished.'

*Lord Hartington to Mr. Gladstone.*

'WAR OFFICE, *December* 31, 1883.

'I certainly did not attempt in my letter of the 27th
inst., or in the memorandum which it enclosed, to state
what course I thought the Cabinet ought, under present

circumstances, to take; and I will endeavour to explain further what my object in sending them to you was. On each occasion when the business of next session was discussed in the Cabinet, I raised some objections to the proposal to proceed with a simple Franchise Bill, and especially to the inclusion of Ireland in such a Bill. At the last meeting of the Cabinet, when the question was discussed at somewhat greater length, I endeavoured to urge some of the objections to the proposed measure. I have already admitted, and I most deeply regret, the inadequate character of the opposition which I then made. I may say, not in justification, but to some extent in explanation of my deficiencies in this respect, that I had not expected the discussion to be so completely one-sided as it proved to be. I had expected from what had fallen from the Chancellor, and from what others had said to me in private, that there would have been at least some discussion. But your memorandum, stating the arguments for the single Bill in the most powerful and condensed form, was read. I certainly did not feel able to reply to such a paper at the moment; the few observations I did make appeared to meet with no support, and not much attention, and, so far as I could judge, the Cabinet appeared to have made up its mind. On the next day, however, I wrote to you that I was not convinced, and that I doubted whether it would be possible for me to concur in the course which was proposed. Then came Chamberlain's and my speeches, making public to a certain extent the difference of opinion which existed. Immediately afterwards I wrote to you to the effect that, having regard to this difference of opinion, and to the fact of its having been made public, there occurred to me to be only one course for me to take. Since that time you, Granville, Spencer, and Harcourt have remonstrated strongly against my proposed action, attaching, as I think, an exaggerated importance to my remaining a member of the Government. I had no wish to be unreasonable, and was anxious that, if possible, some means might be found of enabling me to

meet the wishes of my colleagues, without entirely sacrificing my own judgment on this matter. I thought that
the best course would be to state as clearly as I could what
was the chief point which I considered essential, in the
hope that such a statement might indicate the means of
coming to an agreement. It was scarcely, I think, for
me under the circumstances to offer advice to my colleagues
on the course which they should take on the matter, which,
as far as I know, they had already decided.

I confess that, in the position in which we stand, I do
not see what advice it is possible for me to give, which
it is possible for them to accept. Had my objections had
more weight at an earlier period, I should have advised the
postponement of the Franchise Bill till 1885, when the
Redistribution Bill might have been prepared and introduced at the same time. As regards Great Britain, I
think it possible (though not a desirable course) that, by
means of a statement made with the authority of the
Cabinet, the necessity for simultaneous dealing with the two
subjects might be dispensed with. With regard to Ireland,
I do not think that a simple statement or declaration of
intentions would be sufficient, and I think that either the
consideration of the case of Ireland should be postponed
till it can be treated in a complete manner, or else that it
should be made the subject of a complete measure in the
present session.

I have only ventured to state these opinions in response
to your definite request. They appear to me to be so far
removed from those which are entertained by the Cabinet,
and from the decisions which, I think, were practically
carried out, that I can hardly hope that they will be of
any value in removing the present difficulties.

*Lord Hartington to the Duke of Devonshire.*

'Dᴇᴠᴏɴsʜɪʀᴇ Hᴏᴜsᴇ, *January* 14, 1884.

'I think I told you that, when Harcourt saw Mr. Gladstone
after coming to Chatsworth, he said that he was ready to

stay on, in order to pass the Redistribution Bill, if possible. I said that was not much satisfaction to me, unless I knew what sort of Redistribution Bill it would be, and after some letters Mr. Gladstone came up to London to see me. I had a very long talk with him. On redistribution generally his opinions are very much the same as mine; and he does not want to go in for anything like electoral districts, or a larger amount of change than is absolutely necessary, and is opposed to a sweeping disfranchisement of the smaller towns. He undertook to make a statement of his own opinions on the subject in introducing the Bill; and he stated the substance of it in the Cabinet. He said that he could not hold the Cabinet as a body to be bound by his statement, but that he considered himself bound by it, to me; and no one in the Cabinet made any serious objections to it.

'Although I think it would have been much better to have had a complete measure in 1885, I thought he had gone as far about redistribution as I could expect, having regard to the difficulties which there certainly would be in passing a complete Bill in one session.

'As regards Ireland, he was less satisfactory; but, on the other hand, his arguments had some effect upon me. He spoke more strongly than I had ever heard him before of the utter impossibility of the English and Scotch majority assenting to the legislative separation of the two countries. He denies that with the extended franchise Parnell will get the whole representation of Ireland. I pressed him, however, very much on this point, and on the possibility of the practical disfranchisement of the whole Protestant and loyal population of Ireland. He would not admit that any practical plan of representation of the minority had ever been proposed, and would object to any plan for that purpose which should not apply to England as well as Ireland, but he undertook in his statement in Parliament to refer to the question of the representation of minorities as an open one, on which there was much difference of opinion on both sides; and to admit that it might become of practical importance with reference to the representation of Ireland.

'He made a statement to the effect of all this in the Cabinet, which was received without any serious objection, even from Chamberlain. I do not know whether it amounts to much, but I think that I may rely, if we pass the Franchise Bill and remain in another session, which I should think is extremely unlikely, that he will next session bring in a moderate Redistribution Bill both as regards England and Ireland, which I should on the whole approve of, though perhaps without any special minority representation plan.

'If the Bill does not pass this session, Gladstone will be committed to the lines of the redistribution measure, and it will not be possible for the Radicals to use his authority for a more extensive measure.

'On the whole I thought that he had made as great concessions to my objections as I could expect, and I agreed to go on. He is also inclined to preserve the 40s. freeholders in the counties, who would almost certainly be extinguished if he does not remain in office to pass the Franchise Bill.

'I can't say that I am satisfied with the prospect of the session ; but, after the concessions which he made, I thought it better to accept them than to split up the party against Gladstone. There is no doubt that, if a split is to come, it will be much better that it should be caused by the Radicals against the Whigs and Gladstone, than by the Whigs against the Radicals and Gladstone.'

Lord Hartington in these discussions held the same position as that occupied in the summer of 1884 by the House of Lords. It will be necessary to return to these matters at a later point in this story.

Burke defined party as 'a body of men united for promoting by their joint endeavour the national interest upon some particular principle on which they are all

agreed.' The events of 1883 made it clear that this defini-
tion applied imperfectly to the Whig-Radical combination.
In October 1883 appeared a powerful article in the *Quarterly
Review* called 'Disintegration,' written, it was understood,
by Lord Salisbury. The writer said :—

'The present Whig party is a mere survival kept alive
by tradition after its true functions and significance have
passed away. A Whig, who is a faithful member of the
present Liberal party, has to submit to this peculiar fate,
not only that he inherits the political opinions he pro-
fesses—a lot which befalls many Englishmen—but that he
also inherits a liability to be compelled to change them at
the bidding of the leader whom the Radical party may
have chosen for him. There are many strange and
unattractive functions which, under the law of caste, a
Hindoo cheerfully accepts as the inherited burden of his
life, but probably few of them suffer more than an educated
Englishman, who thinks that it does not consist with the
honour of his family to profess in public the opinions he
really holds, or to oppose the political changes on which,
in his heart, he looks with horror. . . . The majority have
neither the courage to abandon their Whig professions,
nor to part with their Radical allies. They may often be
met with helplessly lamenting their fate, for the only solution of their difficulties that has yet presented itself to
them is a combination of public loyalty with private
imprecation.'

Lord Hartington must have had in mind this caustic
attack when, in a speech at Accrington on 2nd December
1883, the day on which he told Mr. Gladstone that his
resignation seemed to be inevitable, he thus defined the
functions of the Whig party :—

'I confess I am not dissatisfied with the position that
the Whig party have in former times occupied, and that I
believe they occupy at the present time. I admit that the

Whigs are not the leaders in popular movements, but the Whigs have been able, as I think, to the great advantage of the country, to direct, and guide, and moderate those popular movements. They have formed a connecting link between the advanced party and those classes which, possessing property, power, and influence, are naturally averse to change, and I think I may claim for the Whig party that it is greatly owing to their guidance and to their action that the great and beneficial changes, which have been made in the direction of popular reform in this country, have been made not by the shock of revolutionary agitation, but by the calm and peaceful process of constitutional acts. That is the part which the Whigs have played in the past, and which I believe the Whigs or those who represent them now, may be called upon to play with equal advantage in the future.'

The name of 'Whig' is now no longer applied to any connected association, but many men of wealth still, under the Liberal flag, try to 'direct, and guide, and moderate popular movements.' How far do they succeed, or how far do they merely serve as cover to masque the approaches of forces dangerous to the classes 'possessing property, power, and influence'? The difference between the present time and that before the schism of 1886 is that far fewer representatives of great families are to be found among modern Liberals. A Cavendish or a Russell took that side mainly because his fathers were concerned in the revolution of 1688; a modern plutocrat who is a Liberal must be so by personal conviction. Whigs of the old hereditary type accompanied Radicals far along the road of 'progress,' but there was for them a limit to the comradeship. Is there any such limit for the modern 'moderate' Liberal? If he has not the strength to break at any point with those whose policy he disapproves, he may do more harm than good.

# CHAPTER XVIII

## THE WAR OFFICE, 1883-1885

LORD HARTINGTON left the War Office in the summer of 1866, and returned to it at the close of 1882, sixteen years later. Mr. Cardwell had carried through the army reform, involving shorter term of service, establishment of the reserve, and the system of linked battalions in each line regiment, one serving abroad, and the other acting as a nursery at home. The system of purchase of promotion had also been abolished. There was little change in the method of central administration. The Duke of Cambridge was still commander-in-chief, as he had been in 1866, and his naturally close relation to the Queen, and his dislike for all innovations, sometimes made difficulties for the Secretary of State. Lord Wolseley, the victor of Tel-el-Kebir, was now at the War Office as adjutant-general. Sir Ralph Thompson was permanent Under-Secretary. No war was, for the moment, in progress; the chief question was whether the troops still in Egypt should be reduced, and, if so, to what extent, or wholly withdrawn, and, if so, when? Sir Evelyn Wood was engaged in reorganising a portion of the shattered army of the Khedive; Valentine Baker, who had once been in the British service, and had afterwards won distinction against the Russians in the Turkish army, was at the head of a force of Egyptian gendarmerie. General Sir Frederick Stephenson commanded the British force of occupation.

Nothing was more sincere than the intention of the British Government in 1883 to retire from the military occupation of Egypt, in pursuance of the pledges given to the world, and in conformity with their general principles of policy. Lord Hartington, in June 1883, told Lord Granville that both Lord Dufferin, recently returned from his Egyptian mission, and Lord Wolseley, thought that a battalion might be withdrawn, and the British troops in Egypt reduced to about 6000 men. Sir Evelyn Baring was appointed to succeed Sir Edward Malet as British Consul-General, and took up his new post at Cairo on the 11th September. Lord Granville wrote on 10th October to Lord Hartington, 'Baring is going to report that we should withdraw all the troops, excepting 3000 to be left at Alexandria, so the sooner you give confidential orders to prepare for this withdrawal, probably the better.' There was, however, a difficulty with the Queen, who sent to Lord Granville a strong protest against this withdrawal. The Queen always opposed any movement of retreat. In this instance her instinct proved to be true. The whole position was changed in a moment by the message flashed from Khartoum to Cairo on the 22nd of November, and from Cairo on to London, confirming the rumour that General Hicks Pasha, with his European staff and 10,000 Egyptian troops, had been slain in the Soudan.

The modern Egyptian dominion over the Soudan, a country twice as large as France and Germany put together, had degenerated or developed, especially after Gordon left the country in 1879, into a mere system of plunder under the masque of taxation, and the discontent of oppressed natives and half-restrained slave-traders had fused with the religious zeal stirred up from the year 1881 by Mohammed Ahmed, the son of the boatbuilder of Sennar, who claimed to be the

Mahdi, or foretold Prophet, predestined to lead Islam to new glory and power. The tribesmen flocked to his standard; the Egyptian Government was disorganised and almost bankrupt; and, in February 1883, El Obeid, the capital of the province of Kordofan, west of the Nile, fell before his arms. General Hicks, a British officer in the Khedive's service, commanding in Khartoum, was ordered to move against the Mahdi. His own opinion condemned the operation; so did that of Colonel Stewart, who knew the country well. Sir Edward Malet, at Cairo, suggested, on 5th June, though not with much emphasis, to Lord Granville, that the Egyptian Government should instruct Hicks to 'confine himself to maintaining the present supremacy of the Khedive in the region between the Blue and White Niles.' Had this advice been pressed by the British Government on the Egyptian, subsequent history might have been very different. Lord Granville, however, following the general bias of the existing policy, that of avoiding further entanglement in Egyptian affairs, held to the decision, communicated to Egypt on 7th May 1883, that the British Government were 'in no way responsible for the operations which have been undertaken under the authority of the Egyptian Government, or for the appointment or actions of General Hicks.' The flaw in this position was that the British Government were, in fact, since Tel el Kebir, the dominant power in Egyptian affairs. Lord Salisbury said, 'Those who have the absolute power of preventing lamentable events and, knowing what is taking place, refuse to exercise that power, are responsible for what happens.' Lord Granville, says Lord Cromer, 'failed to see this. Instead of recognising the facts of the situation, he took shelter behind an illusory abnegation of responsibility which was a mere phantasm of the diplomatic and parliamentary mind. The result was that the facts asserted themselves in defiance of diplomacy and parliamentary convenience.'[1]   It is a way they have.

The unfortunate Hicks marched from Khartoum at the beginning of September, oppressed by the sense of coming doom.   'In two days,' wrote Power, the *Times* correspondent, 'we start on a campaign that even the most sanguine look forward to with the greatest gloom. We have here 9000 infantry that fifty good men could rout in ten minutes, and 1000 cavalry that have never learnt even to ride, and these, with a few Nordenfeldt guns, are to beat the 69,000 men whom the Mahdi has got together.'   What wonder that the Egyptians perished in the wilderness before the spears of the fanatic swarm of tribesmen.   The scene must have been appalling.   Hicks' 10,000 men are said to have been killed in fifteen minutes. The Mahdi by this magnificent victory gained vast prestige and a large stock of arms and ammunition. Had the British Government, acting on the advice of their agents in Egypt, forbidden the expedition, and restricted Hicks, as he desired, to the defence of Berber, Dongola, Khartoum, Sennar, and the Nile, the thousands of lives and millions of money squandered then and afterwards would, Lord Cromer believes, have been saved.[2] When the destruction of Hicks' army had been accomplished, the British Government abandoned, too late, its attitude of non-interference in Soudanese affairs, and compelled that of Egypt to take a step fraught with *still* greater disaster.

The defeat of Hicks left the various Egyptian garrisons at Khartoum, Sennar, and other places isolated and cut off from each other.   There were still in the country some 32,000 Egyptian soldiers, and a considerable non-native civil

---

[1] *Modern Egypt*, vol. i. p. 367.
[2] Vol. i. p. 366.

population.[1] Khartoum, at the junction of the two Niles, a flourishing trade centre, with a population of about 50,000, was garrisoned by some most inefficient Egyptian troops and a few rather better black troops.  Was the Soudan to be abandoned to the Mahdi, or was any, and, if so, what part of it?  There was general agreement that, under the existing conditions, it was impracticable, at present, to reconquer the whole Soudan, or to maintain the outlying garrisons.  But were Khartoum and the province south of it lying between the two Niles, and was the line of the Nile from Khartoum to Egypt proper, to be held or to be abandoned?  Lord Dufferin, in his report on his mission to Egypt in 1883, made before the Hicks disaster, had advised that the rest of the Soudan should be abandoned, and that Egypt should be content with maintaining her jurisdiction in the provinces of Khartoum and Sennar.  This was also the opinion of Lord Wolseley.  After the Hicks disaster he sent a memorandum to Lord Harting-ton urging that a good garrison should be established at Assouan, that reinforcements should be sent to Suakin, Berber, and Khartoum, and that the two last places should be strongly held under British officers.  Lord Hartington was of the same opinion.  On the 23rd November 1883 he wrote to Lord Granville :—

'When men talk of withdrawing from the Soudan, not many of them know exactly what extent of country it is they mean by that expression.  Egypt will never volun-tarily give up the provinces east of the White Nile, which she has held for over sixty years, and I don't think she should be asked to do so, but to give up the provinces of Kordofan, Darfour, and Fashoda to the west of that river

---

[1] In the further instructions given to Gordon at Cairo by Baring, it was esti-mated that in Khartoum only, some 10,000 to 15,000 civilians would wish to leave when the evacuation was effected ; native Christians, Egyptian employés, their wives and children, &c. (Wingate).

would be a very reasonable measure. . . . I think, however, that the district included in the great bend made by the Nile from Khartoum to Debbeh should be retained as part of Egyptian territory, although it is to the west of the Nile.'

This reasonable *via media* between holding and abandoning the whole Soudan was that which the Egyptian Government desired, but to carry it out was beyond their unassisted power. Khartoum was, by the Nile route, distant 1600 miles from Cairo ; the tribes were up in the Eastern Soudan ; and the short route from Suakin to Berber had become difficult ; besides, the Khedive's Government were almost insolvent, and had already sent their last man who could even be called a soldier to the Soudan. Sir Evelyn Baring reported that, *unless* the British Government were prepared to assist with English or Indian troops, the Egyptian Government would be unable to hold Khartoum, and had better accept defeat, and fall back to some point on the Nile. Lord Granville informed Sir Evelyn Baring, on December 13th, that the Government had no intention of employing British or Indian troops in the Soudan, but had no objection to the employment of Turkish troops, provided the cost was met by the Sultan—really a prohibitive condition. 'Excepting for securing the safe retreat of the garrisons still holding positions in the Soudan' the Government could not agree to any charge on Egyptian revenues for operations in the Soudan.[1] Sir Evelyn Baring was to advise the Ministers of the Khedive to abandon all territory south of Assouan or, at least, of Wadi Halfa. This advice was an order. On 22nd December, Chérif Pasha replied by a memorandum stating that the Egyptian Government could not 'agree to the abandonment of

---

[1] See *Modern Egypt*, vol. i. p. 373. The military authorities at Cairo agreed that Egypt could not hold Khartoum *unassisted*.

territories which they consider absolutely necessary for the security, and even for the existence of Egypt itself.' The Government in London then came to a fateful decision. Baring was instructed (4th January 1884) that, unless the Egyptian Ministers agreed to evacuate Khartoum as well as the interior Soudan, they must forfeit their offices. It was intimated that, if no other Egyptians could be found to carry out this policy of retreat, English Ministers would, in the last resort, have to be appointed to carry on the affairs of Egypt. This ultimatum overthrew Chérif's Ministry, and Nubar Pasha consented to form an administration which would, at the command of England, abandon Khartoum. Lord Hartington appears to have acquiesced at the time in this momentous decision, but it was contrary to the view which he had expressed in November, and he soon came to regard it as an error. The long defence of Khartoum by Gordon single-handed proved that it could have been saved altogether by a very moderate strengthening of the garrison. It might even have been sufficient to send up a certain number of British officers and non-commissioned officers. Had a statesman then been at the head of affairs whose chief concern was not parliamentary strategy but the imperial business of England, so much, at the very least, would surely have been risked to save Khartoum and the line of the Nile for Egypt and civilisation. But that dark leaf was not to be torn from the book of Fate.

The decision of January made the British Government responsible before the world, as a matter of honour and humanity, for the evacuation of the whole Soudan. The Egyptian troops had to be extracted, together with all the alien civilians who might not wish to be plundered or massacred. How was the evacuation to be carried out? This question led to the mission of Charles Gordon.

General Gordon was on the active list of the army, but his career had lain for the most part outside of the regular service of the 'Sappers.' He had acquired by his deeds in the service of the Chinese Government against formidable rebels, and of the Egyptian Government in the Soudan (1874–79), and by his reputation as a religious genius of a singular kind, a somewhat indefinite and mysterious reputation. He was in Switzerland, and a little later in England, in March 1880, and among the Devonshire papers are two letters which he addressed to Lord Hartington, whom he had once met, at the moment when it became evident that the Liberals would be returned to power. In one of these he expressed his disapproval of the whole policy of Lord Beaconsfield's Government with regard to the 'Eastern question' and to Egypt, and said that 'a definite arrangement with France with respect to Egypt and Syria, a firm conviction that the Turkish Government is irrevocably bad and past redemption, and that Bulgaria and Greece should be supported, are what is required.' In the other letter he expressed the view that the Beaconsfield Government were intending to promote the extension of Egyptian territorial dominion on the Red Sea coast in order to counteract Italian ambitions, and he said that Egyptian revenues were incapable of supporting a policy of this kind, and that 'the extension of Egyptian rule is an unmitigated evil.'

At the time of the Hicks disaster Gordon was in Palestine, where he had spent some months in study and meditation. On the 29th May 1883 he had written from Jerusalem to his sister : 'I sometimes wonder what is written in the roll of futurity about me. I scarcely think I am to dwell thus for long. It is too quiet to last.' In October Gordon was asked by Leopold, King of the Belgians—and this is singular also—to go to the

Congo to manage things there. He telegraphed to his
brother in England that, as he was on the active list, he
could not accept the offer without permission, and asked
him to consult the War Office. Lord Wolseley wrote to
Lord Hartington (16th October) : ' Looking at the fanatic
character of the man, and the chance of collision with
French adventurers, I think it very doubtful whether the
permission should be given.' Lord Granville thought that
permission should be refused, and the War Office telegraphed a negative to Gordon. By a strange chance the
telegram, which was worded ' Secretary of State declines to
allow you to accept employment,' was received by Gordon
at Jerusalem in the form ' Secretary of State decides to
allow you,' &c.[1] Gordon accordingly came back from
Syria to take up the Congo appointment. When he discovered that the War Office were not willing to grant
permission, he asked leave to resign his commission in
order to redeem his promise to the King of the Belgians.
The idea of employing Gordon in Egypt in connection
with the Soudan trouble had already been mooted. Lord
Granville asked Sir Evelyn Baring by a telegram, on 1st
December 1883, whether, if Gordon would consent to go
to Egypt, he would be of any use, and, if so, in what
capacity. The Prime Minister, Chérif, was averse to
employing Gordon in the Soudan, and the first impressions of Sir Evelyn Baring were also unfavourable to the
suggestion. He thought that it would be better to send to
Khartoum Abdul-Kader Pasha, a soldier and ex-Governor.
After the fall of the Chérif Ministry, Lord Hartington again
raised the question. On the 8th January he wrote to Lord
Granville :—

'You know that Gordon has accepted employment on

[1] Lord Hartington to Lord Granville, 11th January 1884. Gordon also
mentions this mistake in a letter to his sister.

the Congo. We, on your advice in the autumn, told him
that we declined to allow him to accept this. He will be
privately told that he ought, under these circumstances,
to resign his commission in the army, but, under our
admirable regulations, he will retire on *nothing*. If he
declines to retire we ought to remove him, but this may
be awkward. What do you say?'

Two days later he wrote again: 'I believe that Nubar
is a friend of Gordon's, and therefore may be more disposed than Chérif was to employ him. . . . Wolseley
thinks that his employment would be most desirable.'
Later, on the same day, Lord Hartington wrote again:—

'Gordon has now formally sent in his resignation. I
do not think that there is now any possible compromise
between accepting it and approving his employment. An
officer in full pay belongs to us. We have a right to his
services, and might require them at any moment. If we
allow him to accept other employment it is because we
approve of it and think it of advantage to the public
service. I don't know how long it is since Baring expressed an opinion adverse to his employment in the
Soudan. Present circumstances might alter his opinion.
I understand that Gordon would probably postpone his
Congo employment if asked to go to the Soudan. I believe
that some people think highly of the value he would be
of there. Do you think it would be worth while asking
Baring again? I have directed that his resignation is
not to be accepted till we hear again from you. I do
not think that there will be any quarrel, as he appears to
understand the necessity for resignation; but I have an
idea that it will not be generally understood, and will be
unpopular.'

On the following day Lord Hartington again wrote,
after perusing a still adverse memorandum from the
Foreign Office:—

'I return Pauncefote's memorandum. I don't think we
can delay a decision about Gordon till the 21st, as I believe

he leaves for the Congo very shortly afterwards.   I should think you had much better withdraw your recommendation that permission should be refused, and let him go.   But I don't think you can say in that case that he has not gone with the approval of the Government.'

Lord Granville now gave way on receiving a reluctant assent from Sir Evelyn Baring,[1] who also conveyed in his telegram of the 16th the formal request of the Khedival Government for a British officer 'to go to Khartoum,' adding, ' He would be given full powers, both civil and military, to conduct the retreat.'   Mr. Gladstone, also with hesitation, signified his concurrence.   On 18th January, Lord Wolseley brought Gordon to the War Office to see some Ministers then in town.   They were Lord Hartington, Lord Granville, Lord Northbrook, and Sir Charles Dilke. Gordon wrote to a friend : 'At noon he, Wolseley, came to me and took me to the Ministers.   He went in and talked to the Ministers, and came back and said, " Her Majesty's Government want you to undertake this.   Government are determined to evacuate the Soudan, for they will not guarantee future government.   Will you go and do it ? " I said, " Yes." He said, "Go in." They said, "Did Wolseley tell you our orders ? " I said, " Yes." I said, " You will not guarantee future government of the Soudan, and you wish me to go up and evacuate now." They said " Yes," and it was over, and I left at 8 p.m. for Calais.'[2]

Lord Hartington, on the same day, sent the following account to Mr. Gladstone.   Gordon's narrative in the preceding letter cannot be easily reconciled with his notes of the 18th January as to his mission.   The idea on the

---

[1] Lord Cromer's *Modern Egypt*, vol. i. pp. 425–6.

[2] While Gordon waited in the anteroom occupied by the official private secretary, and stood with his back to the fire, he said suddenly to the private secretary, 'Do you ever tell a lie?' Before the astonished secretary could ascertain the purpose of this difficult question Lord Wolseley re-entered and took Gordon in.

18th seems to have been that he should first report, and that there should then be a further decision as to action by the Government.

*Lord Hartington to Mr. Gladstone, 18th January 1884.*

'Gordon, on being pressed by Lord Wolseley as to what he would do if he had the direction of affairs, said that he would send himself out direct to Suakin without going to Cairo. The enclosed notes written by himself sketch the terms on which he would be willing to go. He was unable to indicate the nature of the advice which he would give to Government until he had learned the state of things on the spot. He might recommend the Government to appoint him Governor-General of the Soudan. The expenditure of a large sum of money was not an absolute necessity. Some money, no doubt, would be required, but time would probably do much.

'Or he might recommend absolute and immediate withdrawal. He could give no opinion without seeing state of affairs on the spot. If anything were to be done, it should be done at once.'

*Enclosed Copy of Notes written by General Gordon.*

'1. To proceed to Suakin and report on military situation of Soudan and return. Under Baring for orders, and to send through him letters, &c., under flying seal.

2. Government not indebted beyond passage money and £3 per diem travelling expenses.

3. Notify public.

4. Nubar and Baring to be notified, so as to give all assistance.

5. Admiral Hewett to give me an account up to £500 to be accounted for.

6. Letters to Brussels saying leave is given me to go to Congo after my mission to Suakin.

7. I understand H.M.G. only wish me to report and are in no way bound to me.

8. Telegraph Egypt to Government to send Ibrahim Bey to meet me at Suez with a writer to attend on me.

C. E. GORDON.'

Lord Wolseley, on the 14th February 1884, reported to
Lord Hartington the results of conversations on the 15th
and 18th January with Gordon, which he had noted at the
time.  Gordon had clearly stated that, in his opinion, it
would be far better to evacuate the Soudan than to reconquer it '*if* such reconquest was to entail again handing
it over to the government of Egyptian Pashas,' whose
injustice, extortions, and military tyranny had, he believed,
caused the rebellion.  (In that word ' if ' lay all the difference
in the world.)  He disbelieved in the Mahdi's power, and
thought that *if* it were made known to the people of the
Eastern Soudan that it was henceforth to be governed by
English officers, independent of the Cairo Pashas, that
'power and strength would soon melt away.'  Gordon
evidently thought that, so far, at any rate, as regarded the
Eastern Soudan, this course, administration by English
officers, should be that chosen and pursued.  He told Lord
Wolseley that ' in all dealings with the Soudan it was most
necessary to do everything very deliberately, and nothing in
a hurry.'  The tribes now gathered round the Mahdi would
not long hold together, nor undertake very distant expeditions far from their own sheep, camels, and families, and
for this reason he did not fear an invasion by them of
Egypt.  He also said to Lord Wolseley that the Government had better send him to Suakin to study the condition
of affairs, and then advise.  He might find that the best
course was complete evacuation ; or, on the other hand, that
some attempt should be made to ' constitute some settled
government before we come to any final determination as
to the future of the country.  In this latter case he might
recommend his own reappointment as Governor-General.'

Lord Wolseley added in his report :—

'From the first he expressed an earnest desire to help
Mr. Gladstone's Government in the Soudan complication

and said that he was prepared, as a soldier, to obey the orders that might be given to him, and would do his best to carry out whatever policy might be determined upon.  He took the deepest interest in the Soudanese people, whom he had learnt to love whilst among them.  He was very glad that they had thrown off the yoke of the Cairo Pashas, and was proud of them for having done so.  He regarded the re-establishment of a settled government in the Eastern Soudan as by no means a difficult operation, if it were attempted by British officers in a spirit of justice and moderation, but the undertaking must not be "rushed." '

Lord Granville, soon after he had consented to the deed, thought that it had been a great mistake to send Gordon, and Lord Cromer to this day, it seems, regrets his own reluctant acquiescence.[1]  But how could the British Government, after compelling that of Egypt to surrender the Soudan, refuse, when asked, to assist in removing the garrisons and the alien civilised population ?  Gordon was the Englishman who best knew the Soudan, and had most influence there.  The sad error of the Gladstone Cabinet surely lay, not in sending Gordon, but in failing, notwithstanding the strong representations made by Baring and Wolseley, to take timely steps to support him, when it became clear that, without such support, his mission would fail.  They refused to accept the unpleasant consequences of the wise step which they had taken.

For reasons explained by Lord Cromer in his book, *Modern Egypt*, Gordon went, at Baring's request, approved by Lord Granville, not to Suakin but to Cairo.  There he saw the Khedive, Sir Evelyn Baring, and others, was formally appointed by the Khedive to be Governor-General of the Soudan 'for the time necessary to accomplish the evacuation,' and went straight on to Khartoum. Now, therefore, he was acting in a double capacity, as

[1] *Modern Egypt*, vol. i. p. 438.

Governor-General under the Khedive, and as an officer on the active list with certain instructions from Her Majesty's Government. This Government, reluctantly or not, acquiesced in the construction given to Gordon's mission at Cairo.[1] Gordon's instructions from the Khedive (in a letter dated 26th January 1884), never revoked or altered, were—

' to carry into execution the evacuation of those territories, and to withdraw our troops, civil officials, and such of the inhabitants, together with their belongings, as may wish to leave for Egypt. We trust that Your Excellency will adopt the most effective measures for the accomplishment of your mission in this respect, and that, after completing the evacuation, you will take the necessary steps for establishing an organised government in the different provinces of the Soudan.'

Lord Cromer says in his *Modern Egypt :*—

' I believe that the original intention of the British Government was that General Gordon should limit himself to reporting, and that Lord Granville did not see that, in authorising General Gordon to accept the appointment of Governor-General, he changed the spirit of the instructions which he had issued on 18th January. He was, therefore, surprised to find what he had done.'

It is the kind of thing which sometimes happens in the offices which transact imperial business for want of *real* knowledge of the countries with which they deal. The Foreign Office, not then practically acquainted with the administration of African dominions, treated the appointment to be Governor-General as a mere detail which could be left to their agent at Cairo. The contents of the word were not the same to officials in Whitehall

---

[1] Gordon himself, on his way from London, suggested that he should be made Governor-General. Lord Granville left it to Sir Evelyn Baring to decide whether the British Government should agree. Baring, when Gordon arrived at Cairo, moved the Khedive to make the appointment. See *Modern Egypt*, vol. i. p. 450.

as they were to Gordon, who had already ruled that vast region with almost absolute and independent power. Thus, in London, Gordon was regarded as an officer on the active list, with a special task in hand. But his real, or dominant, position was that of Governor-General of the Soudan, under the Khedive, charged with the task of evacuation. Unless the British Government compelled the Khedive to withdraw the appointment or the instructions, this contention, constantly made by Gordon in his Journal, is undeniable.[1]   The British Government were free to support Gordon, or not to support him. They had no right to order him, and they never did explicitly and finally order him, to disobey, by leaving Khartoum without effecting the evacuation of the Soudan, the instructions received from the Khedive on his appointment as Governor-General, and formally acquiesced in by themselves. They had the right, or at least the power, if they chose, and if they dared take a step like this in the face of English opinion, to compel the Khedive to revoke the decree of appointment, and then themselves expressly to recall Gordon. Lord Granville was in favour of directly recalling Gordon. Mr. Gladstone advised him 'not to press an opinion which it was clear the Cabinet would not adopt.'[2]

---

[1] *e.g.* entry in Gordon's Journal for 25th October 1884, p. 237 : ' Put yourself in my position. If you say "rapid retreat and leave Sennar to its fate," I will say " No, I would sooner die first," and will resign my commission, for I could not do it. If you say " Then you are no longer Governor-General," then I am all right, and all the responsibility is on you, for I could not be supposed, if you turn me out of Governor-General, to be obliged to aid in such a movement, which I think is disgraceful. You will then be face to face with the people.' And see his entry on 22nd November, p. 353.

On the 3rd March 1884, Gordon wrote to Baring: ' How could I look the world in the face if I abandoned them and fled? As a gentleman could you advise this course?' No gentleman, and, surely, no Gordon, could, in fact, have done it, unless he had the most explicit orders both from the English Government and the Khedive. And Gordon had nothing except hints, and permission, from the former to run away.

[2] See *Life of Lord Granville*, vol. ii. p. 401.

What Gladstone really wished was that Gordon should
abandon Khartoum without direct orders from Government. Gordon was often, and still is, accused by writers
and speakers of 'disobedience to orders.' Gladstone himself diffused this view. He wrote to Lord Granville in
1888 that 'Gordon ought, at a very early date, to have
come away of his own motion. He really remained in
defiance of the whole mind and spirit of our instructions.
To remain beleaguered in Khartoum was only the proof
of his failure. It was his absolute duty to withdraw if he
could, and I have never heard his power to do so dis-
puted. For us to have complied with his demands was
madness and crime.'[1] Gladstone, then, thought, in 1888,
that the Nile expedition was an act of 'madness and
crime, and actually felt remorse for nothing except that
he had reluctantly tried to save Gordon. This mad
and criminal act was the deed of Hartington, who,
at the last ditch, overcame his chief's obstinate refusal.
Gladstone chose, or allowed himself, to believe and say
that the dead Gordon had been guilty of disobedience.
But what are the ethics of belief? If, for political
reasons, he dared not openly and explicitly recall Gordon,
what *right* had Gladstone to believe that it was Gordon's
duty to desert his post? Was Gordon, then, to abandon
to slavery or the sword those who put their trust in him in
order that the Prime Minister might satisfy his Radicals
without offending the rest of the Liberal party? Gordon
remained at Khartoum in the endeavour to fulfil instructions received from the Khedive, confirmed by the British
Government, and never explicitly revoked. That was sufficient justification ; but he also remained there to save those
whom he ruled, and to maintain the honour of England.
He was no hireling shepherd. Critics may sophisticate over

[1] *Life of Lord Granville*, vol. ii. p. 401.

details, but the broad truth stands forever and nobly in-
scribed upon Gordon's monument in St. Paul's Cathedral :—

'He saved an empire[1] by his warlike genius; he ruled
vast provinces[2] with wisdom, justice, and power; and
lastly, obedient to his Sovereign's command, he died in
the attempt to save men, women, and children from imminent and deadly peril. "Greater love hath no man than
this, that a man lay down his life for his friends."'

But this is a digression, and one must return to the story.

When the Foreign Office heard of the extended instructions given to Gordon at Cairo they sent a despatch to the
effect that the Government—

'bearing in mind the exigencies of the situation, concurred in these instructions, which virtually altered
General Gordon's mission from one of advice to that of
executing, or at least directing, the evacuation not only
of Khartoum, but of the whole Soudan, and they are
willing that General Gordon should receive the very
extended powers conferred upon him by the Khedive
to enable him to effect this very difficult task.'[3]

One can almost hear the conversations in the Foreign
Office which preceded the framing of this despatch. It
was a grudging assent, worded so as to throw as much
responsibility as possible upon the 'men on the spot.'
It *was* a clear and formal assent, all the same, and the
question soon arose whether, if Gordon were unable to
accomplish this task, the British Government, who had
ordered and compelled the evacuation, were morally bound
to assist him.

While Gordon was on his way to Khartoum a disaster

---

[1] China.　　　　　　　　　[2] First government of the Soudan.
[3] Lord Cromer quotes this despatch in *Modern Egypt*, vol. i. p. 447, and
makes some valuable observations. He says, 'The statement that I altered
General Gordon's instructions without authority from the British Government, is
wholly void of foundation.'

occurred near the Red Sea coast of the Soudan. Osman Digna and his tribesmen, after some successes against small detachments of Egyptian troops, invested the fortified posts of Tokar and Sinkat, not far from the port of Suakin. General Baker, with a force of Egyptian gendarmerie, was sent to effect a relief. He was attacked near Tokar by a smaller body of dervishes, on the 5th February, and was utterly defeated with a loss of 2000 killed. His Egyptians hardly made an attempt to resist the onslaught of the sons of the desert. A few days later Sinkat fell. Obviously this event might imperil Gordon's personal safety, or injure his mission. Lord Hartington wrote to Lord Granville on February 6th :—

'I know that the Cabinet would not agree to any effectual measure for the support of Gordon, and I doubt whether an expedition to Suakin would really assist him in his mission, but it would be as well to settle what sort of line we are going to take, both in and out of the House, in the event of Gordon coming to grief.'

Two days later Lord Wolseley submitted the following memorandum to the Secretary of State :—

'The defeat of Baker Pasha on the 4th instant alters most materially the position of affairs generally in the Soudan. General Gordon when he reaches Khartoum will find himself in a worse position than he anticipated when he left Cairo on the 27th January. The idea amongst the people will be that the English have been defeated, as it will be known everywhere that the red-coated British troops now occupy Suakin from which Baker started on his unfortunate expedition.

'Our occupation of that port and of the works erected on the mainland for its defence, gives us directly as a nation the position of belligerents in the war which Egypt has been for some time waging in the Soudan.

'British troops are besieged in Suakin : they dare not go even a few miles outside their intrenchments. This will be proclaimed throughout the Soudan, and the people will see that the garrison of Khartoum commanded by English officers at one end of the line is besieged, and Suakin occupied by English troops is besieged at the other end of it.

'We have proclaimed our intention of clearing out of the Soudan ; it is not therefore to be expected that any chiefs will throw in their lot with us. They will consider what their position will be when all the Egyptian garrisons are destroyed and the country left to itself, and their line of conduct will be adopted with a view to the future. In the general scramble after we are gone, what can they do to secure power and influence, and in the meantime, at present in fact, what should they do to secure that end ? They will naturally care nothing for us or for our policy ; why should they ?

'General Gordon will have to treat with them in the position of a suppliant, and any man who knows Easterns is fully alive to what that means—our experiences at Cabul in 1840, and at Cawnpore in 1857, teach us what reliance can be placed upon the most solemn promises and sworn-to agreements of Easterns who believe themselves to be masters of the position.

'To enable General Gordon to treat with the rebels on good terms you must show yourselves strong, and no Eastern will believe in your strength as long as you allow your troops to be cooped up in Suakin, not daring to leave the protection of its defences and the gunboats stationed there.

'Unless "something" is now done, and done at once, to manifest your power and strength in the most un-mistakable manner, it is tolerably certain that Gordon will soon find himself shut up in Khartoum, unable to do more than hold his own there as long as his provisions last, even assuming he is able, with his genius for command, to infuse sufficient courage into the miserable troops that now constitute the garrison of that place.

' I think the time has now come for a revision of the policy previously come to with reference to the Soudan.

'General Gordon has been constituted Governor-General of that country. Giving him that position was clearly a step in the right direction, but it does not accord with your declared intention of abandoning the Soudan ; and the expression used in the Queen's Speech in reference to this policy, "the interior of the Soudan," would seem to have been devised to enable you to retain possession of the Eastern Soudan, with Khartoum as its capital, while you evacuate the western provinces, which have only been added to the Egyptian possessions in very recent years.

' I would advise, therefore, that Gordon, in announcing to the inhabitants of the country his appointment as Governor - General, should announce his intention to retain possession of the country to the east of the White Nile; that, in future, it will not be ruled by Egyptian Pashas; that it will be ruled by Soudanese officials under British officers until a stable native government can be established, when it may be possible for England to hand it over to the government of its own native rulers.

' To enable General Gordon to carry out this policy it is absolutely necessary to show your strength at once by proving your determination and your ability to support him . . .'

Lord Wolseley then proposed, with details, an advance of an English brigade to Wadi Halfa, a despatch of additional troops to Suakin, and operations in that district. He continued :—

'These operations would, I believe, so strengthen General Gordon's hands that he would be enabled to carry out whatever policy he deemed advisable at Khartoum.

'Unless this is done, I do not see what he can effect there. He will be besieged, and, with troops such as those

recently employed near Tokat, it is folly to imagine he
would be able to cut his way out. The result I foresee
is an irresistible demand on the part of our people to
have him relieved, and to relieve Khartoum under such
circumstances would mean a costly war of considerable
proportions.

'No army can march from Suakin to Berber if it be
opposed, as about the last hundred miles of the route is
almost entirely destitute of water, and at other positions of
the road water is so scarce that only detachments could
move over it at one time.

'If Khartoum is besieged in force, and its relief has
to be undertaken, the army employed will have to advance
from Assouan, in Egypt proper, along the Nile valley—a
very long and tedious operation.

'It is because I would avoid this war on a large scale
that I propose the immediate execution of the smaller
operations I have here recommended.

'My dread is that, unless action is at once taken, we
shall be forced into war before many months elapse.

'It is bold measures and a decided policy at moments
like the present that stave off wars with all their horrors
and their attendant cost. It is half measures, and no
policy beyond waiting upon events, that causes us in-
sensibly to drift into war.

'It is easy to persuade ourselves to do nothing, and
we can always find many plausibly sounding arguments
for supineness. At present we may persuade ourselves
that the adoption of any decided line of action, such as
that I recommend, might complicate matters that it might
be desirable General Gordon should deal with diplomatically—but any one who has ever had to deal with
Easterns must know you can never weaken your diplomatic
position by a display of military strength and determination.
The more you can do in the next fortnight to make both
apparent, the more you will strengthen General Gordon
and aid him in carrying out any policy, no matter what may
be its main features, that he may resolve upon adopting.

'I am no politician and have no concern with party, but it is evident even to an outsider that the feeling increases, every hour almost, that some step should be taken by the Cabinet to save human life in the Soudan and to put a stop to these massacres. One after another the Egyptian garrisons will have to surrender, the men to have their throats cut, the women to be debauched, and the children sold into slavery.

'Are we to stand by with folded arms within the entrenchments at Suakin whilst this is taking place? Is it wise, is it right for us to do so?

'This feeling that something should be done, like a rolling snowball, will go on increasing until the Government will be forced to adopt measures to save the Khartoum garrison. A small, but determined and well carried out, effort on our part, if made now, would in all probability enable General Gordon to treat with wavering chiefs, and so to become master of the position at Khartoum, but if nothing is done that place will be besieged, and we shall be, in my humble opinion, forced into a war on a large scale.'

Tory speakers and writers were fiercely attacking the Ministry for allowing the Egyptians to be sent like sheep to the slaughter, and for doing nothing while Sinkat fell, and while an audacious foe threatened Suakin. There was also a strong feeling among many Liberals, headed by W. E. Forster, in favour of active steps, partly because the possession of Suakin stopped an outlet for the Red Sea slave trade. The Cabinet accordingly decided to send a brigade under Sir Gerald Graham. The force came too late to save Tokar; the garrison there surrendered a few days before Graham reached Suakin. But on the 29th February the British attacked the Arab force, and slew some 3000. Osman Digna, undaunted, remained near Suakin. Another fight took place on 13th March, and 2000 more Arabs were slain.

In both fights, especially in the first, the British force sustained severe loss. Graham now commanded the Suakin end of the comparatively short route to Khartoum *via* Berber, on the Nile, a place held till the 26th May by an Egyptian garrison. The distance from Suakin to Berber is 240 miles, across a desert supplied at intervals with wells. It was an old trade route, and that by which Egyptian troops had always been sent to the Soudan. From Berber to Khartoum by river the distance is about 200 miles, navigable throughout by Gordon's steamboats.

Gordon arrived at Khartoum on the 18th February, thirty-one days after his departure from London. His first decision was to ask that the great slave-trader of former Soudan days, Zobeir, might be sent up from Cairo to co-operate with him. The outlying provinces might be recovered by members of the old dynasties, but Khartoum and Sennar, the country between the two Niles, had, since the conquest, always been under direct Egyptian control, nor was there any family to which these provinces could be transferred. Gordon believed that Zobeir was the one man strong enough to hold his own there. It was a wonderfully bold proposal, for Gordon had, in his previous government, shot Suleiman, son of Zobeir, for rebellion and slave-trading, and knew that he was still hated by Zobeir. It was difficult for an English Government, more especially for a Liberal Government, to grant the request, since Zobeir was the king of slave-traders. If, on the other hand, the alternative were anarchy, there was no doubt that slave-trading would flourish in other hands. Gordon's request was sent on by Sir Evelyn Baring with an expression of his own concurrence. Mr. Gladstone was for the moment unwell and unable to attend Cabinet meetings. He was in favour of the scheme, and believed that he would be able to induce the House of Commons to accept it.

Possibly, if he had been well, the thing might have been
done. But the request had to be refused, because the
members of the Cabinet who best knew the House of
Commons were convinced that the sanction of that
Assembly could not be obtained. Gordon had cited the
precedent of Abdurrahman, in whose hands we had left
Afghanistan without any inquiry into his character or
methods of administration. But, in that case, the dread
word 'slavery' did not occur, the word whereby an emotional section of the English nation can be driven to
rage as the sea by the whip of the wind. These people
had already been excited by the sensible step taken by
Gordon on his arrival at Khartoum in proclaiming that
he had no intention to interfere with domestic slave-
holding.[1]

At the end of February, Gordon, knowing that Zobeir
was not to come, made two other proposals. One was that
200 British troops should be sent to Wadi Halfa; the
other that Indian troops should be employed to open up
the Suakin-Berber road. It was now that Gordon used
the phrase about 'smashing up'[2] the Mahdi, which alarmed
so much the advocates of a rapid and pacific evacuation.
Sir Evelyn Baring at the same time continued to press for
a reversal of the decision as to Zobeir, and received on
5th March that Foreign Office telegram, a masterpiece of
official procrastination, asking him how he reconciled this
proposal with the discouragement of slave-trading, with the

---

[1] The Committee of the Anti-Slavery Society wrote (10th March) to Lord
Granville that 'countenance in any shape to such an individual (Zobeir) would be
a degradation to England and a scandal to Europe.' Evidently they thought the
idea 'shocking,' and a leading Nonconformist journal must have regretted its
previous advice to its readers to 'trust in God and in His Ministers, Gladstone
and Gordon.'

[2] February 26, 1884.—'If Egypt is to be quiet, the Mahdi must be smashed
up. . . . Remember that once Khartoum belongs to the Mahdi, the task will be
far more difficult.'

policy of complete evacuation, and with the security of
Egypt, and requesting information, with full details, as
to the progress made in extricating each garrison. Sir
Evelyn Baring read this telegram 'with a feeling akin to
despair.'[1]

On the 9th March, fatal day, Lord Granville sent a
telegram finally declining either to let Zobeir go up or
to send troops to Berber. But, he said, in view of the fact
that the withdrawal of the garrisons would take a considerable time (and this by reason of the doubts felt by the
'inhabitants of the Soudan with regard to the future
government of the country'), the Government had 'no
desire to force General Gordon's hand prematurely,' and
proposed, therefore, 'to extend his employment for any
reasonable period which may be necessary to enable him
to carry out the objects of the mission with which he has
been entrusted.' Correspondence continued until the
middle of April. Sir Evelyn Baring still pressed Zobeir
as the best solution, while the Foreign Office took the line
that, if Gordon could make no better suggestion, he should
at once evacuate Khartoum with all that he could save
from the wreck. Baring also supported Gordon's other
proposal. He advised (24th March) that a detachment
from Graham's victorious force at Suakin should be pushed
across to Berber. The military advisers at Cairo, Stephenson and Evelyn Wood, thought that the operation was
practicable, though not, of course, without risk. Lord
Granville replied that, in view of the climate, the time of
the year, and the dangers, the Government did not think
it justifiable to send an expedition to Berber. They left
full discretion to General Gordon to 'remain at Khartoum
if he thought it necessary, or to retire by the southern, or
any other route which might be found available.' It was

---

[1] See *Modern Egypt*, vol. i. p. 508.

little use to keep a brigade at Suakin if it was to serve no purpose. Sir Gerald Graham was ordered (26th March) to re-embark the bulk of his force as soon as possible. Some thousands of Arabs had been killed and many English lives had been lost with no justifying results.

Sir Evelyn Baring had already telegraphed (25th March) to Lord Granville the rumour that the rebels were between Khartoum and Berber.  He sent on the 26th March a very strongly worded telegram :—

'Let me earnestly beg Her Majesty's Government to place themselves in the position of Gordon and Stewart. They have been sent on a most difficult and dangerous mission by the English Government.  Their proposal to send Zobeir, which, if it had been acted upon some weeks ago, would certainly have entirely altered the situation, was rejected.  The consequences which they foresaw have ensued.  If they receive the instructions contained in your Lordship's telegram of the 25th, they cannot but understand them as meaning that they and all with them are to be abandoned and to receive no help from the British Government.  Coetlogon, who is here, assures me that, so long as the rebels hold both banks of the river above the Sixth Cataract, it will be quite impossible for boats to pass.  He ridicules the idea of retreating with the garrison to Equator, and we may be sure that Gordon and Stewart will not come away alone.  As a matter of personal opinion, I do not believe in the impossibility of helping Gordon, even during the summer, if Indian troops are employed, and money is not spared.  But, if it be decided to make no attempt to afford present help, then I would urge that Gordon be told to try and maintain his position during the summer, and that then, if he is still beleaguered, an expedition will be sent as early as possible in the autumn to relieve him.  This would, at all events, give him some hope, and the mere announcement of the intention of the Government would go a long way to ensure his safety by keeping loyal tribes who may still be wavering.  No one can regret more than I do the necessity of sending British or Indian troops to the Soudan, but, having sent Gordon to Khartoum, it appears to me that it is our bounden duty, both as a matter of humanity and policy, not to abandon him.'

This was strong and clear.  After its despatch all responsibility for the disasters, miseries, and massacres of Berber and Khartoum fell upon the Government of England. The writer of this telegram, many years later, wrote in his book, *Modern Egypt*, ' There can scarcely be a doubt that if the decision to send an expedition to General Gordon's relief had been taken in April or May, instead of in August, the objects of the expedition would have been obtained. The main responsibility for this delay rests upon Mr. Gladstone.'

If Queen Victoria had not only reigned but had been able to decide the course of action, Khartoum would have been saved.[1]  The following telegram shows how strongly she supported the view of the civil and military advisers in Egypt ; and Lord Hartington's reply gives the view taken at the War Office and by the Cabinet.

*Telegram from the Queen to Lord Hartington,*
*March 25, 1884.*

' Referring to No. 246 from Sir E. Baring—It is alarming ; General Gordon is in danger : you are bound to try to save him.  Surely Indian troops might go from Aden and could bear climate though British cannot.  You have incurred fearful responsibility.'

---

[1] In a letter to Miss Gordon, on the 17th February 1885, after the catastrophe at Khartoum, the Queen wrote, ' That the promises of support were not fulfilled— which I so frequently and constantly pressed upon those who asked him (Gordon) to go—is to me grief inexpressible.'  This is printed in the book called *Gordon's Letters to his Sister.*

Lord Hartington replied to the Queen on the following day :—

'Lord Hartington, with his humble duty and in reference to Your Majesty's telegram of yesterday, begs to state that he understands that Lord Granville wrote an account to Your Majesty of the deliberations of the Cabinet on the position of General Gordon at Khartoum. Lord Hartington begs to add that, in his opinion, however critical may be General Gordon's position, and however strongly the Government would desire to render assistance to him, the risk and difficulty of despatching a military force to Berber and thence to Khartoum would be so great as to make the attempt an unjustifiable one. At this time of year, in addition to the sufferings to which the troops would be exposed from the great heat, it would be impossible on account of the difficulties of the water supply to send more than very small bodies of troops from Suakin to Berber ; and in the present condition of the country surrounding that place, it is doubtful whether a small force could render any effectual assistance to General Gordon, or whether it would even be able to maintain its own position. Although it is possible that General Gordon may be surrounded and besieged in Khartoum, there is no reason at present to doubt that he will be able to defend himself there, and the place is known to be well supplied with provisions and stores. If it should be eventually necessary to relieve him by force, such an operation could be more effectually carried out, and with less risk to the health and safety of the troops engaged, in the autumn than now when the great heat is commencing. H.R.H. the Duke of Cambridge concurs with Lord Hartington in the opinion that an expedition to Berber would be too hazardous and would also involve too great a loss of life by sickness to be undertaken at present. General Gordon certainly, when he left England, distinctly understood that no British troops would be employed in relieving him or the garrisons and was confident of his ability to accomplish his task without such assistance.'

Lord Wolseley concurred in these opinions. At a later date he explained that he had, at that time, been opposed to the despatch of a small force to Berber, because he understood that the Government did not propose to support the movement by a larger expedition in the early autumn, so that a small force at Berber or Khartoum would be 'in the air,' and might only add to the complications. Apart from this just consideration, when one remembers what was done in India, in the Mutiny, by English troops in the hot weather, it is difficult to suppose that the feat of sending Indian, or even English, troops across 240 miles of desert track, while Berber was still held by friends, should have been impossible. [1]

Lord Granville, in his reply (March 28th) to Baring's telegram of 26th March, adhered, under the decision arrived at in the Cabinet, to his former position, and said that the Government were not prepared to take any new step until they heard from Gordon what was 'his actual condition and prospects as to security, and also, if possible, his plans of proceeding and his desires under present circumstances.' His 'actual condition,' at this moment, was that, with a garrison of mostly incompetent officers and feeble soldiers, he was surrounded on all sides by a numerous and courageous enemy well supplied with munitions of war, though deficient in discipline and organisation. On the 29th March Gordon's troops suffered a bad surprise and defeat near Khartoum. On April 7th he sent a famous telegram :—

'As far as I can understand, the situation is this; you state your intention of not sending any relief up

---

[1] Suakin to Khartoum is about the distance of London to Perth, and for the last 200 miles there was easy navigation on the Nile, and Gordon's steamers to maintain communications.

here or to Berber, and you refuse me Zobeir. I consider myself free to act according to circumstances. I shall hold out here as long as I can, and if I can suppress the rebellion I shall do so. If I cannot I shall retire to the Equator, and leave you the *indelible disgrace* of abandoning the garrisons of Sennar, Kassala, Berber, and Dongola, with the certainty that you will ultimately be forced to smash up the Mahdi under great difficulties if you would retain peace in Egypt.'

Sir Evelyn Baring, on 14th April, strongly urged on Lord Granville that, if the Nile route were chosen for an expedition, no time should be lost in making preparations so that the movement might begin directly the water rose.

In a debate in the House of Commons in the first week of April, Lord Hartington stated the case of the Government. He gave their reasons for refusing to accede to Gordon's request for Zobeir. It was, he said, this request and this refusal which led the Government to ask Gordon to stay at Khartoum so long as he deemed this to be necessary for the purpose of withdrawing the Egyptian troops and handing the country over to native rulers. Gordon had never suggested that British troops should be sent to Khartoum itself. Hartington said:—

'He left this country with a most clear and distinct understanding, repeated over and over again by himself, that the mission . . . was one which he was prepared to undertake with such resources as he might find on the spot, and he distinctly understood that it was not the policy of the Government to send a fresh expedition for the relief of Khartoum or any similar garrisons.'

Lord Hartington then stated the military reasons against sending a small unsupported force to Berber.

He went on to say that 'the Government have accepted the responsibility for General Gordon's actions, so far as they have sanctioned them, and they feel also that they are greatly responsible for his safety.' But their information, he added, was not yet sufficient to allow them to state what measures might ultimately have to be taken. The time had not yet come when it could definitely be said that Gordon had failed in his mission.

The following letters show more vividly than could any résumé the position at this critical moment. The writer of the first letter had seen a good deal of Gordon :—

*The Hon. Reginald Brett, M.P., to Lord Hartington,*
*April 1, 1884.*

'I heard from General Gordon this morning. Letter dated March 3rd, Khartoum. He asks to be remembered to you. The following are extracts from his letter :—

"(1) As for Zobeir, I wish with all my heart he was here. He alone can ride the Soudan horse, and if they do not send him, I am sentenced to penal servitude for my life up here.

"(2) Bear this in mind, that it is impossible to hope for any compromise between H.M.'s Government and the Pasha tribe ; I know it by experience, and I smite them with unrelenting severity because I know it is hopeless to try and deal with them. I rejoice in so doing. It is no use trying to work with them, and I wish our Government would see this.

"(3) A French Consul will be here in two days. He will not bother me, but you may expect he will push the French Government to bother our Government.

"(4) We *must* evacuate the Soudan. It is absolutely necessary. In a year the slaves up here will rise and will emancipate themselves. What a wonderful dénouement! And how my prayers will have been then heard."

'I wish again to say that nothing will, I am convinced, induce Gordon to leave Khartoum until all those persons who have been faithful to him can leave with him; and any policy based on the assumption that such an order would be obeyed is predestined to fail.

'I am also sure that Gordon neither wants nor expects an army to be sent to Khartoum to relieve him.

'At the same time it never will strike him that the Government could be capable of allowing it to be believed for twenty-four hours that England had "abandoned" him.

'He would, of course, assume that the English Government would let it be known far and wide that they are prepared to support him with all the force at their disposal if he should require and ask it; and the knowledge of this, permeating through Egypt and the Soudan, would in all probability be sufficient for his purpose.

'If it were not, H.M. Government would only then have to do what, if they were by some mischance to try and leave Gordon to his fate, they would have to do notwithstanding.'

### Lord Hartington to Mr. Gladstone.

'HOLKER HALL, *April* 11, 1884.

'After Gordon's message contained in Baring's No. 289 we can scarcely say any longer that we know that he does not want troops. I presume that he would prefer British to Turkish.

'Lord Wolseley has, at my request, prepared (confidentially) a rough sketch of an expedition which he thinks practicable by the Nile. The movement could not take place before the Nile rises in a month or six weeks; but preparations would have to be made almost immediately. Sir C. Wilson thinks that Wolseley has underrated the difficulties and delay of the Nile route, and thinks that the Suakin-Berber route, which has always been used by

the Egyptians, should be used, at all events in part. I have
sent Wolseley's memo. to Northbrook.

'But I do not know whether the time has not come when
we ought to ask Baring to consult Stephenson and Wood
on the practicability and scope of an operation to relieve
Gordon, and on the nature of the preparations which
should be made. It is very probable that the effect
of the mere announcement that preparations were being
made would have a great effect on the "trumpery revolt"
which Gordon describes.'

### Mr. Gladstone to Lord Hartington, April 13, 1884.

'I have never heard mention in the Cabinet or otherwise of sending English troops to Khartoum, unless in
the last and sad necessity of its being the only available
means of rescuing him.

'The despatch of Turkish soldiers is, of course, a different
matter, but a serious one not yet accepted in Egypt or by us.

'As far as I see the sending English troops to
Khartoum, except as above, would be the most vital and
radical change that could be made in our policy. ₁

'What I do think we ought to set about is sending a set
of carefully prepared questions to Gordon about his future
condition and plans ; all the more so because it appears to
me that in his telegrams he takes very little notice indeed
of any general questions that we put to him.

'I *hope* to see Granville to-morrow at Holmbury, and I
will show him your letter.'

### Lord Hartington to Lord Granville, April 15, 1884.

'As to Mr. Gladstone's letter it seems doubtful whether
we can receive replies to any questions "carefully prepared," or otherwise, addressed to Gordon, in time to be
of any use to us in making up our minds. We do not
know that he has received *any* message from Cairo since
the 10th March. I think that it is clear enough that,
whether he has a right to do so or not, he expects help in

some shape or another, and it is also, I think, clear that he will not be able to leave Khartoum without some such help.'

*Lord Wolseley to Lord Hartington, April* 13, 1884.

'The enclosed telegram has just been sent to me with a request that I would state my views on the subject it deals with. Before I can do so to any useful purpose, I should know what are the intentions of the Government regarding General Gordon and Khartoum.

'His position at present is that of an officer commanding a besieged garrison.

'Putting the possibility of his dying or being killed within the next six months out of the question, the siege must end in one of the three following ways, viz. :—

' 1. The surrender of Khartoum
    (*a*) Being taken by assault, a most improbable contingency.
    (*b*) By treachery from within, also improbable.
    (*c*) By the garrison being starved out, which, if blockaded long enough, may be regarded as a certainty.
    (*d*) Owing to the want of ammunition ;
' 2. The relief of Khartoum by a British force ;
' 3. The raising of the siege through some change of Soudanese feeling towards General Gordon ; in fact, a sort of political revolution.

'I have not included as a possible contingency the garrison under Gordon being able to cut its way through their besiegers and making good their retreat to Berber, and so down the Nile, as owing to the miserable stuff of which their garrison is composed, no such gallant feat is to be expected from it.

'I presume the Government is not prepared to allow General Gordon and his garrison to fall into the hands of the cruel and barbarous enemy now besieging Khartoum,

if he can hold out until the march of an English force to
relieve him becomes climatically possible.   I understand,
from some of the telegrams from Gordon which I have seen,
that he had provisions for six months, and that, when he
said this, he was still receiving supplies from without, as
the investment of the place was by no means complete.   I
presume therefore that, as far as provisions are concerned,
he can hold out until October, and that, if now informed
that he would be relieved early in November, he could still
obtain from the surrounding country enough supplies of
food to enable him to hold out, say to middle of November.
This telegram tells us that he had 1400 rounds of ammunition for his two Krupp guns—that would allow for an
average expenditure of about seven rounds per diem until
he was relieved, say 200 rounds per mensem.   This is
small, but would, I should say, suffice, provided he has an
ample supply of small arm ammunition.   It is also to be
expected that he has some camel guns and ammunition for
them.

'The question of sending him ammunition as proposed
by Sir E. Baring therefore resolves itself into the question
of what the Government proposes doing to relieve Gordon
from his present difficult position.   If no attempt is to be
made in the autumn to relieve Khartoum, then by all
means send him more ammunition, telling him you are
doing so because he wished for it, but above all things
impressing on him that he must not under any circumstances expect any expeditionary force to be sent to help
or relieve him.

'As I regard the position of affairs in the Soudan, what
I consider to be now of the first importance is that the
Government should at once determine upon the line of
action or inaction it means to pursue, and that Gordon
should be immediately informed of the determination
arrived at.   Gordon would then be enabled to shape his
course accordingly.   He might resolve to hold on to
Khartoum, trusting to the chapter of accidents to bring
his garrison some opportunity of escape, or he might

determine upon that retreat up the White Nile which at first you forbad him to attempt, but which prohibition I lately understood from you the Government had withdrawn. If you contemplate sending an expedition in the autumn to Gordon's relief, the sooner he is informed the better it will be for him and for your interests. A garrison that knows an English force will come to its relief within a given time will eat its boots before surrender. This knowledge will give life and courage and the power of endurance even to cowards, whereas the feeling that no such promise is, or will be, made, that surrender is merely a matter of time, to be spent in misery, privation, danger, and hopelessness, will go far to depress the spirit and the courage even of the strong and daring of heart.

'My own opinion is that a telegram should be sent to Berber without delay addressed to Gordon, in clear, to the care of the Governor of that place (Hassein Khalifa) saying that as soon as the climate admitted of British troops moving, an expeditionary force would be sent to Khartoum. No further information to be given in clear, but a message in cipher to Gordon should accompany this telegram in clear telling him he might calculate upon being relieved before the 15th November next.

'Upon this there cannot be two opinions, that the English people will force you to do this, whether you like it or not, and therefore you had better make all your arrangements accordingly, and have the credit of determining upon it of your own free will, and of enabling Gordon to reap as soon as possible all the advantage which an authoritative announcement when made will afford him.

'At the same time, I think every endeavour should be made to avoid the necessity of having to send this British force to Khartoum. This brings me to the consideration of the third of the three ways in some one of which, I said at the beginning of this letter, the siege of that place must end.

'There is only one means of bringing about the raising

of the siege that I can think of, and that is to announce
that Gordon is to remain on as Governor-General of the
Soudan to rule the country for the benefit of the Soudanese
people.

'What has, in my opinion, deprived Gordon of power
was his fatal announcement that he meant to clear out of
the Soudan as quickly as possible. This has prevented all
men of any influence from helping, much less from throwing in their lot with him. Who would do so in the East
for a Giaour who was about to desert them? Knowing
that anarchy, or possibly anarchy plus the Mahdi, must
follow upon Gordon's departure, every one thought only of
his own future and the future safety of his family and his
fortune. To help Gordon under such circumstances would
have been suicidal on any man's part. This is so strongly
impressed upon my mind that I have, every day since our
troops left Suakin, been expecting to hear that Hassein
Khalifa at Berber had deserted our cause and made terms
with his neighbours or the Mahdi. It was very much with
a view to retaining him in his allegiance to us that I was
so anxious for Major Kitchener and one or two other
officers who spoke Arabic well to be sent to Berber.

'If we even now made it public with authority that a
settled government under Gordon, and after him under
some other English officer was to be established over the
Eastern Soudan (east of the White Nile) with Khartoum as
its capital, and that Gordon was to have £100,000 a year
for the present to start his new government, many strong
men might even now join his standard.

'There are two difficulties in the way of this plan : first,
it might entail increased responsibilities upon England.
Second, Gordon's engagement to the King of the Belgians.

'Is it possible to get over these difficulties? I think so.
Why not ask King Leopold to allow the Eastern Soudan
to be taken over by the great Congo or rather Central
African Association of which he is the head ?

'I know King Leopold tolerably well, and having stayed
a week with him when he was incubating his African

scheme, and having then talked the matter over daily with him for hours each day, I think I know his aims tolerably well. This knowledge leads me to think that it is quite possible he would allow Gordon to rule over the Eastern Soudan as an appanage—if not under his suzerainty, at least under the protection of the African Society that he has created. The King writes to me occasionally, and I should be very glad to sound him on this subject without compromising you or any one else, but merely throwing it out as an idea of my own, and as the most decisive and complete way of for ever killing the slave trade. Indeed I should be very glad to go to Brussels to see the King on this subject on my own hook, if the idea was one that would commend itself to the Cabinet in the event of King Leopold's entering into the idea. Some such plan as this is the only way in which, as far as I can see, there is any chance of Gordon's being able to hold his own at Khartoum without a relieving force being sent to his assistance. The despatch of that force should be avoided if possible. The plan I have roughly sketched out might possibly enable you to avoid the necessity of having to despatch that force : the surest way of having that necessity forced upon you is to do nothing now, to let matters slide, and to formulate no policy and to announce none to Gordon.'

*Lord Hartington to Lord Granville, April 16, 1884.*

'I send you another letter from Wolseley in answer to one which I wrote to him some days since. I do not know on what he founds his inference that the Government intend to relieve Gordon. I may have indicated my own opinion that it will have to be done, but I have not the slightest idea what the Government at present proposes to do.

'But it is nearly time for us to make up our minds what we will do both about Gordon and in Egypt. So far as I can understand, we are now waiting in hopes that Gordon will send us a message to say that he does not

want British troops, and that in some other way he is
going to effect the evacuation of the Soudan without them.
This is rather a broken reed to lean on, and, in my opinion,
was finally shattered by his last telegram.   Can we suppose
that he would not prefer English to Turkish troops.   I do
not agree with Northbrook that it would be of any use to
send Gordon the most positive orders to come away leaving
the main part of the garrison behind him.   I do not think
that he would obey, and I believe that public opinion
in England would support him in disobeying.   In fact, I
think, the first thing we have to do is to decide whether
we intend to leave Gordon to his fate, because, if we do
not, the sooner we begin to make preparations the better.
Then, if we are compelled after all to send an expedition,
I think that we shall have to reconsider our decision to
abandon the Eastern Soudan.[1]   I doubt whether we were
right at first in accepting Baring's opinion that it was
impossible for Egypt to hold it.   Events seem to show
that it would have been easier to hold it than to get out
of it.[2]   But probably it would not be necessary to establish
Egyptian government there, but to replace it by some
sort of independent government under our protection.
Further, I think that we shall have to make a new
departure in Egypt itself; and that it will be impossible
to face the Conference with the policy of a continuation of
the present experiment, which, according to all outside
information, and, I gather, in Baring's opinion, is an
utter failure.'

On the 21st April Lord Hartington circulated to the
members of the Cabinet two memoranda by Lord Wolseley
(dated 8th and 14th April) containing, with full detail, alter-

---

[1] He meant here to include Khartoum and Berber in the expression 'Eastern
Soudan,' as Lord Wolseley did in his previous letter.

[2] What Baring actually had said was that it was impossible for the Egyptian
Government to hold Khartoum and the Upper Nile *without British military
assistance*. Whether such assistance should be given or not was a political
question for the British Cabinet to decide, and Baring left it to them, without
offering advice.   See *Modern Egypt*, vol. i. pp. 372–76.

native schemes for an expedition (1) by the Suakin–Berber route and (2) by the Nile route.   Lord Wolseley expressed his strong preference for the Nile route, notwithstanding its greater length, on account of the facilities given by water transport, and the safe supply of drinking water. He pointed out that, of the total distance of 666 miles by river from Wadi Halfa to Berber, 224 were navigable by steamers, 140 by light steamers at high Nile, leaving only about 200 miles of difficult navigation, which could be traversed by small row-boats.   He estimated the force necessary at 6500 combatants.   If the force left Wadi Halfa on the 1st September it would, he believed, be possible to reach Berber on the 20th October and Khartoum on the 10th November at latest.   On the 23rd and 25th April, more alarming news having been received, Lord Wolseley sent in further memoranda showing how an advance detachment of from 500 to 800 British soldiers could be thrown forward by river steamers to Korosko, and thence on camels across the loop to Berber.   If preparations were begun without a day's delay this force would reach Berber by the 10th of June.[1]   He stated also the preparations which should at once be taken in hand for the larger supporting expedition in the autumn.

The Cabinet, a decisive one, with Lord Wolseley's first two memoranda before it, met on the 23rd April.   Lord Northbrook that evening noted in his diary: 'Cabinet, 3 till 7.   Great difference of opinion.   Question of immediate steps for consideration of expenditure to support Gordon deferred.   A message to him, which will make him quite mad, approved, written by Mr. Gladstone.   I think Government will probably break up.   Decision not

---

[1] Lord Wolseley allowed fifteen days for preparations and thirty days to move this light force from Cairo to Berber.   He pointed out that Gordon did that journey in fifteen days.   The 10th June would have been too late to save Berber.

to send joint expedition to Berber or English troops to Korosko.'[1] Their decision was conveyed to Cairo in the telegram, written by Mr. Gladstone, settled in the Cabinet, and sent by Lord Granville that same afternoon. The message was that Her Majesty's Government could not sanction the despatch of a British force to Berber *via* Korosko. Gordon was to be asked to inform Government as to his immediate prospects and, if Khartoum were in danger, to state the force necessary to secure *his removal.* He was to be told that Government did not propose to supply him with a Turkish or any other force for the purpose of undertaking military expeditions. If, with this knowledge, he continued at Khartoum, he was to state the 'cause and intention' with which he so continued. This decision involved the abandonment of Khartoum and Berber, and, as events proved, the storm and massacre at both places, the death of Gordon, and other disasters and calamities. Lord Hartington wrote on the next day, 24th April 1884, to Lord Granville :—

'Will you let me have copies of the telegram settled yesterday ? I don't think I can agree in the course which is now being taken. Somebody said that we were yesterday at a turning-point in our policy, and I think we were. I look on the decision as one practically to do nothing and make no preparations, and this I cannot acquiesce in. I am glad that Mr. Gladstone is going further than I anticipated in his answer to Bourke. But I cannot agree that there is any real or practical intention. The message to Berber is an instruction to surrender, and the conditions as to Gordon are such as will never be fulfilled.'

Lord Hartington, after seeing the telegram, wrote on the 25th to Lord Granville protesting against the word 'removal,' which 'goes against the grain with me more

---

[1] *Life of Lord Northbrook,* by Bernard Mallet, p. 186.

than I can say,' and to which 'I feel the most intense dislike.' Gordon's feelings as to the word were, as his Journal shows, precisely the same when the message at last reached him. He had no wish to be the 'rescued lamb.' Lord Hartington now proposed to send a telegram to General Stephenson, the purport of which is shown in the following correspondence :—

*Mr. Gladstone to Lord Granville, April 25, 1884.*

'I by no means object in principle to Hartington's proposed telegram, but I think its form has a character we did not intend, and looks so much in the direction of Wolseley's great scheme, while it overlooks the instruction already sent to Gordon respecting an expedition, that it could not I think be sent without the authority of the Cabinet.

'I wrote yesterday to Northbrook urging him to press his inquiries about the Nile ;
> 'how far it could be available for navigation,
> 'whether continuously or with interruption,
> 'what vessels could be had, and where, to go upon it.

'It seems to me as to the telegram to Stephenson that—

> '(a) It should recite, or embody by reference, the instruction already sent to Gordon.
> '(b) It should, in conformity with that instruction, speak of his removal, not his relief, as the object of any expedition.
> '(c) Should desire the generals to report on all the same subjects, and whatever else Hartington thinks proper to enumerate.
> '(d) Should ask whether any, and, if so, what preparations (as distinguished from inquiries) should be made immediately.
> '(e) Should enjoin strict secrecy at present.
> '(f) Should more pointedly desire information as to Nile route.

'Of course I assume that Hartington's papers will be sent to them.'

Lord Hartington wrote that same evening to Cairo :—

*Lord Hartington to General Stephenson, April 25, 1884.*

'I shall send you to-night or to-morrow an important telegram asking you to report on the measures which may become necessary for the relief (or removal) of General Gordon from Khartoum. I do not know yet which of these words will be used, and my object in writing to you by the mail which is just going out is to give you some explanation of the sense which either word may be intended to carry. It is the opinion of some here (an opinion which may be a sound one, but in which I do not think that General Gordon will concur), that our obligations to him do not extend further than to secure the safety of himself and his immediate suite, and not to that of the garrison or any part of the population of Khartoum or other places in the Soudan. The use of the word 'removal' would of course indicate that the primary intention of the expedition would be the more limited object, while the use of the word 'relief' would indicate the more extended one. I am inclined to think that, if General Gordon is able to hold out till the time when any expedition could reach him, it is probable he would be able to secure his own safety by means of the steamers which he has at Khartoum when the river rises without any expedition at all. If, however, an expedition should become necessary even for this limited object, I presume that its extent and character would not be greatly affected by the consideration whether its intentions were limited to bringing away General Gordon alone or were extended to enabling the garrison to retreat also. I presume that an expedition, if sent out at all, will have to be organised on a scale mainly calculated on the amount of opposition which it may probably meet with on the road, and that this would be much the same whatever may be the ultimate object. At all events I should wish you to bear this distinction in mind in making your report, and that you should endeavour to inform us what would in the opinion of yourself and your advisers be the difference in the scale of the preparations necessary for the accomplishment of either object.

'I must take this opportunity of congratulating you on the very efficient arrangements made for the Suakin expedition, and on the complete military success which it accomplished. I wish that the political results had been as complete as the military success, but that this has not been the case was not the fault of those who organised and directed the operations.

'With reference again to the possible Khartoum expedition, I fancy that, in the opinion of many here, Lord Wolseley has underrated the difficulties of the Nile route, relying very much as he does on the experience under different conditions of the Red River expedition. All former experience seems to point to the Suakin route, and at the proper time of year I presume that the difficulties of water could be overcome.

'I believe, however, that the Egyptians have never on former occasions had to make use of this route in the face of determined opposition from the tribes which would probably have to be reckoned on now.'

The purport of the telegram which Lord Hartington had obtained leave to send is shown by the Commanding Officer's reply :—

*General Sir F. Stephenson to Lord Hartington, May 5, 1884.*

'The difference in the amount and composition of a force for the removal or release of General Gordon, and that required for the relief of the garrison, is nil.

'The difficulties to be encountered in either case would exist on the road to Khartoum, and would not be affected by the consideration of the number of men to be withdrawn from the place after we had once reached it.

'If, however, I understand General Gordon's character at all correctly, I do not imagine that he would ever contemplate coming away from Khartoum accompanied by his suite only, and leaving the garrison to their resources, provided they remained true to him, or unless favourable terms could be made with the enemy for their future safety.

'It is, I believe, even doubtful whether he would come away unless similar provision were made for the safety of Sennar and the other garrisons.

'I venture to submit this as my own private opinion, although it is one which is entertained by others who are more intimately acquainted with his character.

'The state of affairs in this country is not very satisfactory ; it is very unsettled, and advantage is being taken of the present condition of things to carry on intrigues and foment disaffection, an instance of which has lately occurred in the battalion of Blacks lately formed at Abassiyeh for service in the Egyptian army, who have been incited to what I can call by no other name than mutiny by some outside influence.

'They were called upon to give up their arms for other and better ones, which, in the first instance, they refused to do, a serjeant stepping out, as I am informed, and calling upon the men not to do so. The serjeant is now under sentence of ten years' penal servitude.

'The arms were eventually given up without further trouble, but, in the meantime, I had to warn General Davis to keep a sharp watch upon this battalion and be ready to turn out the English troops if required.

'I have no doubt that these circumstances have been already brought to your notice, but I mention them, as they entail additional watchfulness and responsibility upon the Queen's troops.

'I beg to thank you very sincerely for the complimentary remarks which you have been good enough to make upon the manner in which the preparations were made for the recent expedition to the Eastern Soudan.

'I only wish that the results of General Graham's brilliant successes were more marked and likely to be more lasting than seems to be the case at present.'

*Memorandum by Lord Wolseley to the Marquis of Hartington,*
*May 9, 1884.*

'During General Graham's recent operations in the neighbourhood of Suakin nothing that I am aware of was put in writing upon the subject of his advancing upon Berber. Indeed, I am not aware that the propriety or possibility of such an advance was ever seriously discussed.

'Owing—I think it was—to General Gordon having urged the Government to send a few squadrons of cavalry from Suakin to Berber, the question of whether some force of cavalry should, or should not, be pushed on to that place was referred to in conversation with Lord Hartington.

'I was always opposed to any such operation, unless it was to be made as part of a large and serious attempt to relieve Khartoum. I asked what could be the advantage of sending a few hundred men to Berber as an isolated operation ? They would either have to remain all the summer at that place, which would have entailed considerable risk, or, after staying there a few days, would have had to return to Suakin, giving the people the idea that a force, which they would have imagined had been despatched to help Gordon in Khartoum, had been forced to retreat without accomplishing its object.

'To have sent a few hundred, say 500, men from Suakin to Berber after Graham's last action could most certainly have been accomplished, but would have been a very silly move unless it was intended to follow it up, and especially unless it were intended to announce most emphatically that we meant to relieve Gordon by moving a column of troops to Khartoum.

'We knew that Gordon was then in no immediate danger. We had made no preparations for the march of a strong column upon Khartoum, and, without such preparations, we should not have been justified in attempting such an operation unless Gordon were in dire straits.

'What we could have done then to strengthen Gordon was to announce publicly that we intended to move troops to his assistance, and to prove our sincerity by at once beginning to make the most open preparations for that operation. Had we done so, I think it may be asserted that Berber would not have fallen, and many who are now Gordon's enemies and arrayed against him would not have joined the Mahdi's cause.

'As far as I understand Gordon's position in Khartoum, he is quite safe there as long as his provisions and ammunition last, and as long as the popular sentiment in that place is for him. His great danger is that our abandonment of Berber will give rise to the notion that we have abandoned him, an idea that is sure to turn the popular feeling against him. In the East the man abandoned by his friends can find few allies or supporters. Few will throw in their lot with the disgraced leader.

'I understood that the Cabinet had come to no decision as to the propriety of sending a force to relieve Gordon at Khartoum, and therefore I thought it would have been unwise to push on a weak detachment to Berber.

'Khartoum can only be relieved after long preparation for moving a force there, and I venture to add here that, in my opinion, we should *at once* begin to make those preparations, for it is evident that we may be forced, whether we like it or not, to undertake that operation before many months elapse.

'To make these preparations at once would not necessarily mean an advance upon Khartoum, but, if the country should force the Government to send an expedition there, those preparations would enable us to accomplish that object.'

The debate in the House of Commons took place on the 12th and 13th May. Sir Michael Hicks Beach moved a vote of censure. With regard to the messages to Gordon, he said :—

'I will venture to say that a more disgraceful suggestion

than the suggestion to a British soldier and a Christian hero
that he should desert those who had placed themselves in
peril for his sake, was never made by a British Government.
. . . General Gordon, beleaguered in Khartoum by hosts of
enemies, bound there even more strongly by those feelings
of honour, of which Ministers never even seem to think,
is asked to state to Her Majesty's Government the cause
and intention with which he continues in Khartoum.'

Gordon may have been a 'Christian hero,' but, in his
place, the most ordinary Major-General surely could not,
and would not, have consented, without, at any rate, most
explicit orders both from the Khedive and British Government, and the appointment of some kind of successor
in command, to steal away from Khartoum leaving the
population entrusted to his care to excellent chances
of being massacred, plundered, and ravished. Gordon
was consistent throughout on the main point. He said,
in a telegram of 3rd March 1884, 'it may have been a
mistake to send me up, but this having been done I have
no option but to see evacuation through . . . even if I was
mean enough to escape I have no power to do so,' and
this view he asserted again and again.[1] If the Government
had boldly said, in reply to Gordon's question in his
telegram of 9th March, 'As your mission has failed, we
do not intend to make any further attempt to save the

---

[1] Early in March the Mahdi had summoned Gordon to surrender Khartoum
and join the true faith. Gordon called together the chief inhabitants and read
the message to them. Sir R. Wingate says, 'The vote was unanimous to trust
to Gordon and to resist. The people declared that this was a false Mahdi.
Gordon accepted the trust. It was to this that he referred so often when refusing
to abandon the town, and it was in the faith of this trust that his faithless and
mutinous soldiers served him so well and truly in his long defence. In those of
the townsmen capable of it, Gordon inspired a sincere feeling of confidence and
affection. Others, and they were the most numerous, viewed him as the Trojans
viewed the statue of Pallas. Even on the most trifling boat journey he was
always accompanied by vigilant townsmen.' (*Mahdism and the Egyptian Soudan*,
p. 111.)

Soudan garrisons. We, therefore, hereby instruct you (and we have obtained the Khedive's consent) to leave Khartoum at once with all those you can bring away,' Gordon would have received explicit orders, and might, at that date, have been able to save much from the wreck of Khartoum. No such decision was taken; no such orders sent; although at a much later date, when it was too late, Gordon received directions that he, as an individual, should *either* come away *or* explain his reasons for staying.[1] The Government refused to send up Zobeir; they refused to allow a light expedition to be sent from Suakin to Berber; they refused to listen to Wolseley's suggestion to send an advance force by Korosko to Berber; they did not listen to Baring; they refused to begin preparations for a larger expedition in the autumn; they had hardly accepted a single suggestion made by their civil and military agents in Egypt, or by their best soldier in London.

It was in this debate that Mr. Gladstone said that the reconquest of the Soudan would be 'a war of conquest against a people struggling to be free. Yes, those people are struggling to be free, and they are rightly struggling to be free.' It was in this debate also that Mr. Forster, in his blunt way, said, ' I believe that every one but the Prime Minister himself is already convinced of that danger (Gordon's) . . . and I attribute his not being convinced to his wonderful power of persuasion. He can persuade most people of most things, and, above all, he can persuade himself of almost anything.'[2] Lord Hartington, when he

---

[1] Gordon discusses the question at length in his Journal under date of 5th October 1884. He says that if he had received positive orders in March that the other garrisons were to be abandoned, before the war had become envenomed by so much resistance and fighting, he might then have left them to take their chance, and have saved that of Khartoum.

[2] Mr. Gladstone did not resemble the great financier, Mr. Neufchatel, in Disraeli's novel, who was ' too sagacious to be deceived by any one, even by himself.' Thomas Carlyle, in 1873, thought Gladstone an 'almost spectral kind of

spoke, regretted that Mr. Forster should have 'thought it necessary to make a bitter, personal, and long-reflected-over attack upon the sincerity of the Prime Minister under whose leadership he has so long served, and perhaps by means of whose support he has been assisted in acquiring some part of the position which he so deservedly occupies.' Mr. Forster meeting Lord Hartington in the lobby afterwards, said, 'You were very unfair to me to-night, but you had such a bad case that I suppose you could not help yourself.' Lord Hartington was, no doubt, in an ill-temper because he had to make officially a case of the merits of which he was not convinced, or, rather, he was convinced of its demerits. He said that the Prime Minister's speech, ' while it contained the repudiation of a policy of military action for purposes inconsistent with the mission of General Gordon, contained at the same time the fullest and most absolute recognition of the responsibility of the Government and of this country for his safety.' No one can have felt more than Lord Hartington the weakness of this attitude. Referring to the 'indelible disgrace' telegram, he said 'it would be indelible disgrace if we should neglect any means at the disposal of this country to save General Gordon ; but if General Gordon tells us that indelible disgrace attaches to the Government with reference to those other garrisons, I do not consider that he is, on this point at least, a better authority than any one else.' It was not yet certain, he added, that Gordon could not effect, unassisted, the evacuation of Khartoum. If an expedition should be necessary, the Government would have to consider the scale of preparations to be made, the route, and the time of year at which operations could commence.

phantasm of a man ; . . . incapable of seeing veritably any fact whatever, but seeing, crediting, and laying to heart the mere clothes of the fact, and fancying that all the rest does not exist.'

'The Government are thinking now, and have long been thinking' (much too long he must have thought) 'what measures they can take for the relief of General Gordon. Is the House aware that by the river route the distance from Cairo to Khartoum is 1600 miles, intercepted by cataracts, and that many parts of the river are very little known, and have never been traversed by large bodies of men, or used for the carriage of large forces?'

Mr. Goschen asked, as well he might, 'Is it not an unique operation in history which he (Gordon) is conducting, to hand back to barbarism a city of 50,000 people?' Other powerful attacks were made on the Ministry—one of especial force by that truly eloquent and patriotic Northumbrian Liberal, Joseph Cowen—and this debate drove the reluctant Prime Minister to some extent out of his previous position. He wrote on the 13th May to Lord Hartington:—

'I have read Lord Wolseley's interesting memorandum. The first question that arises is whether in reference to preparations he means preparations for an expedition up the Nile, or preparations for an advance from Suakin to Berber. These respective routes would, I apprehend, require very different measures, and also very different times.

'The paper circulated the other day for the Cabinet left on my mind the impression that the conditions of the river at the different cataracts made it impossible for a large force such as Lord Wolseley had contemplated.'

How could the soldiers say what the preparations should be until the Government had decided whether to make an expedition at all, and, if so, by which route? Lord Wolseley much preferred the river scheme, but, if he had received 'marching orders,' he would have thrown himself at once and with zeal into the task of relieving Khartoum by the Suakin-Berber route.

Lord Hartington, on 15th May, wrote to Lord Granville :—

'We have sent you an official letter in reply to yours enclosing Egerton's last telegram on the subject of the command of the force in Egypt. The position in Upper Egypt will soon be serious if Berber has fallen and Dongola is about to be evacuated. There is at present a confusion of authority and responsibility which may lead to the worst results. We have some boats patrolling the Nile under the orders of the Admiral; some Egyptian troops occupying Assouan and Wadi Halfa, and some Bedouins under Kitchener and Stuart Wortley wandering about somewhere in the desert, under Sir E. Wood's orders; and, finally, the British troops under Stephenson. It is not sufficient to say that troops are not to be moved in Upper Egypt without Stephenson's concurrence. If he is to be responsible, as he will ultimately have to be, for the defence of Upper Egypt and for keeping order there, he ought to have the supreme control of the military forces of all kinds; and he ought to see, which he does not now, the reports of Wood's officers on frontier questions.'

On the same day (15th May) Lord Hartington circulated the following memorandum to the members of the Cabinet :—

'We have now got all the information we are likely to get on the subject of the possibility of an expedition for the relief of General Gordon. We have Lord Wolseley's memoranda, Generals Stephenson's and Wood's reports, Sir S. Baker's scheme, and the Admiralty comments upon it.[1] Whether any expedition be ultimately despatched or not, I think that it is clear that if we admit the possibility of having to send an expedition, no time should be lost in making some preparations, whatever the route which may be adopted.

'I should propose that a Committee should at once be appointed, to consist of Lord Northbrook, myself, and any

---

[1] Sir S. Baker, the Nile explorer, had a scheme for relief by a volunteer force.

other member of the Cabinet who may desire to join, Lord
Wolseley, some Naval authority, Sir C. Wilson, Mr. Brand,
and any others who may be suggested.

'We should decide, in the first instance, on the route to
be adopted, and, of course, subject to the approval of the
Cabinet, on any immediate measures to be taken.

'I would add Sir A. Clarke to those whom I have named.
If this is approved, I do not think that we could meet too
soon, and I should suggest to-morrow afternoon at the
War Office.

'I do not think it is necessary to obtain the approval of
the whole Cabinet to this. I stated in my speech, to which
Mr. Gladstone has referred as expressing the views of the
Government, that we were engaged in the collection and
examination of information, and in consultation with the
best authorities.'

Mr. Gladstone wrote to Lord Hartington on 16th May :—

'I received and read yesterday General Stephenson's
report. It appeared to me an honest and able paper ;
conclusive, together with other documents, against the
idea of any large operation by the river, but most alarming
in regard to English treasure and life, and giving occasion
for much reflection and deliberation.

'Granville tells me you think of proposing a Committee
of the Cabinet, but will not the *first* thing be for the War
Office to go to work and frame its estimates ? taking care,
I make no doubt, to frame them as was done in the case of
the China Vote of Credit (1860) and of the Ashantee War
(1866) so as to bring out the full charge.

'Also, ought there not to be a medical report on the
degree of risk to life which will have to be encountered ? '

It was most unfortunate that Mr. Gladstone had served
during so much of his administrative career as Chancellor
of the Exchequer, and had acquired the 'Treasury mind.'
Lord Wolseley now made an important proposal, in a
letter to Lord Hartington (18th May). He wrote :—

'With reference to the discussion at our meeting yesterday, it strikes me that, if the Cabinet decide upon announcing that immediate preparations will be made for the eventual despatch of an expedition to Khartoum, and that you were to follow up that announcement by beginning the construction of a railroad to Berber, it would be a good move to send me to Suakin as soon as the railroad is to be begun. The announcement that I was to start without delay for Suakin would make every one feel you were thoroughly in earnest. In Egypt this would do good, and might even tend to relieve Gordon from some of the pressure he now suffers from at Khartoum.

'It is very necessary you should have some military officer of position at Suakin to reconcile all the various interests; our Army, the Egyptian Army, the Navy and political dealings with the Arab tribes, the work connected with the building of the railroad, render it very necessary to focus in one man the general direction of affairs at Suakin and in its neighbourhood.

'My own idea is that, if the business be well managed all serious fighting might be avoided. Once you begin your railroad, negotiations ought to be possible with the Arab tribes, and through their aid we ought to be able to open out the road to Berber in a short time after the first ten miles of rails are laid. With the road to Berber opened, a small force could be pushed on there very soon, and with British troops there and the assured fact that more were behind waiting to be sent forward, it is in my opinion quite possible that Khartoum would be relieved of its besiegers long before the railroad was half finished. I do not believe that these results are to be expected from a general with a reputation to make, or unless you have a head that will be recognised as an authority by all at Suakin.

'I know that I make this proposal to you having only the public interests in view, and I earnestly hope that both you and Mr. Gladstone will give me credit for this feeling.

'The proposed operation is a serious one, and I should contemplate with a certain sense of dread its being confided to some young ambitious man if you wish to avoid conquest and possibly a big war.

'I make this proposal with a full sense of the responsibility attaching to it, and with the knowledge that those who do not know me well, may think me self-conceited because of the manner in which I make it.'

The effect of the debate in the House of Commons, and of the threatening attitude of some more independent Liberal members of Parliament, like Forster and Goschen, was shown in the Foreign Office telegram to Sir Evelyn Baring of 17th May. Gordon was now to be asked to '*report on*' the best measures to be taken not only for his own 'removal' but that of the Egyptians who had served him at Khartoum, their wives and their children. This was a step, a very little one, in advance of the decision of 23rd April.

While discussions went on in London, Berber on the Nile was in its last agony. In London there were words and 'minutes,' at Berber realities. The Arabs stormed the town on the 26th May. The massacre of soldiers, merchants, townsmen, lasted for two days.[1] Their wives and daughters were, of course, divided among the victorious chiefs. Sir Reginald Wingate, the most competent judge, thinks that, after Graham's defeat of the Arabs on 13th March, a force might easily have been sent from Suakin to Berber. 'The weather was cool, the wells on the road were open ; everything pointed to an advance to Berber.' But he thinks that, after Berber fell, this march would have been almost impossible, because the last wells are fifty-eight miles from the river. An exhausted force would have had to meet a well-supplied enemy before they could drink the

---

[1] Wingate, *Mahdism and the Egyptian Soudan*, p. 121.

water of the Nile. The fall of Berber should therefore have brought about a rapid decision in London in favour of the river route so strongly advocated by Lord Wolseley. This was not, however, the result. Controversy dragged on between different departments in the way in which it always does, and must do, if the Prime Minister does not force a decision. Things might have gone better, possibly, if the Imperial Defence Committee had existed in those days.

Lord Wolseley had urged again and again that preparations for an autumn expedition by the Nile should be begun. Sir Evelyn Baring had also urged it. Why was nothing whatever begun until August? It was because Lord Hartington could not get the Prime Minister or the Cabinet to attend to the matter. They would not, partly because most of them, not only the Radicals but some Whigs, were averse to any expedition, and partly because their attention was absorbed by the vastly nearer and superior fascination of the dispute between the House of Lords and House of Commons about Franchise and Redistribution, of which something must be said later. If blame attaches to Lord Hartington, it is that he did not, when the Cabinet came to their fatal decision of 23rd April, or, at least, when news arrived of the fall of Berber, do that which he did at the end of July, and say finally that he would resign at once, if steps were not taken. After the event one sees that he should have done so, but his difficulty was that Mr. Gladstone without saying either yes or no, postponed decision, and even discussion, from Cabinet to Cabinet. In a letter to Lord Granville (in 1888) quoted by Lord Morley in his *Life of Gladstone*, Mr. Gladstone says that 'in the main' Lord Hartington 'got what he wanted.'[1] This impression is as incorrect as anything can well be.

[1] *Life of Gladstone*, vol. iii. p. 164.

What Hartington 'wanted' was a decision on the main issue. Not only the Prime Minister, but the great majority of the Cabinet were either opposed to all action, or were indifferent and uninterested. At the end of May, there was some discussion on paper among members of the Cabinet. Lord Hartington, Lord North-brook, and Sir William Harcourt were for taking preparations in hand at once. At this moment their idea was to make a light railway from Suakin to Berber, or for part of the way. Sir Charles Dilke and Mr. Childers wished to postpone consideration till after the Whitsuntide recess; Mr. Chamberlain thought that the first section of the railway might be authorised; Lord Derby was for not acting without parliamentary sanction. The question was adjourned till after the holiday. The following letter shows what happened next :—

*Lord Hartington to Mr. Gladstone.*

'War Office, *July* 1, 1884.

'As to-morrow is not likely to be a very busy day, I should be very glad if we could have a short Cabinet to consider the question of military preparations for the Soudan, before the Conference and the Franchise Bill again absorb the whole attention of the Cabinet.

'I really do not feel that I know the mind or intention of the Government in respect of the relief of General Gordon; and I also feel that the Government, and especially I, as responsible for the military department, may at any moment be placed in a most painful position from the want of some clear indication of what the policy of the Government is. It is now about three weeks since I was authorised to make some preparations for putting the port of Suakin into a condition to receive the heavy stores required either for a railway or an expedition. Something has been done in this direction; but a telegram has recently been received by the Admiralty from Lord John Hay asking to be allowed to hire 300 or 400 native labourers from Jeddah on the coast of Arabia, which I can scarcely sanction without the Cabinet.

'But towards the construction or preparation for the railway itself, for the organisation of the force to protect it, or for the organisation of an expedition nothing whatever has been done. We may receive any day news from Khartoum which may show the necessity of an expedition for Gordon's release; the time is approaching when military operations would be possible as regards climate; but I may have to tell the Cabinet that for want of preparation nothing can be done.

'I am anxious that the Cabinet should at least share the responsibility of this position with me; and to ascertain, if I can, the circumstances, if any, under which they would consider an expedition necessary.'

Mr. Gladstone did not call a special Cabinet, but he circulated Lord Hartington's letter to his colleagues with a note of his own in which he said that, if the Chancellor of the Exchequer concurred, he was willing to accede to Lord John Hay's request, but that 'the laying of any rails for a permanent way would be a great and serious measure, especially if, as I incline to think, the chances of an expedition thus far are not increasing.' Mr. Childers, using consecrated Treasury language, did 'not object' to an expenditure 'not exceeding' £50,000 on preparations at Suakin port, but from no man did Lord Hartington receive an answer to his question: 'Do the Government intend to relieve Khartoum or not?' On 15th July Lord Hartington wrote to Lord Granville :—

'I enclose the result of our deliberations to-day. I hope there may be a Cabinet to-morrow or very soon to decide on this. At the last Cabinet when it was mentioned, summoned as I hoped to decide on it, I got five minutes at the fag end, and was as usual put off. Another fortnight has passed, and the end of the session is approaching. I cannot be responsible for the military policy in Egypt under such conditions.'

The enclosed memorandum ran as follows :—

'I have had a long conversation to-day with Lord Northbrook, Sir E. Baring, and Lord Wolseley on this and other questions of the military policy in Egypt.

'The conclusion at which I think we unanimously arrived is that it is impossible to come to a decision on the question of the instructions to be given about Dongola or on any of the other pending military questions until the Cabinet will decide whether or not an expedition is to be undertaken to bring away General Gordon and the garrison from Khartoum. There is, I conceive, now no reason for further delay in deciding on this point. It is now more than three months since we have had any message from General Gordon. The last messengers despatched to him left Cairo on May 21st, Korosko on June 5th, and, about June 26th, were allowed to pass through the rebel lines at Abu Ahmed. The periods which have elapsed since these dates are 55, 40, and 19 days respectively. But there is little hope that news can now be received direct from General Gordon. It is not to be supposed that if there were any possibility of sending a message out of Khartoum General Gordon, Colonel Stewart, and Mr. Power would have omitted to avail themselves of it. It is to be feared that this silence points to a close investment of Khartoum, and probably to an investment by a more fanatical enemy than had been anticipated, for I believe that this impossibility of transmitting a message is almost unprecedented in the East.

'So far, therefore, as we can judge, it appears that the possibility, even if he were likely to avail himself of it, of peacefully withdrawing from Khartoum is not open to General Gordon, and the Cabinet must decide whether

he is to be left to his fate, or to be rescued by force.
The delay in deciding any action on the Suakin-Berber
route has been so great that the conditions of the problem
have been materially changed since the proposal to operate
on that line and by means of a railway was first put
forward. The railway could now only be constructed
within the cool season for a very short portion of the
distance. Osman Digna has again collected a considerable force near Suakin, and Berber is probably in the
hands of the rebels. We must calculate on having to
fight one or more battles at each end of the route, and
at Berber we shall have to fight under considerable
difficulties, as the desert which extends for the last
hundred miles can only be crossed by troops in small
detachments.

'Further, the alarm which has been caused by the
reports of the rebellion, has necessitated the despatch of
a considerable force, British and Egyptian, up the Nile
to Assouan, and Wadi Halfa; and more troops are
asked for. A movement by Suakin and Berber will do
little to protect or tranquillise Upper Egypt. On the
other hand a movement by the Nile to Khartoum, or to
whatever point might be necessary to secure the retreat
of General Gordon would, incidentally, completely protect
Upper Egypt. Notwithstanding all the difficulties of the
river route Lord Wolseley is confident that a force of
6000 or 7000 men collected at Wadi Halfa on the 1st
October could reach Khartoum in three months. I
should not like to commit myself to this estimate, but I
have little doubt that the operation is practicable, and, at
the period we have reached, it appears on the whole to
afford the most advantages. If this operation were
decided upon, it would be worth while to make every
effort to keep Dongola out of the hands of the rebels;
if not, I agree with Lord Northbrook and Sir E. Baring,
that it should be made clear to the Egyptian Government
that it should be absolutely abandoned.

'But the first and indispensable condition of forming

an opinion on any of the military questions in Egypt is a decision whether Gordon is to be rescued or abandoned, and I submit that there is no reason for any further delay in coming to a decision on this.'

The question of route was still under departmental discussion. On 23rd July Lord Wolseley wrote to Lord Hartington that nothing said by the Admiralty in any way abated his 'complete faith in being able to reach either Dongola or Khartoum as may be necessary by water.' He based his belief, from the first, on the success of his Red River expedition in Canada, when troops were hauled in small boats over difficult sections of a long waterway. August had almost arrived; Parliament and the Cabinet would soon disperse; yet no decision had been reached. In one memorandum submitted to the Secretary of State at this time Lord Wolseley wrote:—

'As no preparations have yet been begun to place us in a position of readiness to send an expeditionary force to Khartoum, should such an undertaking be forced upon us, it seems to me that General Gordon's position is not well understood.

'Every one naturally hates the idea of such an expedition, but being intimately acquainted with the present condition of our army, and having given the military problem which that operation involves the closest study, I think I can conscientiously say that no one is better aware of the difficulties which surround it, no one can be more anxious to avoid undertaking it than I am.

'But, on the other hand, my military experience tells me that in all such affairs the worst course to pursue is to shirk the question, and to imagine you dispose of it by shutting your eyes and trying to ignore or forget it. As a recent example I may point to our position at Alexandria in 1882. If it had been properly studied then, and the military results of our intended bombardment duly provided for, I am justified in saying we should have been able to have avoided the campaign which the fault of failing to provide for the future subsequently forced upon us.[1] Had the bombardment been dealt with as a military problem before it was ordered and the necessary military preparations made, no campaign upon the scale of that we undertook would ever have been necessary.

'We should take a lesson from that recent page of our history, and avoid in 1884 the risks we ran in 1882.

' My contention is, that if you refuse to make all reasonable preparations now for what is certainly a very possible, if not a very probable, military operation this autumn or winter, you will be let in for what may become a very big affair, and which, under those circumstances, will certainly be a very costly operation, fraught with great difficulty and danger to all who have to take part in it.

' The longer the relief of Gordon is postponed—assuming for the moment that it will become eventually necessary—the greater will be the armed resistance to be overcome, the greater will become the number of enemies surrounding Khartoum. Tribes which are now either friendly or neutral, will have been forced to throw in their lot with what will seem to them the only powerful party in the Khartoum district. The more exhausted will become the garrison of that place, the weaker and less able to assist will Gordon become.

' The high Nile, during which alone steamers can be sent up the Cataracts, will wait for no one, neither will the period of cool weather, when alone an English force can operate in the Soudan. If Khartoum is to be relieved, the troops required must be sent from England, as both Mr. Egerton and General Stephenson assert you cannot safely diminish the force we now have in Egypt proper. You will have to obtain 1000 rowing boats or else about 50,000 camels. I doubt the possibility of being able to obtain that number of camels on any terms, no matter

---

[1] He means by having a military force at hand to follow up the bombardment immediately.

how costly those terms may be, and I do not see how or where you could feed them, even supposing you could collect them.

'The 1000 boats have to be purchased, the greater proportion to be built, and, unless you now decide to obtain them as soon as possible, you will not have them above the Second Cataract sufficiently early to enable you to get a force to Khartoum during the cool weather.

'Then again, as regards military stores and supplies, it is only during high Nile, when steamers are able to ply easily, that a sufficient quantity of provisions, &c., can be collected above the Second Cataract to enable an expeditionary force to reach Khartoum at any season.

'If you decide upon not making the necessary preparations now, please remember that you must abandon all hope of being able to relieve Khartoum.

'I state this deliberately after a most careful study of the problem which is before me, and feeling that we have already postponed making these preparations to a dangerous limit of time.

'Looking to the assurances that Ministers have given in Parliament as to their acceptance of all responsibility for the safety of Gordon and Stewart, is it wise, is it honest, to refuse to look the difficulties of the position straight in the face, to refuse to make the necessary preparations now when you have time to do so; in fact, to postpone their consideration to a period when all preparation will be in vain?

'Is it wise to ignore or even to make light of the danger in which Gordon now finds himself?

'In order to avoid the cost of making these preparations we wish to persuade ourselves that Gordon is in no danger; are we justified in doing so?

'Every idle rumour coming percolated to us through rebel sources that in any way supports the view which we wish to believe regarding Gordon's position we eagerly grasp at as true, whilst we turn our face from the facts which are patent to every impartial observer.

'What are these facts? We know to a certainty that Gordon is so closely shut in that not even for enormous rewards can we get a message to him or an answer from him. This one fact speaks aloud for itself and tells his whole story. It is quite possible that he makes sorties on the Nile. This is doubtless his best means of defence, and may be his only means of obtaining subsistence for his garrison and the besieged people, but it in no way contradicts the assertion that the cordon of enemies round him is so closely drawn that no messenger can pierce it.

'Then again, even supposing he can by sorties obtain provisions, how about the ammunition by means of which he is doubtless alone able to make these sorties, and by means of which he is still able to keep his enemies at bay?

'He told us on the 28th March last that he only had 1400 rounds of gun ammunition, and he asked us to send him some. If he has fired since then ten rounds a day, he has now only 200 rounds left, and at that same rate of expenditure will have fired his last round on the 20th of this month.

'His last round will be his death-knell.

'Is the Government prepared to accept this responsibility in order to avoid asking Parliament for a supplementary estimate to enable it to save Gordon and Stewart from the fate which is possibly, and I believe most probably, before them?

'It is to my mind, as a soldier, horrible to reconcile this condition of things to one's conscience by assuming the fact that those gentlemen, who are soldiers, can avoid such a fate by quitting Khartoum and deserting their followers. To a soldier such a reflection is as repugnant as the idea that they could save themselves by becoming Mahomedans would be to a believing Christian.'

At the end of another memorandum, dated 29th July, Lord Wolseley wrote:—

'I do not wish to overload this paper with details, but to confine myself to a general outline of the necessary proceedings. What is now required is the decision of Her Majesty's Government upon this all-important point, namely, do they contemplate the possibility of having to send a force this autumn or winter to Dongola or Khartoum for any purpose whatsoever ?

' If they consider that such a contingency is possible, I cannot urge upon them in terms too strong the absolute necessity of at once making preparations to meet that possible contingency, and in the papers I have lately written on the subject I have sketched out in general terms what the nature of those preparations should be. Perhaps I may be pardoned for saying that if, in the opinion of the Cabinet, any such operations may possibly during the next six months become necessary, it is in a military point of view the height of folly not to make the necessary preparations forthwith.

' In conclusion, I can only add that, in coming to a decision on this all-important point, every day is of the utmost consequence, if those preparations are to be made at all. . . .'

On the same day, 29th July, Lord Hartington circulated to the Cabinet his own final memorandum on the subject. He said :—

' I wish before Parliament is prorogued, and it becomes absolutely impossible to do anything for the relief of General Gordon, to bring the subject once more under the consideration of the Cabinet.

'On the last occasion when it was discussed, although an opinion was expressed that the balance of probability was that no expedition would be required to enable General Gordon and those dependent on him to leave Khartoum, I gathered that a considerable majority were in favour of making some ,preparations, and taking some steps which would make a relief expedition to Khartoum possible. I believe that I have already stated the grounds on which I think that if anything is now attempted, it must be by the Valley of the Nile, and not by the Suakin-Berber line.

'The delay which has taken place makes it impossible that the railway should be constructed for any considerable distance on that line during the next autumn and winter, the period during which military operations would be practicable without great suffering and loss of life to the troops. The renewed concentration of the tribes under Osman Digna near Suakin, and the fall of Berber, make it inevitable that severe fighting would have to be done at both ends of the march, and, in consequence of the necessity of crossing the desert in small detachments, the engagement near Berber would be fought under great disadvantages.

'On the other hand, we have for the defence of Egypt itself been compelled to send a considerable force of British and Egyptian troops up the Nile ; and the positions which are now occupied by those troops are so many stages on the advance by the Nile Valley. It would be impossible, I think, to withdraw these forces if an advance by the Suakin-Berber line were decided on. On the contrary, it is more probable that they will have to be increased. An advance by the Nile will therefore in any case have the effect of strengthening the defence of Egypt, which would not be the case if the other plan were adopted.

'Lord Wolseley has drawn up certain proposals for the despatch of a brigade to Dongola, by means of steamboats, railroad, and row-boats, so far as those means are available, and by small row-boats from Wadi Halfa, where those resources would terminate. These proposals have been examined by General M'Neill, General Redvers Buller, and Colonel Butler, three officers who accompanied Lord Wolseley in the Red River expedition, which was accomplished in a similar manner. These officers have reported, after examination of the information available as to the navigation of the Nile, that a brigade can easily be conveyed in small boats from Cairo to Dongola in the time stated by Lord Wolseley (about 1st November), and further that, should it be necessary to send a still larger force by water to Khartoum, that operation will present no insuperable difficulty.

'They say that if it be found necessary to take a fighting force to Khartoum before the end of the year, or the end of January, the Nile will, in their opinion, be found "the easiest, the safest, and immensely the cheapest line of advance to adopt."

'They say, "In our opinion the question resolves itself into this—Is it possible to procure and place on the Nile at Sarras (a place a few miles above Wadi Halfa and the terminus of a railway round the Cataract) 500 boats by the 5th October? Surely this should be possible." I believe that the Admiralty authorities do not regard this scheme with much favour, but I understand that they have regarded the question from an entirely different point of view from that of the military authorities. They have based their estimate of the difficulties of the operation on the assumption that steamers and boats of considerable size will be used, whereas the military proposal is that above the Cataracts small boats shall be mainly, if not exclusively, employed. I submit that officers who have actually conducted a military expedition in the face of much greater physical difficulties on the Red River, are the most competent judges of the practicability of the operation.

'The proposal which I make is that a brigade should be ordered to advance as soon as possible to Dongola by the Nile.

'Further, that, although it is quite possible that no further advance of troops may be necessary, the boats and stores required for the advance of a second brigade to Dongola, and if required to Khartoum, should be provided; but that no order for the actual despatch of the second brigade should be given until further information as to the position at Dongola and Khartoum is received.

'I have had a detailed though necessarily rough estimate prepared of the War Office expenditure for sending a brigade to Dongola with six months' supplies. It amounts to £300,000. If it should be considered necessary to provide at once for the second brigade this should of course be doubled.

'For the two brigades 1000 boats should be provided. I understand that the Admiralty estimate the cost of delivering those at Sarras at £120 each. This is considered an extreme estimate ; but it would amount to £120,000. The Admiralty would incur some further charge in transport of troops to Egypt, and in river transport below the Second Cataract ; but this I cannot state at present. Probably something under £1,000,000 would be a sufficient estimate for the whole operation ; of which a large portion would not be spent unless the necessity were actually found to exist.

'I have not entered into the question whether it is or is not probable that General Gordon can leave Khartoum without assistance. As we know absolutely nothing, any opinion on this subject can only be guess-work. But I do not see how it is possible to redeem the pledges which we have given, if the necessity should be proved to exist, without some such preparations and measures as those which I now suggest.'

Lord Hartington was supported by Lord Selborne, the Lord Chancellor, in a long and powerfully written memorandum now printed in his *Memorials*.[1] It contained the following sentence :—

'I am as much averse as any man possibly can be to sending out an unnecessary and a more or less costly expedition to encounter the difficulties and dangers of any route which may be practicable between Egypt and the Red Sea and Khartoum. But I am still more averse to acting towards a public servant, in whose reputation and safety all England (and I might also say the world) is interested, who has accepted at our instance a mission of extraordinary difficulty, as if we had no real sense of our responsibilities which we had publicly acknowledged, or as if something,

---

[1] That this Cabinet memorandum should have been published twelve years later, in 1898, shows on high authority that there is a time limit for the secrecy of these confidential documents.

of which I can see no evidence at all, had happened to absolve us from these responsibilities.'

Two days later (31st July) Lord Hartington wrote to Lord Granville a letter intended for communication, as an ultimatum, to the Prime Minister :—

'I don't know whether you have read the two boxes which have gone round this week from the Chancellor and me about Gordon.

'I suggested to Mr. Gladstone that we should have a Cabinet here to-morrow on the question, as it is almost hopeless to try to get a discussion on anything else after a long debate on the Conference.

'However, Mr. Gladstone seems to think that there will be time enough on Saturday.

'From what he has written in each case, I infer that his mind is made up and that nothing is to be done.

'This is a conclusion which I do not think it is possible for me to accept. I, with you and Northbrook are more responsible than any other members of the Cabinet for sending out Gordon, but I consider that I had the largest share of the responsibility. I gave the assurance in the debate on the Vote of Censure, which certainly had some effect on the decision. I must attach my own meaning to those assurances, and no explanations by any one else can absolve me from what I consider to be their obligation. I think this is a different sort of question from the numerous ones on which I have differed from the Cabinet. It is a question of personal honour and good faith, and I don't see how I can yield upon it.'

Lord Granville replied (1st August) :—

'Although you first told me of Gordon's advice that he should himself be sent, I share the responsibility with you and Northbrook of sending him. The early doubts I had of the wisdom of what we had done did not diminish this responsibility. But I deny any responsibility resting upon us to rescue Gordon until the declarations were made to Parliament (1) by Gladstone, (2) by you, and (3) by me.[1] I agree with you that these declarations commit us to a certain degree, but not as far as I gather you believe.'

Mr. Chamberlain minuted that he was 'against what is called an expedition, or the preparations for an expedition.' He did not think that the information was sufficient to justify it. He thought that more information should first be obtained, and would wish to strengthen Kitchener's hands to the extent of 1000 men, if necessary, to enable him to communicate with Khartoum, and obtain information on which further action might be based.

Mr. Gladstone minuted (31st July): 'I confess it to be my strong conviction that to send an expedition either to Dongola or Khartoum at the present time would be to act in the teeth of evidence as to Gordon which, however imperfect, is far from being trivial, and would be a grave and dangerous error.' Mr. Gladstone at the same time wrote to Lord Granville a letter, which the latter forwarded to Lord Hartington. He said :—

'I had intended to give much time to-day to collecting the sum of the evidence as to Gordon's position which appears to me to be strangely underrated by some.

'But I have been diverted from this by the receipt of Hartington's letter, which created a very formidable state of things at a moment when we have already on our hands a domestic crisis of the first class likely to last for months, and a foreign crisis of the first class, hardly certain, however, to be developed in a few days.[2]

'It is a difficult but paramount duty for each one of us to ask himself what he can contribute towards meeting

---

[1] These were the declarations made in mid-May.

[2] The domestic crisis was the dispute with the House of Lords about the Franchise Bill. The foreign crisis was as to the Conference of the Powers in London on Egyptian finance, &c.

the present emergency.  Undoubtedly I can be no party to the proposed despatch, as a first step, of a brigade to Dongola.

'I do not think the evidence as to Gordon's position requires or justifies, in itself, military preparations for the contingency of a military expedition.  There are, however, preparations, perhaps, of various kinds which might be made, and which are matters simply of cost, and do not include necessary consequences in point of policy.

'To these I have never offered an insuperable objection, and the adoption of them might be, at the worst, a smaller evil than the evils with which we are threatened in other forms.

'This on what I may call my side.  On the other hand, I hope I may presume that, while we are looking into the matters I have just indicated, nothing will be done to accelerate a Gordon crisis until we see, in the early days of next week, what the Conference crisis is to produce.'

Lord Hartington and Lord Selborne gave it to be understood that they would certainly, and at once, resign unless some preparations and military movements were sanctioned. Lord Carlingford, a member of the Cabinet, was another of Lord Hartington's adherents in this matter.  'I hope,' he wrote to him afterwards, 'that the operations and preparations, which by superhuman perseverance you have extorted, will not be too late for a good Nile.'  For the present there was a compromise, which did not hold for a month, between the smaller section of the Cabinet who agreed with Lord Hartington and the larger section who followed the Prime Minister.  A brigade was not yet to be sent to Dongola, but Parliament was to be asked for a grant of £300,000 in order, as Mr. Gladstone explained to the House on 5th August, 'to enable Her Majesty's Government to undertake operations for the relief of General Gordon, should they become necessary, and to make certain preparations in respect thereof.' These preparations included, when translated into action, an increase of British troops in Egypt, an advance of troops to Wadi Halfa, the passage of steamboats up the First and Second Cataracts, arrangements for Canadian boatmen and West African Kroomen to be sent to Egypt, some improvements of the Egyptian railways south of Cairo, organisation of land transport, &c. The following letters show that the latest meetings of the Cabinet had still left obscure the steps which were to be taken. But the affair was now, at last, virtually in the hands of a determined and patriotic statesman and of an able soldier. The fundamental basis of action having been secured, the autumnal dispersal to the four winds of the House of Commons and the Cabinet was a boon even greater than it is in most years.

*Lord Hartington to Lord Granville, August* 19, 1884.

'. 'I am going back to London to-night for a day or two to settle many arrangements about the proposed movements. I shall tell Buller[1] that long before he can reach Dongola, Northbrook will be in Egypt, and that the general in command will receive the instructions of the Government from him. But that, as at present advised, and subject to any alterations of plan consequent on what we may hear from Gordon, our objects are limited to getting out Gordon and those who have identified themselves with his cause; that Khartoum is to be evacuated by the Egyptian Government and is not going to be occupied by us, and that therefore, unless the Zobeir project, or some more hopeful one, can be carried into effect, Khartoum must be ultimately abandoned to the Mahdi, or to any one who will take it. This I

[1] Sir Redvers Buller was starting for Egypt as Chief of Staff, and second in command to General Earle who was appointed to command the troops at Wadi Halfa, Lord Wolseley's appointment not yet having been made. He had sent written questions to Lord Hartington in order to obtain an idea what Government wished to do, or not to do.

believe to be the policy of the Government; it is not altogether what I should recommend as settled and irrevocable policy, though it may be found necessary ultimately to adopt it. On the contrary, I should say that events seem to be proving the accuracy of Gordon's statements of the weakness of the Mahdi, and that the best solution in the interests of Egypt, and also of the Soudanese, might be the reversal of the peremptory decision to abandon Khartoum, and the maintenance of a self-supporting Egyptian Government there.'

*Mr. Gladstone to Lord Hartington, August* 19, 1884.

'I am not very well to-day, but I will answer your letter to the best of my ability.

'A movement of British troops to Dongola (with or without Egyptian) would be a step of great political importance, and clearly could not be decided on without reference to the members of the Cabinet. It might depend upon the answers whether they need be called together, which would be on more grounds than one inconvenient.

'Next I should like to know *at what date* this forward movement from Wadi Halfa *could* commence supposing it agreed on? While I entirely sympathise with your anxiety that we should not mar any operation which may be proper by delay, I think you would admit that, unless there is a necessity of time, the moment is more unfortunate than not for a decision, inasmuch as the lapse of time, and Gordon's renewed communication with the Mudir, while nothing is sent to us, seem to strengthen the presumption that he purposely refrains from communicating with us. I nearly, though not quite, adopt words received to-day from Granville, " It is clear, I think, that Gordon has our messages, and does not choose to answer them."

'If the time has come when a decision must be taken whether we go to Dongola or not, then I think the Cabinet should know what force you propose to send there, and most of all, for what purpose it is to go. These two questions are to a certain extent connected with one another.

'May we reasonably believe that Gordon, if he thinks fit, can make his way to Dongola ? This I can believe probable. But will he do it ?

'By much the best idea before us at this time is, I think, that of Northbrook that we ought to make the Mudir of Dongola play the part of Zobeir, and take over Khartoum, so putting an end to this most perplexing and distressing affair.

'I think it possible that this may be your view too.

'For one, I should not be unwilling to stretch a point for the purpose of forwarding this plan : though I should have thought it better forwarded by money, and perhaps material, than by a *British* force ; with which I associate the very serious danger of stirring a religious war. Surely it is singular to note that our force, gallant as it was, could not get rid of Osman Digna, and that matters now look as if he might be more easily dealt with since the withdrawal.

'You refer, I believe correctly, to Northbrook's opinion ; but do not appear to have had full communication with him.

'If I might make a recommendation it would be that you should bring your views into full comparison with his, and endeavour to frame a plan in concert with him, which he may endeavour to work out in Egypt.

'Would it be quite fair to the Cabinet, or to certain members of it, to ask them to take a *step* in advance, without a plan, that they might know what they were about, and be assured that they were not about to become unawares the slaves of Gordon's (probably) rebellious ideas.'

*Mr. Gladstone to Lord Hartington, August* 21, 1884.

'With reference to the first paragraph of your letter, I do not doubt that correspondence on Gordon and the Soudan is to all of us a matter of extreme anxiety. I know of no way of alleviating the case except much forbearance and giving eventual credit for the best and most considerate intentions.

'The greatness of the difficulties already surmounted by these means encourages me to hope that we may also overcome what remains, I mean among ourselves, for whether we can survive the Egyptian business in Parliament is indeed very doubtful.

'I shall probably receive from you to-morrow the information for which I asked: and in the meantime I would say a word on two points which I hope will create no difficulty.

'1. I can take upon me to assure you that you are mistaken about Harcourt. He *consented* to the Vote of Credit, and the preparations under it. He certainly so consented out of deference to you, and in this he was not alone : but you would be the last person to say his claims to know what was going on were thereby diminished. I find he is at Oban, and I would have written or telegraphed to him to-day, to name the subject to him, but that I do not like to interfere with you.

'A special reason, I think, for letting him know anything you contemplate is that, if my memory be correct, nothing was proposed definitively about going beyond Wadi Halfa in the Cabinet of the 9*th*. Perhaps my recollection is wrong : I cannot now rely upon it as well as formerly.

'2. You say that you are making preparations of such a character as would make it appear almost absurd not to send the expedition ; but, if these are the preparations stated by you to the Cabinet, we must take the risk. I am sure you would not put them in such a position without their consent.

'I agree in the force of your argument from the silence of Stewart and Power : it has, however, much to meet.'

The lateness of the political decision, such as it was, the peril of Khartoum, and the habits of the Nile, which rises from June till the end of August and then begins to fall, made time of the utmost value. Lord Hartington telegraphed to Mr. Gladstone on the 22nd August :—

'We are at cross purposes here and in Egypt as to the plan of operations on which our preparations are based. Wolseley is responsible for that which we have adopted, and there is risk of failure in unwilling hands. He knows views of Government and extreme unwillingness to send an expedition except in case of absolute necessity. Firmly believe that this would offer best chance of avoiding serious expedition and of success if it must be undertaken.'

On the same day he wrote to Lord Granville :—

'Mr. Gladstone wants me to consult him before deciding on the advance of the detachments to Dongola about which I wrote to you. This is a pleasant way of doing business when every hour may be important.

'I have sent to-day in cipher the enclosed telegram' (that asking sanction to send out Lord Wolseley) 'to Mr. Gladstone and Northbrook. As you are within a reasonable distance, and sometimes answer a letter by return of post, I spare you the cipher. I hope you will all agree. I am very uneasy about the cross purposes we are at. The plan which we have adopted, on which our preparations here are based, *in case an expedition should be ordered*, is Wolseley's. Stephenson and the people in Egypt say it is impracticable, and go on hammering at their own plan. We don't deny that they can get to Dongola by their plan, but we say that it is doubtful whether they can get back again even from Dongola this winter, and that, if we should be forced to go to Khartoum, it is certain that they could not get there and back again during the winter. Wolseley and his Red River men are confident that the boat plan is practicable. At all events we are committed to it, so far as preparations go. I am sorry for Stephenson, but it is not fair either to Wolseley who has proposed, or me who have adopted, or to Stephenson who has to execute the operation, that it should be entrusted to men who do not believe in it rather than to those who do.

'The only objection I can think of is that the appointment of Wolseley, "our only general," to command in

Egypt will be taken as committing us to an expedition. It may be so understood here, perhaps in Egypt, but it will not really be so. He feels no doubt strongly our obligations towards Gordon, but the decision whether the expedition is to go or not will ultimately depend on the political, not the military authorities. Nor does Wolseley in the least want an expedition, if he can get Gordon out without one. He has nothing more to get ; he sees immense difficulties in it, and not much possible honour or glory in the fighting line. Men who have got their reputation to make are much more likely to be keen on an expedition than he is.

'But it is for the efficiency of the preparations which we are making, and for the success of the expedition, *if it should be necessary*, that I am most anxious about this appointment. We are obliged now to give every order from here, and we shall probably have to continue to do so. We cannot conduct this sort of business in Egypt properly from home, and we shall probably fail if we try to do it. If Wolseley goes to Egypt he will be in the proper place to superintend the preparations for his own plan, and he will be responsible for its success or failure.'

Lord Granville replied that he doubted whether Wolseley, on the spot, would be disinclined to go on, and said :—

'I take it war is the most exciting game of skill and chance that ever was invented, and that the attraction of it to a successful soldier is overwhelming, till he becomes fat and gouty.[1] I have no doubt that if Wolseley goes out there will either be an expedition or the moral effect of his appointment will make one unnecessary. But the latter advantage is neutralised by my doubts as to Gordon availing himself of a fair opportunity of coming away.'

Lord Granville said that he could 'hardly conceive Gladstone consenting to the immediate despatch of Wolse-

---

[1] 'La guerre est un grand jeu, une belle occupation,' said Napoleon at Elba to Lord John Russell, of all people.

ley. It will be considered in and out of England as an absolute decision to make the expedition.' Mr. Gladstone did, however, consent, at once and heartily, to the despatch of Lord Wolseley. That officer speedily left for Egypt, and at last the expedition became a practical certainty. Command had been given to the soldier who most wished to make it by the statesman who most decidedly thought that it ought to be made. Both of them were, perhaps, unconscious of the full strength of their desire. The boat was launched on the stream, and passed beyond the control of any who wished to stop or delay it. The supersession for no fault of his own, but in order to avoid misunderstandings, of an excellent officer, Sir Frederick Stephenson, in the active Egyptian command, at the moment before action, was a painful operation. Lord Hartington wrote a frank and kind letter, and General Stephenson accepted the blow with the spirit of a soldier and of a gentleman. The following letter to the Queen, dated 23rd August, is also of interest :—

'Lord Hartington presents his humble duty to Your Majesty, and begs to submit to Your Majesty that the telegrams recently received from Sir F. Stephenson have caused him considerable anxiety. It appears to Lord Hartington that the plan of operation which has been decided on here in the event of its becoming necessary to send an expedition for the relief of General Gordon is imperfectly understood in Egypt, and that, so far as it is understood, great doubts are entertained of its practicability.

'This plan has been adopted on the advice of Lord Wolseley and of other officers who took part in the Red River expedition in 1870, who feel confident that the difficulties of the Nile navigation in boats of small size suitably constructed and fitted are less than those which were then successfully encountered, and the preparations which are now in progress are mainly based upon it.

'Lord Hartington feels that there is considerable risk of failure if the conduct of this operation and of these preparations is entrusted to officers who have little faith in their practicability, and that it is scarcely fair either to those officers who have advised him, or to those whose duty it will be to execute the plan in Egypt that it should be so entrusted.

'Lord Hartington therefore proposes to ask Lord Wolseley temporarily to assume command of the troops in Egypt, not necessarily of an expedition if it should be despatched, but to direct and superintend the preparations and the organisation of the force.

'In Lord Hartington's opinion there would be this additional advantage in this measure, that he has been in very confidential communication with Lord Wolseley for some time past upon this subject, that this officer is very fully acquainted with the views of Your Majesty's Government and the extreme unwillingness which they would feel in despatching an expedition except in case of absolute necessity, although they consider it necessary to make such preparations as will place them in a position to undertake it without further delay.

'Lord Hartington therefore feels that he could rely with much confidence on Lord Wolseley's complete co-operation with Lord Northbrook and the Government on what may be considered the political side of any questions which may arise.

'Lord Hartington would propose, if Your Majesty approves of this appointment, to communicate it to Sir F. Stephenson in the manner least likely to wound that officer's feelings. Sir F. Stephenson has most ably discharged the very difficult duties in Egypt, and he has only done his duty in pointing out the objections which he sees to the plan which has been adopted. Lord Hartington proposes to express a hope that Sir F. Stephenson will remain in Egypt, but if he should be unwilling to do so, he would suggest that he should temporarily undertake the duties of the Adjutant-General during Lord Wolseley's absence.

'H.R.H. the Duke of Cambridge is out of town, and Lord Hartington has not therefore been able to consult him before writing to Your Majesty, as time presses, but he is writing to H.R.H. on the subject to-day.'

Lord Hartington, before the appointment of Wolseley was sanctioned, had already, as the following letters show, proposed an advance of troops to Dongola :—

### Lord Hartington to Mr. Gladstone, August 18, 1884.

'From recent telegrams from Sir F. Stephenson and Mr. Egerton it appears probable that the former will shortly be in a position to direct the advance of a small force, British and Egyptian, from Wadi Halfa to Dongola or Debbeh. If there should be no military objections do you see any political reasons for delaying this step? It appears to me extremely desirable, and I think that there is some possibility that it may avoid the necessity for more extensive operations later. It will be as well to consider what should be the instructions to the officer commanding this force when he reaches Dongola, but there is no great hurry about this, as they can always be communicated by telegram; but the decision as to the advance should not be long delayed. I have sent a copy of this to Granville.'

### Lord Hartington to Mr. Gladstone, August 21, 1884.

'I have seen Dilke to-day, who entirely concurs in what I wrote to you yesterday about the opinion of the Cabinet. He thinks that, if you assent, no one would object, and as to Harcourt he understood that, though objecting to any expedition for the relief of General Gordon, he had waived that objection, and would not oppose any measure of this character.

'You will see in the Foreign Office telegrams of to-day

how much at Dongola appears to depend on the despatch
of some troops there. I am sorry to say that there is a
good deal of misunderstanding between us and Stephenson about our respective plans of operations; but I assume
that the Cabinet will wish these details to be settled by me
with the help of my military advisers. Our differences
relate chiefly to the organisation of an expedition on a
considerable scale for the relief of General Gordon, if it
should ultimately become necessary, and, I hope, will be
to a great extent removed when the officers going out
from England have arrived.

'But what I hope I may receive to-morrow is authority
from you to send forward such a limited force from Wadi
Halfa to Dongola as we and Stephenson may consider safe.

'I believe that in this step lies the best chance of averting
the necessity of sending a considerable expedition.'

*Lord Hartington to Mr. Gladstone, August* 26, 1884.

'I have received your letter of the 19th, which has
caused me considerable anxiety, and does not diminish
the anxieties with which I have to deal.

'I have sent a telegram to-day to Stephenson (copy of
which I enclose) the answer to which will probably give
the information you ask for as to the time and the force
with which an early advance on Dongola could be made.
It is, however, obvious that the longer the orders for such
an advance are delayed, the longer it will be before it can
be commenced, and before its advantages (if there are
advantages) can be secured. As to its purpose, I conceive
it to be that described in Egerton's telegrams, especially
his 528 of August 6 and 540 of August 16. It was on the
former of these that Northbrook's and Granville's opinion,
referred to above, was given. I do not know that I can
add anything to what is contained in those telegrams, but
I may say that the object appears to me to be to give confidence and support to the Mudir of Dongola, who, by an
extraordinary piece of good fortune, appears to be loyal,
and to a certain extent powerful, who has, notwithstanding

the instructions to surrender which have been sent to him, held his own, defeated the Mahdi's forces, but is still threatened by them.  It is not only to support the Mudir in retaining Dongola which, at all events till Gordon's retreat is assured, must be a matter of the first importance, but also to influence the tribe with whom Kitchener is now endeavouring to communicate, and who apparently hold the road to within three days' journey to Khartoum. Whether Gordon can make his way to Dongola, or whether, being able, he will do so, must be a matter of pure conjecture, but it is quite certain that his ability to do it will be increased by anything which will strengthen the Mudir, and which tends to secure the support of the Kababish.  I cannot agree with Granville that it is clear that Gordon has our messages but will not answer them.  Of course the messages to the Mudir without any to us are perplexing, but there may be explanations.  There may be some complicity between the Mudir and the rebels, or between Zobeir and the rebels ; some messengers may be allowed to pass and others may not ; or, again, Gordon may have sent a large number of messengers of whom some may have got through and others have not.  (It is probable that one messenger could only take a very small number of messages concealed about him.)  Again, it is almost inconceivable that Stewart and Power should abstain from sending messages if possible.  A message from Power to the *Times* would be worth thousands of pounds.[1]  I maintain, therefore, that there is no proof that Gordon is ignoring, or acting in opposition to, our instructions. At all events, I am quite sure that public opinion here will not be satisfied if our action is in any degree based on this supposition, until it can be conclusively proved to be accurate.

    ₄ 'I quite agree that all possible use should be made of the Mudir of Dongola, and I thought that he might be the Zobeir of Dongola, though Kitchener's report con-

----

[1] Stewart and Power left Khartoum 10th September, and were killed below Berber.

tained in Egerton's telegram of to-day is not encouraging. But there is no reason to suppose that he has any influence at Khartoum, and before he left London, Northbrook distinctly told me that he did not think he could be used at Khartoum.

'I do not think we need be afraid of raising a religious war by sending troops to Dongola. The Mudir asks for them; and Kitchener appears to have been well received by the people at Dongola and Debbeh. No doubt Osman Digna's people were fanatical; but we had crushed him; and it was our hurried departure which set him up again. I feel quite sure that with your, Granville's, and Northbrook's assent the Cabinet would not object to the despatch of a moderate force as now proposed to Dongola. The case would be different if it was a question of immediately despatching the brigade which is being prepared, and the transport for which is being provided, for Dongola or perhaps eventually for Khartoum. Chamberlain has several times advocated sending a small force to support Kitchener. I know of no one who has dissented except Harcourt, who objects to everything, including the Vote of Credit and preparations.

'If, when the Cabinet is scattered all over the country, I have to wait in the case of every decision of any importance to collect the opinions of Ministers, subject perhaps, in the case of difference, to the delay of summoning a Cabinet, I despair of acquitting myself of the responsibility which will be placed on me by my colleagues and by Parliament.

'I have already taken a great responsibility in authorising preparations, on very meagre instructions from the Cabinet, which were, however, in my opinion, absolutely necessary to be undertaken without delay, if the possibility of an expedition during the winter was contemplated. I have spent, and am spending, a great deal of money (I will endeavour shortly to let the Cabinet know at what rate); but what is more important, perhaps, is that they are preparations of such a character as will make it appear almost absurd not to send the expedition when they are complete, except on the clearest proof that Gordon's position does not require it.

'On reading this over, I think I should add that I did not support, and would not support now, Chamberlain's proposal to send a small force to Dongola unless it could be supported within some reasonable period, and with some degree of certainty by a larger force in case of necessity. The preparations which are now in progress will enable this to be done if necessary, and my objection is therefore removed, provided that Stephenson recommends it.

'I should also like to call your attention to Egerton's telegram, No. 522 of August 6.

'Messenger who brought Gordon's letter says . . . no news had come to Gordon from outside.'

After a long interval, unbroken save by a message or two to the Mudir of Dongola, some communications from Gordon reached Cairo towards the end of September. Gordon replied to the Foreign Office enquiry of April. 'You ask me to state cause and intention of staying at Khartoum knowing Government means to abandon Soudan, and in answer I say: I stay at Khartoum because Arabs have shut us up and will not let us out.' He complained that the English telegrams gave no information as to intentions of Government 'and only ask for information and waste time.' He said that he intended to retake Berber, and then send to the Equator 'to withdraw the people who are there.' These messages were sent before the decisive disaster to Gordon's troops at El Fun on 4th September. They were difficult to reconcile in London with the view that Gordon was hard pressed and in need of relief. Lord Hartington wrote to Lord Granville on the 16th September 1884 :—

'No fresh instructions were given to Wolseley. Such verbal instructions as he required from me were, like yours to Northbrook, "of a negative kind," *i.e.* he is not to undertake an expedition except in case of absolute necessity; he is not to send more than a small force beyond Wadi Halfa, and not to send any force at all beyond Dongola without instructions from the Government. . . . The exact object of the expedition, if it shall take place, is, I conceive at present, to enable General Gordon and General Stewart, with the Egyptian garrison of Khartoum, to leave that place, if it should appear that they cannot do so by any other means.

'I have, however, my own opinion that, if it is necessary to go to Khartoum, and if that operation is successfully accomplished, it will be found desirable and necessary to hold Khartoum, Berber, and Dongola in some form or another. I have for some time thought that our decision to abandon those places was a mistake.

'However, there are no stronger advocates for the abandonment of the whole of the Soudan than Northbrook and Baring, and therefore the Cabinet is safe against any change of policy in that direction without the fullest consideration. I have, however, asked Northbrook to keep his mind open on the subject.'

On the 24th September, Lord Hartington wrote to Lord Granville, from Newmarket. He said :—

'I have read Gordon's telegrams again, and I confess that I am utterly unable to understand them. I can neither accept Mr. Gladstone's paraphrase, nor can I supply any other.

'I think that all we can do is to look at the position as it is known to us from other sources, and to pay no attention to what he says. We have no proof that he could have done anything different from what he has done and is doing, or that he has wilfully disobeyed or disregarded our instructions. We know that the despatch of the Egyptian employés, invalids, women, &c., from Khartoum was followed by the rising of the country between Khar-

toum and Berber, and by the attack on and fall of Berber.[1]
It is not probable that, since those events, he could have left
Khartoum without sacrificing the lives of himself and those
who followed him, and also of those whom he left behind.
He had no alternative but to hold on at Khartoum and to
keep the insurgents at bay. We have no knowledge that,
even now, he could make any movement of retreat without
bringing down the tribes upon him and on the garrison.

'I think, therefore, that our troops must go on to Dongola at least, and if possible get into free communication
with Gordon. Whether they will have to go beyond
Dongola, or to Khartoum itself, I do not think it is possible
to say now.

'If we are not in a position to say to him (as I do not
think we are now), "You must come away from Khartoum
with the garrison and inhabitants who want to come with
you," I see no use in giving him further general and vague
instructions. Neither do I think that we can attempt to
limit his action strictly to Khartoum, disregarding the fate
of all the other Egyptian garrisons in the Soudan. If it
should hereafter appear that, by allowing Gordon to remain
somewhat longer at Khartoum, and to follow up his successes, the whole of the Soudan might have been pacified
or the garrisons peacefully withdrawn, and that this result
has been prevented by our precipitate action, what excuse
shall we have ?

'I am sorry that I have not anything more definite to
suggest, but the long and the short of it is that I would
not give any orders in a hurry, or till we can give them
through Wolseley or a British officer at Dongola with a
British force ; and that I would ask, as I wrote yesterday,
for a full report of the opinions and advice of our officers
in Egypt.

'You know that Baring and Northbrook are as strong
for evacuation of the Soudan as you can be, and are not,
like me, infected with a weakness for its partial retention,
and you can therefore trust their advice.'

---

[1] Some cargoes of these had been sent down to Berber, where they must have
been killed or enslaved at the sack of that town.

This letter shows that Gordon's action in holding on at Khartoum appeared to Lord Hartington to be correct in the circumstances, nor did he agree with Mr. Gladstone that Gordon was a wilful rebel. His view, indeed, of the whole matter was much the same as Gordon's. In another note Lord Hartington suggested that Lord Granville should telegraph to Northbrook and Baring to get their impressions as to Gordon's 'wild telegrams,' and suggested that they should consult Wolseley, and added :—

'He knows Gordon well, and is more likely to be able to interpret his dark sayings. At all events I am convinced that we should be wrong in sending Gordon a message out of our own heads without consulting our people in Egypt. Gordon has never understood us, nor we him.'

Hartington understood Gordon far better than did most of his colleagues, because he did not deceive himself, nor allow himself to be deceived by others, and because he knew that, in Gordon's position, he would not himself have abandoned his post. But Gordon's Khartoum Journal shows that this man of action and thought, who had been taught by real and world-wide experience to know men and their motives, and lived outside the region of talk and mundane seductions, and could see through forms and phrases into realities, did, in fact, understand the feelings of those other mere politicians at home infinitely better than they could understand those which moved him. Gordon's heart was disinterested, and, therefore, his eyes were clear.

END OF VOL. I.

Printed by BALLANTYNE, HANSON & CO.
Edinburgh & London

EGYPT

Toski  Korosko
Argin  Halfa
Sarras
Ambuyol  Akasha
Ginnis  Firket
Suarda  Kosha
Dalgo
Hannek  Kerma
Hafir  Argol
Dongola
Khandak
d. Dongola
Debba
Merowe
Korti
Jakdul
Abu Hamed
Wreck of Stewart's Steamers
El Gab
Kirbekan
Berti
Obak
Ariab (W)
Berber
El Damer  Nakheila
Adarama
Abu Tleh
Metemma
Gubat
Shendi
Kereri
Omdurman  KHARTOUM
El Eilafun
Kamlin
Masselemia  Rufaa
Wad Medani
Baraka
Obeid
El Dueim  Kawa
Gedid
Gaz Abu Guma
Sennar
Roseires
Renk
Talodi
Kodok
Taufikia
Nasser

Tambuk  Mandub
Hashini  Suakin
Tamai
Tebb  Tokar  Agik
Port Sudan (Sheikh Burghut)

ERITREA

Kassala
Gedaref
Gera
Gallabat
Sinhit  Keren
Massaua
Amadib
Asmara

ABYSSINIA

LADO ENCLAVE
Lado  Mongalla
Rejaf  Gondokoro
New Dufile
UGANDA
Mahagi  ALBERT NYANZA

Stanford's Geog. Estab. London

# THE POLITICAL HISTORY
## OF ENGLAND.

Edited by the Rev. W. HUNT, D.Litt., and
REGINALD LANE POOLE, M.A., LL.D.

8vo. 12 vols. 7s. 6d. net per volume.

Vol. I. **FROM THE EARLIEST TIMES TO THE**
NORMAN CONQUEST (to 1066). By THOMAS HODGKIN, D.C.L., Litt.D., Fellow
of University College, London ; Fellow of the British Academy. With 2 Maps.

Vol. II. **FROM THE NORMAN CONQUEST TO THE**
DEATH OF JOHN (1066 to 1216). By GEORGE BURTON ADAMS, Professor of History
in Yale University. With 2 Maps.

Vol. III. **FROM THE ACCESSION OF HENRY III.**
TO THE DEATH OF EDWARD III. (1216 to 1377). By T. F. TOUT, M.A., Professor of Mediæval and Modern History in the University of Manchester. With
3 Maps.

Vol. IV. **FROM THE ACCESSION OF RICHARD II.**
TO THE DEATH OF RICHARD III. (1377 to 1485). By C. OMAN, M.A.,
Chichele Professor of Modern History in the University of Oxford; Fellow of the
British Academy. With 3 Maps.

Vol. V. **FROM THE ACCESSION OF HENRY VII.**
TO THE DEATH OF HENRY VIII. (1485 to 1547). By H. A. L. FISHER, M.A.,
Fellow and Tutor of New College, Oxford; Fellow of the British Academy. With
2 Maps.

Vol. VI. **FROM THE ACCESSION OF EDWARD VI.**
TO THE DEATH OF ELIZABETH (1547 to 1603). By A. F. POLLARD, M.A.,
Fellow of All Souls' College, Oxford ; Professor of English History in the University of
London. With 2 Maps.

Vol. VII. **FROM THE ACCESSION OF JAMES I.**
TO THE RESTORATION (1603 to 1660). By F. C. MONTAGUE, M.A., Professor
of History in University College, London, formerly Fellow of Oriel College, Oxford.
With 3 Maps.

Vol. VIII. **FROM THE RESTORATION TO THE**
DEATH OF WILLIAM III. (1660 to 1702). By RICHARD LODGE, M.A., LL.D.,
Professor of History in the University of Edinburgh; formerly Fellow of Brasenose
College, Oxford. With 2 Maps.

Vol. IX. **FROM THE ACCESSION OF ANNE TO**
THE DEATH OF GEORGE II. (1702 to 1760). By I. S. LEADAM, M.A., formerly
Fellow of Brasenose College, Oxford. With 8 Maps.

Vol. X. **FROM THE ACCESSION OF GEORGE III.**
TO THE CLOSE OF PITT'S FIRST ADMINISTRATION (1760 to 1801). By the
Rev. WILLIAM HUNT, M.A., D.Litt., Trinity College, Oxford. With 3 Maps.

Vol. XI. **FROM ADDINGTON'S ADMINISTRATION**
TO THE CLOSE OF WILLIAM IV.'s REIGN (1801 to 1837). By the Hon.
GEORGE C. BRODRICK, D.C.L., late Warden of Merton College, Oxford, and J. K.
FOTHERINGHAM, M.A., Magdalen College, Oxford; Lecturer in Classics at King's
College, London. With 3 Maps.

Vol. XII. **THE REIGN OF QUEEN VICTORIA**
(1837 to 1901). By SIDNEY LOW, M.A., Balliol College, Oxford ; formerly Lecturer on
History at King's College, London ; and LLOYD C. SANDERS, B.A. With 3 Maps.

LONGMANS, GREEN & CO., 39 Paternoster Row, London.
New York, Bombay, and Calcutta.

# RECENT BIOGRAPHIES, Etc.

**THE LIFE OF GEORGE JOACHIM GOSCHEN,**
FIRST VISCOUNT GOSCHEN. 1831-1907. By the Hon. ARTHUR
ELLIOT. With Portraits and other Illustrations. 2 vols. 8vo. 25s. net.

**GARIBALDI AND THE MAKING OF ITALY.** By
GEORGE MACAULAY TREVELYAN. With 4 Maps and Numerous Illustrations. 8vo. 7s. 6d. net.

*By the Same Author.*

**GARIBALDI'S DEFENCE OF THE ROMAN**
REPUBLIC. With 7 Maps and 35 Illustrations. 8vo. 6s. 6d. net.

**GARIBALDI AND THE THOUSAND.** With 5
Maps and numerous Illustrations. 8vo. 7s. 6d. net.

**KING EDWARD VII. AS A SPORTSMAN.** By ALFRED
E. T. WATSON. With Contributions by Captain the Hon. Sir SEYMOUR
FORTESCUE, C.M.G., K.C.V.O., the MARQUESS OF RIPON, G.C.V.O.,
LORD WALSINGHAM, LORD RIBBLESDALE, and others. With 10 Plates
in Colour and 92 other Illustrations. 8vo. 21s. net.

**LIFE OF THE MARQUISE DE LA ROCHEJA-**
QUELEIN, THE HEROINE OF LA VENDÉE. By M. M.
MAXWELL SCOTT. 8vo. 7s. 6d. net.

**THE LIFE OF GRANVILLE GEORGE LEVESON**
GOWER, SECOND EARL GRANVILLE, 1815-1891. By Lord
FITZMAURICE. With 8 Portraits (3 Photogravures). 2 vols. 8vo.
30s. net.

**GATHORNE HARDY, FIRST EARL OF CRAN-**
BROOK. A Memoir, with Extracts from his Diary and Correspondence.
Edited by the Hon. ALFRED E. GATHORNE-HARDY. With Portraits
(3 Photogravures) and other Illustrations. 2 vols. 8vo. 24s. net.

**NAPOLEON I.: A BIOGRAPHY.** By AUGUST FOURNIER,
Professor of History at the University of Vienna. Translated by ANNE
ELIZABETH ADAMS. 2 vols. 8vo. 21s. net.

**THE LETTERS OF JOHN STUART MILL.** Edited,
with an Introduction, by HUGH S. R. ELLIOT. With a Note on Mill's
Private Life by MARY TAYLOR. With 6 Portraits. 2 vols. 8vo.
21s. net.

**A MEMOIR OF THE RIGHT HON. WILLIAM**
EDWARD HARTPOLE LECKY, M.P., O.M., LL.D., D.C.L.,
Litt.D. By his WIFE. With 5 Portraits. 8vo. 12s. 6d. net.

**THE RIGHT HON. CECIL JOHN RHODES:** a
Monograph and a Reminiscence. By Sir THOMAS FULLER, K.C.M.G.,
formerly Agent-General for the Cape of Good Hope. With Rembrandt-
gravure Frontispiece and 12 other Illustrations. 8vo. 6s. net.

**JOHN VIRIAUM JONES, AND OTHER OXFORD**
MEMORIES. By EDWARD BAGNALL POULTON, D.Sc., M.A., etc.,
Hope Professor of Zoology in the University of Oxford, Fellow of Jesus
College, Oxford, etc. With 5 Illustrations. 8vo. 8s. 6d. net.

LONGMANS, GREEN & CO., 39 Paternoster Row, London.
New York, Bombay, and Calcutta.